CONTENTS

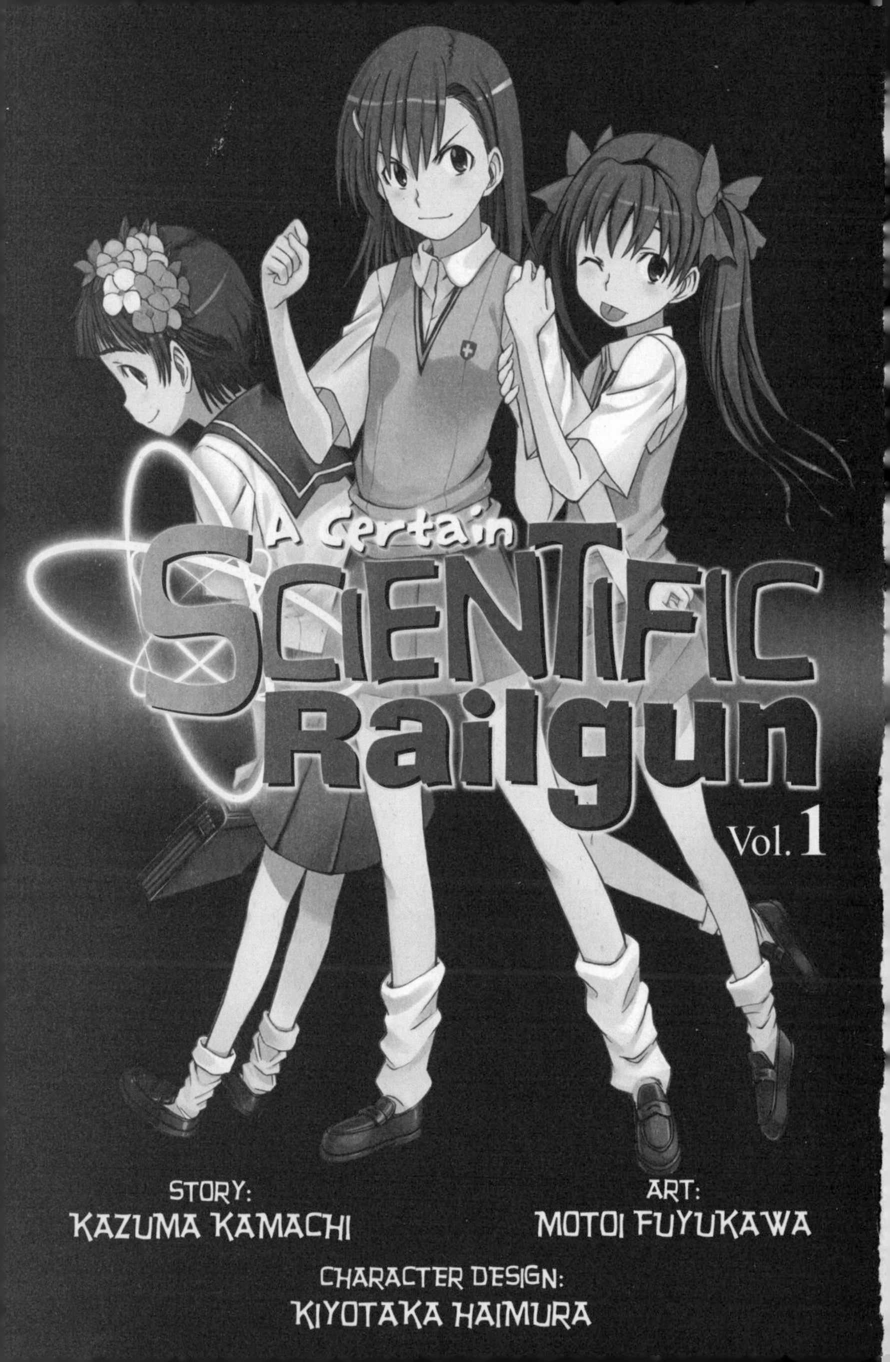

A Certain SCIENTIFIC Railgun

Vol. 1

STORY:
KAZUMA KAMACHI

ART:
MOTOI FUYUKAWA

CHARACTER DESIGN:
KIYOTAKA HAIMURA

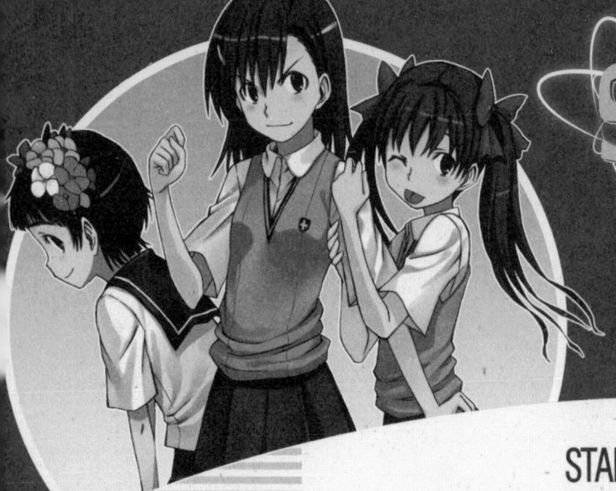

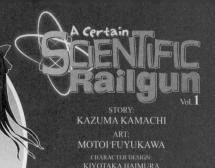

A Certain SCIENTIFIC Railgun

Vol. 1

STORY:
KAZUMA KAMACHI

ART:
MOTOI FUYUKAWA

CHARACTER DESIGN:
KIYOTAKA HAIMURA

STAFF CREDITS

translation	Andrew Cunningham
adaptation	Janet Houck
retouch & lettering	Roland Amago
cover design	Nicky Lim
layout	Bambi Eloriaga-Amago
copy editor	Shanti Whitesides
editor	Adam Arnold
publisher	Jason DeAngelis Seven Seas Entertainment

Visit us online at www.gomanga.com.

ISBN: 978-1-935934-00-4

Printed in Canada

First Printing: June 2011

10 9 8 7 6 5 4 3 2 1

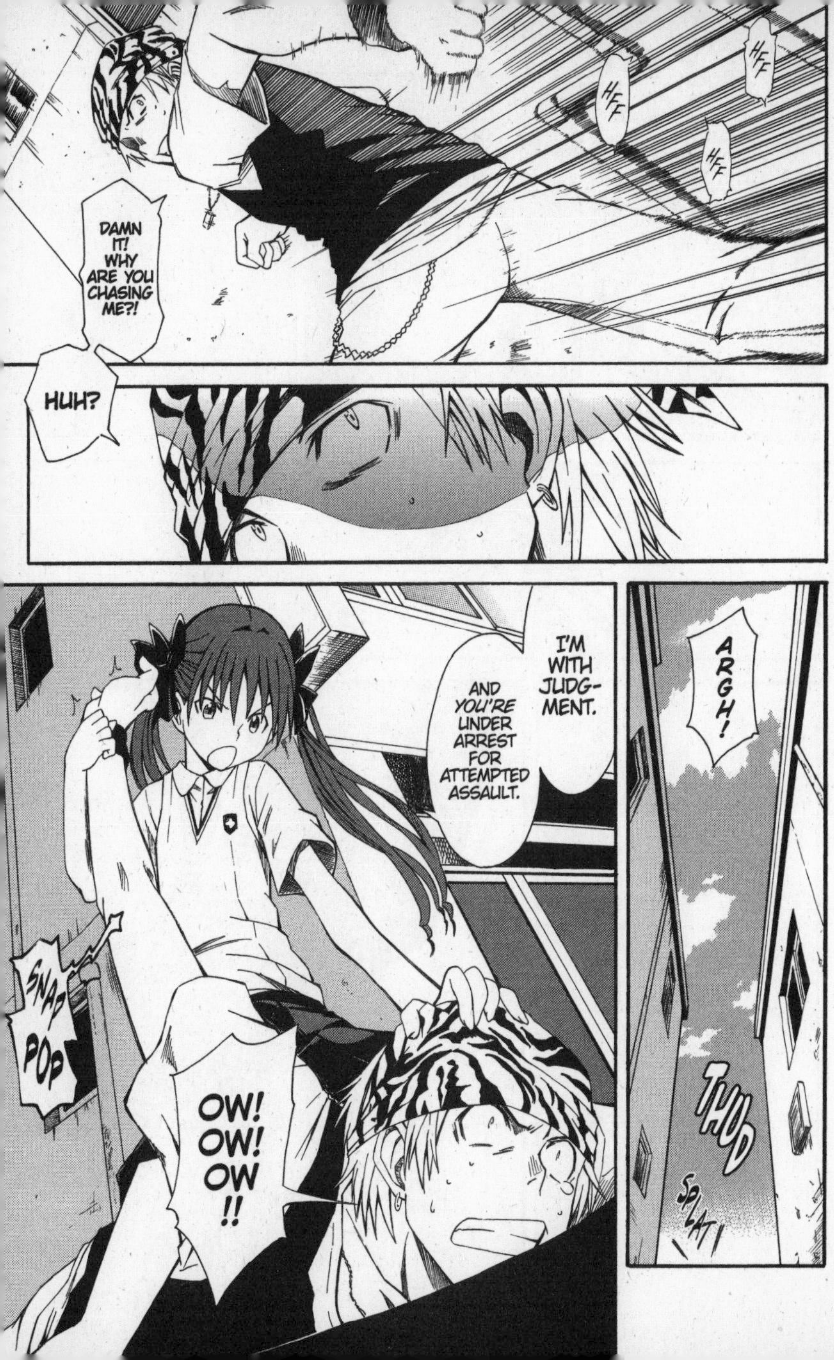
HFF
HFF
HFF
DAMN IT! WHY ARE YOU CHASING ME?!
HUH?
ARGH!
THUD
SPLAT
I'M WITH JUDGMENT.
AND YOU'RE UNDER ARREST FOR ATTEMPTED ASSAULT.
SNAP
POP
OW! OW! OW!!

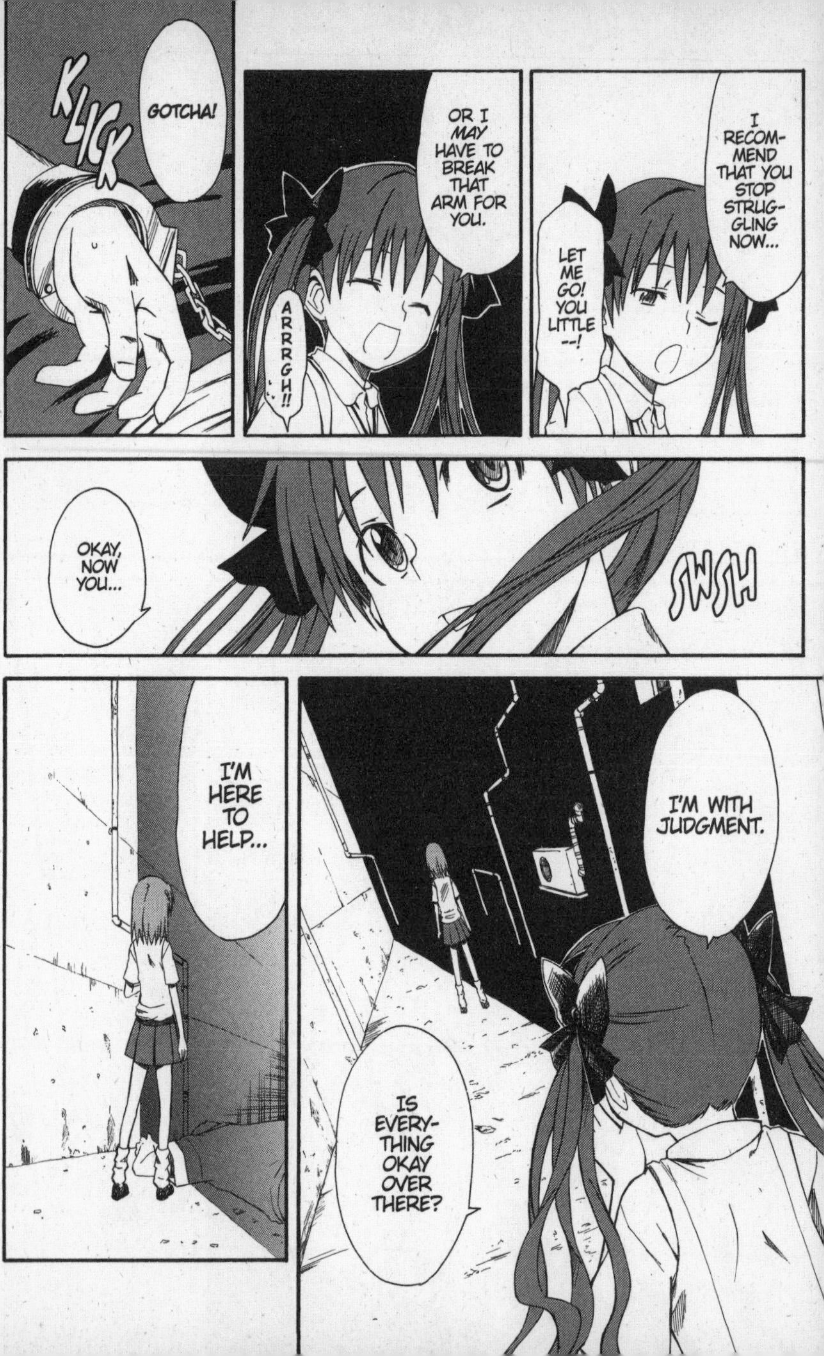
I RECOMMEND THAT YOU STOP STRUGGLING NOW...
LET ME GO! YOU LITTLE --!
OR I *MAY* HAVE TO BREAK THAT ARM FOR YOU.
ARRRGH!!
KLICK
GOTCHA!
SWSH
OKAY, NOW YOU...
I'M WITH JUDGMENT.
IS EVERYTHING OKAY OVER THERE?
I'M HERE TO HELP...

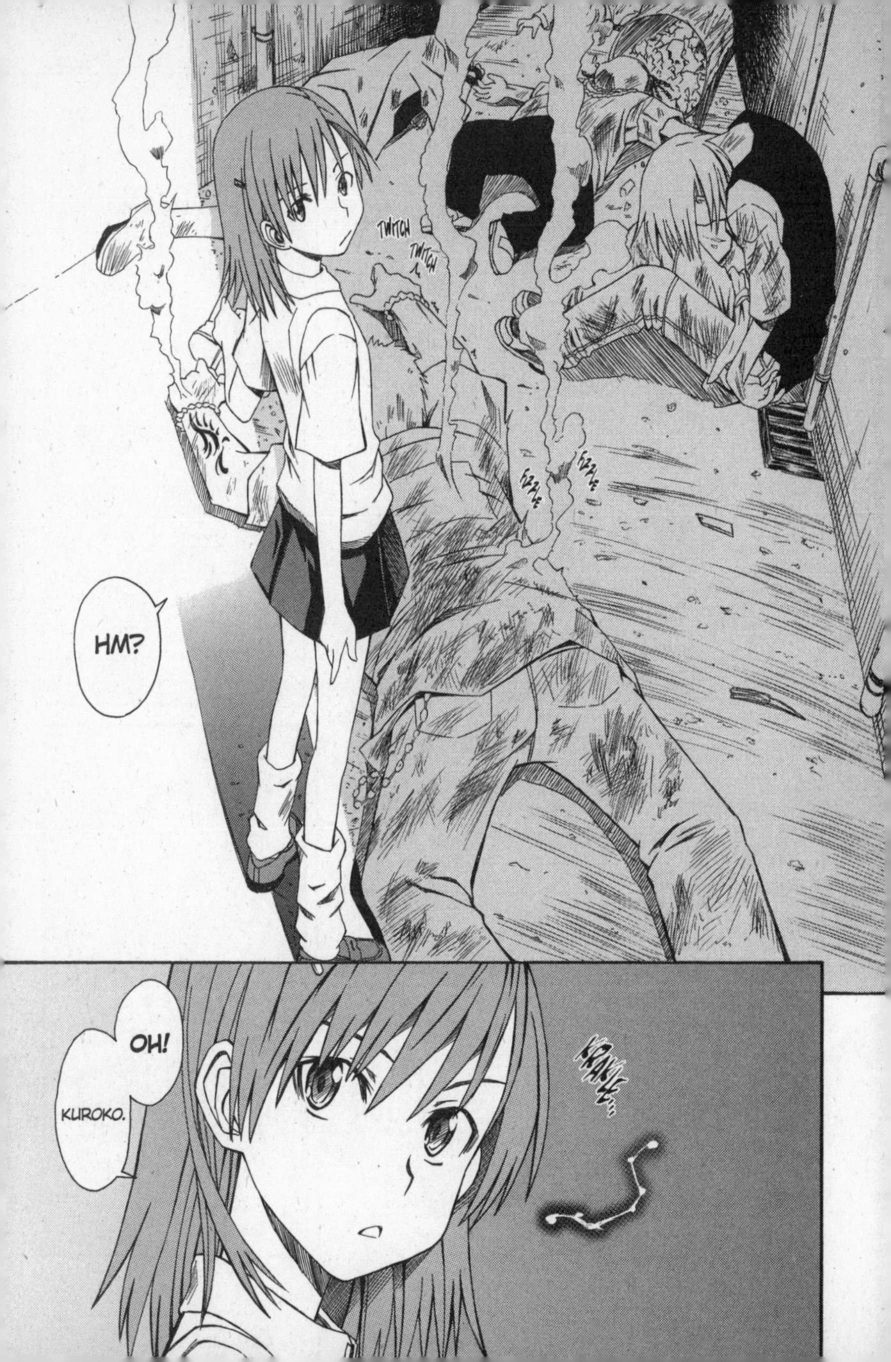
TWITCH
TWITCH
FIZZLE
FIZZLE
HM?
KRACKLE...
OH!
KUROKO.

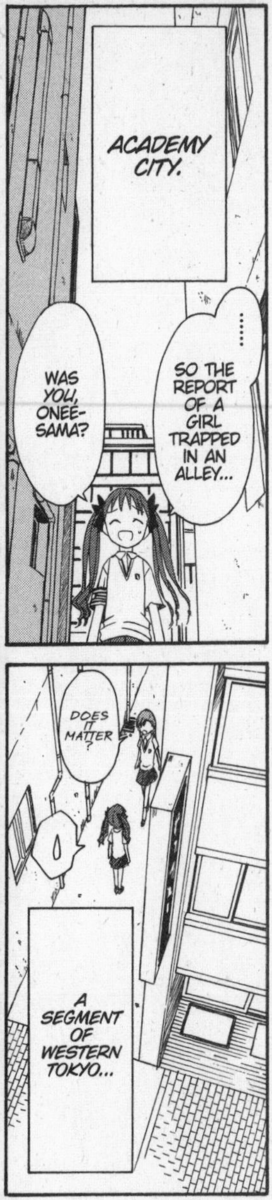
ACADEMY CITY.
......
SO THE REPORT OF A GIRL TRAPPED IN AN ALLEY...
WAS YOU, ONEE-SAMA?
DOES IT MATTER?
A SEGMENT OF WESTERN TOKYO...

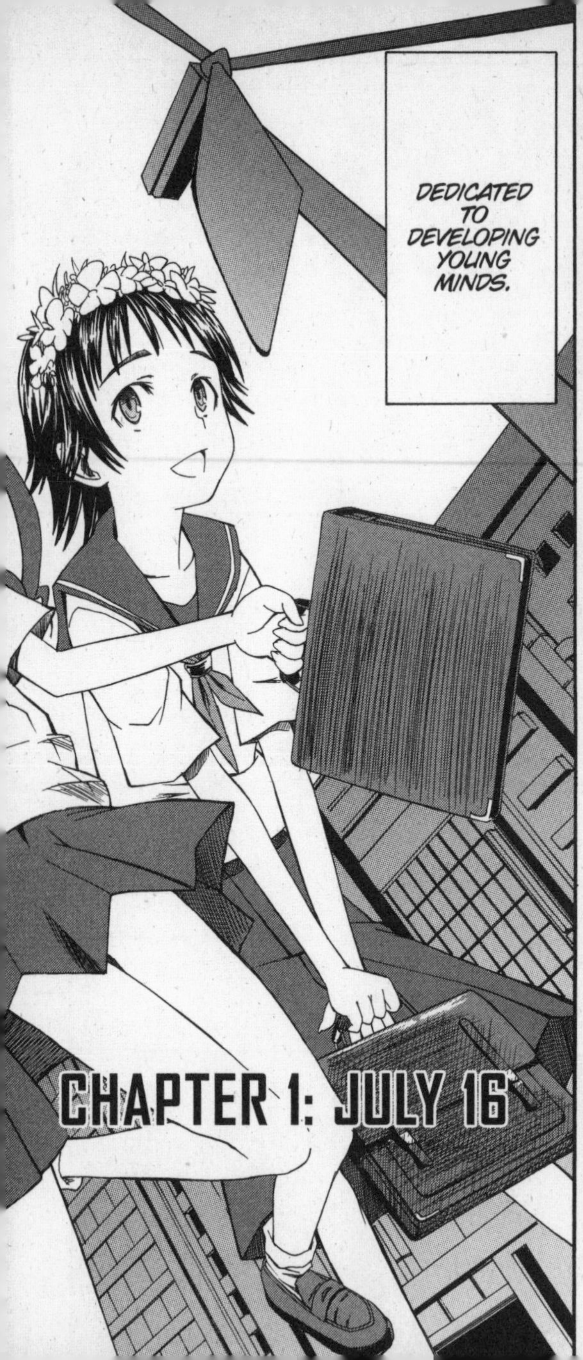
DEDICATED TO DEVELOPING YOUNG MINDS.
CHAPTER 1: JULY 16

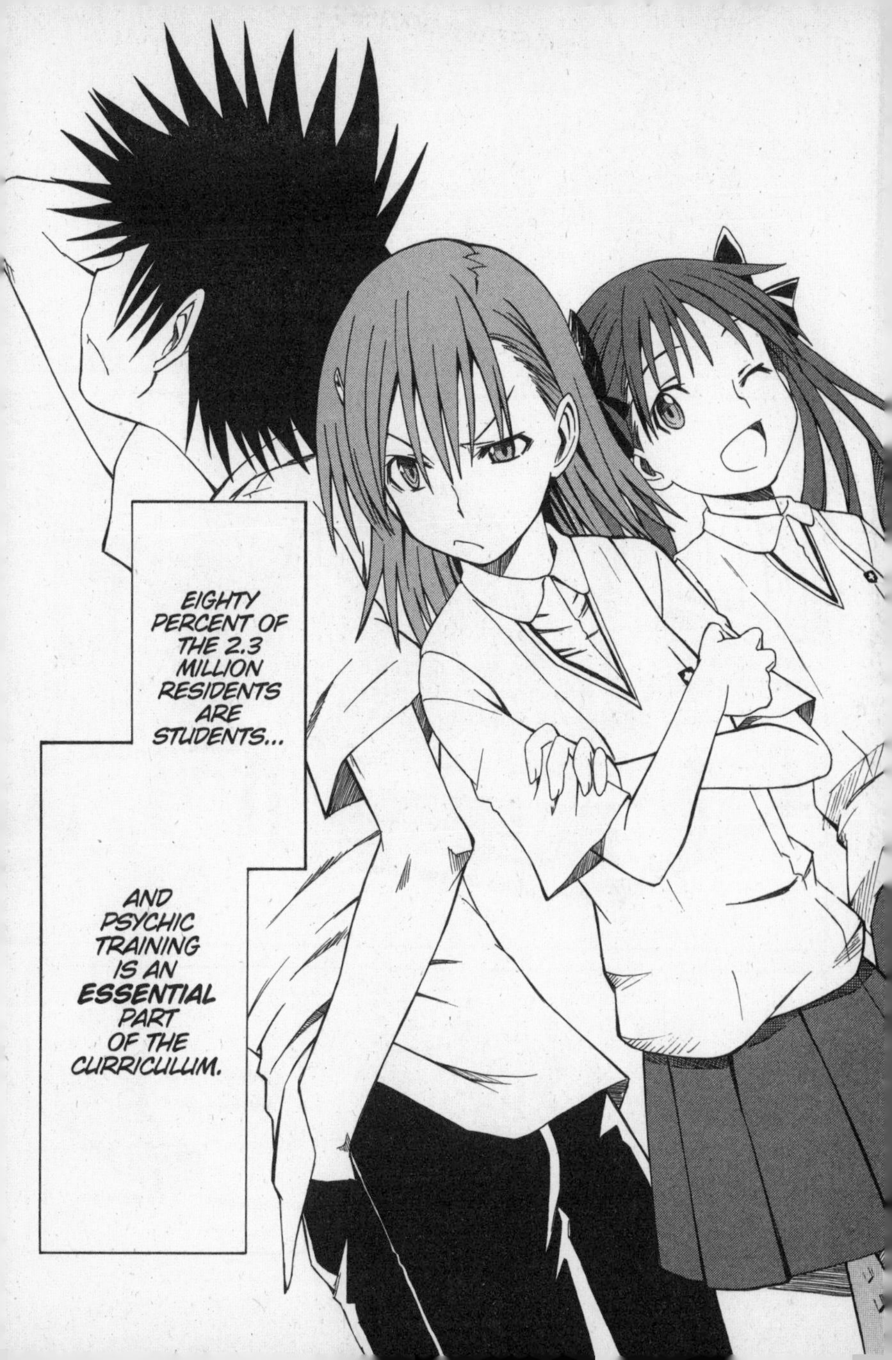
EIGHTY PERCENT OF THE 2.3 MILLION RESIDENTS ARE STUDENTS...
AND PSYCHIC TRAINING IS AN **ESSENTIAL** PART OF THE CURRICULUM.

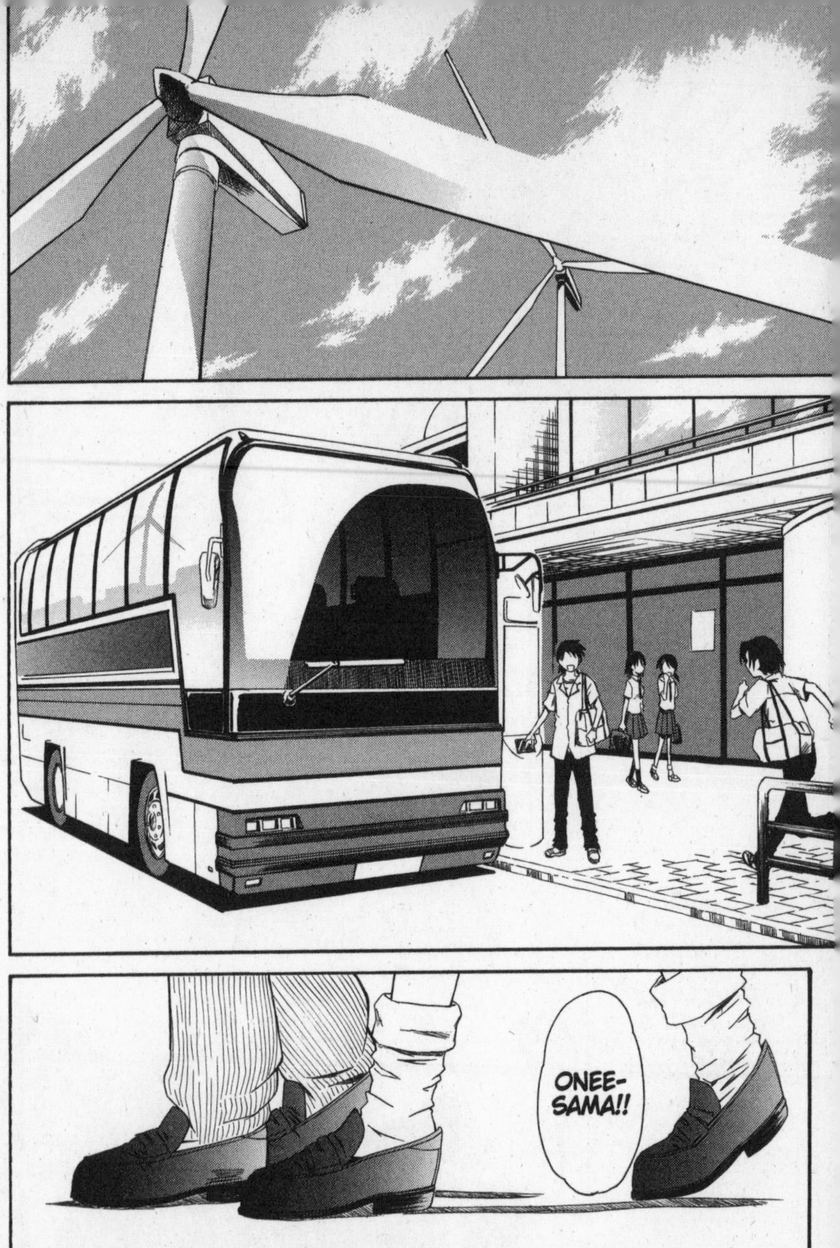
ONEE-
SAMA!!

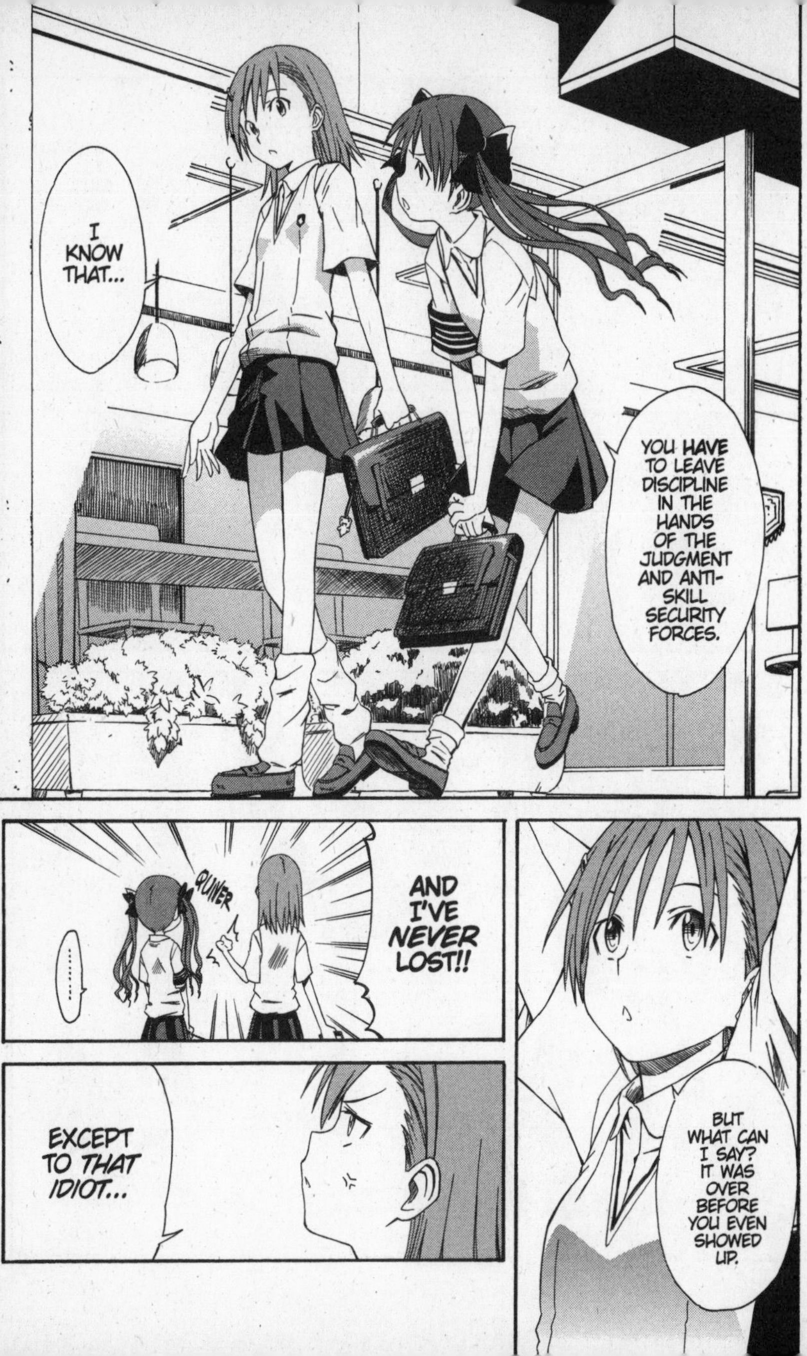
YOU HAVE TO LEAVE DISCIPLINE IN THE HANDS OF THE JUDGMENT AND ANTI-SKILL SECURITY FORCES.
I KNOW THAT...
BUT WHAT CAN I SAY? IT WAS OVER BEFORE YOU EVEN SHOWED UP.
AND I'VE NEVER LOST!!
QUIVER
......
EXCEPT TO THAT IDIOT...

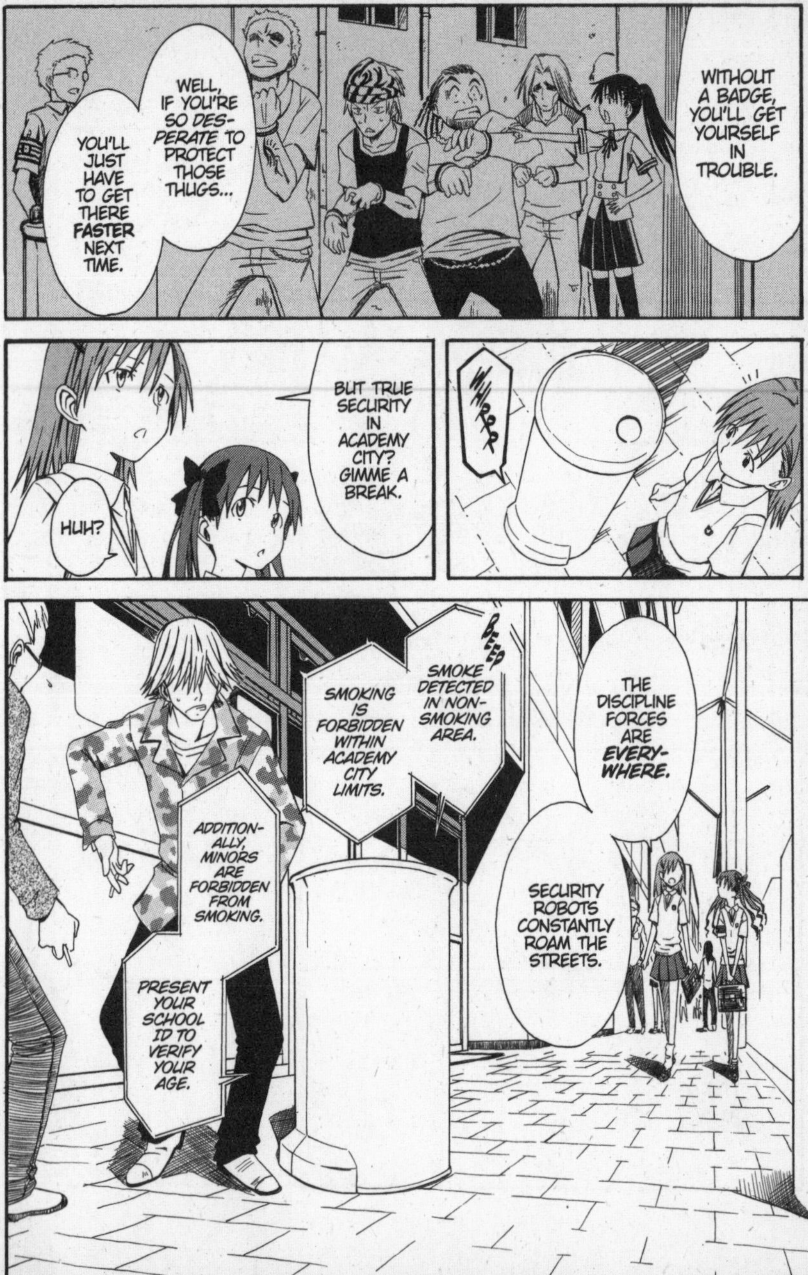
WITHOUT A BADGE, YOU'LL GET YOURSELF IN TROUBLE.
WELL, IF YOU'RE SO DESPERATE TO PROTECT THOSE THUGS...
YOU'LL JUST HAVE TO GET THERE FASTER NEXT TIME.
WHIRRR
BUT TRUE SECURITY IN ACADEMY CITY? GIMME A BREAK.
HUH?
THE DISCIPLINE FORCES ARE EVERYWHERE.
SECURITY ROBOTS CONSTANTLY ROAM THE STREETS.
BEEP
SMOKE DETECTED IN NON-SMOKING AREA.
SMOKING IS FORBIDDEN WITHIN ACADEMY CITY LIMITS.
ADDITIONALLY, MINORS ARE FORBIDDEN FROM SMOKING.
PRESENT YOUR SCHOOL ID TO VERIFY YOUR AGE.

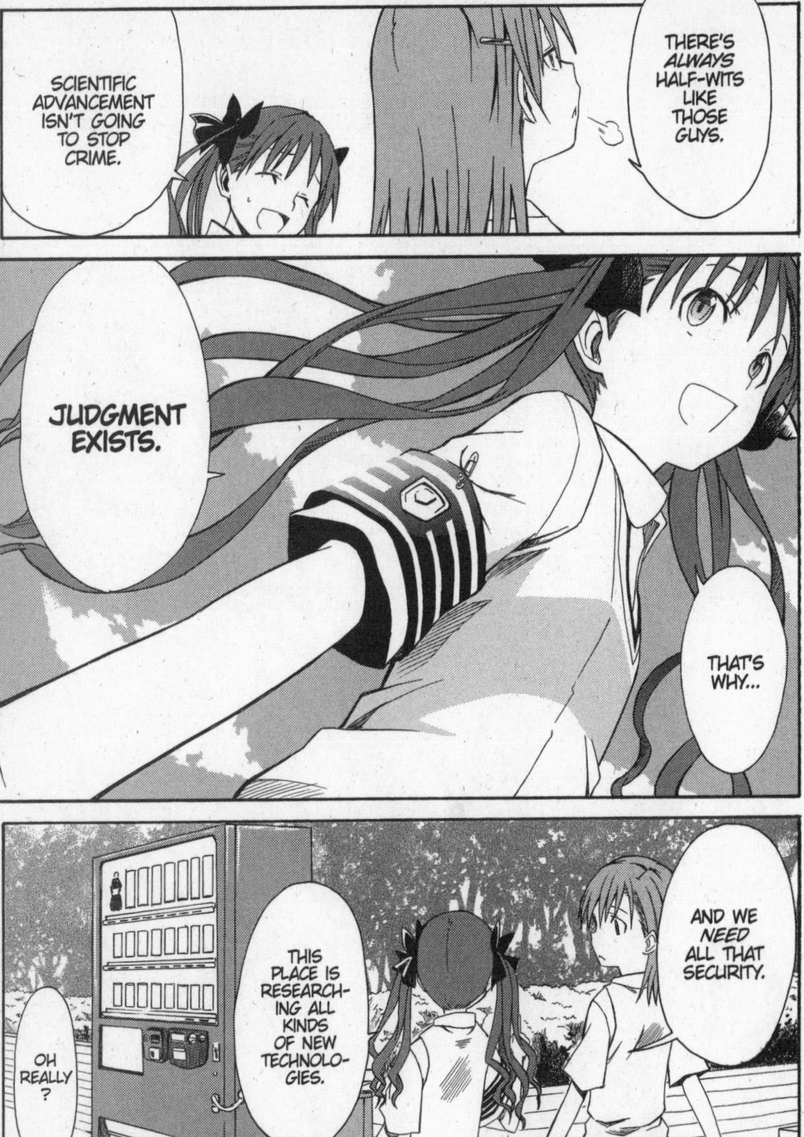
THERE'S *ALWAYS* HALF-WITS LIKE THOSE GUYS.
SCIENTIFIC ADVANCEMENT ISN'T GOING TO STOP CRIME.
THAT'S WHY...
JUDGMENT EXISTS.
AND WE *NEED* ALL THAT SECURITY.
THIS PLACE IS RESEARCHING ALL KINDS OF NEW TECHNOLOGIES.
OH REALLY ?

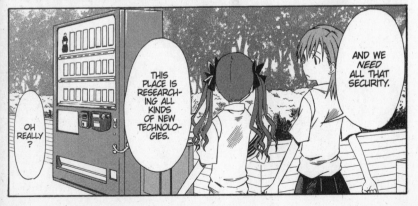

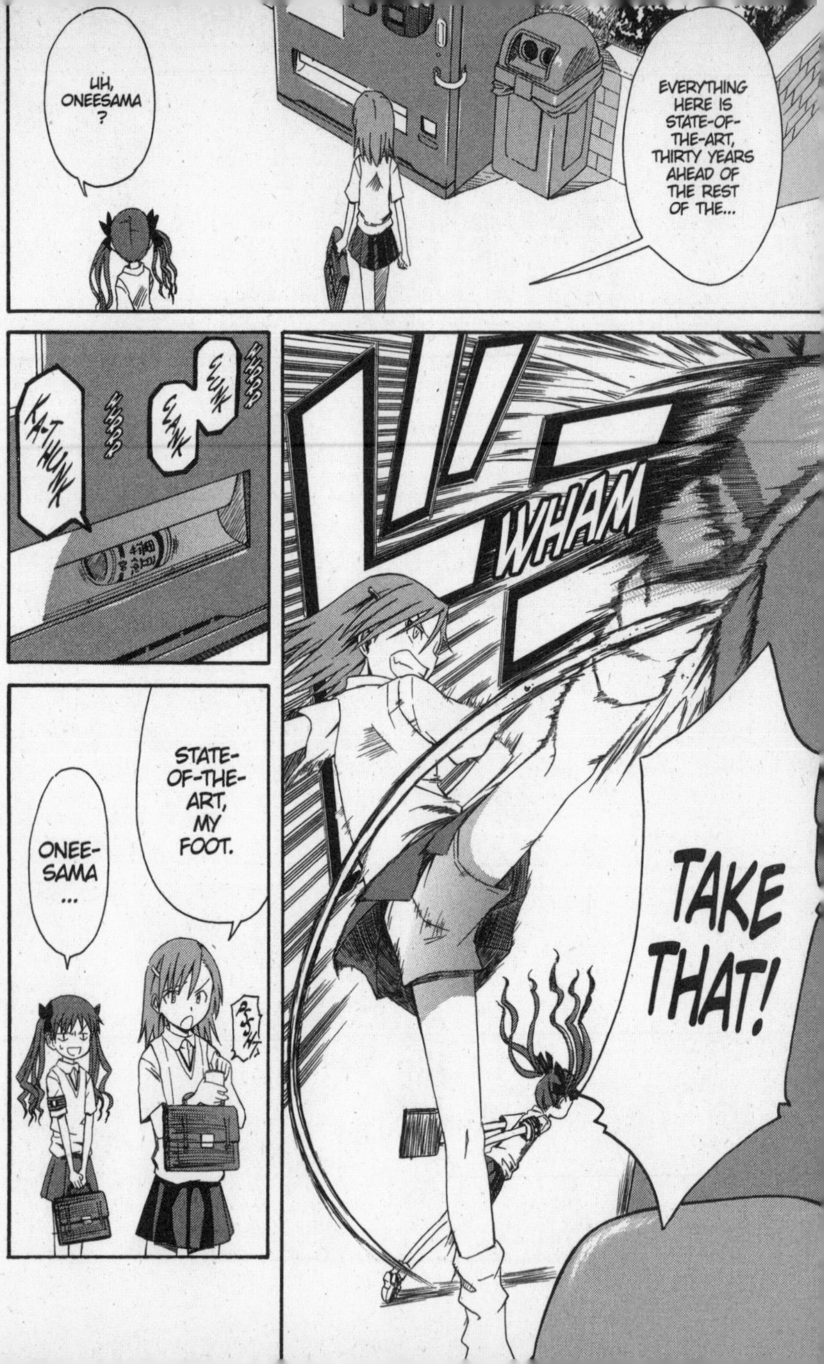
EVERYTHING HERE IS STATE-OF-THE-ART, THIRTY YEARS AHEAD OF THE REST OF THE...
UH, ONEESAMA?
WHAM
TAKE THAT!
WHRRR
CLUNK CLANK
WHRRR
KA-THUNK
STATE-OF-THE-ART, MY FOOT.
ONEE-SAMA...

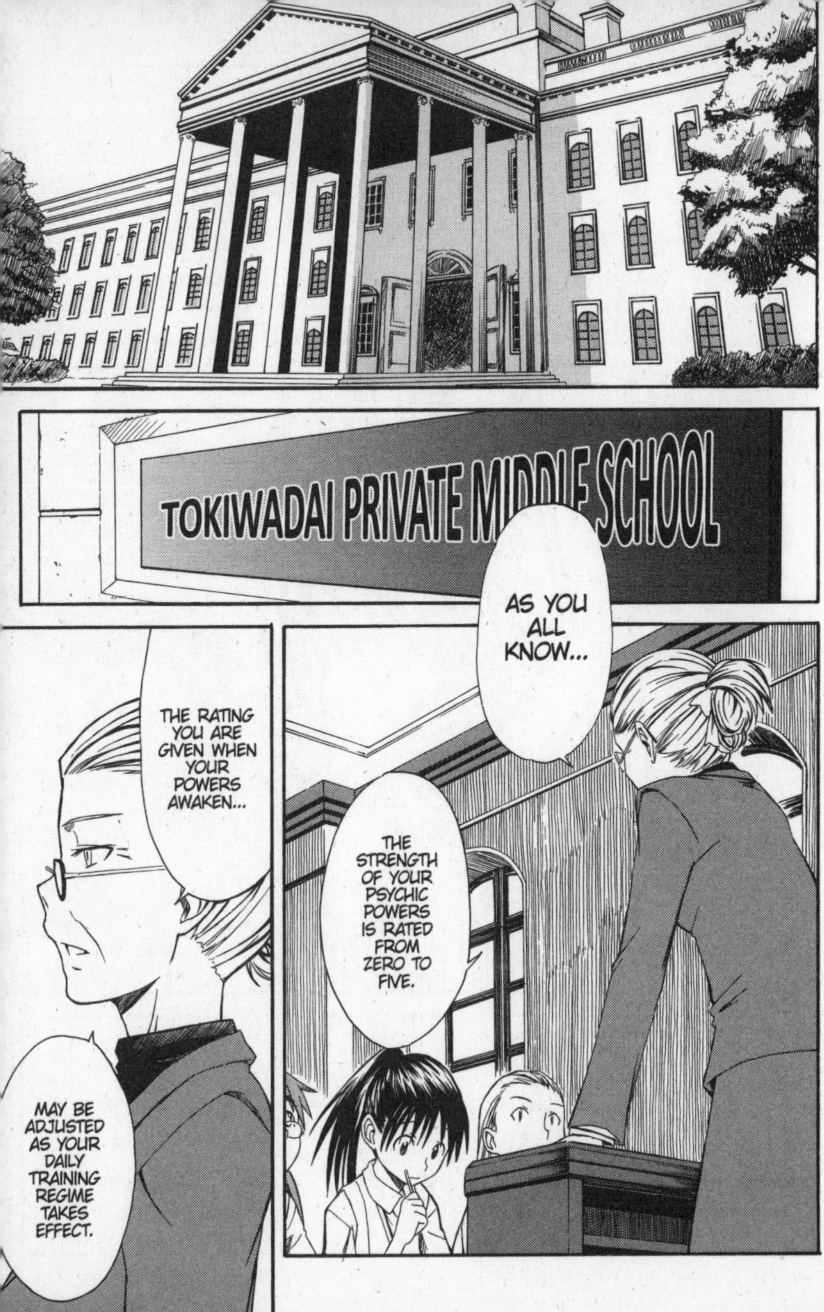
TOKIWADAI PRIVATE MIDDLE SCHOOL
AS YOU ALL KNOW...
THE STRENGTH OF YOUR PSYCHIC POWERS IS RATED FROM ZERO TO FIVE.
THE RATING YOU ARE GIVEN WHEN YOUR POWERS AWAKEN...
MAY BE ADJUSTED AS YOUR DAILY TRAINING REGIME TAKES EFFECT.

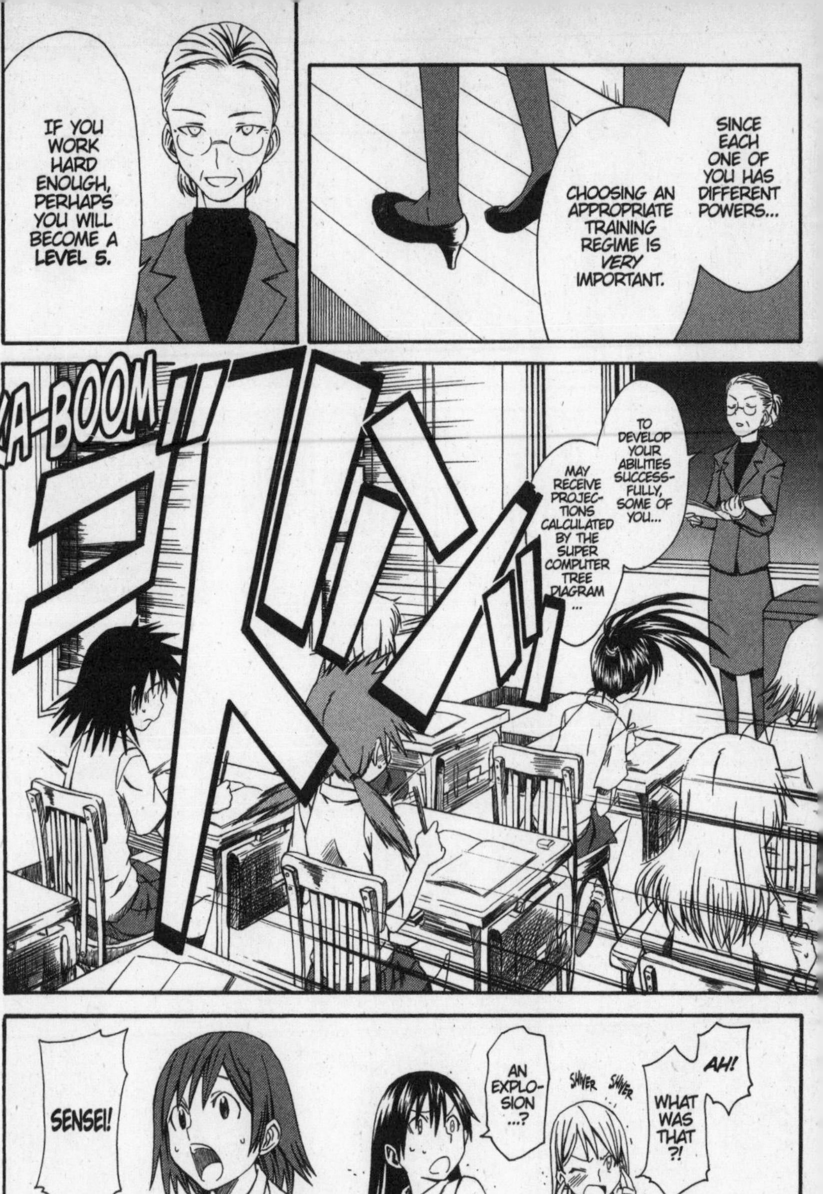
SINCE EACH ONE OF YOU HAS DIFFERENT POWERS...
CHOOSING AN APPROPRIATE TRAINING REGIME IS VERY IMPORTANT.
IF YOU WORK HARD ENOUGH, PERHAPS YOU WILL BECOME A LEVEL 5.
TO DEVELOP YOUR ABILITIES SUCCESSFULLY, SOME OF YOU...
MAY RECEIVE PROJECTIONS CALCULATED BY THE SUPER COMPUTER TREE DIAGRAM ...
KA-BOOM
AH!
WHAT WAS THAT ?!
TREMBLE
SHIVER SHIVER
AN EXPLOSION ...?
SENSEI!

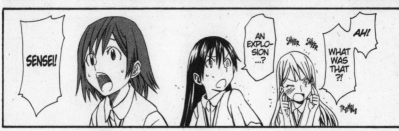

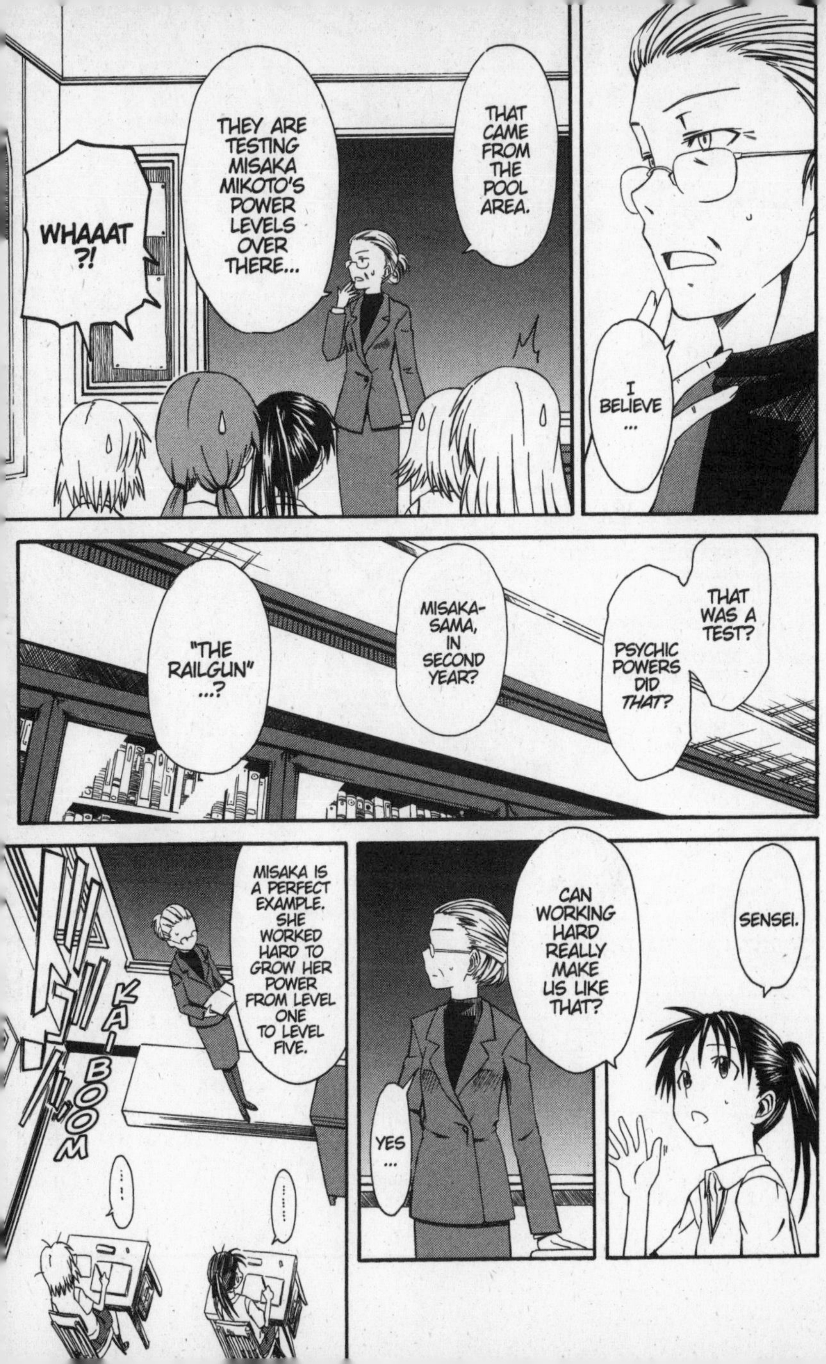
I BELIEVE ...
THAT CAME FROM THE POOL AREA.
THEY ARE TESTING MISAKA MIKOTO'S POWER LEVELS OVER THERE...
WHAAAT ?!
THAT WAS A TEST?
PSYCHIC POWERS DID THAT?
MISAKA-SAMA, IN SECOND YEAR?
"THE RAILGUN" ...?
SENSEI.
CAN WORKING HARD REALLY MAKE US LIKE THAT?
YES ...
MISAKA IS A PERFECT EXAMPLE. SHE WORKED HARD TO GROW HER POWER FROM LEVEL ONE TO LEVEL FIVE.
KAIBOOM
......
...

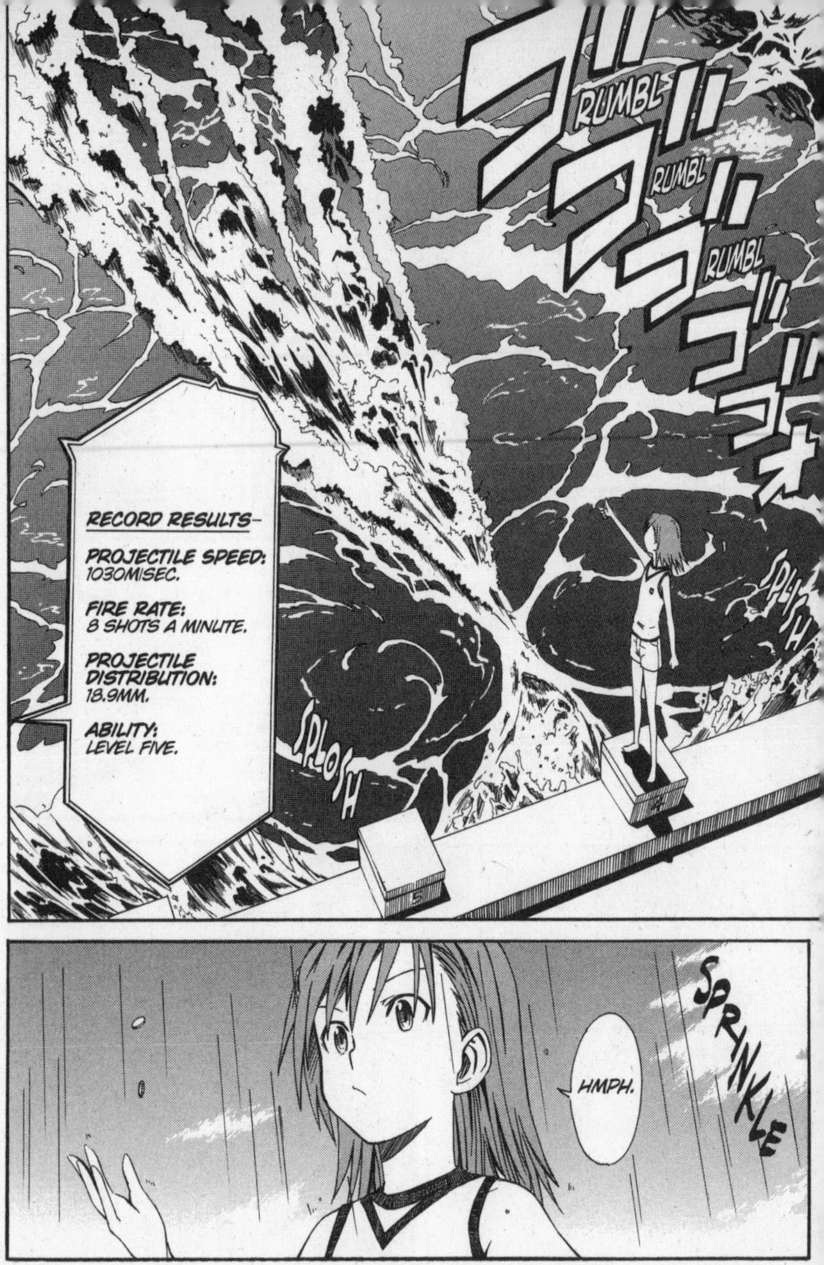
RUMBL
RUMBL
RUMBL
SPLISH
RECORD RESULTS—
PROJECTILE SPEED: 1030M/SEC.
FIRE RATE: 8 SHOTS A MINUTE.
PROJECTILE DISTRIBUTION: 18.9MM.
ABILITY: LEVEL FIVE.
SPLOSH
SPRINKLE
HMPH.

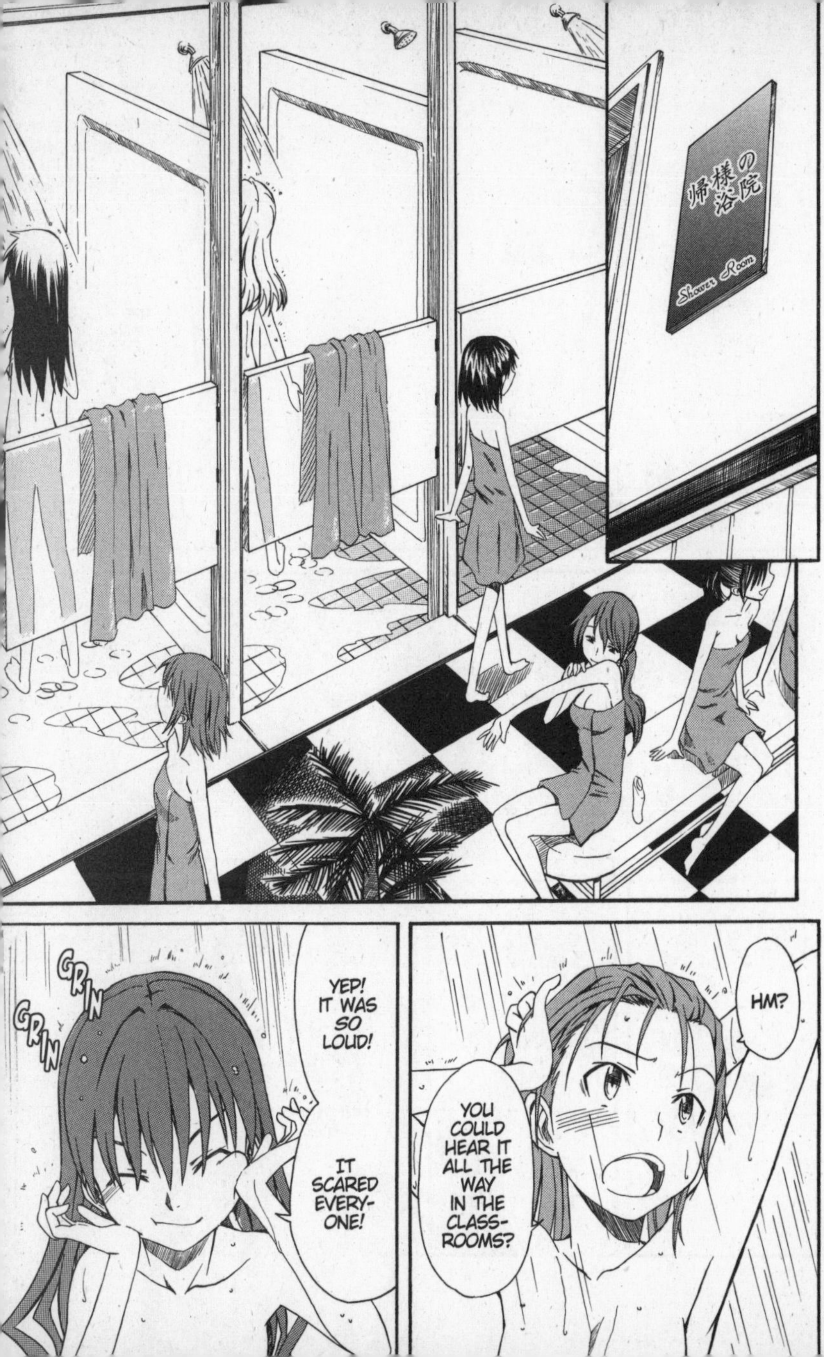
帰様の浴院
Shower Room
HM?
YOU COULD HEAR IT ALL THE WAY IN THE CLASS-ROOMS?
YEP! IT WAS SO LOUD!
IT SCARED EVERY-ONE!
GRIN GRIN

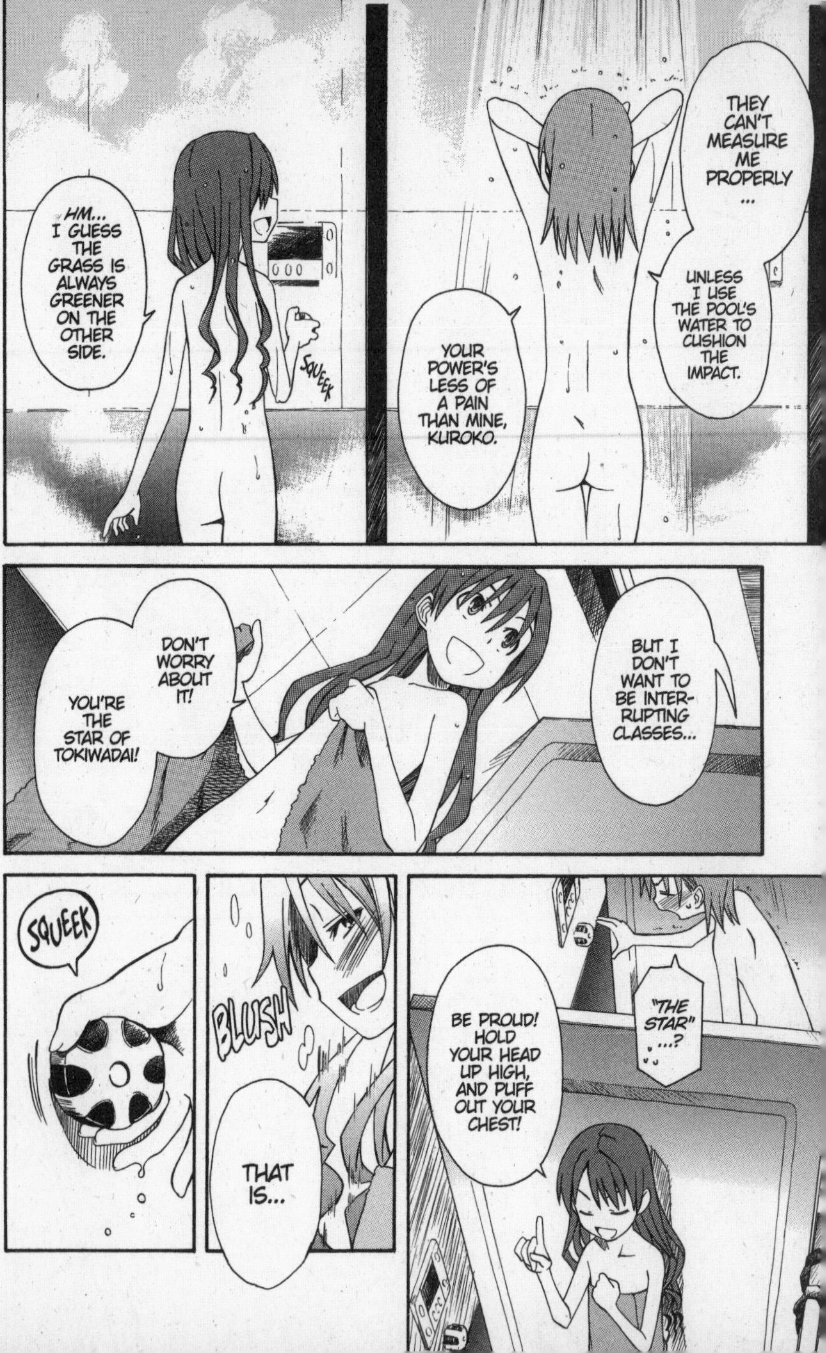
THEY CAN'T MEASURE ME PROPERLY...
UNLESS I USE THE POOL'S WATER TO CUSHION THE IMPACT.
YOUR POWER'S LESS OF A PAIN THAN MINE, KUROKO.
HM... I GUESS THE GRASS IS ALWAYS GREENER ON THE OTHER SIDE.
SQUEEK
BUT I DON'T WANT TO BE INTER-RUPTING CLASSES...
DON'T WORRY ABOUT IT!
YOU'RE THE STAR OF TOKIWADAI!
"THE STAR"...?
BE PROUD! HOLD YOUR HEAD UP HIGH, AND PUFF OUT YOUR CHEST!
BLUSH
THAT IS...
SQUEEK

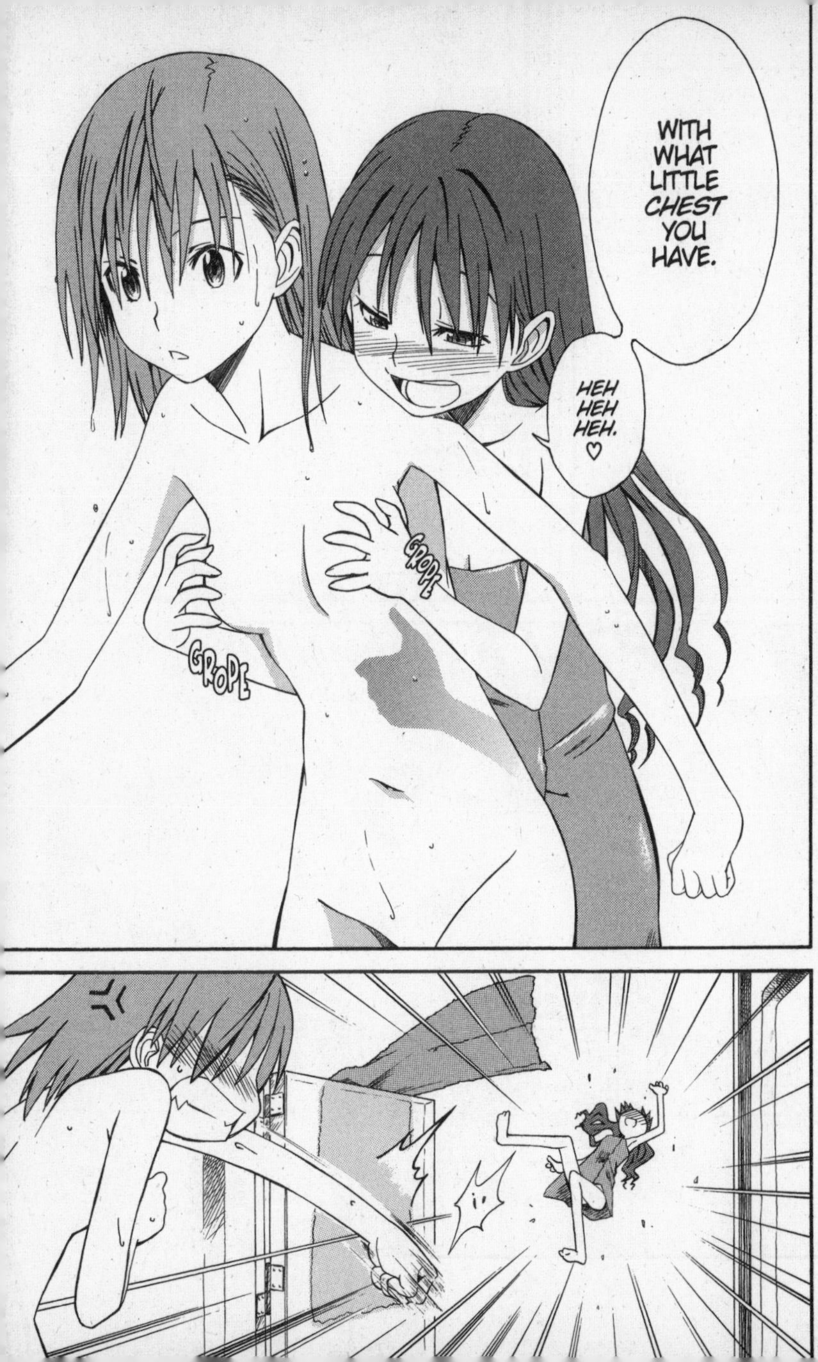
WITH WHAT LITTLE CHEST YOU HAVE.
HEH HEH HEH. ♡
GROPE
GROPE

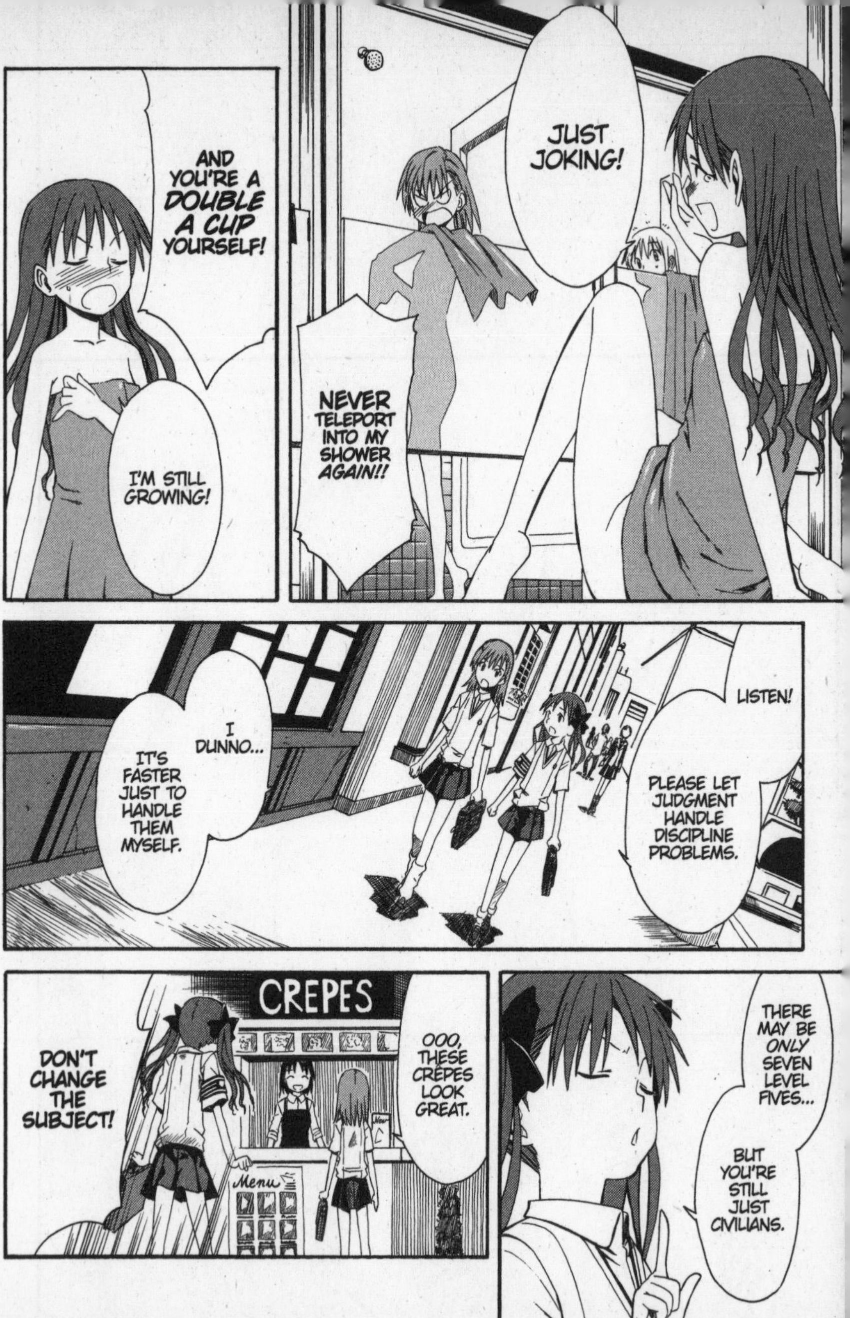
JUST JOKING!
NEVER TELEPORT INTO MY SHOWER *AGAIN!!*
AND YOU'RE A *DOUBLE A CUP* YOURSELF!
I'M STILL GROWING!
LISTEN!
PLEASE LET JUDGMENT HANDLE DISCIPLINE PROBLEMS.
I DUNNO...
IT'S FASTER JUST TO HANDLE THEM MYSELF.
THERE MAY BE *ONLY* SEVEN LEVEL FIVES...
BUT YOU'RE STILL JUST CIVILIANS.
CREPES
Menu
OOO, THESE CREPES LOOK GREAT.
DON'T CHANGE THE SUBJECT!

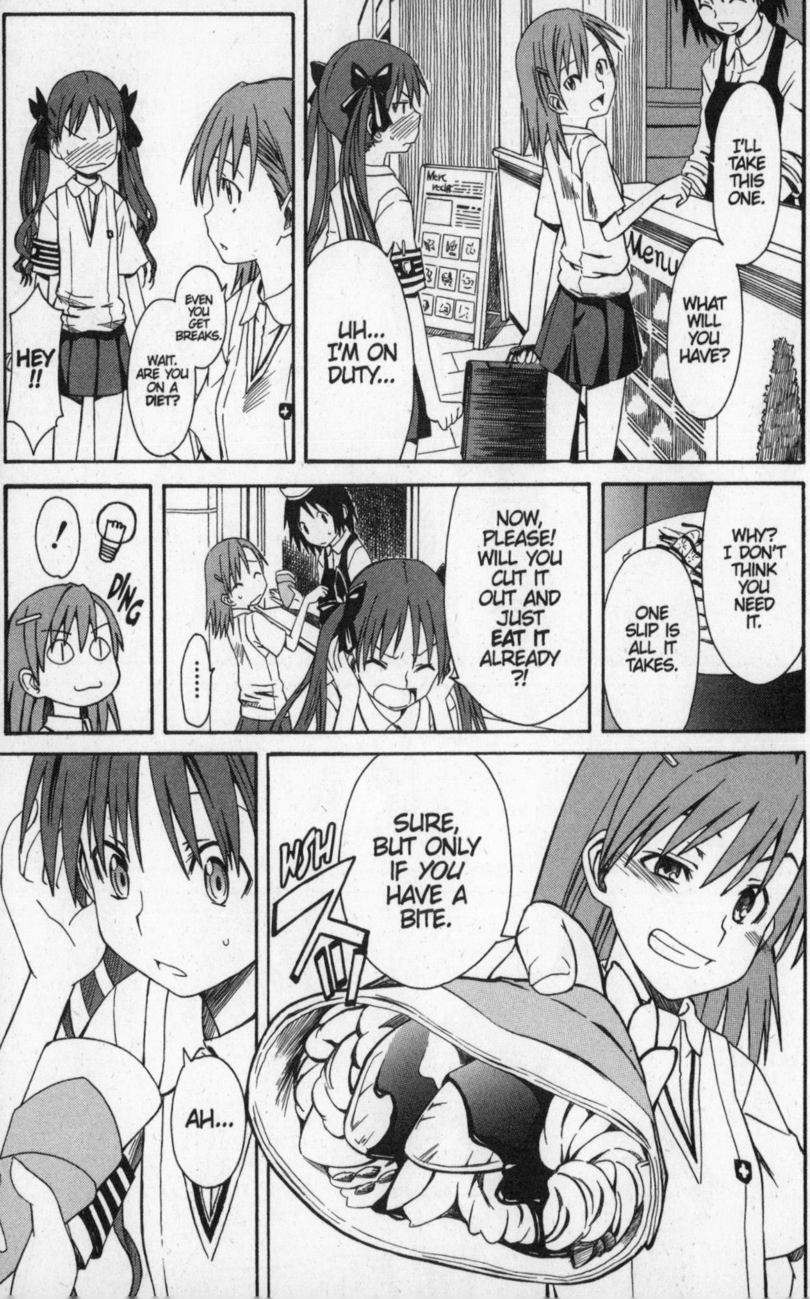
I'LL TAKE THIS ONE.
WHAT WILL YOU HAVE?
Menu
UH... I'M ON DUTY...
EVEN YOU GET BREAKS.
WAIT. ARE YOU ON A DIET?
HEY!!
WHY? I DON'T THINK YOU NEED IT.
ONE SLIP IS ALL IT TAKES.
NOW, PLEASE! WILL YOU CUT IT OUT AND JUST EAT IT ALREADY?!
......
!
DING
WSH
SURE, BUT ONLY IF YOU HAVE A BITE.
AH...

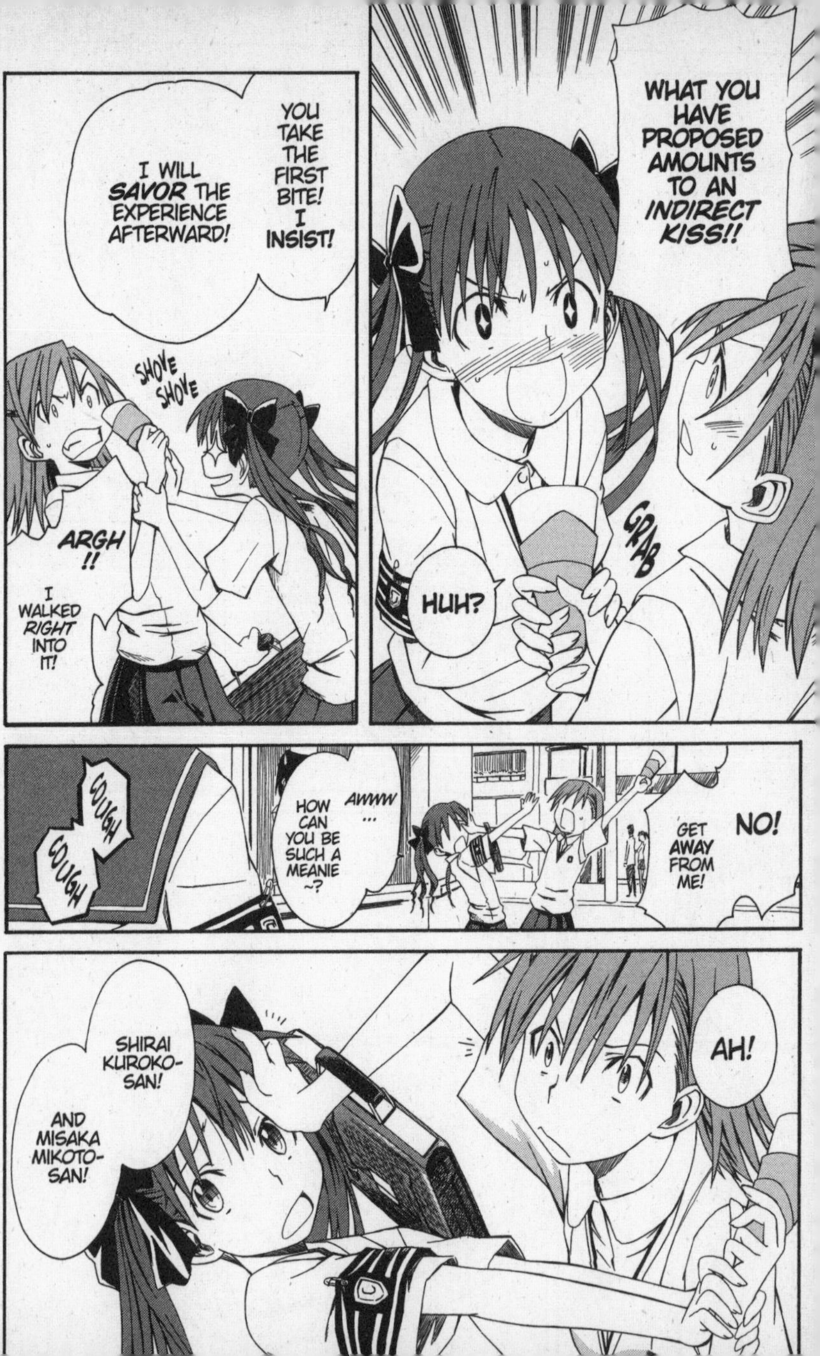
WHAT YOU HAVE PROPOSED AMOUNTS TO AN INDIRECT KISS!!
GRAB
HUH?
YOU TAKE THE FIRST BITE! I INSIST!
I WILL SAVOR THE EXPERIENCE AFTERWARD!
SHOVE SHOVE
ARGH!!
I WALKED RIGHT INTO IT!
NO!
GET AWAY FROM ME!
AWWW...
HOW CAN YOU BE SUCH A MEANIE~?
COUGH COUGH
AH!
SHIRAI KUROKO-SAN!
AND MISAKA MIKOTO-SAN!

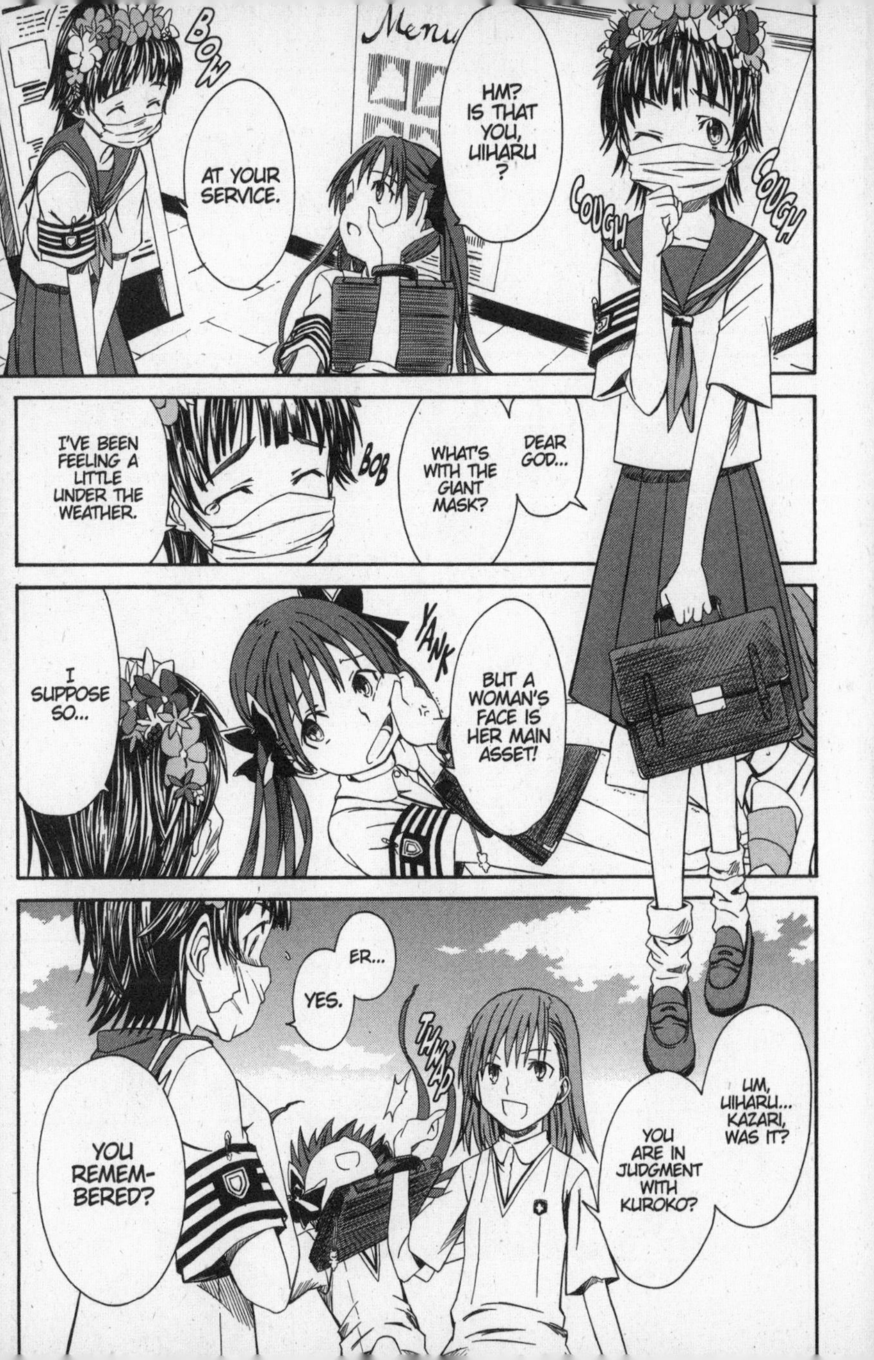
COUGH
COUGH
HM? IS THAT YOU, UIHARU?
AT YOUR SERVICE.
BOW
DEAR GOD...
WHAT'S WITH THE GIANT MASK?
BOB
I'VE BEEN FEELING A LITTLE UNDER THE WEATHER.
YANK
BUT A WOMAN'S FACE IS HER MAIN ASSET!
I SUPPOSE SO...
UM, UIHARU... KAZARI, WAS IT?
YOU ARE IN JUDGMENT WITH KUROKO?
THWAP
ER...
YES.
YOU REMEMBERED?

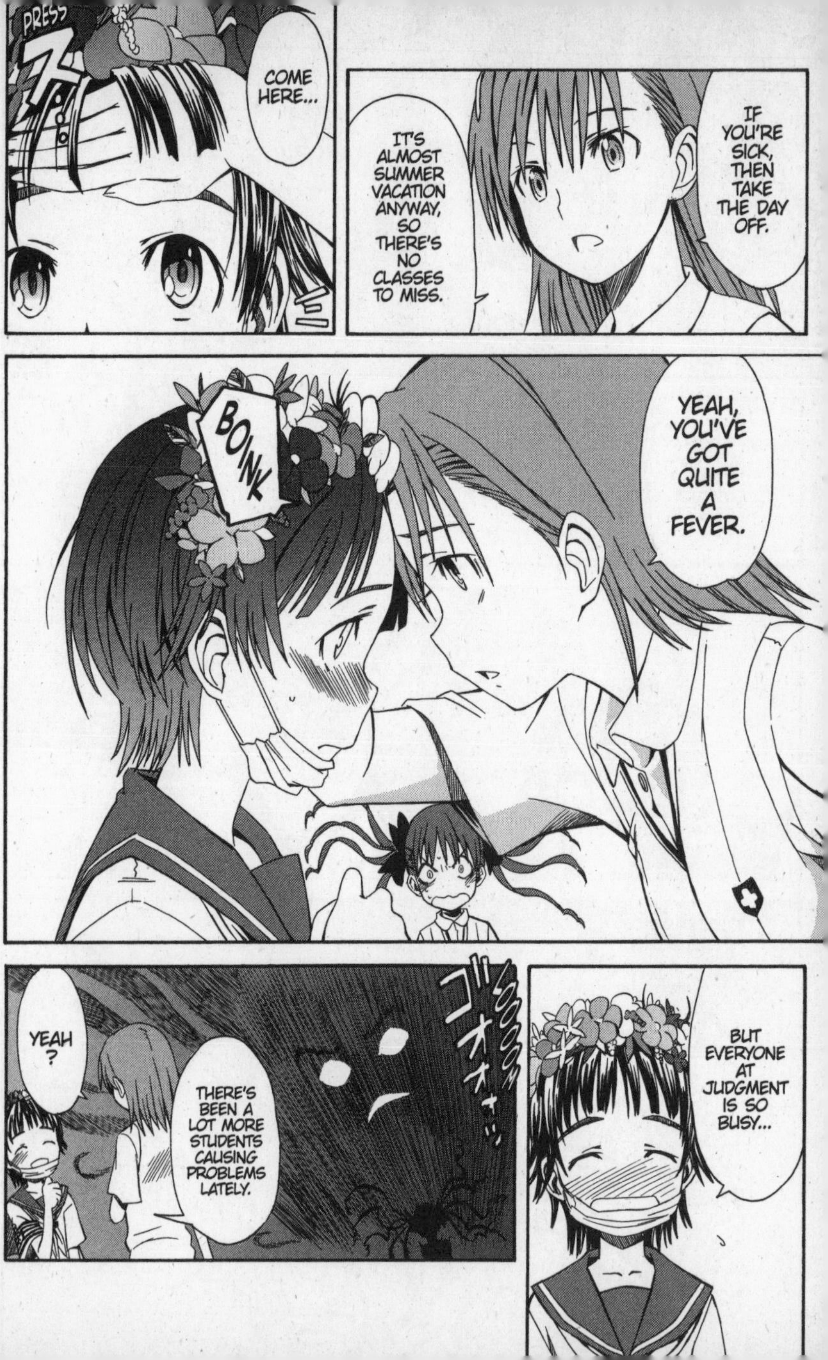
IF YOU'RE SICK, THEN TAKE THE DAY OFF.
IT'S ALMOST SUMMER VACATION ANYWAY, SO THERE'S NO CLASSES TO MISS.
PRESS
COME HERE...
YEAH, YOU'VE GOT QUITE A FEVER.
BOINK
BUT EVERYONE AT JUDGMENT IS SO BUSY...
ゴオオオッ
LOOOOM
THERE'S BEEN A LOT MORE STUDENTS CAUSING PROBLEMS LATELY.
YEAH?

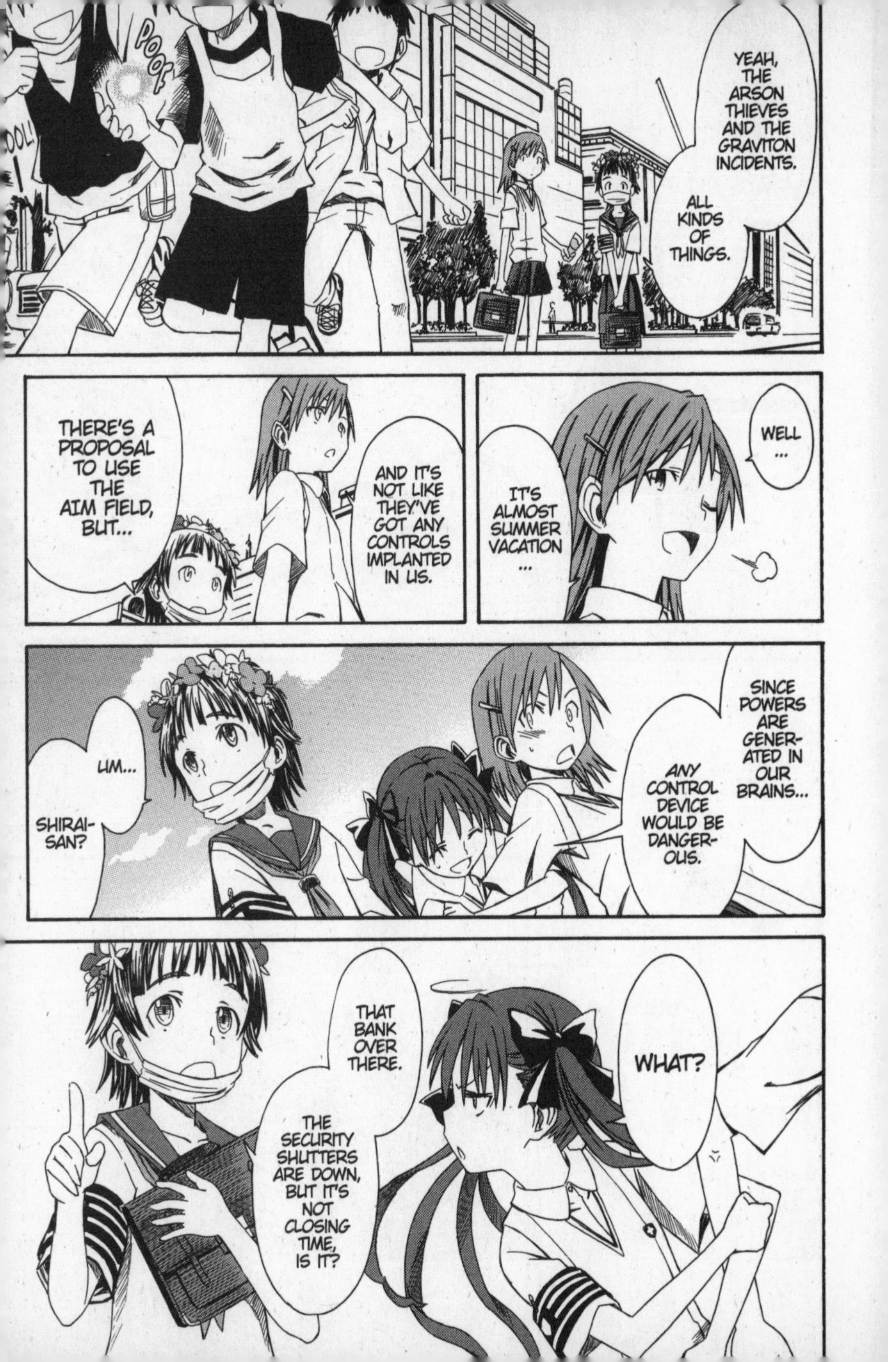
YEAH, THE ARSON THIEVES AND THE GRAVITON INCIDENTS.
ALL KINDS OF THINGS.
POOF
WELL ...
IT'S ALMOST SUMMER VACATION ...
AND IT'S NOT LIKE THEY'VE GOT ANY CONTROLS IMPLANTED IN US.
THERE'S A PROPOSAL TO USE THE AIM FIELD, BUT...
SINCE POWERS ARE GENERATED IN OUR BRAINS...
ANY CONTROL DEVICE WOULD BE DANGER-OUS.
UM...
SHIRAI-SAN?
WHAT?
THAT BANK OVER THERE.
THE SECURITY SHUTTERS ARE DOWN, BUT IT'S NOT CLOSING TIME, IS IT?

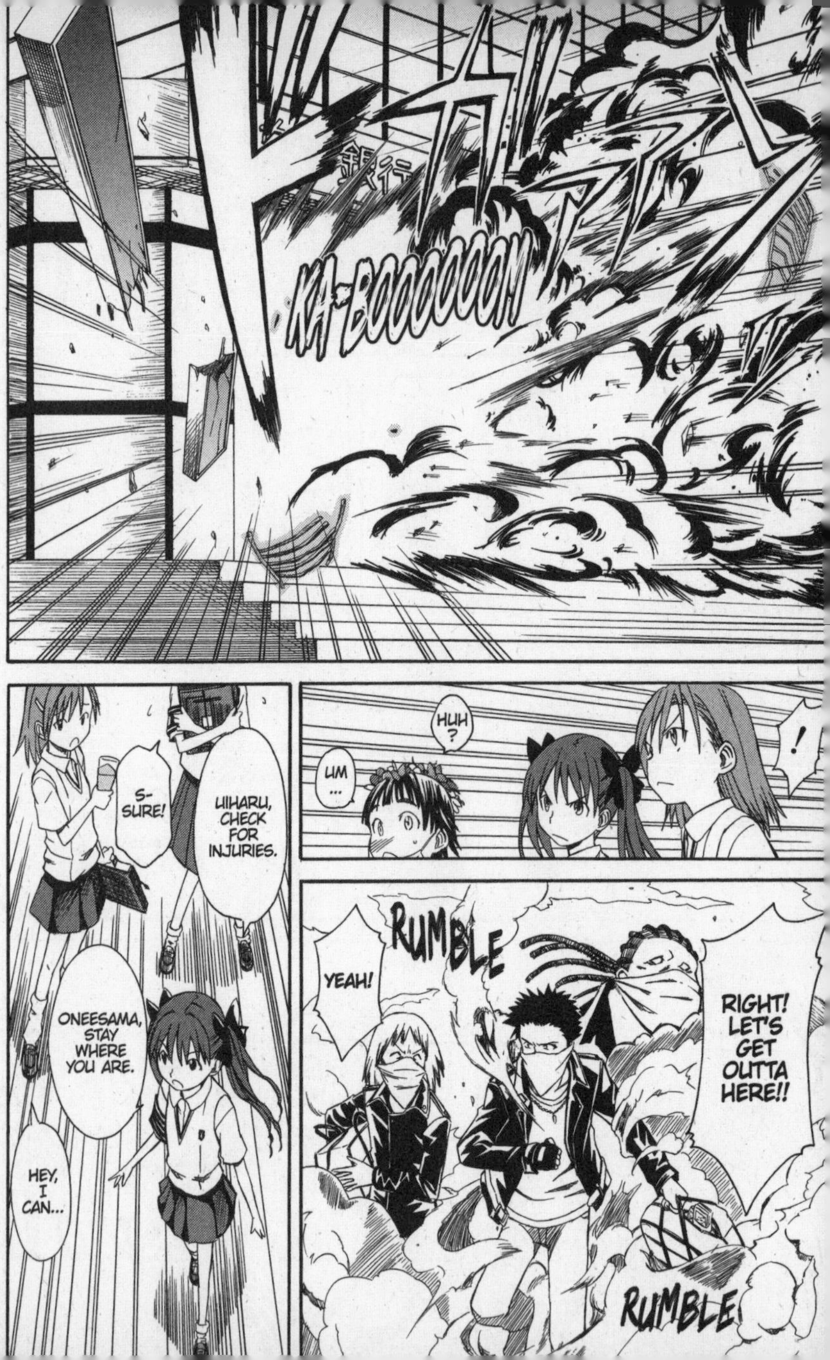
銀行
KA-BOOOOOOM
!
HUH?
UM...
RIGHT! LET'S GET OUTTA HERE!!
RUMBLE
YEAH!
RUMBLE
UIHARU, CHECK FOR INJURIES.
S-SURE!
ONEESAMA, STAY WHERE YOU ARE.
HEY, I CAN...

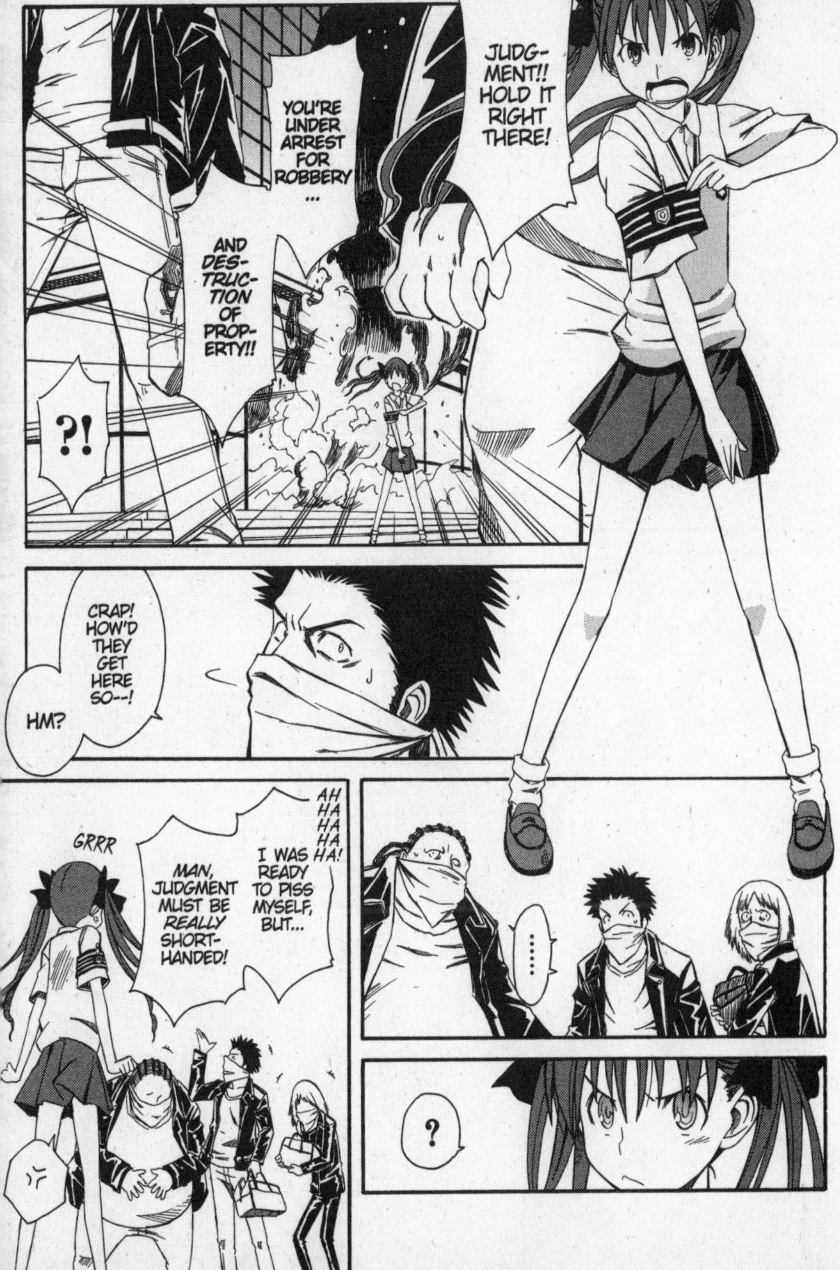

JUDGMENT!! HOLD IT RIGHT THERE!
YOU'RE UNDER ARREST FOR ROBBERY...
AND DESTRUCTION OF PROPERTY!!
?!
CRAP! HOW'D THEY GET HERE SO--!
HM?
......
?
AH HA HA HA HA HA!
I WAS READY TO PISS MYSELF, BUT...
MAN, JUDGMENT MUST BE *REALLY* SHORT-HANDED!
GRRR

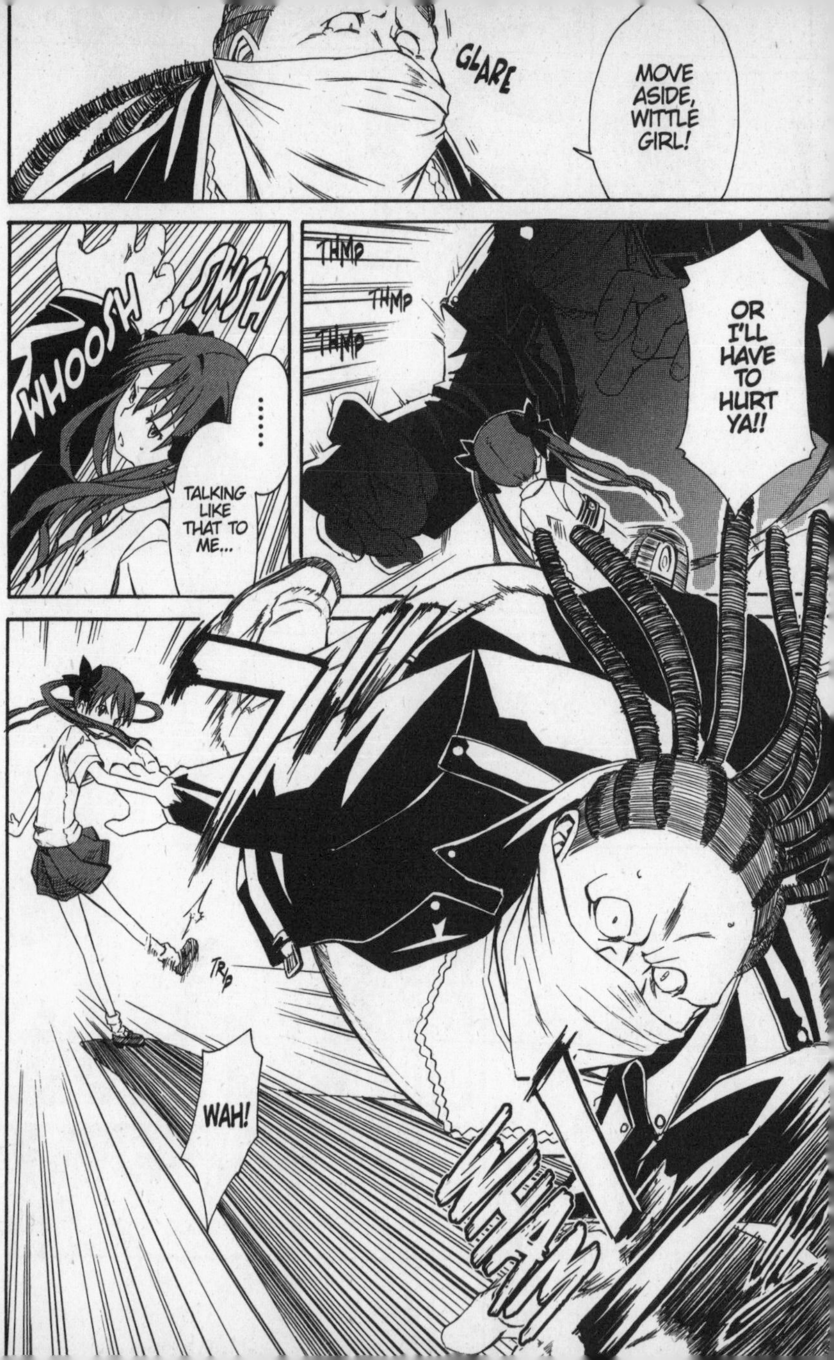
GLARE
MOVE ASIDE, WITTLE GIRL!
THMP
THMP
THMP
OR I'LL HAVE TO HURT YA!!
WHOOSH
SWSH
......
TALKING LIKE THAT TO ME...
TRIP
WAH!

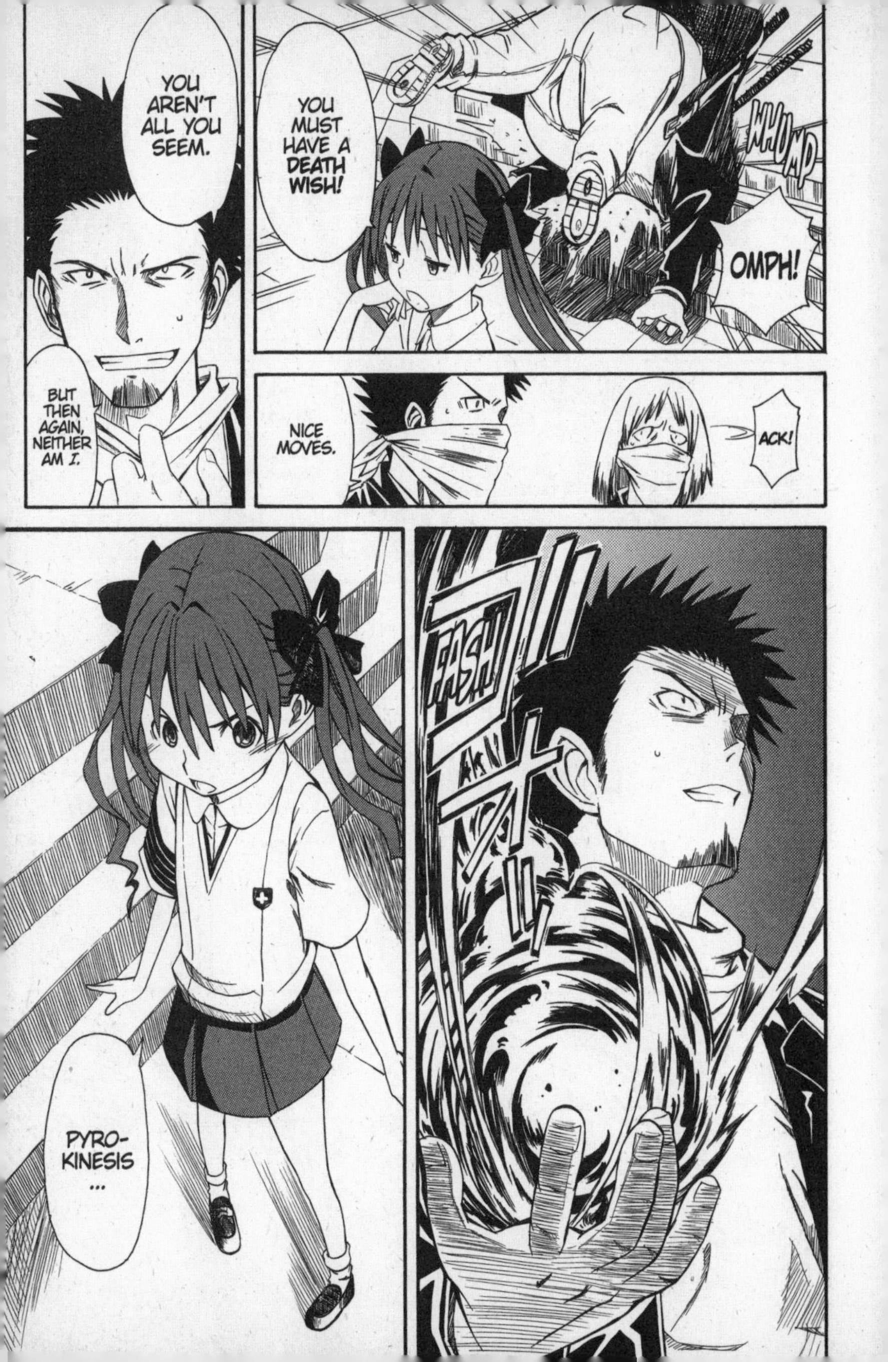
WHUMP
OMPH!
YOU MUST HAVE A DEATH WISH!
ACK!
NICE MOVES.
YOU AREN'T ALL YOU SEEM.
BUT THEN AGAIN, NEITHER AM I.
FASH
PYRO-KINESIS ...

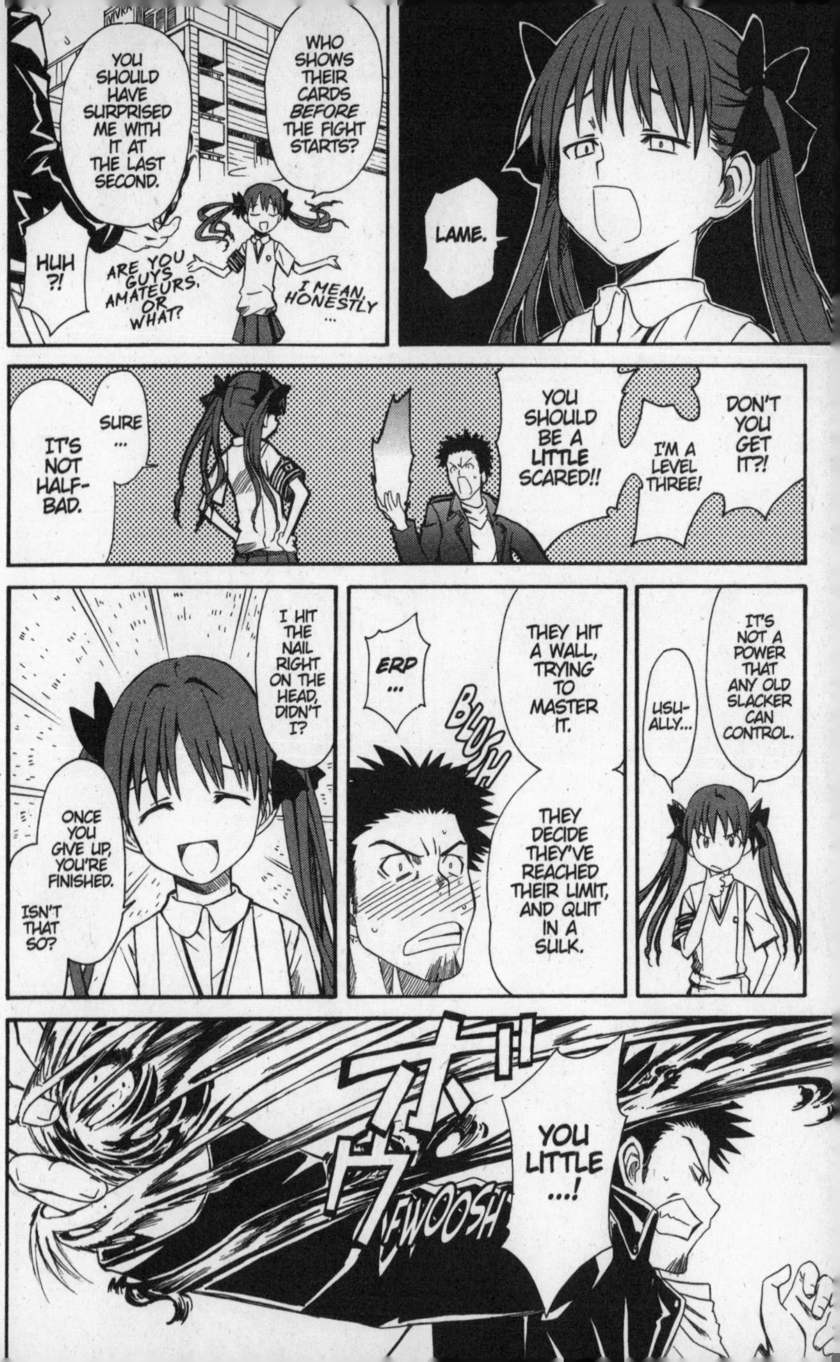
LAME.
WHO SHOWS THEIR CARDS BEFORE THE FIGHT STARTS?
YOU SHOULD HAVE SURPRISED ME WITH IT AT THE LAST SECOND.
I MEAN, HONESTLY ...
ARE YOU GUYS AMATEURS, OR WHAT?
HUH ?!
DON'T YOU GET IT?!
I'M A LEVEL THREE!
YOU SHOULD BE A LITTLE SCARED!!
SURE ...
IT'S NOT HALF-BAD.
IT'S NOT A POWER THAT ANY OLD SLACKER CAN CONTROL.
USU-ALLY...
THEY HIT A WALL, TRYING TO MASTER IT.
THEY DECIDE THEY'VE REACHED THEIR LIMIT, AND QUIT IN A SULK.
ERP ...
BLUSH
I HIT THE NAIL RIGHT ON THE HEAD, DIDN'T I?
ONCE YOU GIVE UP, YOU'RE FINISHED.
ISN'T THAT SO?
YOU LITTLE ...!
FWOOSH

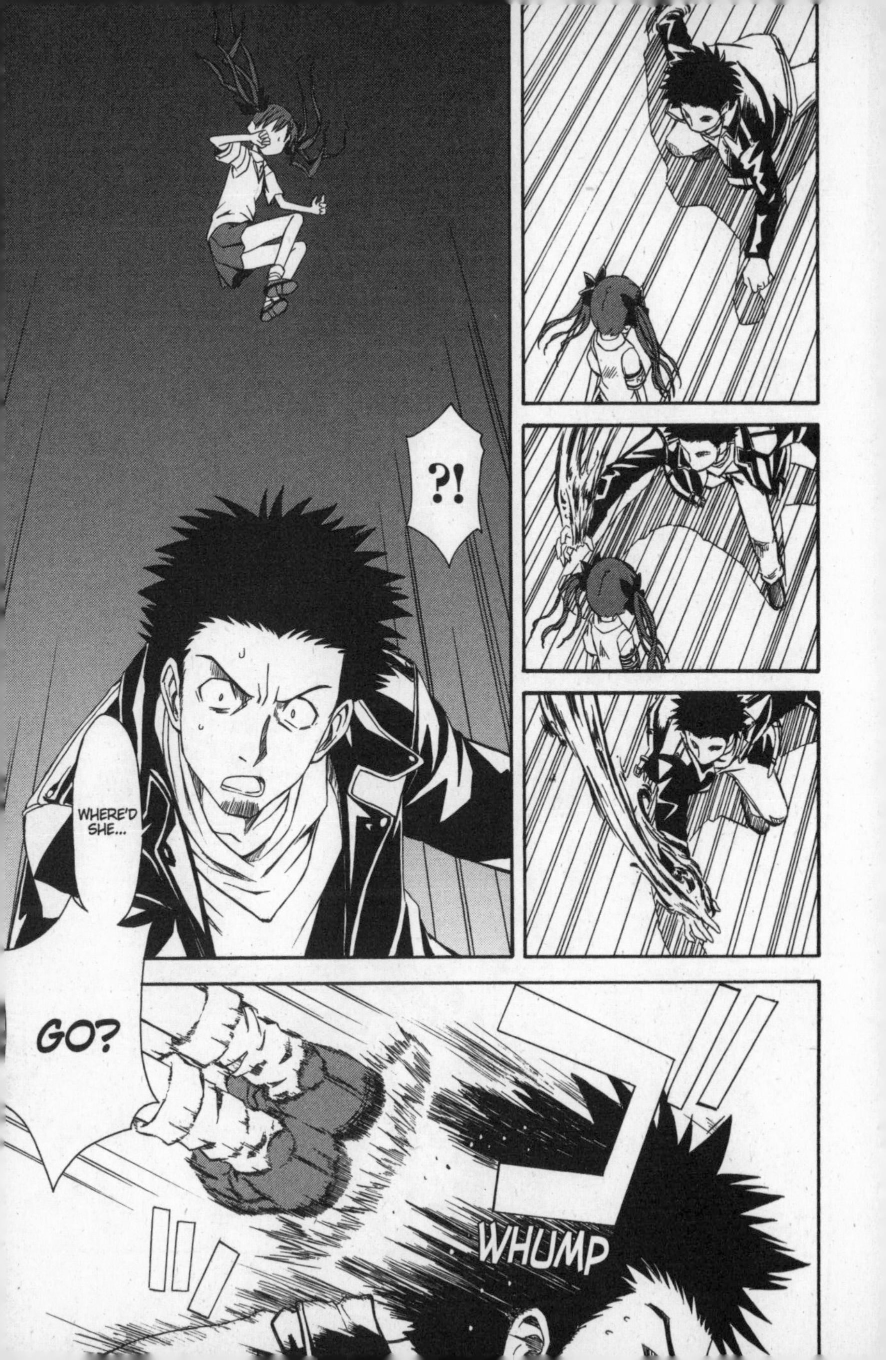
?!
WHERE'D SHE...
GO?
WHUMP

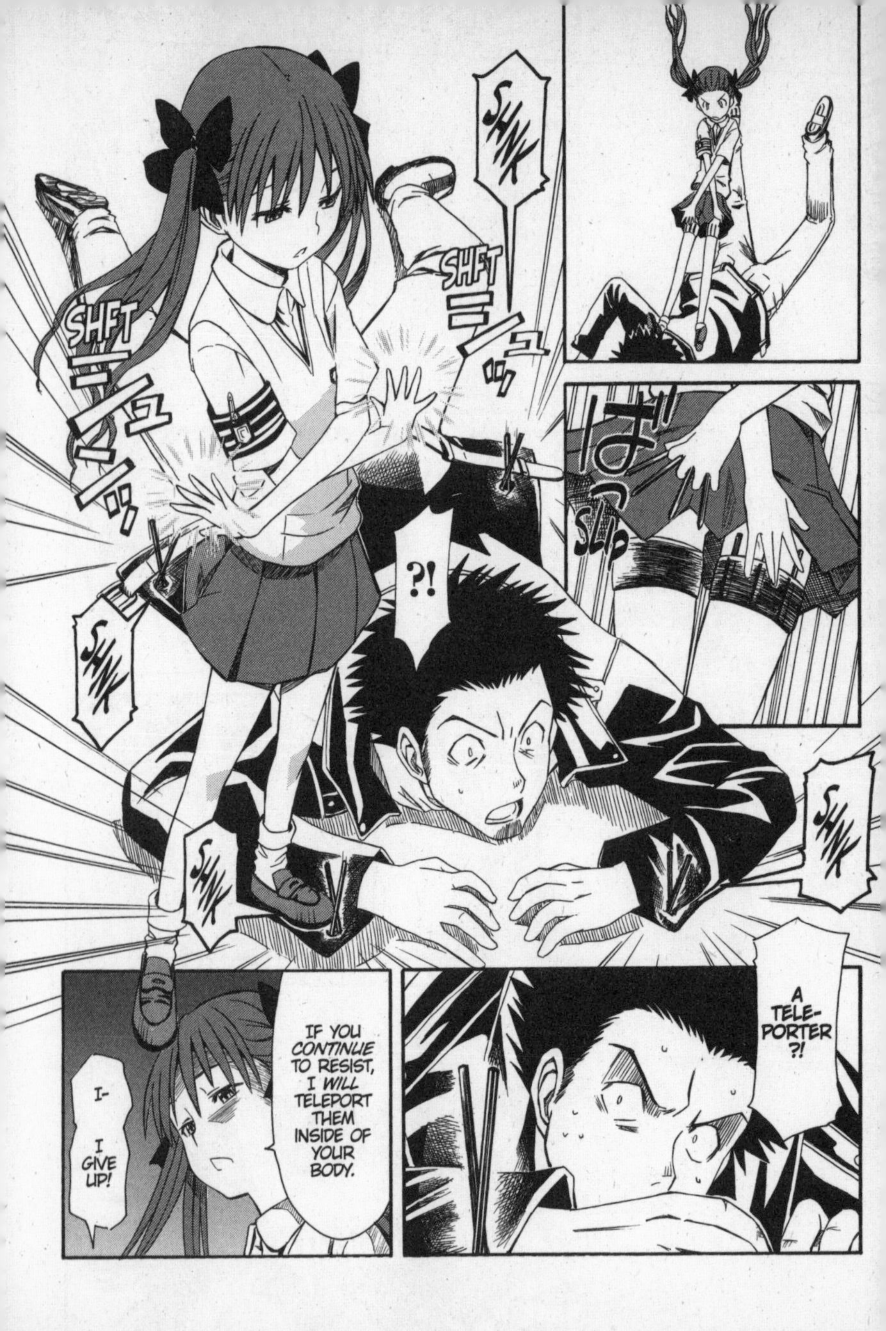
ばっ
SLIP
SHNK
SHFT
SHFT
?!
SHNK
SHNK
SHNK
A TELE-PORTER?!
IF YOU CONTINUE TO RESIST, I WILL TELEPORT THEM INSIDE OF YOUR BODY.
I-
I GIVE UP!

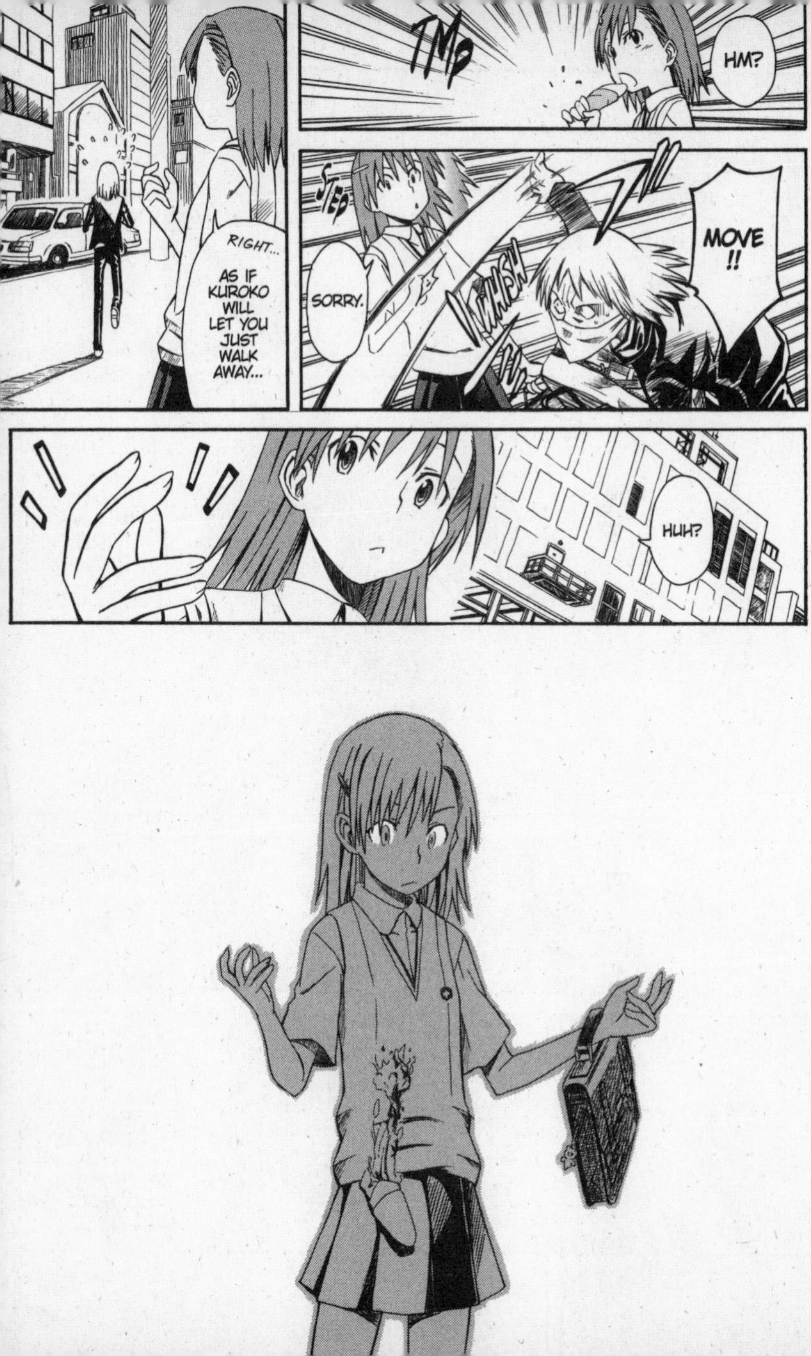

TMP
HM?
MOVE !!
STEP
WHISH
SORRY.
RIGHT...
AS IF KUROKO WILL LET YOU JUST WALK AWAY...
HUH?

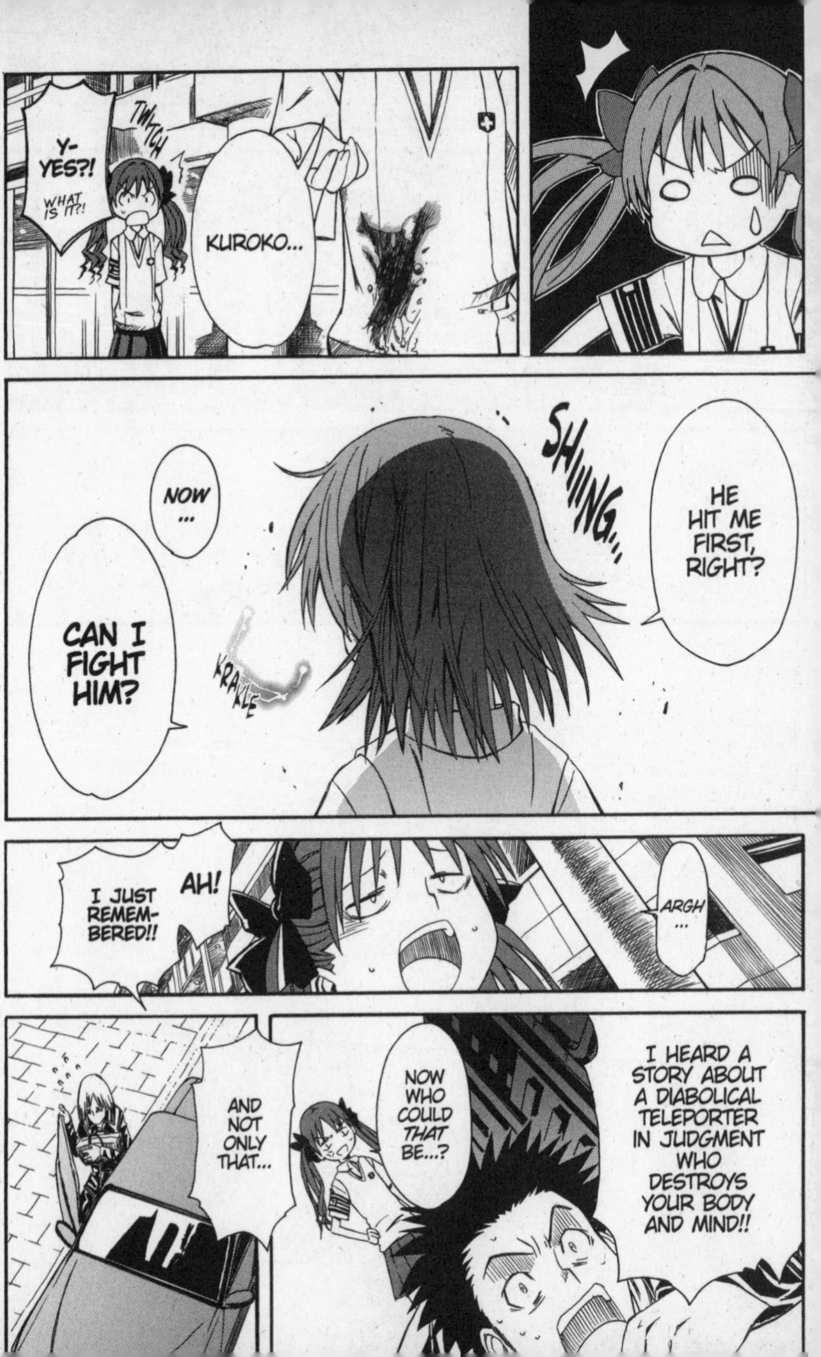
TWITCH
KUROKO...
Y-YES?!
WHAT IS IT?!
HE HIT ME FIRST, RIGHT?
SHIIING...
NOW...
CAN I FIGHT HIM?
KRAKLE
ARGH...
AH!
I JUST REMEMBERED!!
I HEARD A STORY ABOUT A DIABOLICAL TELEPORTER IN JUDGMENT WHO DESTROYS YOUR BODY AND MIND!!
NOW WHO COULD THAT BE...?
AND NOT ONLY THAT...

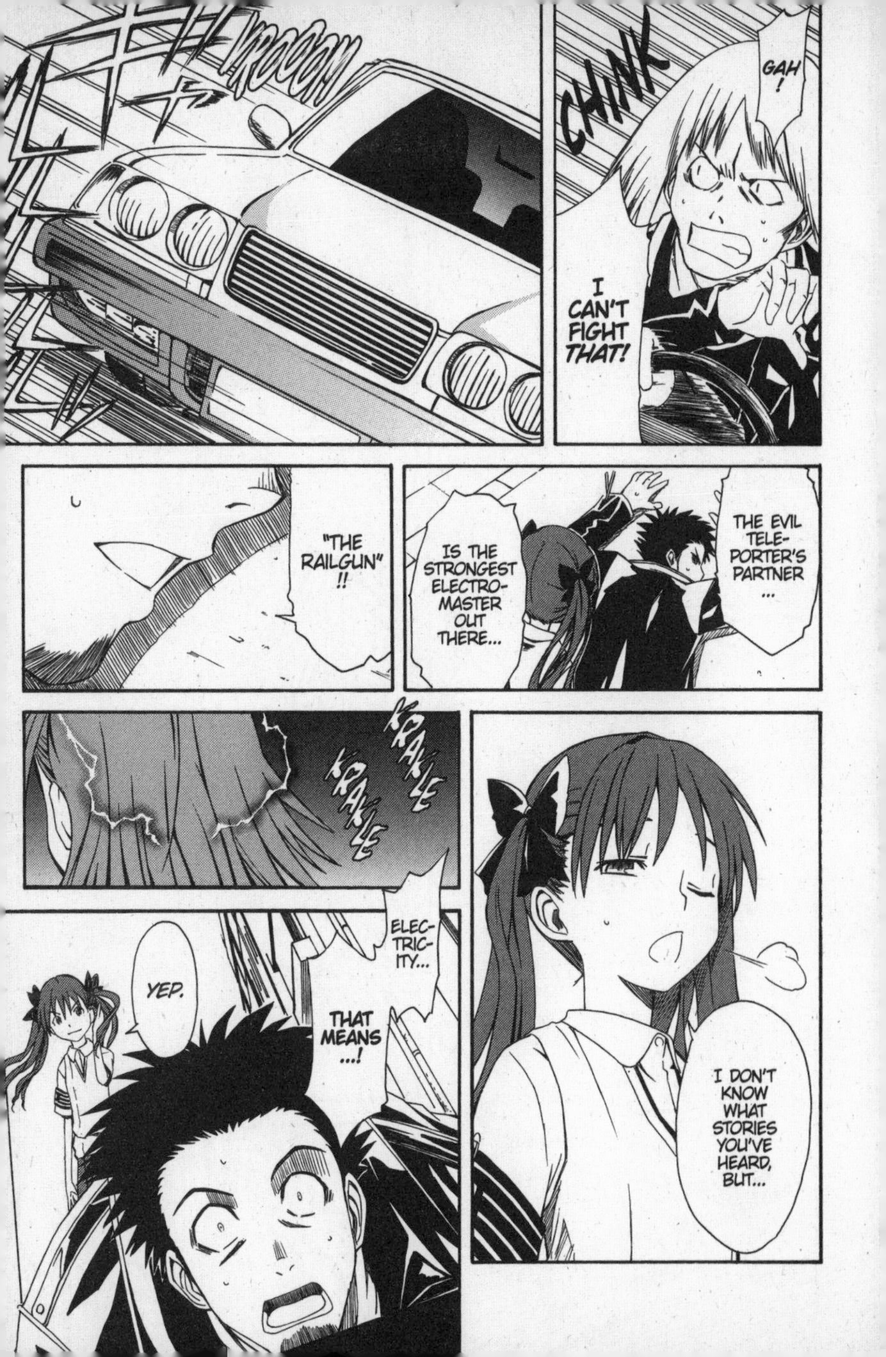
GAH!
CHINK
I CAN'T FIGHT THAT!
VROOOM
THE EVIL TELE-PORTER'S PARTNER ...
IS THE STRONGEST ELECTRO-MASTER OUT THERE...
"THE RAILGUN" !!
I DON'T KNOW WHAT STORIES YOU'VE HEARD, BUT...
KRAKLE
KRAKLE
ELEC-TRIC-ITY...
THAT MEANS ...!
YEP.

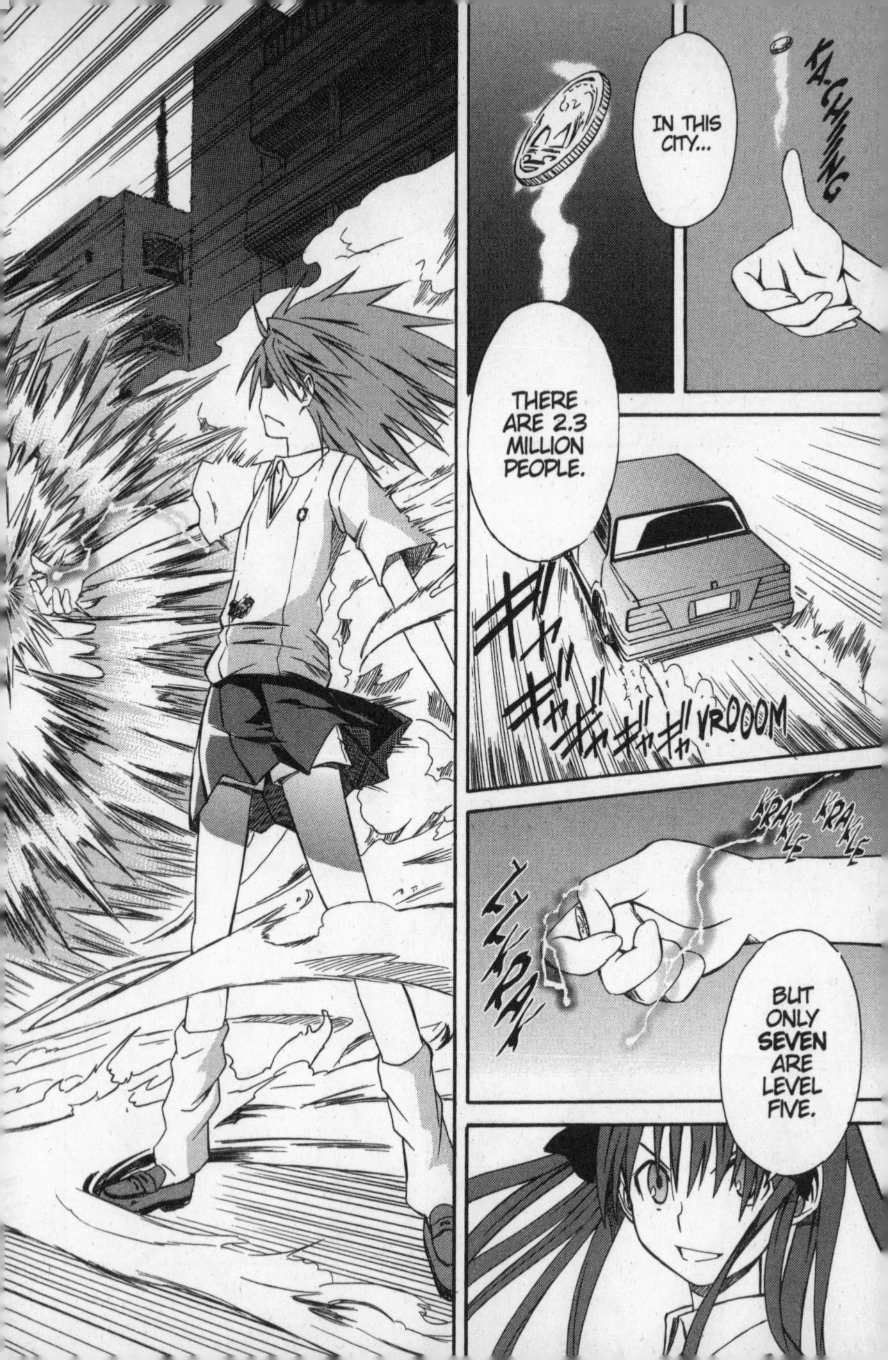

KA-CHING
IN THIS CITY...
THERE ARE 2.3 MILLION PEOPLE.
VROOM
KRAKLE KRAKLE
BUT ONLY SEVEN ARE LEVEL FIVE.

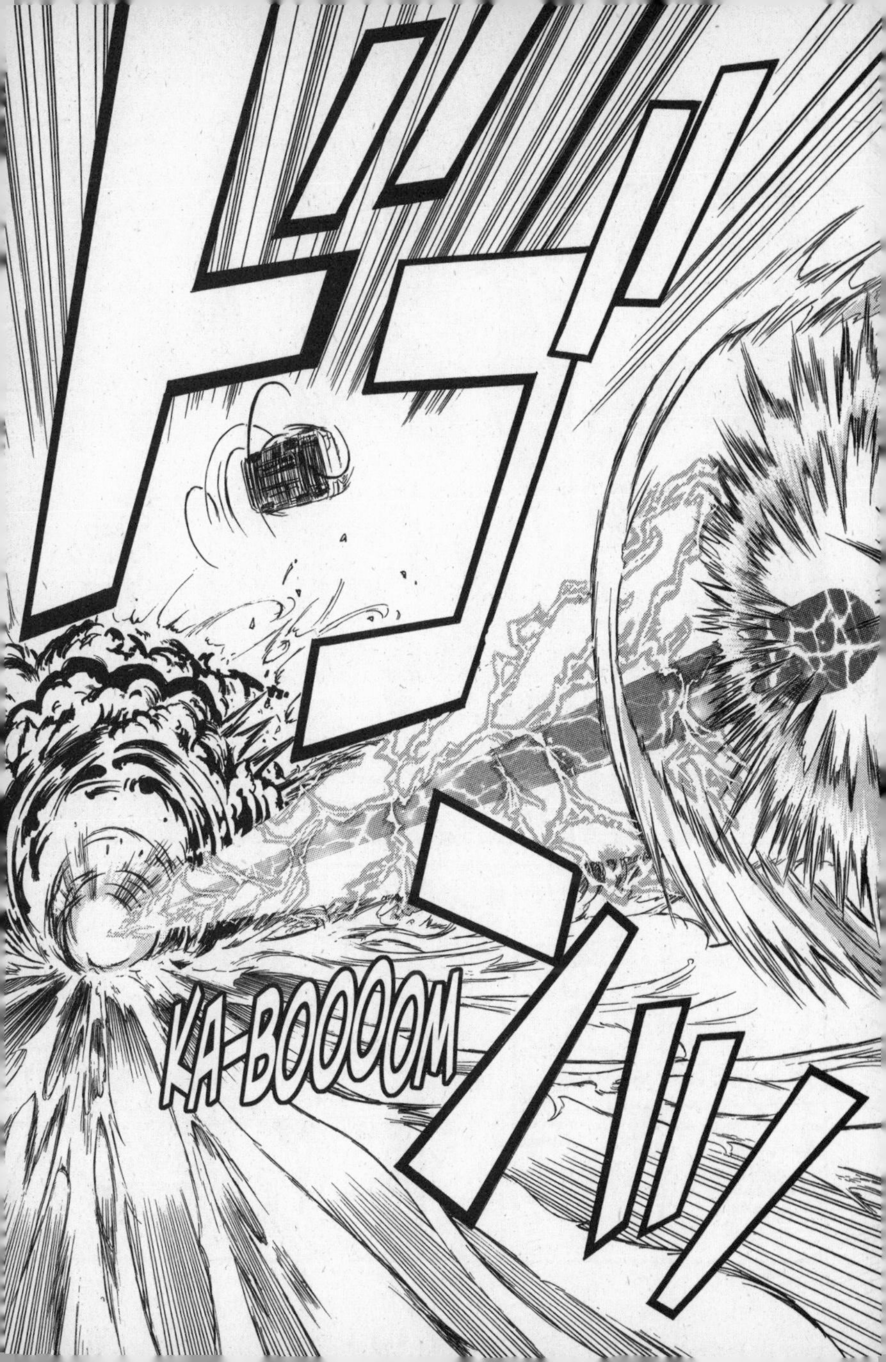
KA-BOOOOM

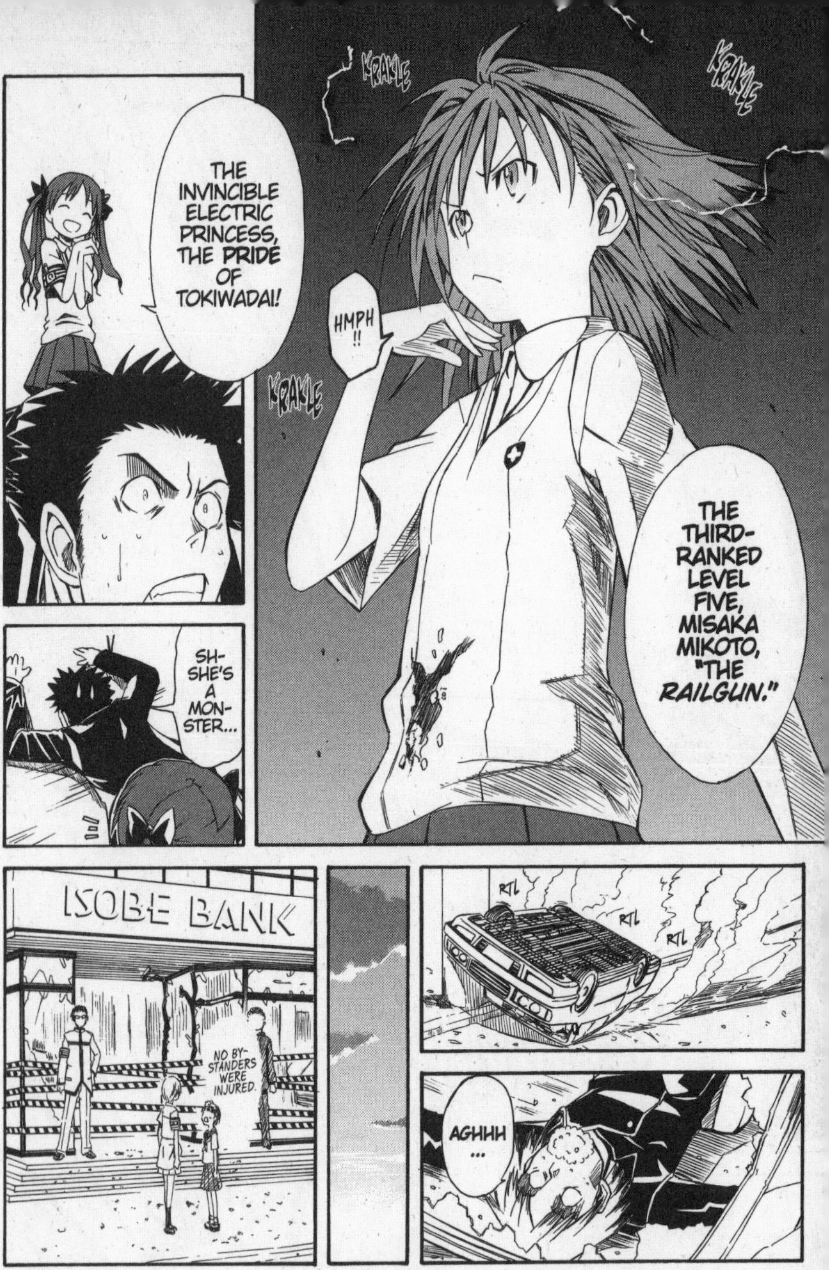
KRAKLE
KRAKLE
HMPH !!
KRAKLE
THE THIRD-RANKED LEVEL FIVE, MISAKA MIKOTO, "THE RAILGUN."
THE INVINCIBLE ELECTRIC PRINCESS, THE PRIDE OF TOKIWADAI!
SH-SHE'S A MON-STER...
RTL
RTL
RTL
AGHHH ...
ISOBE BANK
NO BY-STANDERS WERE INJURED.

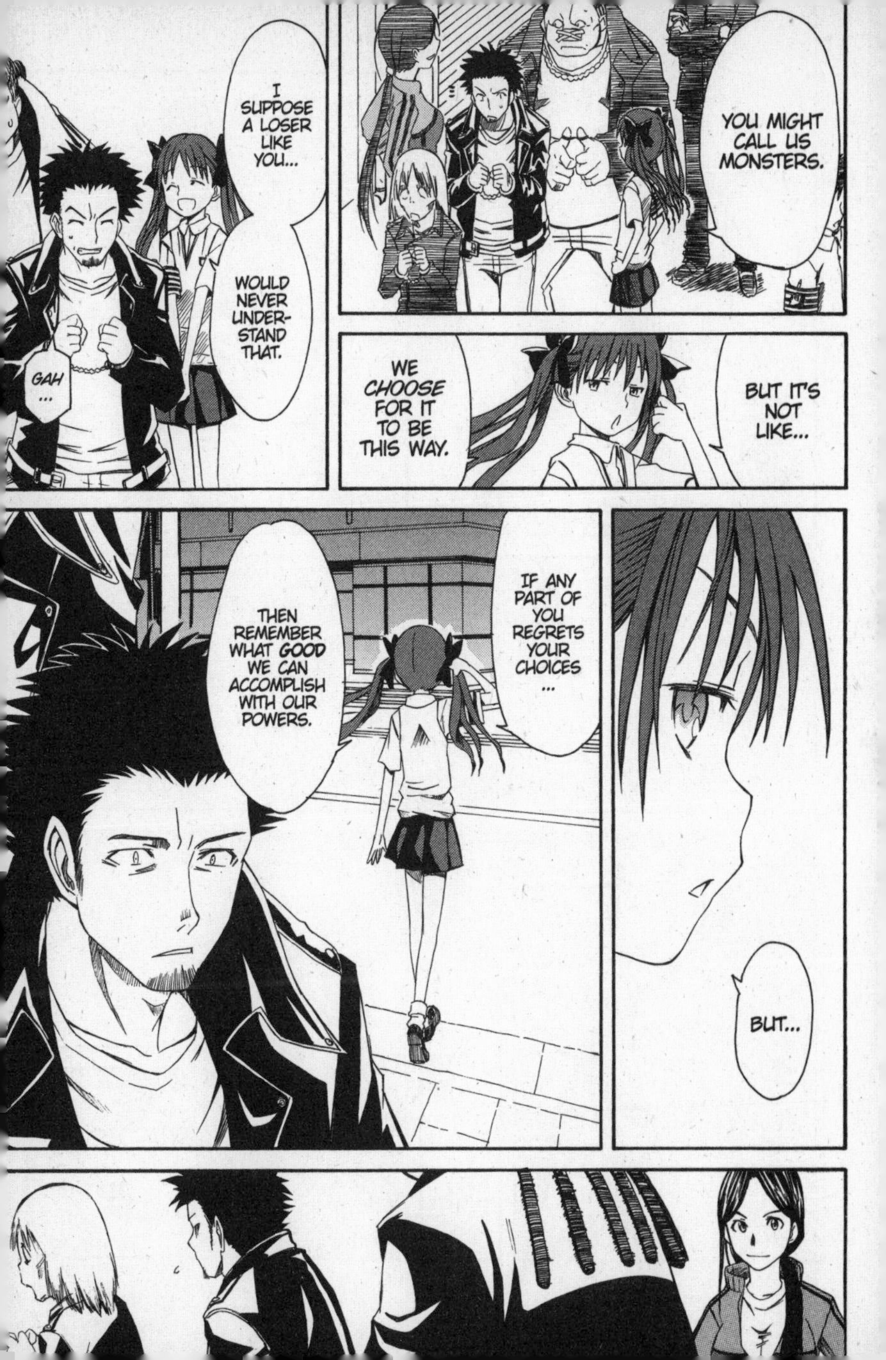
YOU MIGHT CALL US MONSTERS.
BUT IT'S NOT LIKE...
WE CHOOSE FOR IT TO BE THIS WAY.
I SUPPOSE A LOSER LIKE YOU...
WOULD NEVER UNDERSTAND THAT.
GAH ...
BUT...
IF ANY PART OF YOU REGRETS YOUR CHOICES ...
THEN REMEMBER WHAT GOOD WE CAN ACCOMPLISH WITH OUR POWERS.

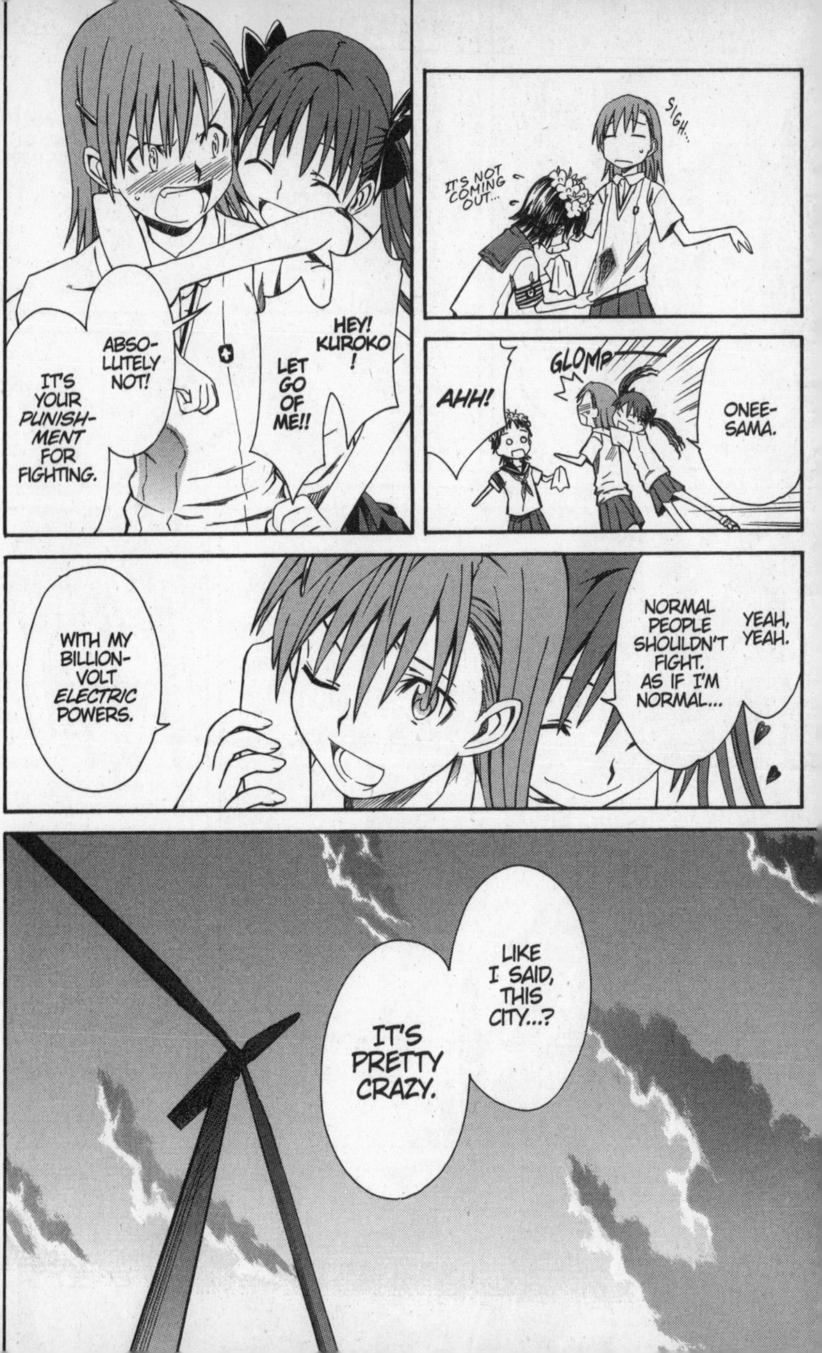
SIGH...
IT'S NOT COMING OUT...
ONEE-SAMA.
GLOMP
AHH!
HEY! KUROKO!
LET GO OF ME!!
ABSOLUTELY NOT!
IT'S YOUR PUNISHMENT FOR FIGHTING.
YEAH, YEAH.
NORMAL PEOPLE SHOULDN'T FIGHT. AS IF I'M NORMAL...
WITH MY BILLION-VOLT ELECTRIC POWERS.
LIKE I SAID, THIS CITY...?
IT'S PRETTY CRAZY.

CHAPTER 2: JULY 17 (1)

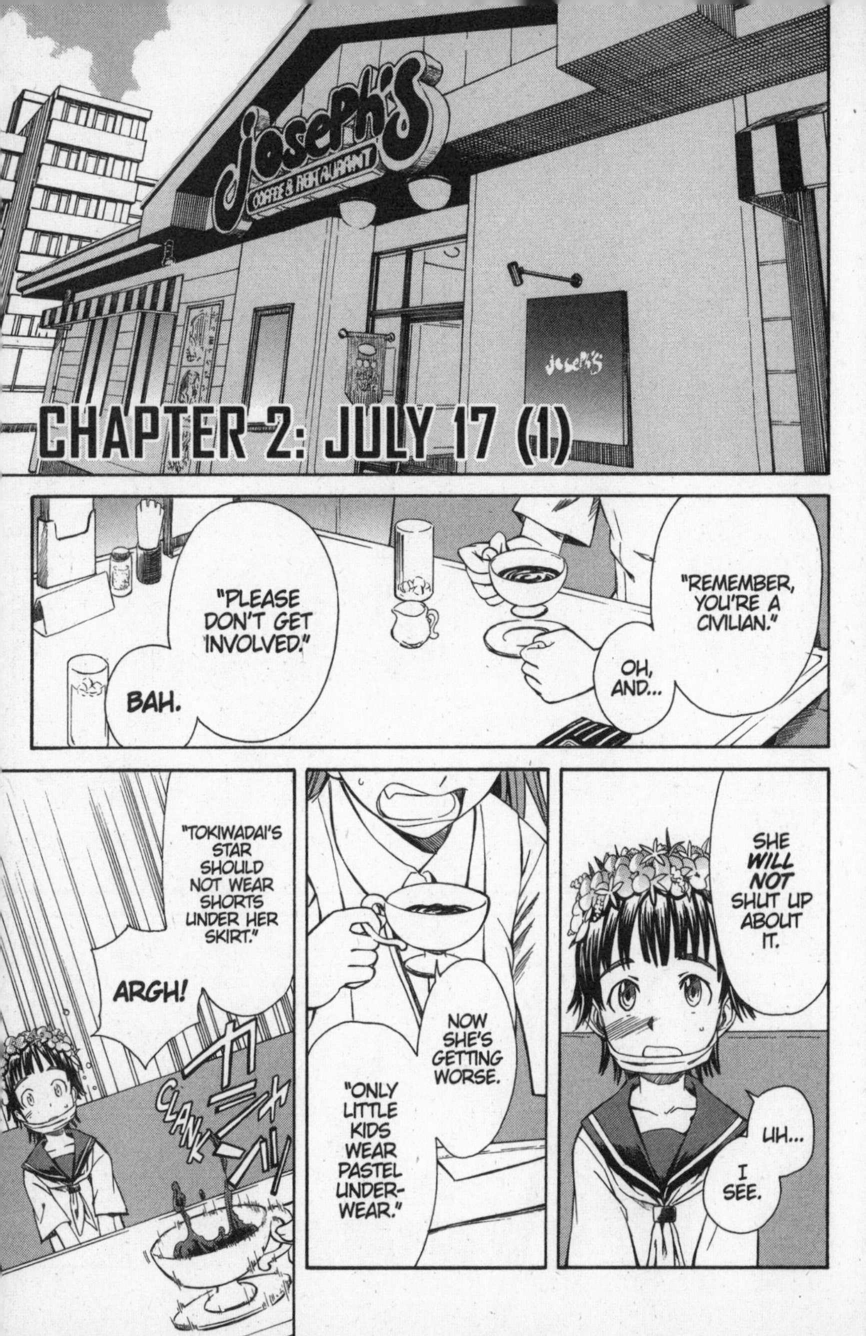
JOSEPH'S
COFFEE & RESTAURANT
JOSEPH'S
"REMEMBER, YOU'RE A CIVILIAN."
OH, AND...
"PLEASE DON'T GET INVOLVED."
BAH.
SHE WILL NOT SHUT UP ABOUT IT.
UH...
I SEE.
NOW SHE'S GETTING WORSE.
"ONLY LITTLE KIDS WEAR PASTEL UNDER-WEAR."
"TOKIWADAI'S STAR SHOULD NOT WEAR SHORTS UNDER HER SKIRT."
ARGH!
CLANK

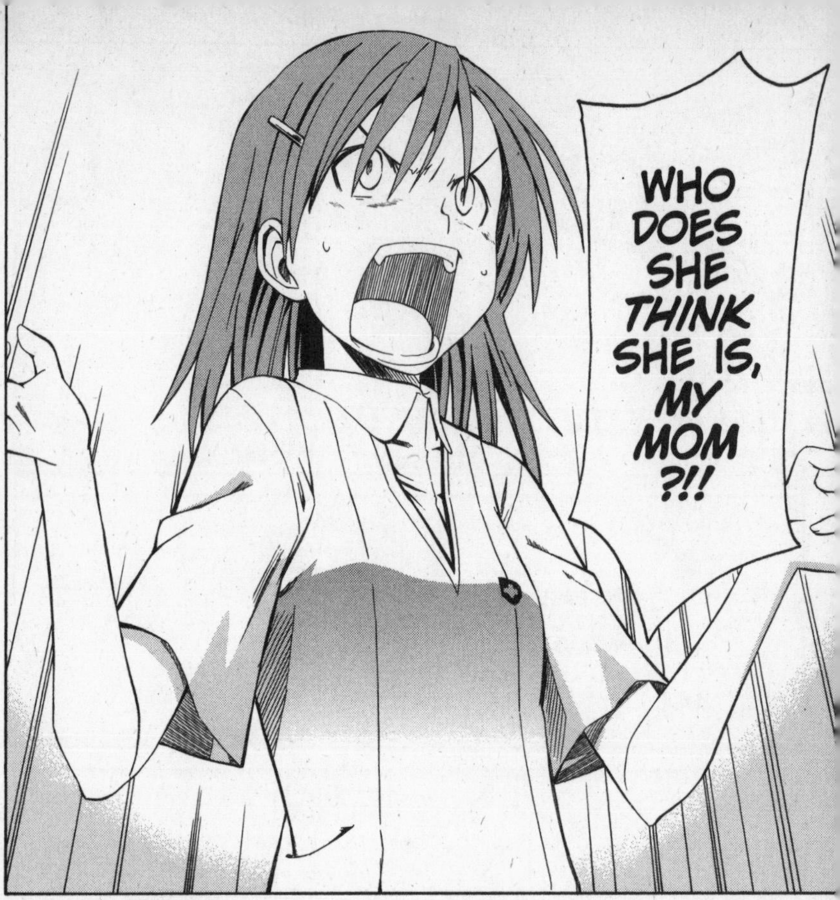
WHO DOES SHE THINK SHE IS, MY MOM ?!!

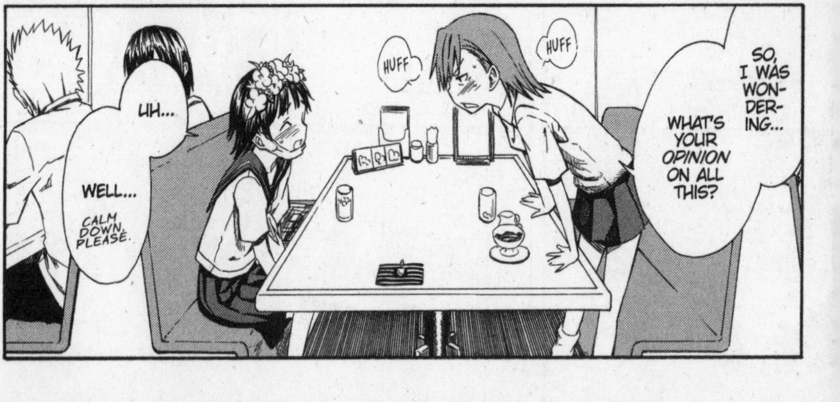
SO, I WAS WON-DER-ING...
WHAT'S YOUR OPINION ON ALL THIS?
HUFF
HUFF
UH...
WELL...
CALM DOWN, PLEASE.

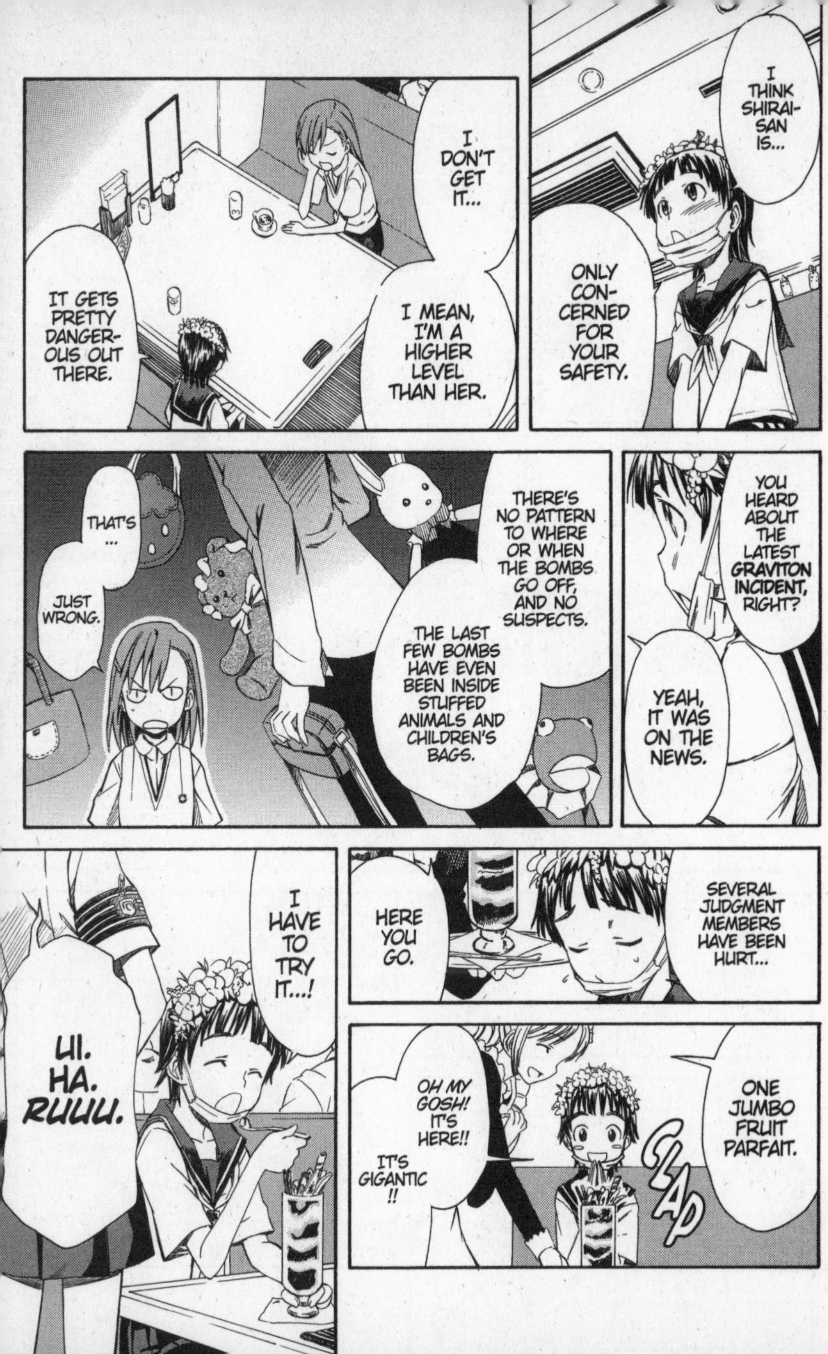
I THINK SHIRAI-SAN IS...
ONLY CONCERNED FOR YOUR SAFETY.
I DON'T GET IT...
I MEAN, I'M A HIGHER LEVEL THAN HER.
IT GETS PRETTY DANGEROUS OUT THERE.
YOU HEARD ABOUT THE LATEST GRAVITON INCIDENT, RIGHT?
YEAH, IT WAS ON THE NEWS.
THERE'S NO PATTERN TO WHERE OR WHEN THE BOMBS GO OFF, AND NO SUSPECTS.
THE LAST FEW BOMBS HAVE EVEN BEEN INSIDE STUFFED ANIMALS AND CHILDREN'S BAGS.
THAT'S ...
JUST WRONG.
SEVERAL JUDGMENT MEMBERS HAVE BEEN HURT...
HERE YOU GO.
ONE JUMBO FRUIT PARFAIT.
CLAP
OH MY GOSH! IT'S HERE!!
IT'S GIGANTIC !!
I HAVE TO TRY IT...!
UI. HA. RUUU.

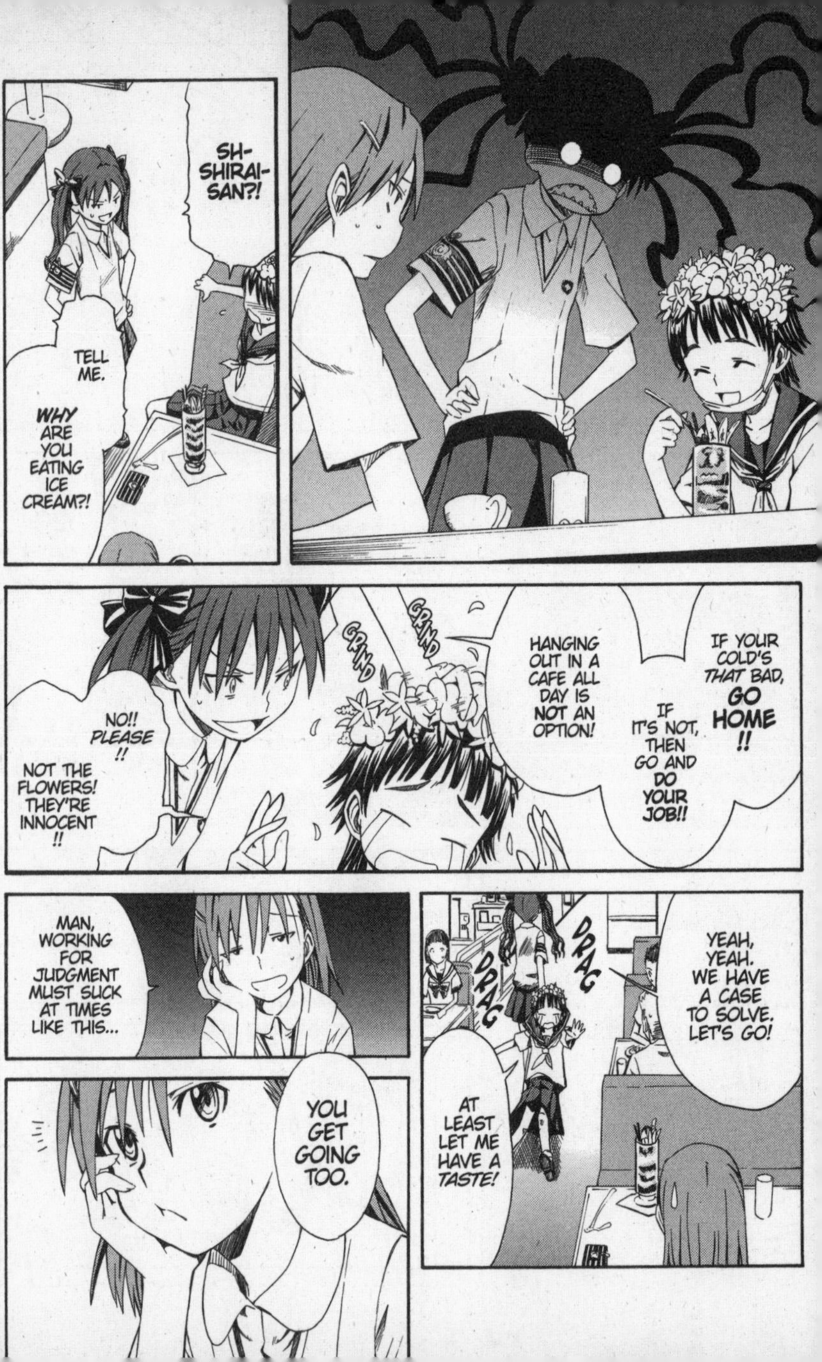
SH-SHIRAI-SAN?!
TELL ME.
WHY ARE YOU EATING ICE CREAM?!
IF YOUR COLD'S THAT BAD, GO HOME!!
IF IT'S NOT, THEN GO AND DO YOUR JOB!!
HANGING OUT IN A CAFE ALL DAY IS NOT AN OPTION!
GRIND
GRIND
NO!! PLEASE!!
NOT THE FLOWERS! THEY'RE INNOCENT!!
YEAH, YEAH. WE HAVE A CASE TO SOLVE. LET'S GO!
DRAG
DRAG
AT LEAST LET ME HAVE A TASTE!
MAN, WORKING FOR JUDGMENT MUST SUCK AT TIMES LIKE THIS...
YOU GET GOING TOO.

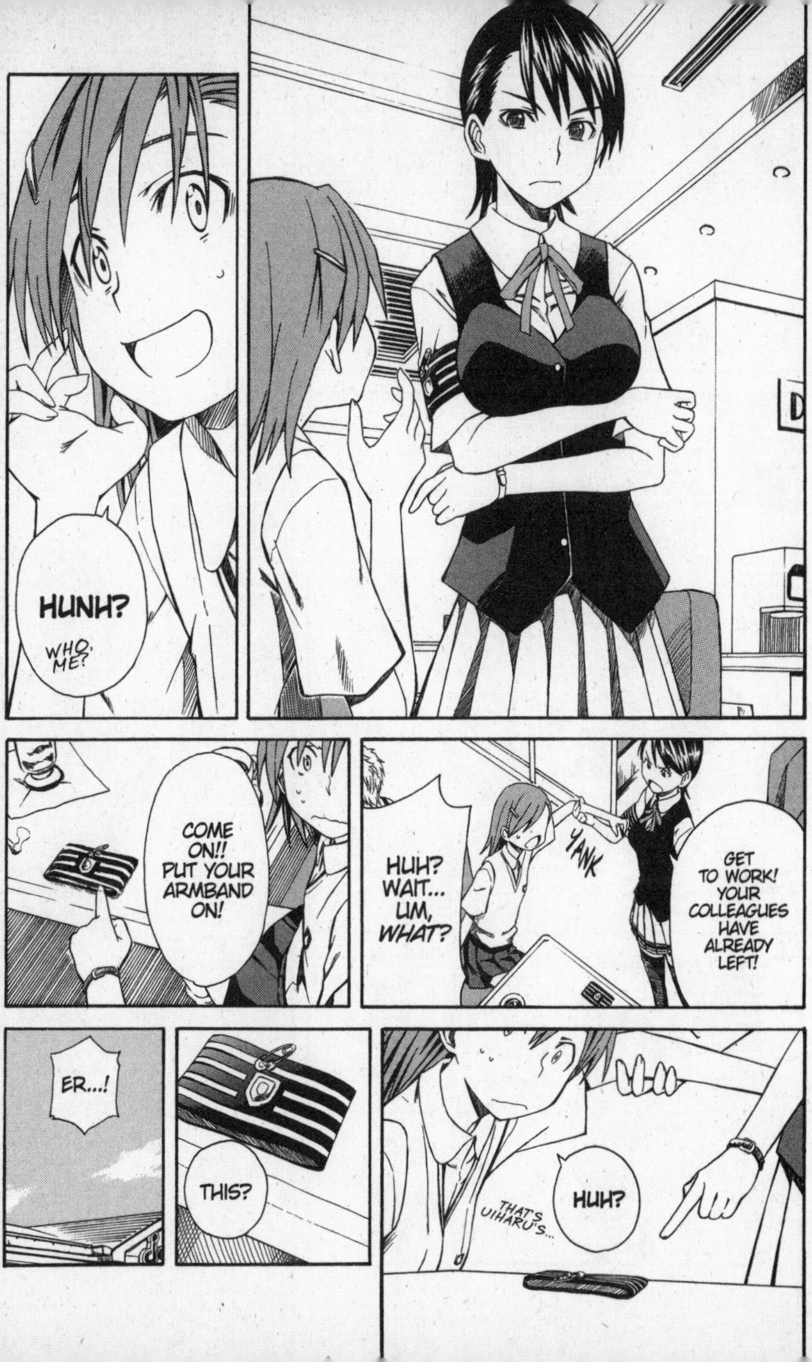
HUNH?
WHO, ME?
GET TO WORK! YOUR COLLEAGUES HAVE ALREADY LEFT!
YANK
HUH? WAIT... UM, WHAT?
COME ON!! PUT YOUR ARMBAND ON!
HUH?
THAT'S UIHARU'S...
THIS?
ER...!

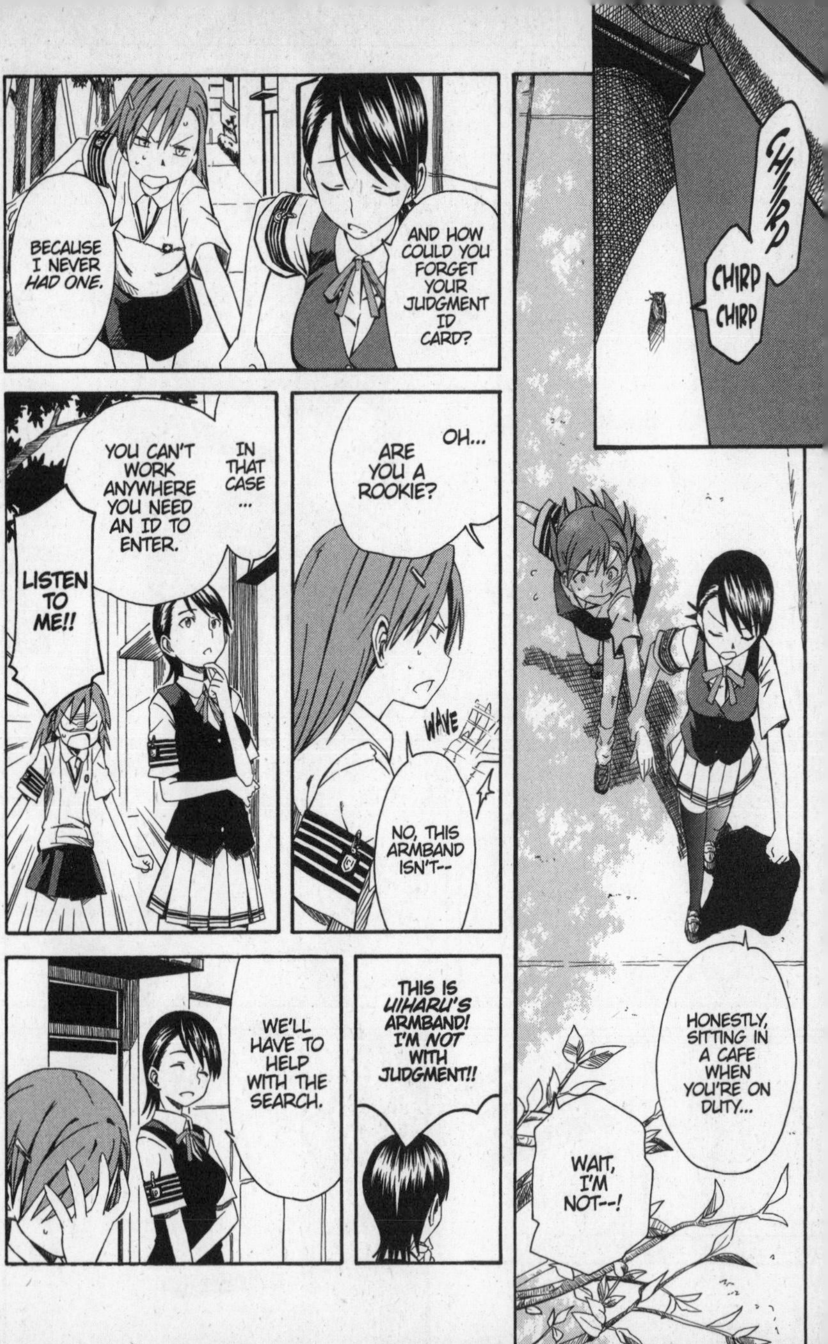
CHIRP
CHIRP CHIRP
HONESTLY, SITTING IN A CAFE WHEN YOU'RE ON DUTY...
WAIT, I'M NOT--!
AND HOW COULD YOU FORGET YOUR JUDGMENT ID CARD?
BECAUSE I NEVER *HAD ONE.*
OH...
ARE YOU A ROOKIE?
WAVE
NO, THIS ARMBAND ISN'T--
IN THAT CASE...
YOU CAN'T WORK ANYWHERE YOU NEED AN ID TO ENTER.
LISTEN TO ME!!
THIS IS *UIHARU'S* ARMBAND! I'M *NOT* WITH JUDGMENT!!
WE'LL HAVE TO HELP WITH THE SEARCH.

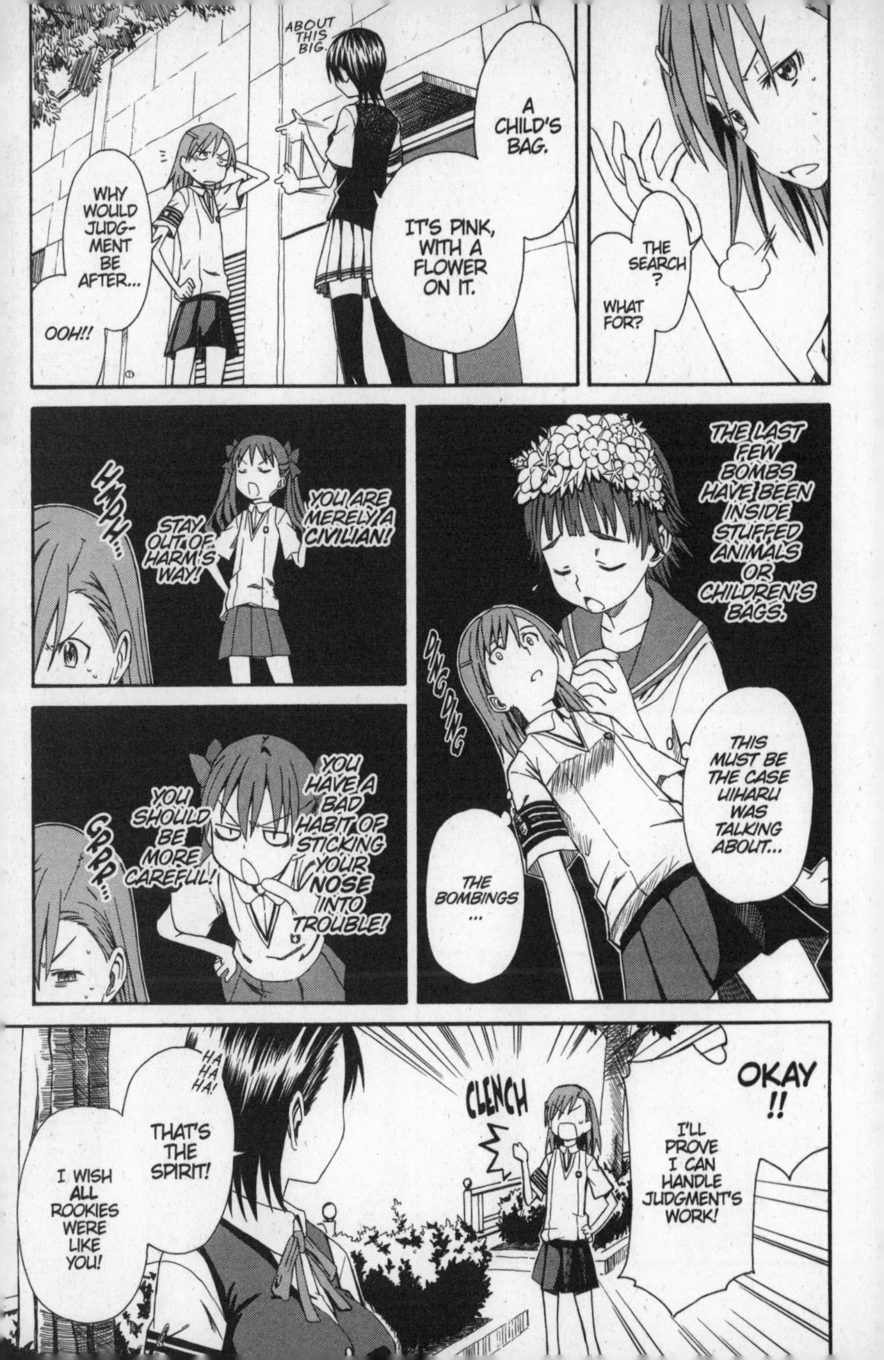
THE SEARCH?
WHAT FOR?
A CHILD'S BAG.
ABOUT THIS BIG.
IT'S PINK, WITH A FLOWER ON IT.
WHY WOULD JUDGMENT BE AFTER...
OOH!!
THE LAST FEW BOMBS HAVE BEEN INSIDE STUFFED ANIMALS OR CHILDREN'S BAGS.
THIS MUST BE THE CASE UIHARU WAS TALKING ABOUT...
DING DING
THE BOMBINGS...
YOU ARE MERELY A CIVILIAN!
STAY OUT OF HARM'S WAY!
HMPH...
YOU HAVE A BAD HABIT OF STICKING YOUR NOSE INTO TROUBLE!
YOU SHOULD BE MORE CAREFUL!
GRRR...
OKAY!!
I'LL PROVE I CAN HANDLE JUDGMENT'S WORK!
CLENCH
HA HA HA!
THAT'S THE SPIRIT!
I WISH ALL ROOKIES WERE LIKE YOU!

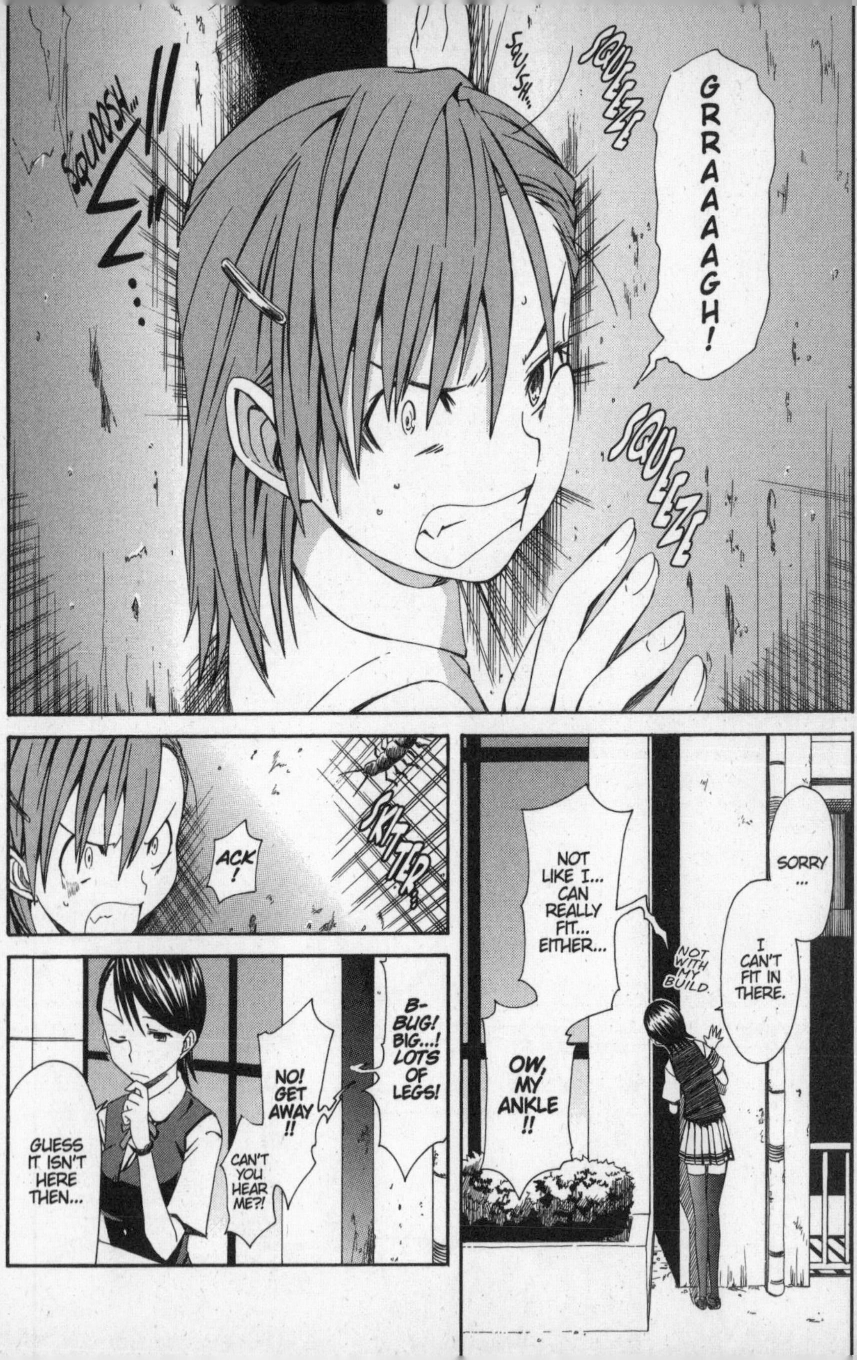
GRRAAAAGH!
SQUEEZE
SQUISH...
SQUEEZE
SQUOOSH...!!
SORRY...
I CAN'T FIT IN THERE.
NOT WITH MY BUILD.
NOT LIKE I... CAN REALLY FIT... EITHER...
OW, MY ANKLE!!
SKITTER
ACK!
B-BUG! BIG...! LOTS OF LEGS!
NO! GET AWAY!!
CAN'T YOU HEAR ME?!
GUESS IT ISN'T HERE THEN...

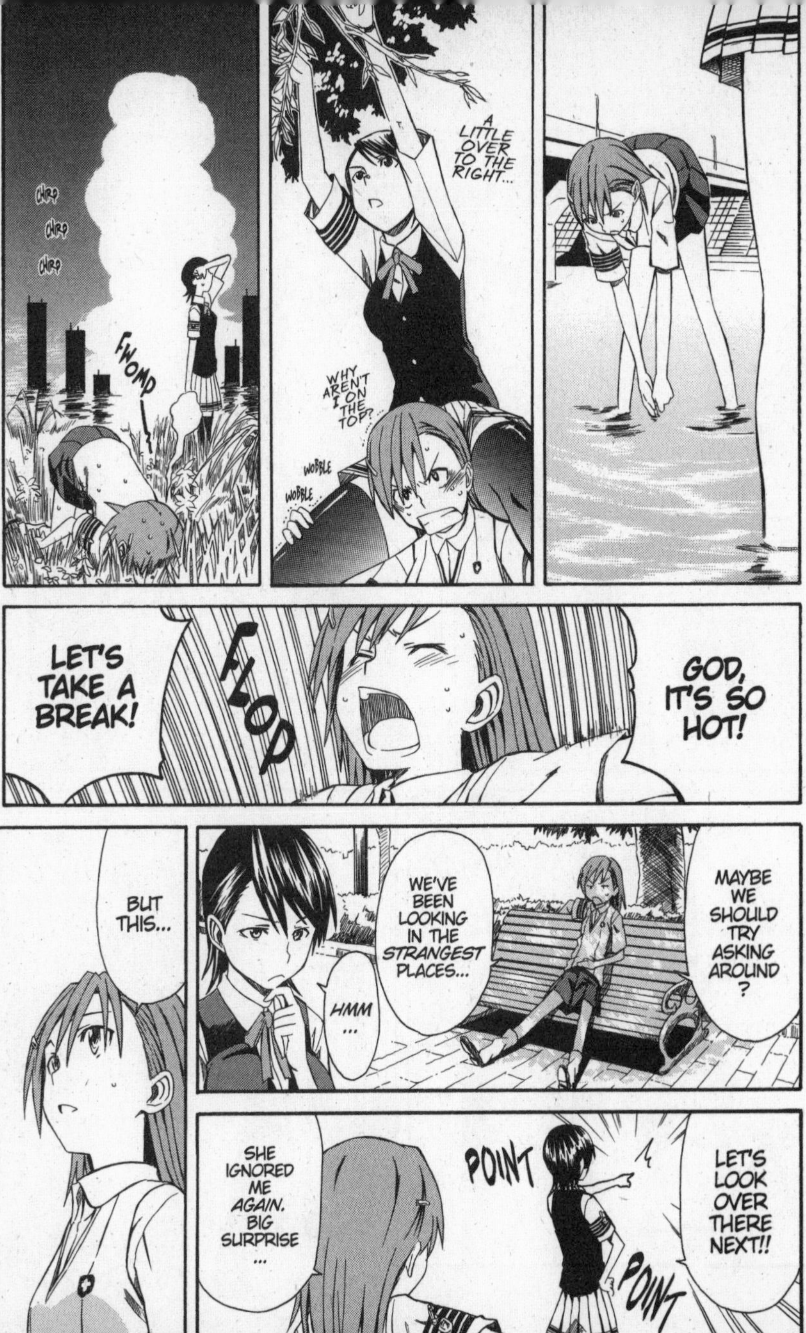
A LITTLE OVER TO THE RIGHT...
WHY AREN'T I ON THE TOP?
WOBBLE
WOBBLE
CHIRP
CHIRP
CHIRP
FWOMP
GOD, IT'S SO HOT!
FLOP
LET'S TAKE A BREAK!
MAYBE WE SHOULD TRY ASKING AROUND?
WE'VE BEEN LOOKING IN THE STRANGEST PLACES...
HMM...
LET'S LOOK OVER THERE NEXT!!
POINT
POINT
SHE IGNORED ME AGAIN. BIG SURPRISE...
BUT THIS...

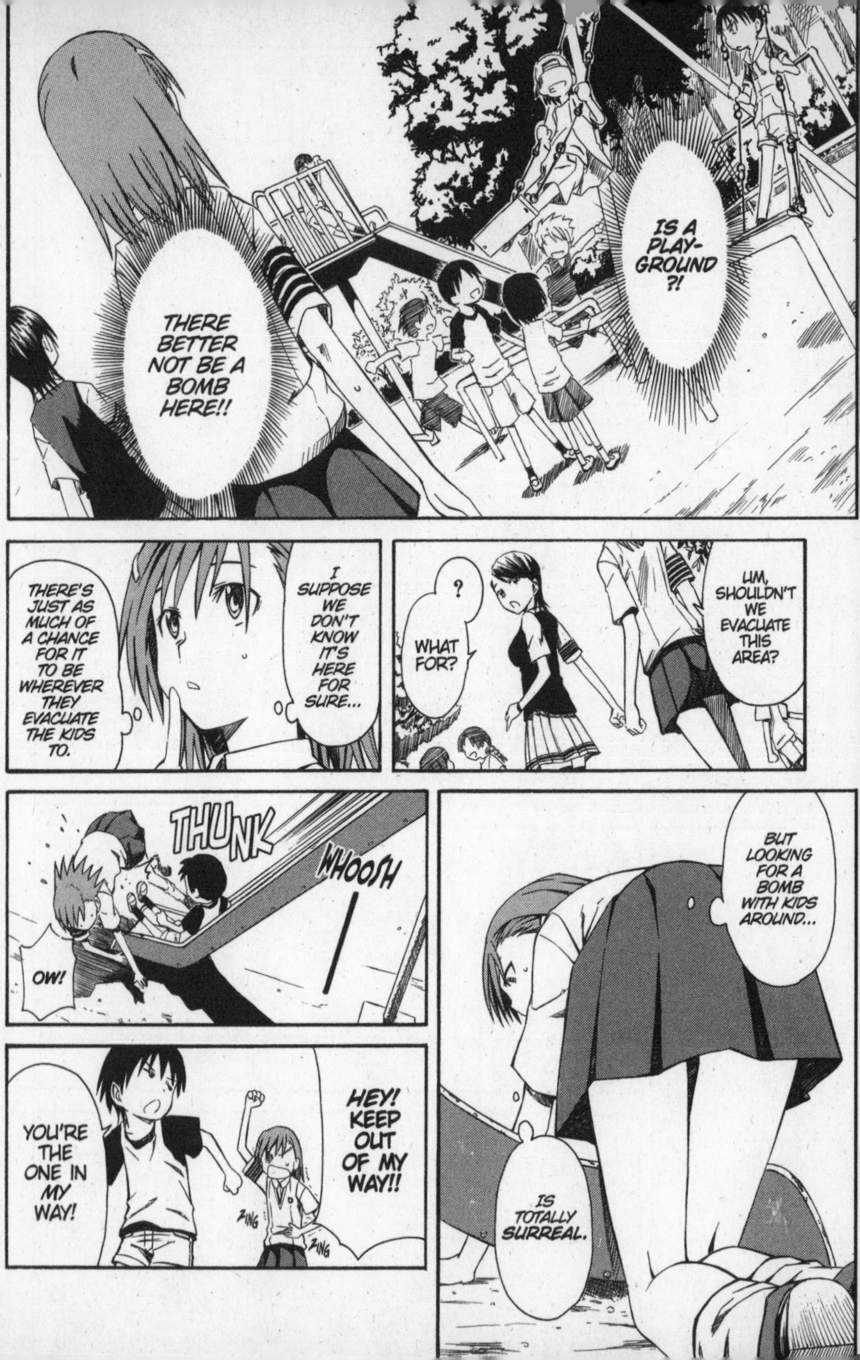
IS A PLAY-GROUND?!
THERE BETTER NOT BE A BOMB HERE!!
UM, SHOULDN'T WE EVACUATE THIS AREA?
?
WHAT FOR?
I SUPPOSE WE DON'T KNOW IT'S HERE FOR SURE...
THERE'S JUST AS MUCH OF A CHANCE FOR IT TO BE WHEREVER THEY EVACUATE THE KIDS TO.
BUT LOOKING FOR A BOMB WITH KIDS AROUND...
IS TOTALLY SURREAL.
THUNK
WHOOSH
OW!
HEY! KEEP OUT OF MY WAY!!
ZING
ZING
YOU'RE THE ONE IN MY WAY!

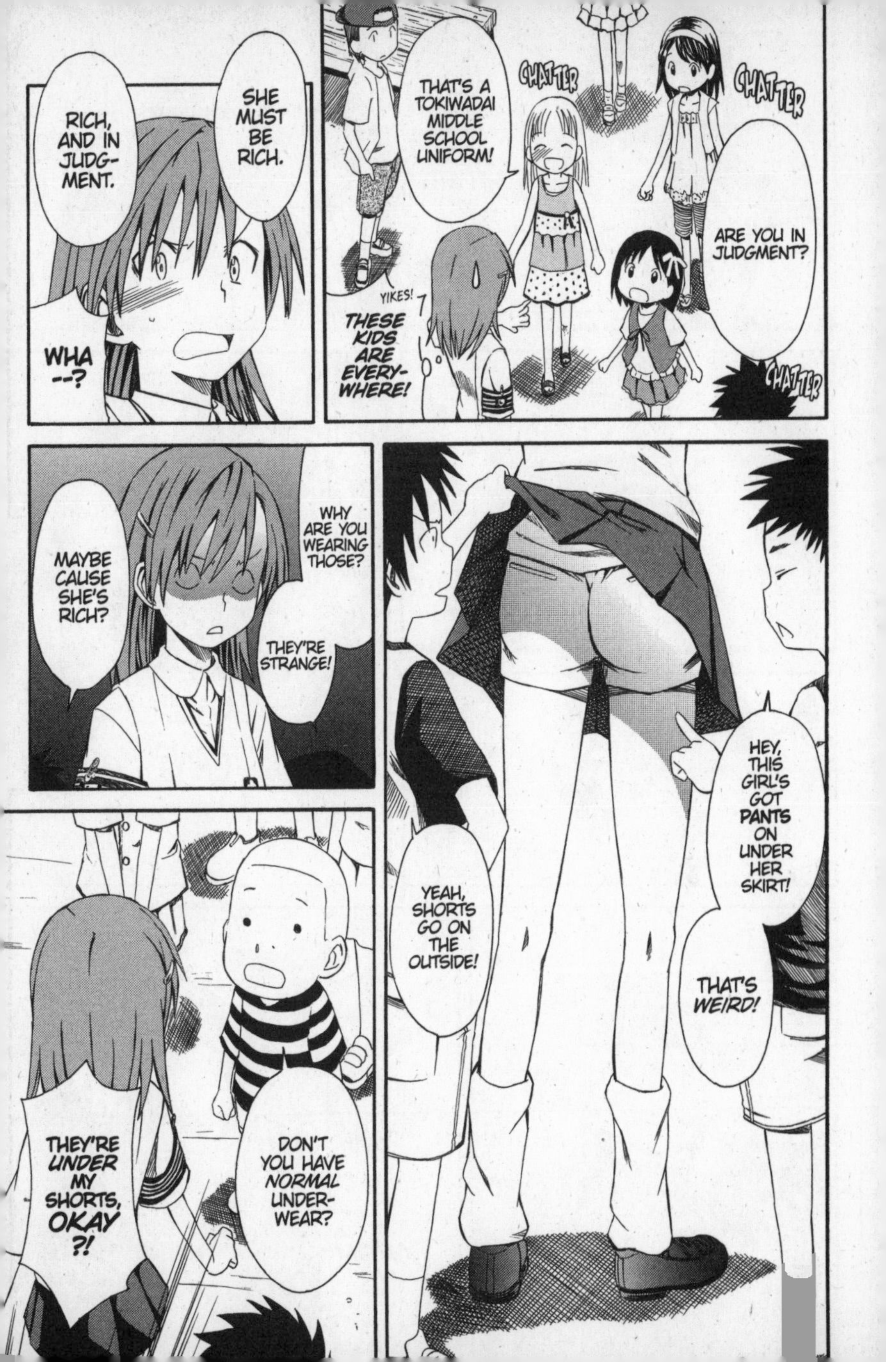
CHATTER
CHATTER
THAT'S A TOKIWADAI MIDDLE SCHOOL UNIFORM!
ARE YOU IN JUDGMENT?
CHATTER
YIKES!
THESE KIDS ARE EVERYWHERE!
SHE MUST BE RICH.
RICH, AND IN JUDGMENT.
WHA--?
HEY, THIS GIRL'S GOT PANTS ON UNDER HER SKIRT!
YEAH, SHORTS GO ON THE OUTSIDE!
THAT'S WEIRD!
WHY ARE YOU WEARING THOSE?
THEY'RE STRANGE!
MAYBE CAUSE SHE'S RICH?
DON'T YOU HAVE NORMAL UNDERWEAR?
THEY'RE UNDER MY SHORTS, OKAY?!

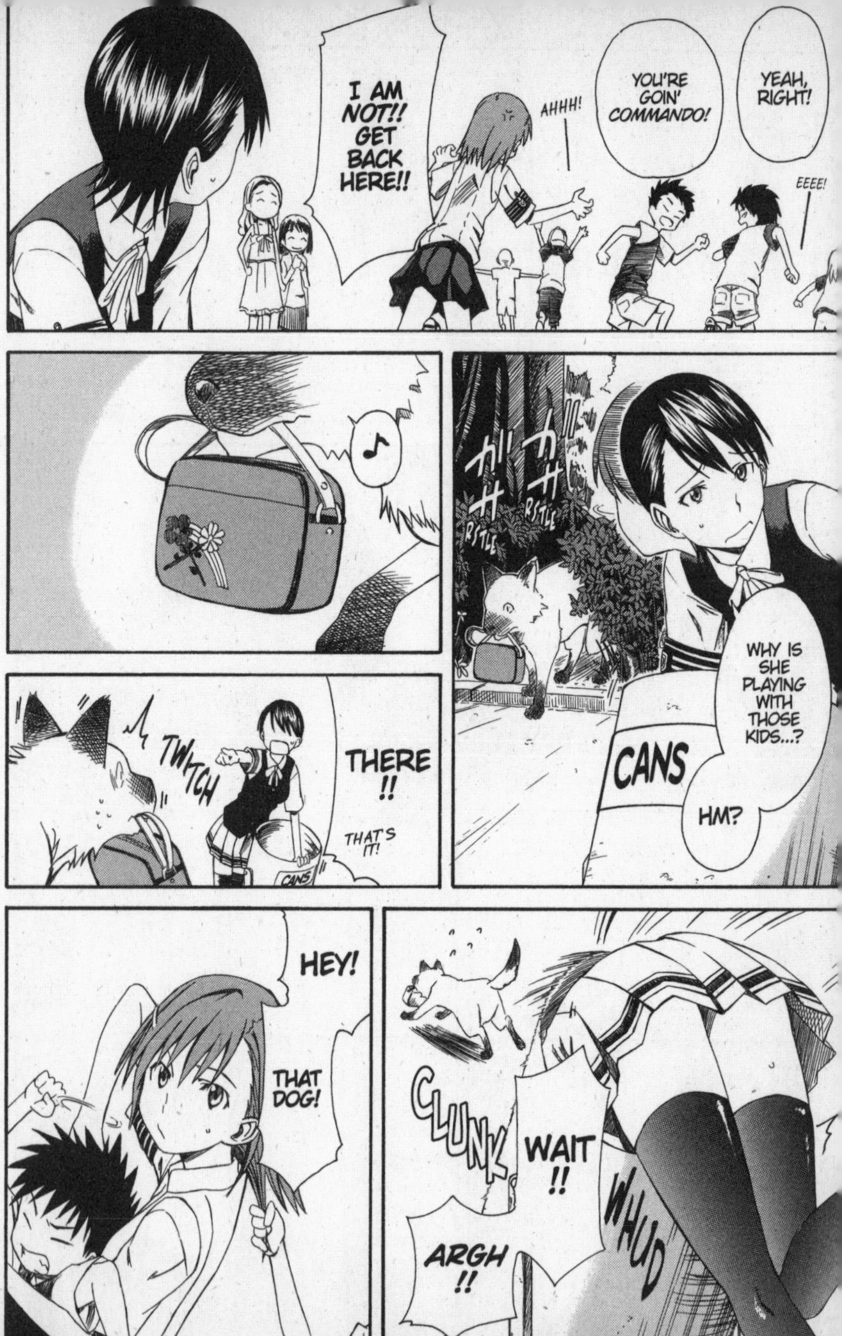
YEAH, RIGHT!
EEEE!
YOU'RE GOIN' COMMANDO!
AHHH!
I AM NOT!! GET BACK HERE!!
WHY IS SHE PLAYING WITH THOSE KIDS...?
HM?
CANS
RSTLE
RSTLE
♪
THERE!!
THAT'S IT!
TWITCH
CANS
WAIT!!
CLUNK
ARGH!!
WHUD
HEY!
THAT DOG!

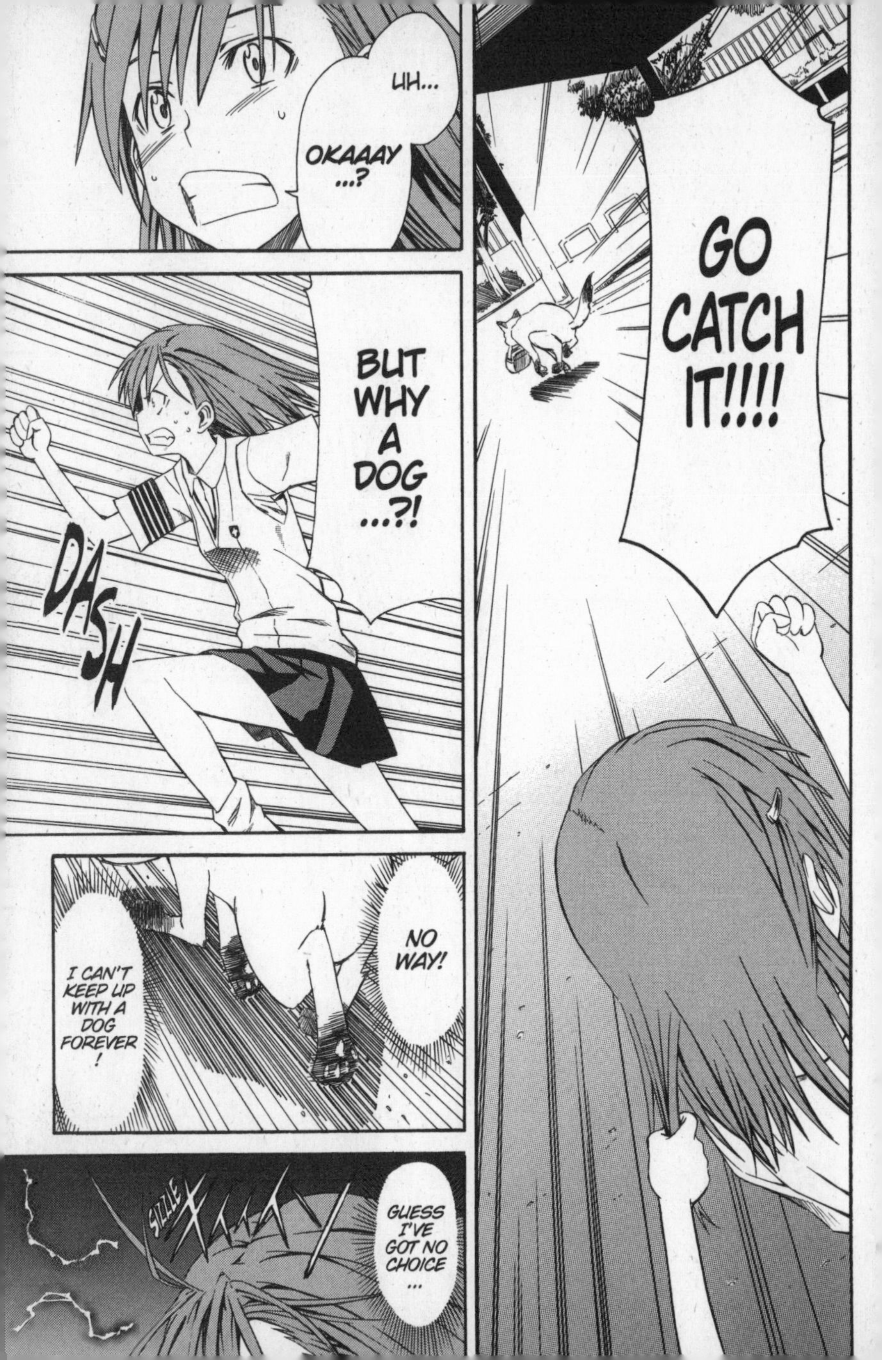
GO CATCH IT!!!!
UH... OKAAAY ...?
BUT WHY A DOG ...?!
DASH
NO WAY!
I CAN'T KEEP UP WITH A DOG FOREVER!
SIZZLE
GUESS I'VE GOT NO CHOICE ...

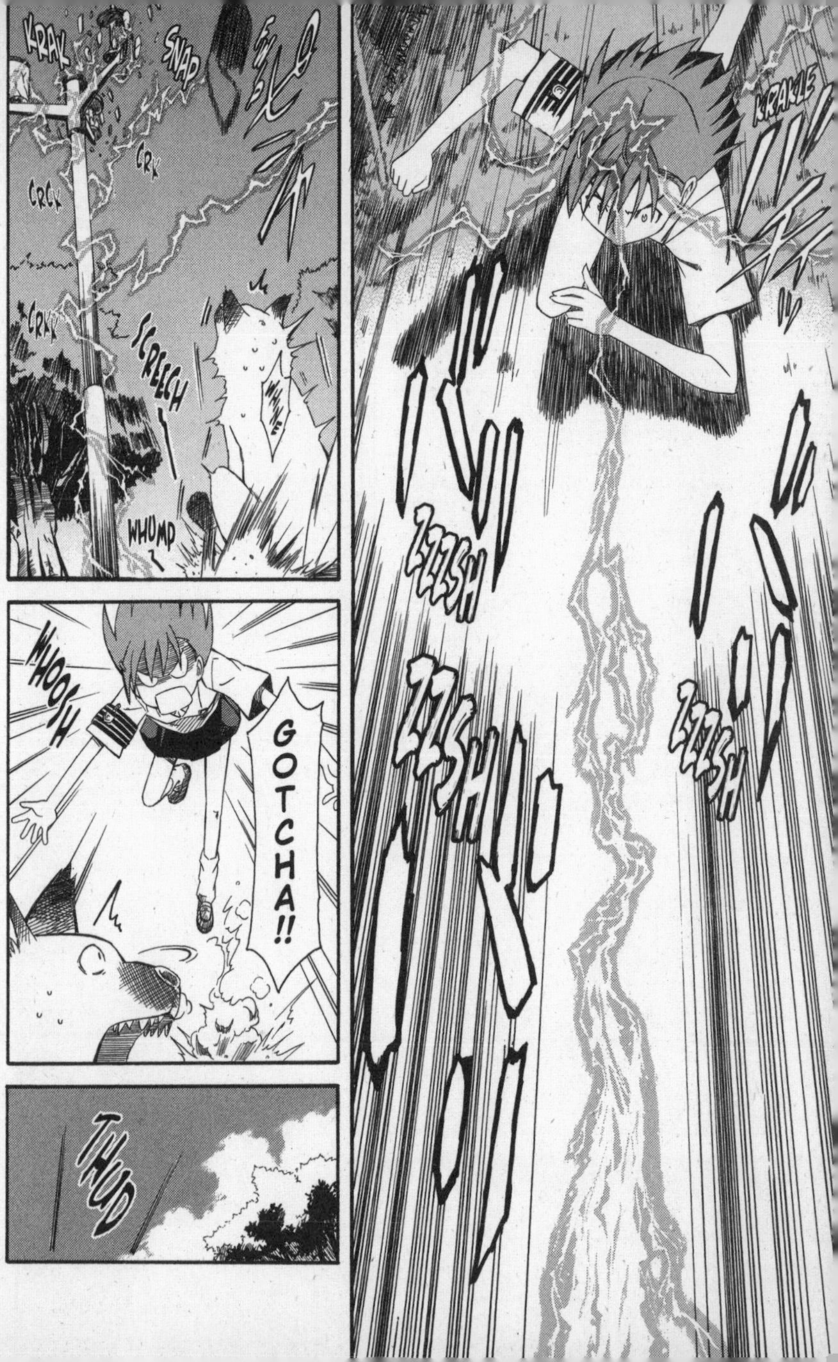
KRAKLE
ZZZSH
ZZSH
ZZZSH
KRAK
SNAP
CRK
CRCK
CRKK
SCREECH
WHINE
WHUMP
WHOOSH
GOTCHA!!
THUD

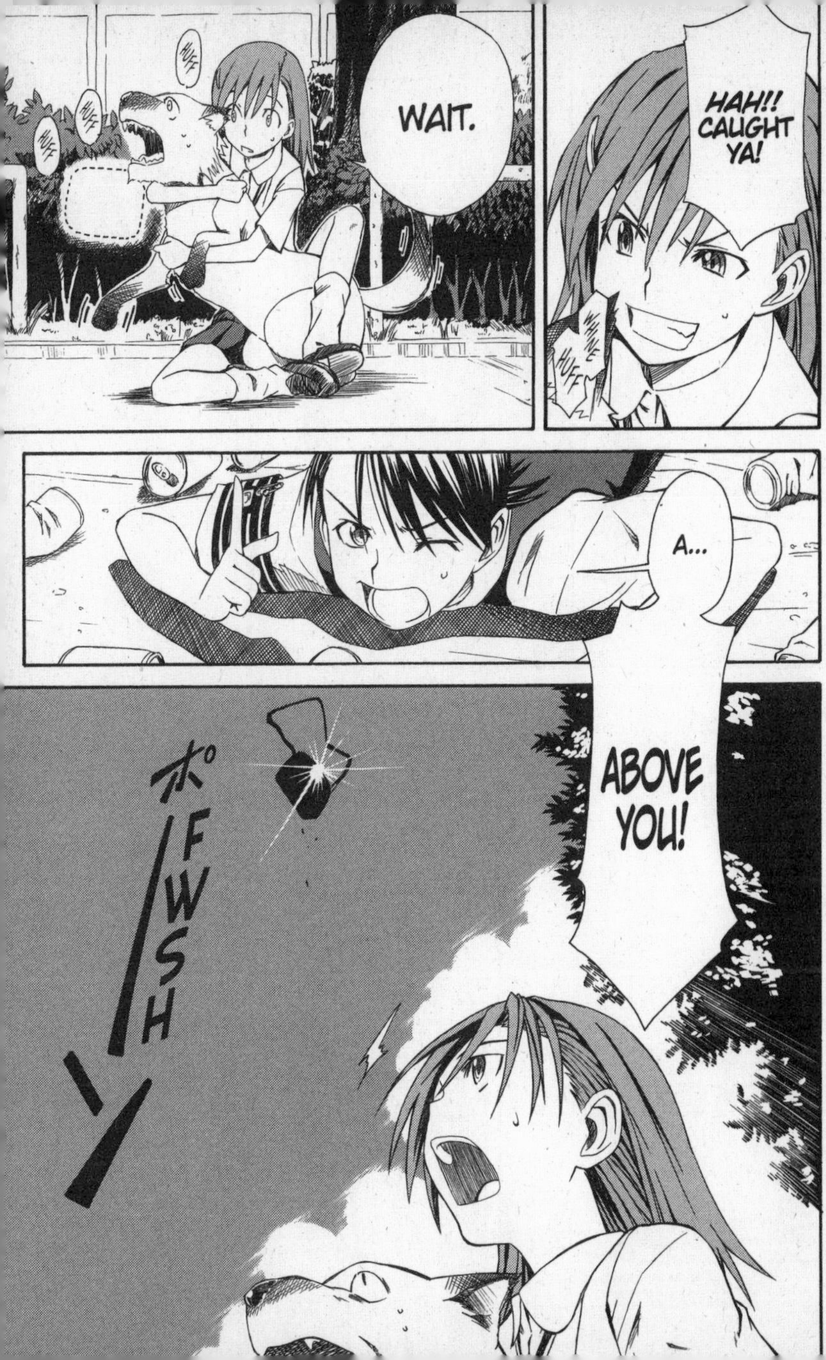
HAH!! CAUGHT YA!
WHINE
HUFF
HUFF
HUFF
HUFF
WAIT.
A... ABOVE YOU!
ポ
FWSH
ン

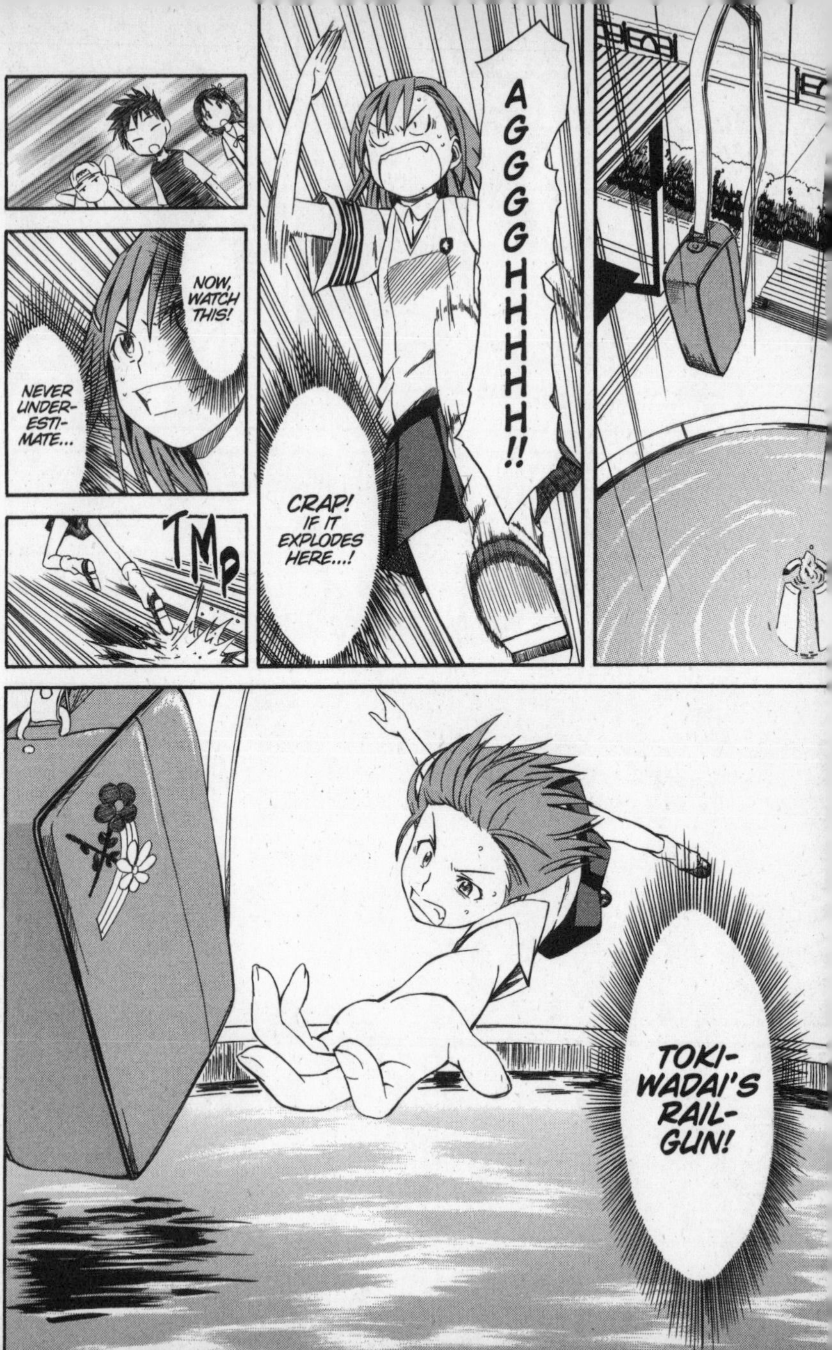
AGGGGHHHHHH!!
CRAP! IF IT EXPLODES HERE...!
NOW, WATCH THIS!
NEVER UNDERESTIMATE...
TMP
TOKIWADAI'S RAILGUN!

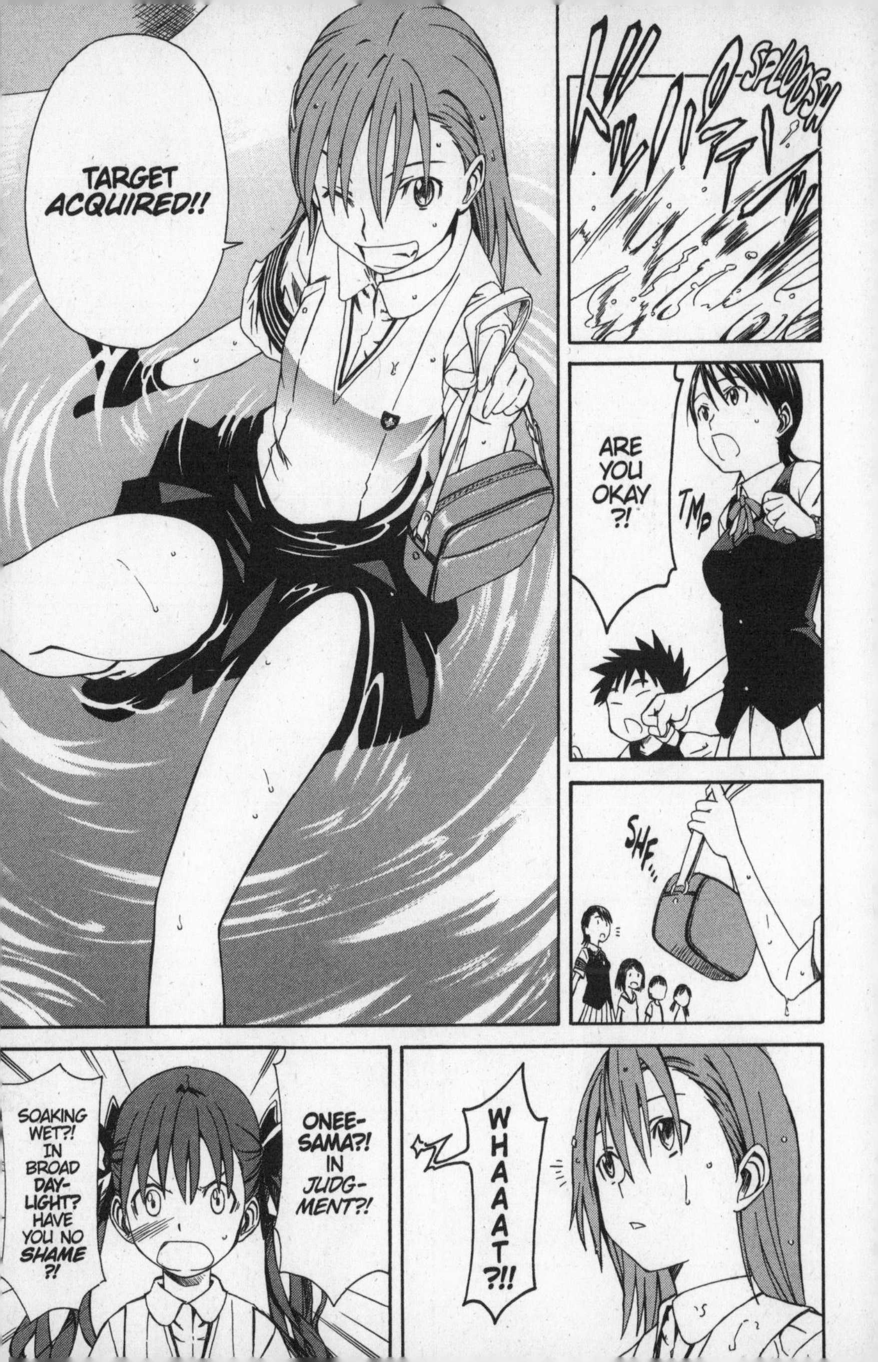
SPLOOSH
ARE YOU OKAY?!
TMP
SHF...
TARGET ACQUIRED!!
WHAAAAT?!!
ONEE-SAMA?! IN JUDGMENT?!
SOAKING WET?! IN BROAD DAYLIGHT? HAVE YOU NO SHAME?!

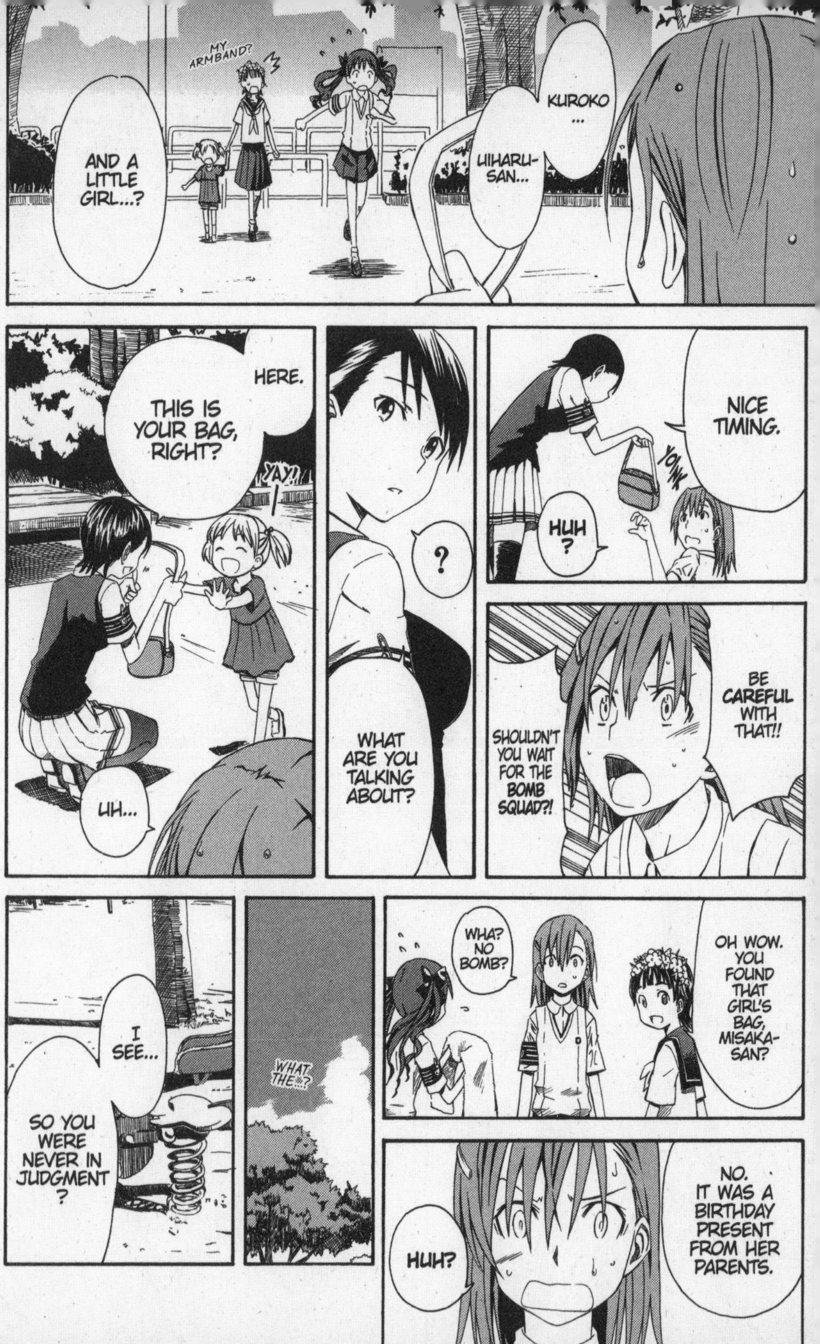
KUROKO ...
UIHARU-SAN...
MY ARMBAND?
AND A LITTLE GIRL...?
NICE TIMING.
YOINK
HUH ?
BE CAREFUL WITH THAT!!
SHOULDN'T YOU WAIT FOR THE BOMB SQUAD?!
?
WHAT ARE YOU TALKING ABOUT?
HERE.
THIS IS YOUR BAG, RIGHT?
YAY!
UH...
OH WOW. YOU FOUND THAT GIRL'S BAG, MISAKA-SAN?
WHA? NO BOMB?
NO. IT WAS A BIRTHDAY PRESENT FROM HER PARENTS.
HUH?
WHAT THE...?
I SEE...
SO YOU WERE NEVER IN JUDGMENT ?

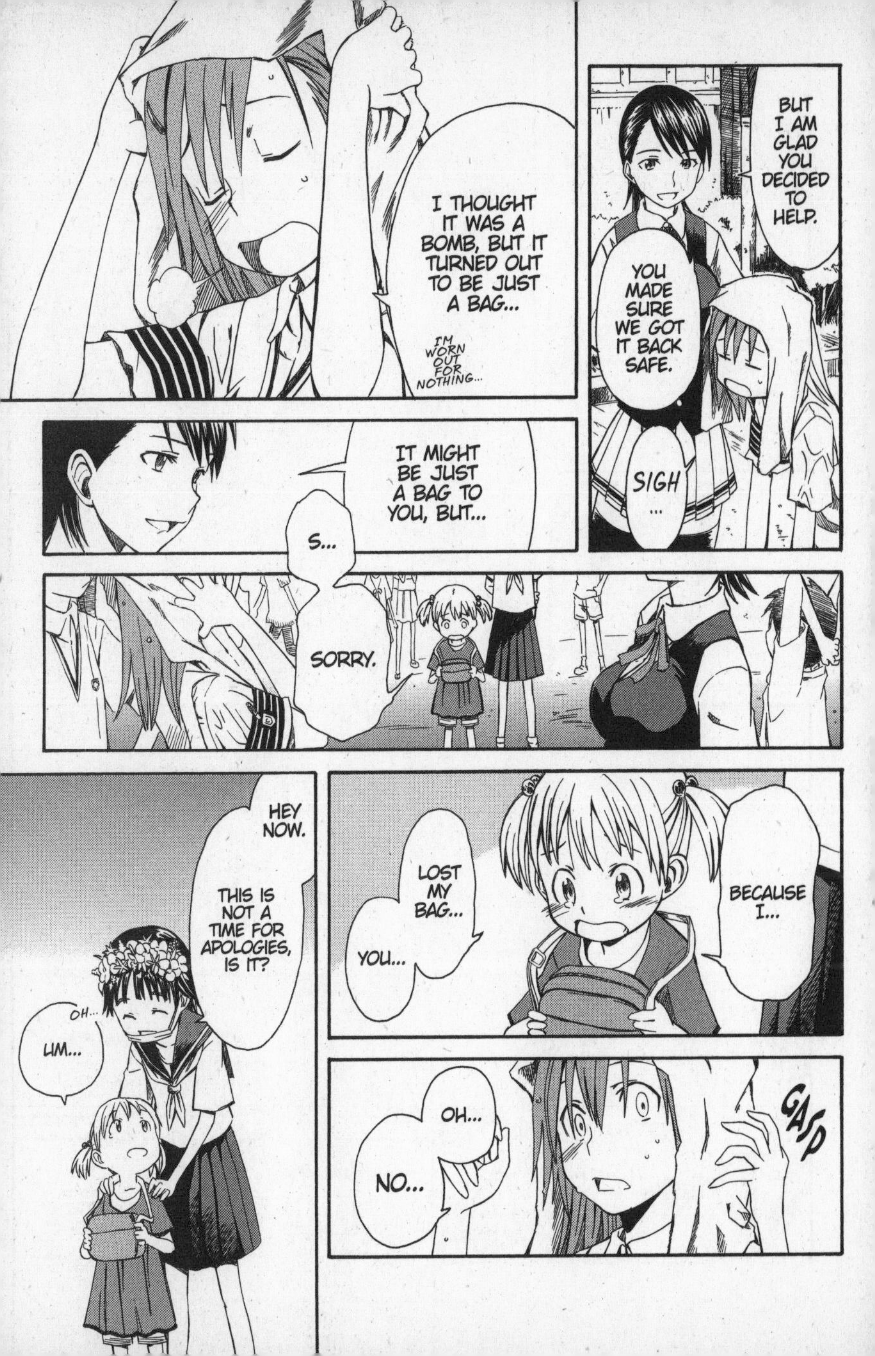
BUT I AM GLAD YOU DECIDED TO HELP.
YOU MADE SURE WE GOT IT BACK SAFE.
SIGH...
I THOUGHT IT WAS A BOMB, BUT IT TURNED OUT TO BE JUST A BAG...
I'M WORN OUT FOR NOTHING...
IT MIGHT BE JUST A BAG TO YOU, BUT...
S...
SORRY.
BECAUSE I...
LOST MY BAG...
YOU...
GASP
OH...
NO...
HEY NOW.
THIS IS NOT A TIME FOR APOLOGIES, IS IT?
OH...
UM...

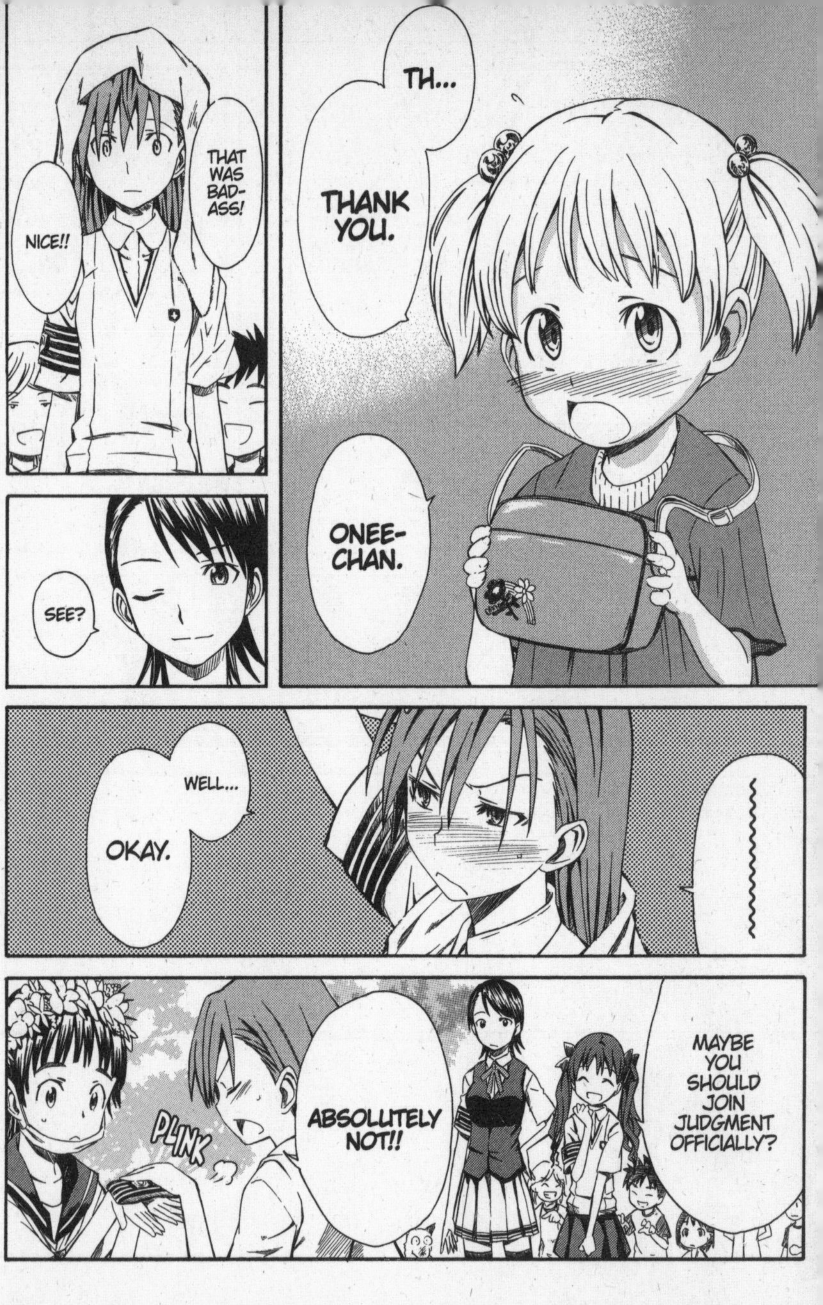
TH...
THANK YOU.
ONEE-CHAN.
THAT WAS BAD-ASS!
NICE!!
SEE?
WELL...
OKAY.
MAYBE YOU SHOULD JOIN JUDGMENT OFFICIALLY?
ABSOLUTELY NOT!!
PLINK

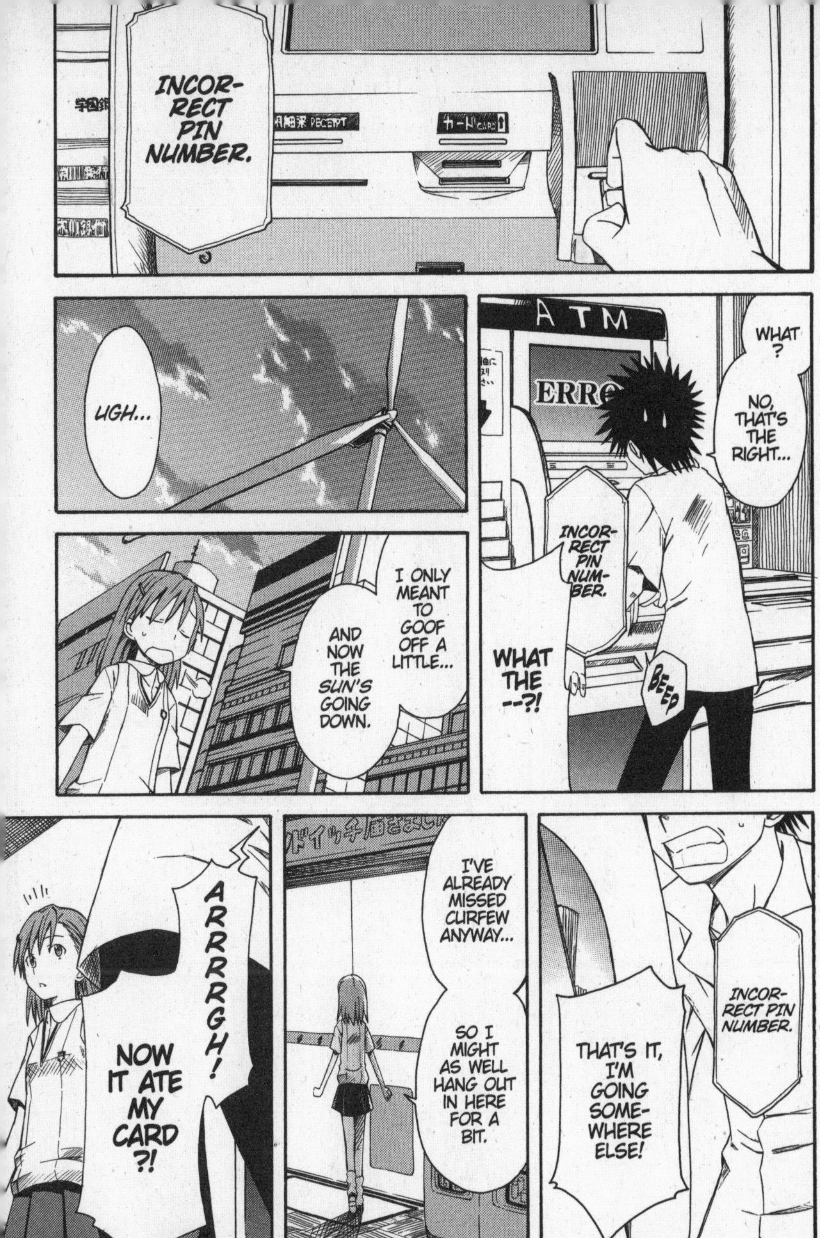
INCORRECT PIN NUMBER.
ATM
WHAT? NO, THAT'S THE RIGHT...
INCORRECT PIN NUMBER.
WHAT THE --?!
BEEP
UGH...
I ONLY MEANT TO GOOF OFF A LITTLE...
AND NOW THE SUN'S GOING DOWN.
INCORRECT PIN NUMBER.
THAT'S IT, I'M GOING SOMEWHERE ELSE!
I'VE ALREADY MISSED CURFEW ANYWAY...
SO I MIGHT AS WELL HANG OUT IN HERE FOR A BIT.
ARRRRGH!
NOW IT ATE MY CARD?!

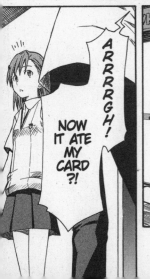

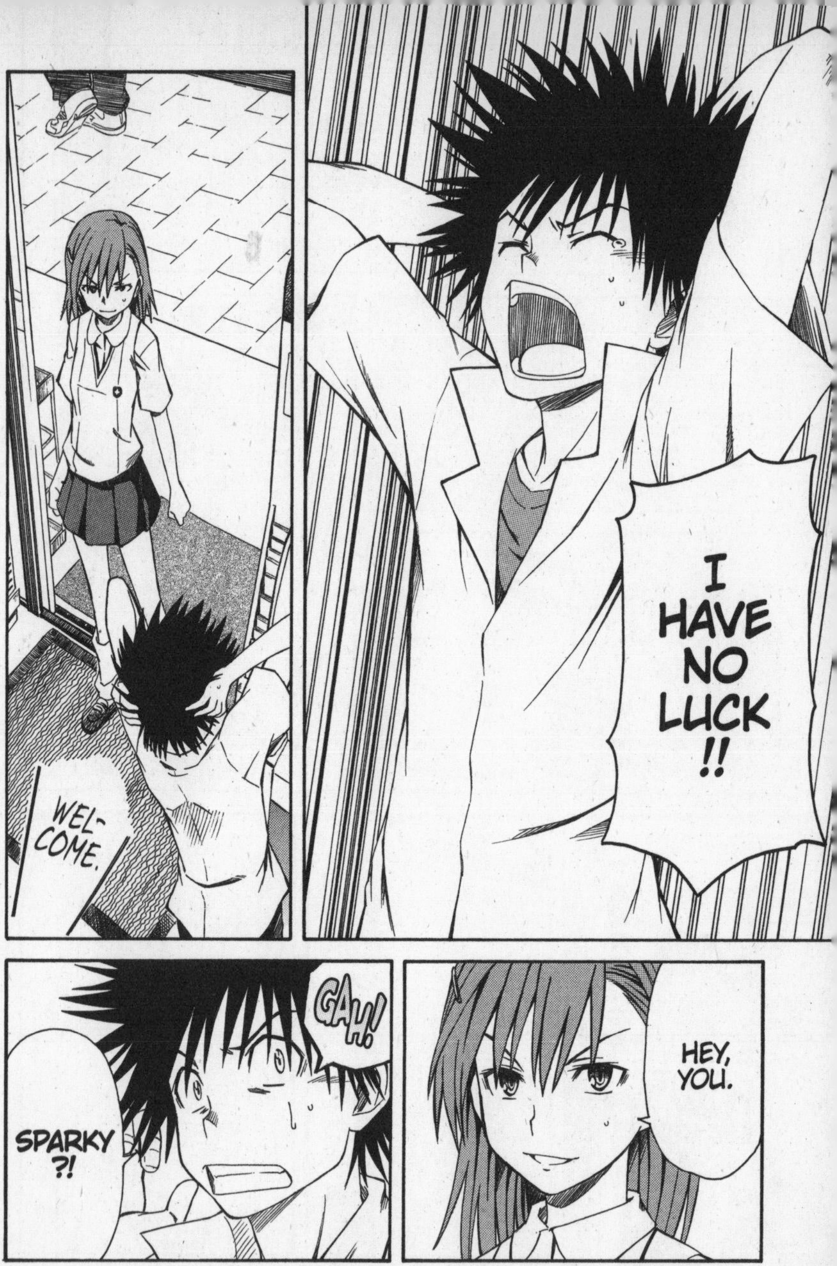
I HAVE NO LUCK!!
WEL-COME.
HEY, YOU.
GAH!
SPARKY ?!

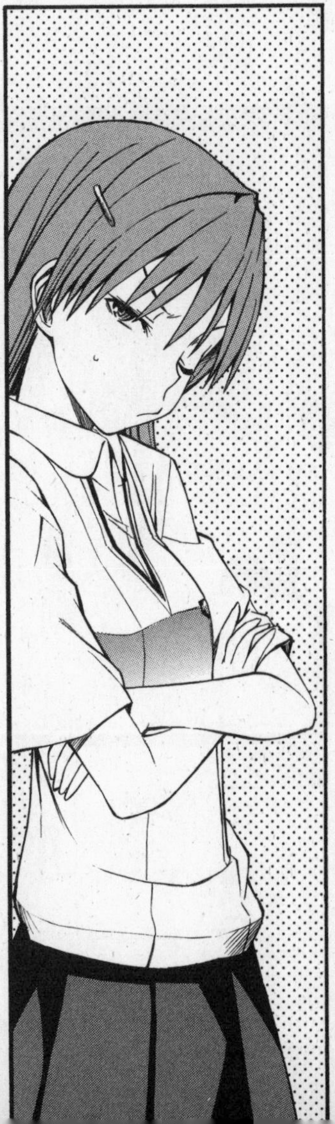

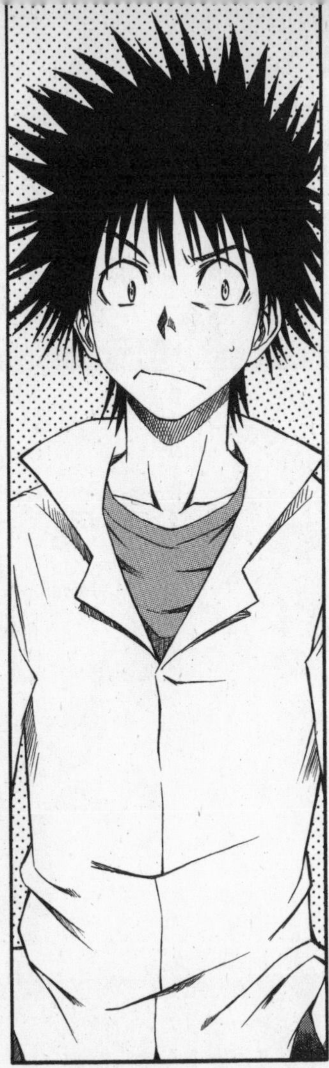

CHAPTER 3: JULY 17 (2)

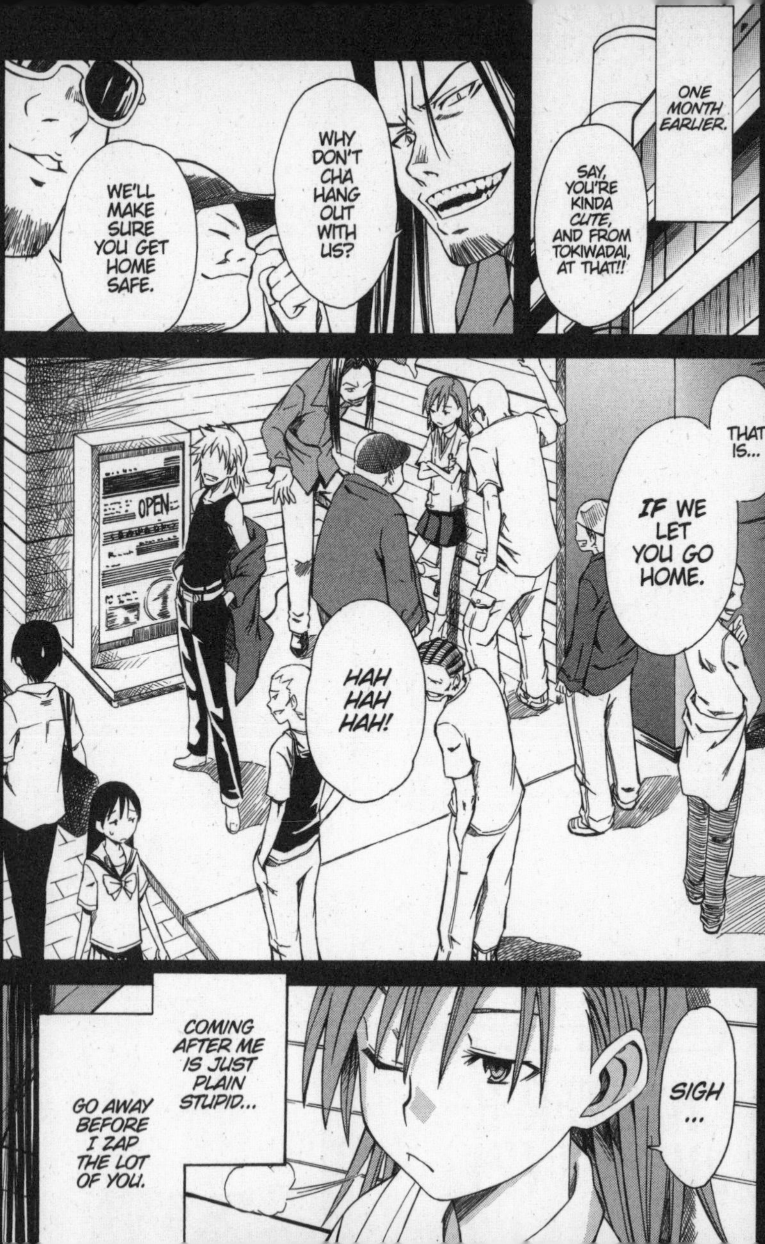
ONE MONTH EARLIER.
SAY, YOU'RE KINDA CUTE, AND FROM TOKIWADAI, AT THAT!!
WHY DON'T CHA HANG OUT WITH US?
WE'LL MAKE SURE YOU GET HOME SAFE.
THAT IS...
IF WE LET YOU GO HOME.
HAH HAH HAH!
SIGH ...
COMING AFTER ME IS JUST PLAIN STUPID...
GO AWAY BEFORE I ZAP THE LOT OF YOU.

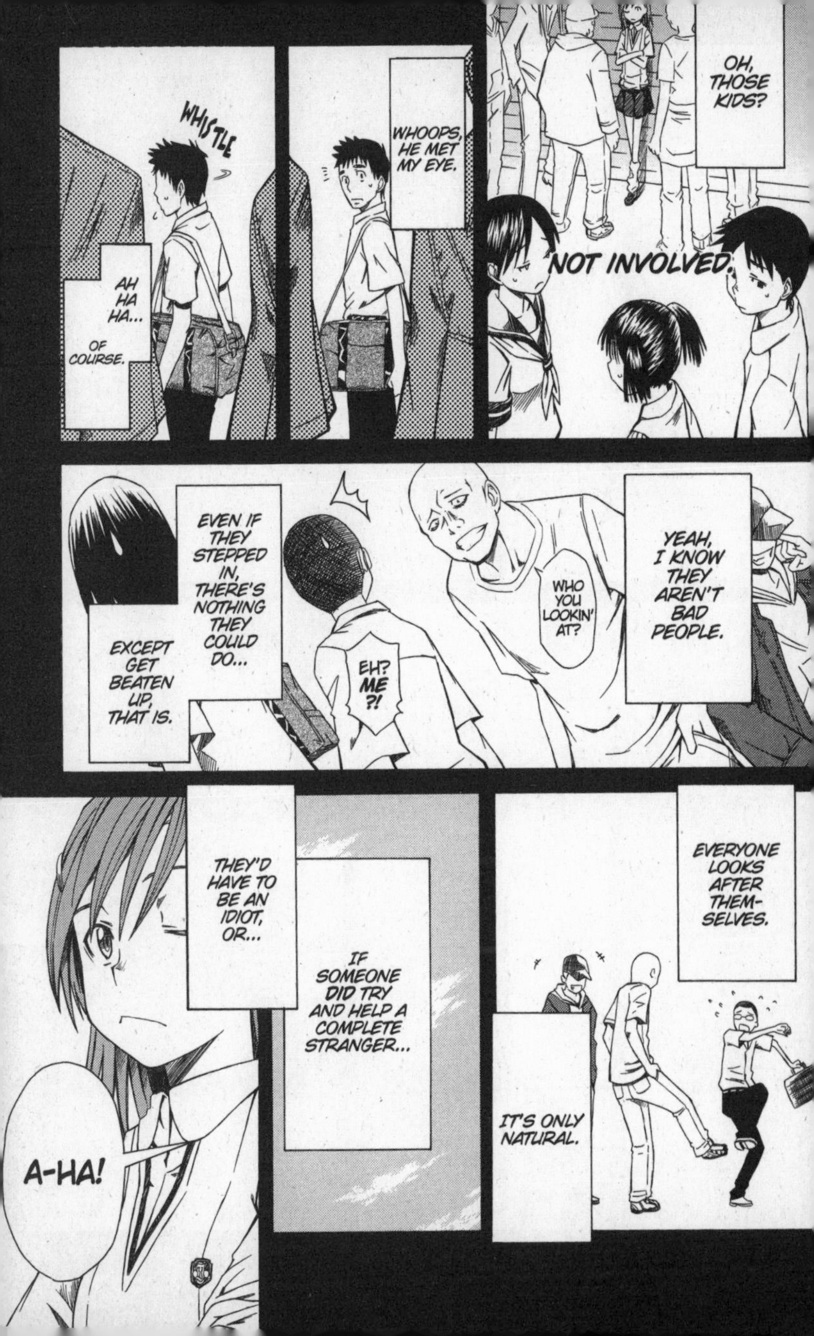
OH, THOSE KIDS?
NOT INVOLVED.
WHOOPS, HE MET MY EYE.
WHISTLE
AH HA HA...
OF COURSE.
YEAH, I KNOW THEY AREN'T BAD PEOPLE.
WHO YOU LOOKIN' AT?
EH? ME?!
EVEN IF THEY STEPPED IN, THERE'S NOTHING THEY COULD DO...
EXCEPT GET BEATEN UP, THAT IS.
EVERYONE LOOKS AFTER THEM-SELVES.
IT'S ONLY NATURAL.
IF SOMEONE DID TRY AND HELP A COMPLETE STRANGER...
THEY'D HAVE TO BE AN IDIOT, OR...
A-HA!

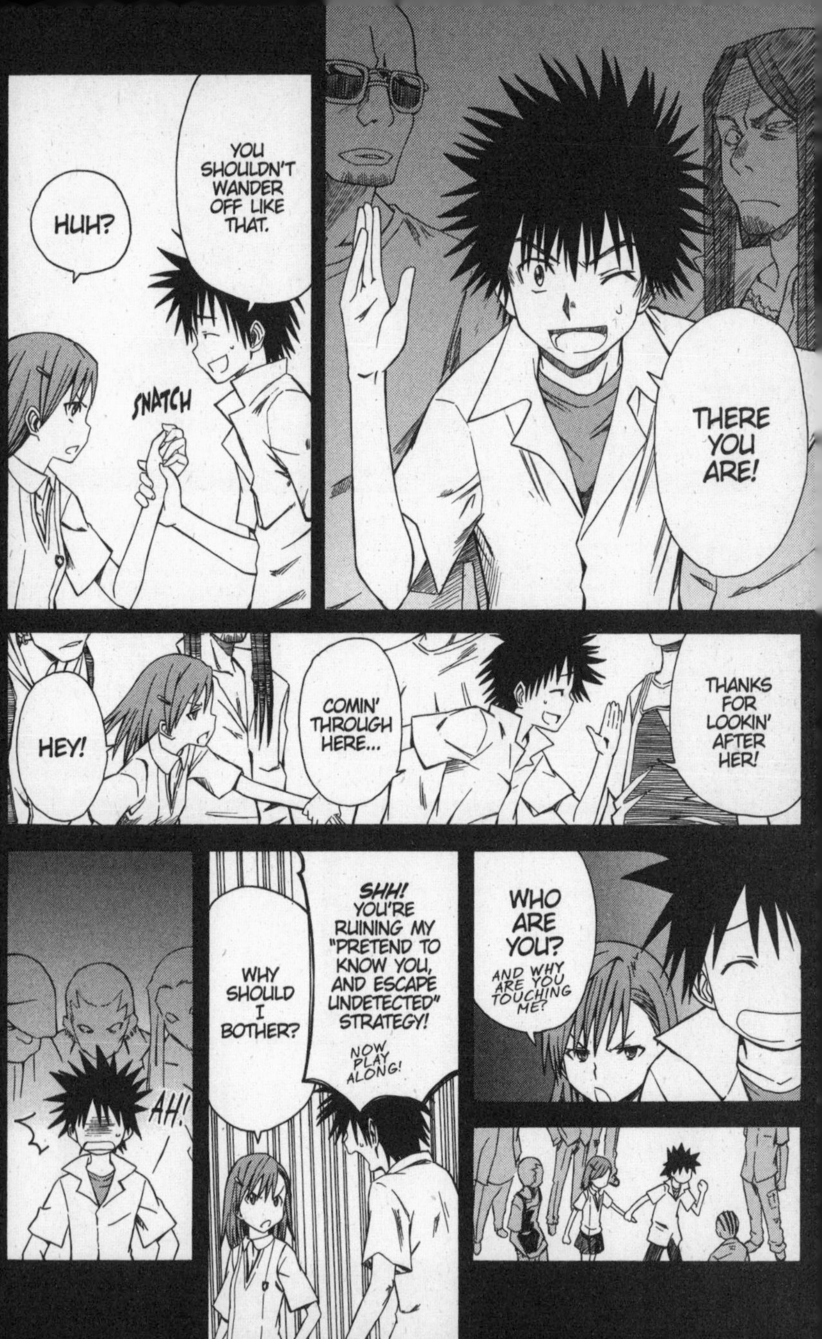
THERE YOU ARE!
YOU SHOULDN'T WANDER OFF LIKE THAT.
SNATCH
HUH?
THANKS FOR LOOKIN' AFTER HER!
COMIN' THROUGH HERE...
HEY!
WHO ARE YOU?
AND WHY ARE YOU TOUCHING ME?
SHH! YOU'RE RUINING MY "PRETEND TO KNOW YOU, AND ESCAPE UNDETECTED" STRATEGY!
NOW PLAY ALONG!
WHY SHOULD I BOTHER?
AH!

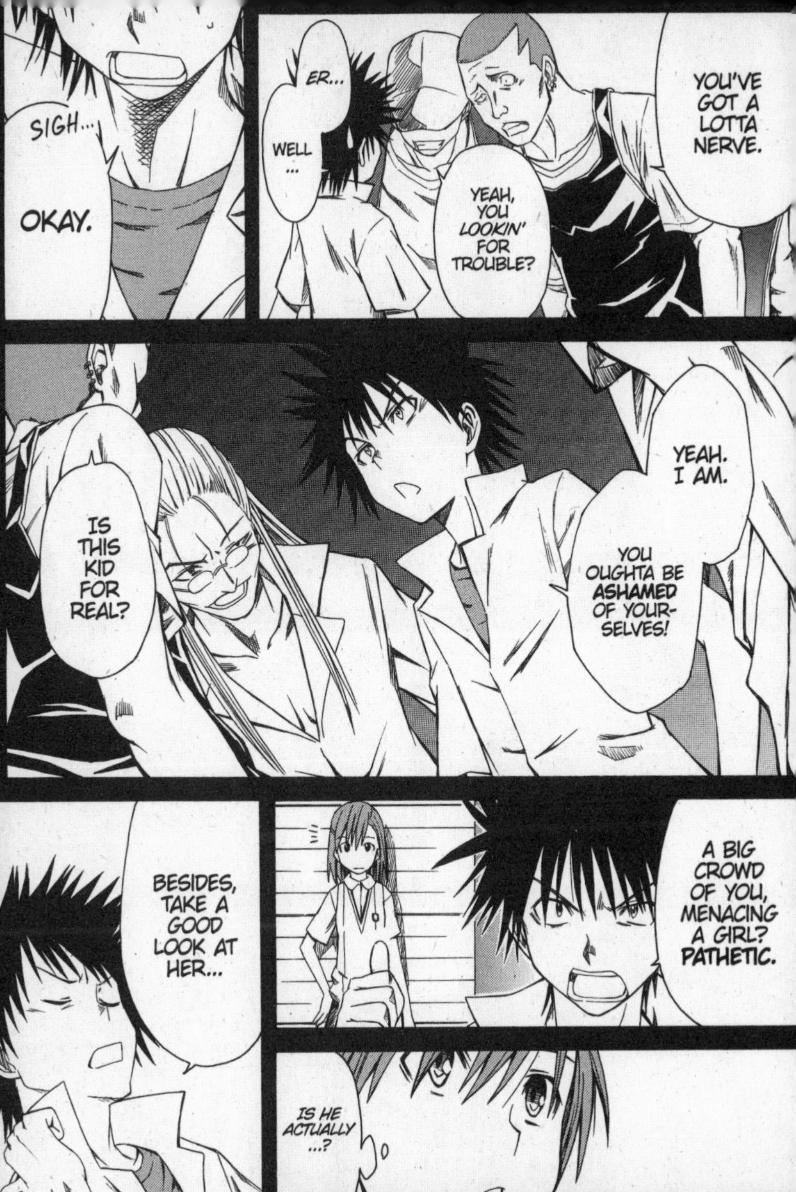
YOU'VE GOT A LOTTA NERVE.
YEAH, YOU LOOKIN' FOR TROUBLE?
ER... WELL ...
SIGH...
OKAY.
YEAH. I AM.
YOU OUGHTA BE ASHAMED OF YOUR-SELVES!
IS THIS KID FOR REAL?
A BIG CROWD OF YOU, MENACING A GIRL? PATHETIC.
IS HE ACTUALLY ...?
BESIDES, TAKE A GOOD LOOK AT HER...

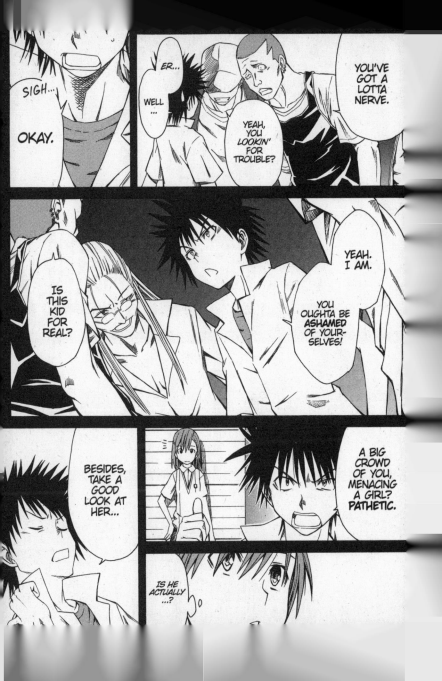

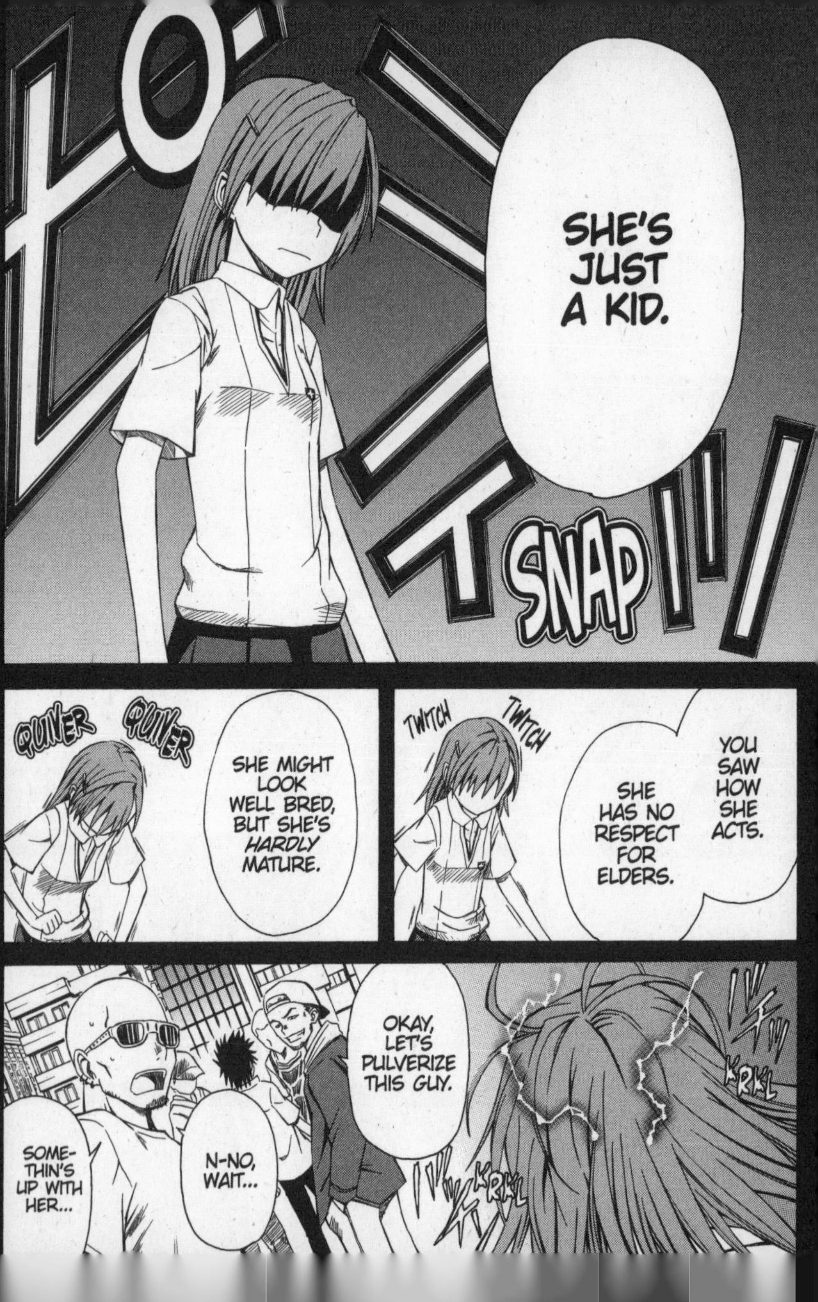
SHE'S JUST A KID.
SNAP
TWITCH
TWITCH
YOU SAW HOW SHE ACTS.
SHE HAS NO RESPECT FOR ELDERS.
QUIVER
QUIVER
SHE MIGHT LOOK WELL BRED, BUT SHE'S *HARDLY* MATURE.
KRKL
OKAY, LET'S PULVERIZE THIS GUY.
KRKL
N-NO, WAIT...
SOME-THIN'S UP WITH HER...

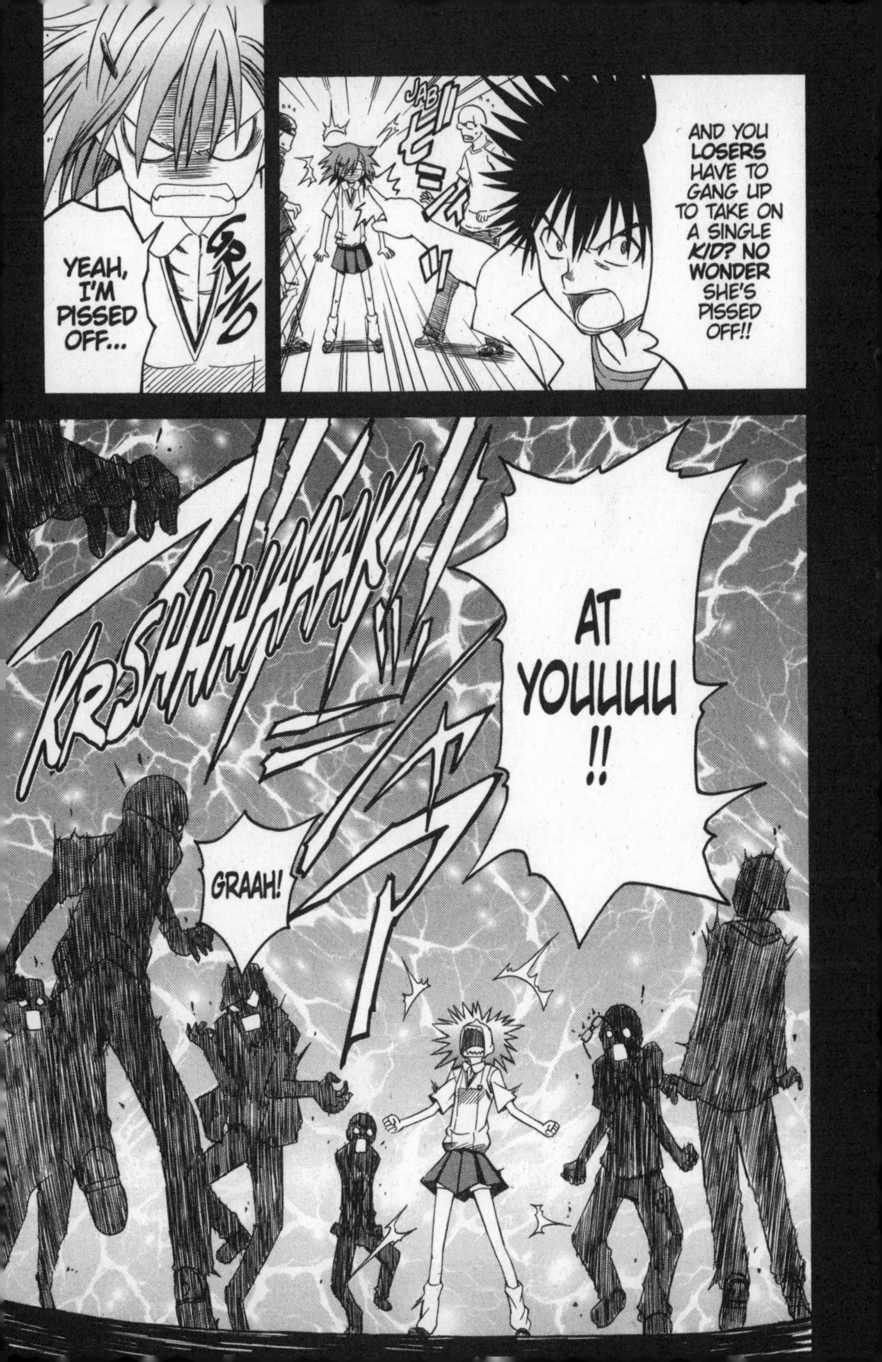
JAB!!
AND YOU LOSERS HAVE TO GANG UP TO TAKE ON A SINGLE KID? NO WONDER SHE'S PISSED OFF!!
GRIND
YEAH, I'M PISSED OFF...
AT YOUUUU !!
GRAAH!

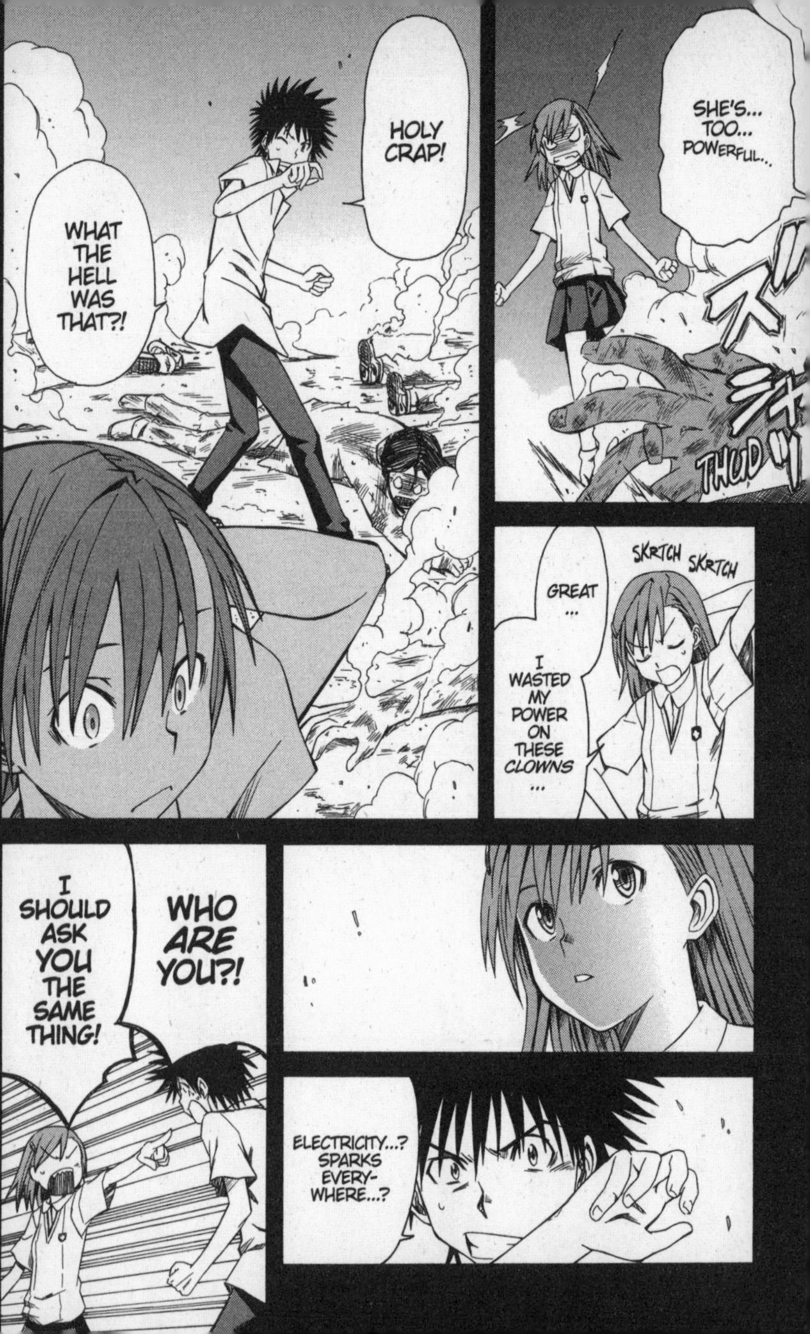

SHE'S... TOO... POWERFUL...
THUD
SKRTCH SKRTCH
GREAT... I WASTED MY POWER ON THESE CLOWNS...
HOLY CRAP!
WHAT THE HELL WAS THAT?!
!
ELECTRICITY...? SPARKS EVERY-WHERE...?
WHO ARE YOU?!
I SHOULD ASK YOU THE SAME THING!

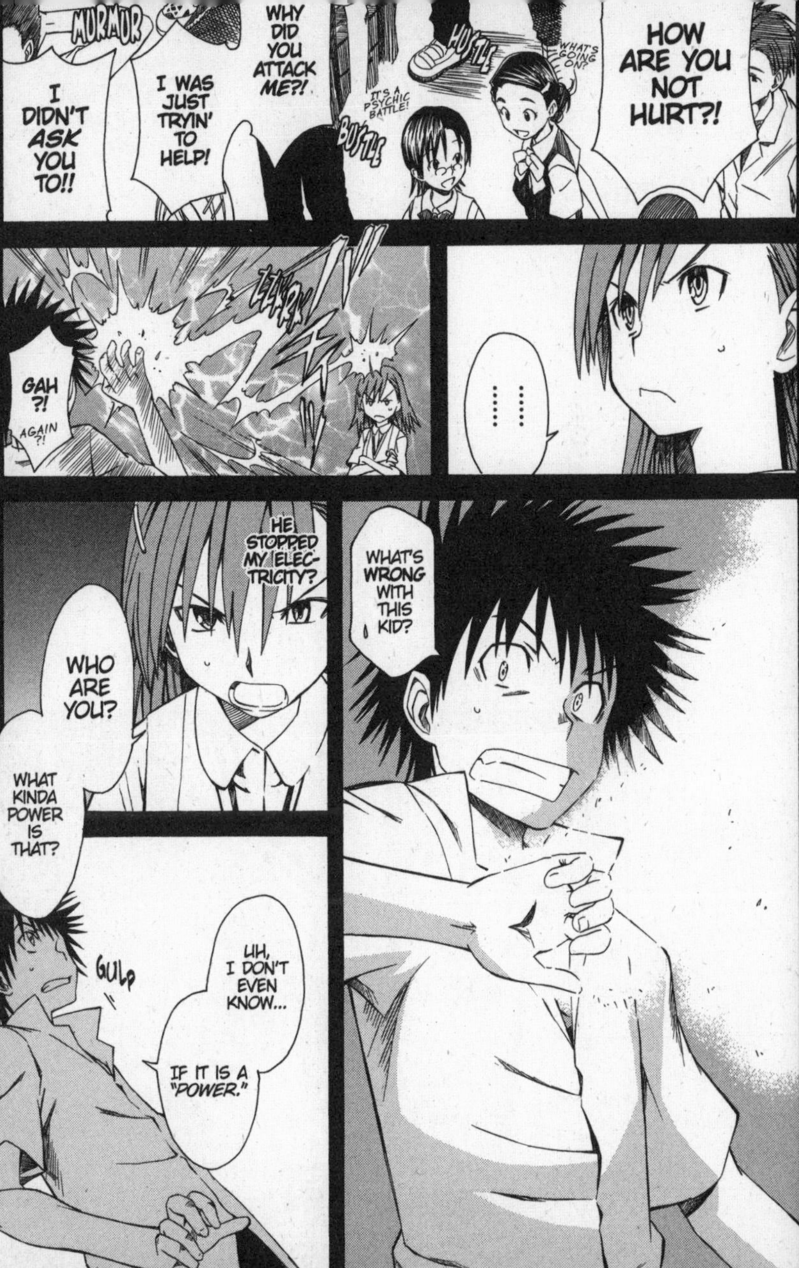
HOW ARE YOU NOT HURT?!
WHAT'S GOING ON?
HUSTLE
IT'S A PSYCHIC BATTLE!
BUSTLE
MURMUR
WHY DID YOU ATTACK ME?!
I WAS JUST TRYIN' TO HELP!
I DIDN'T ASK YOU TO!!
......
GAH?!
AGAIN?!
WHAT'S WRONG WITH THIS KID?
HE STOPPED MY ELECTRICITY?
WHO ARE YOU?
WHAT KINDA POWER IS THAT?
UH, I DON'T EVEN KNOW...
IF IT IS A "POWER."
GULP

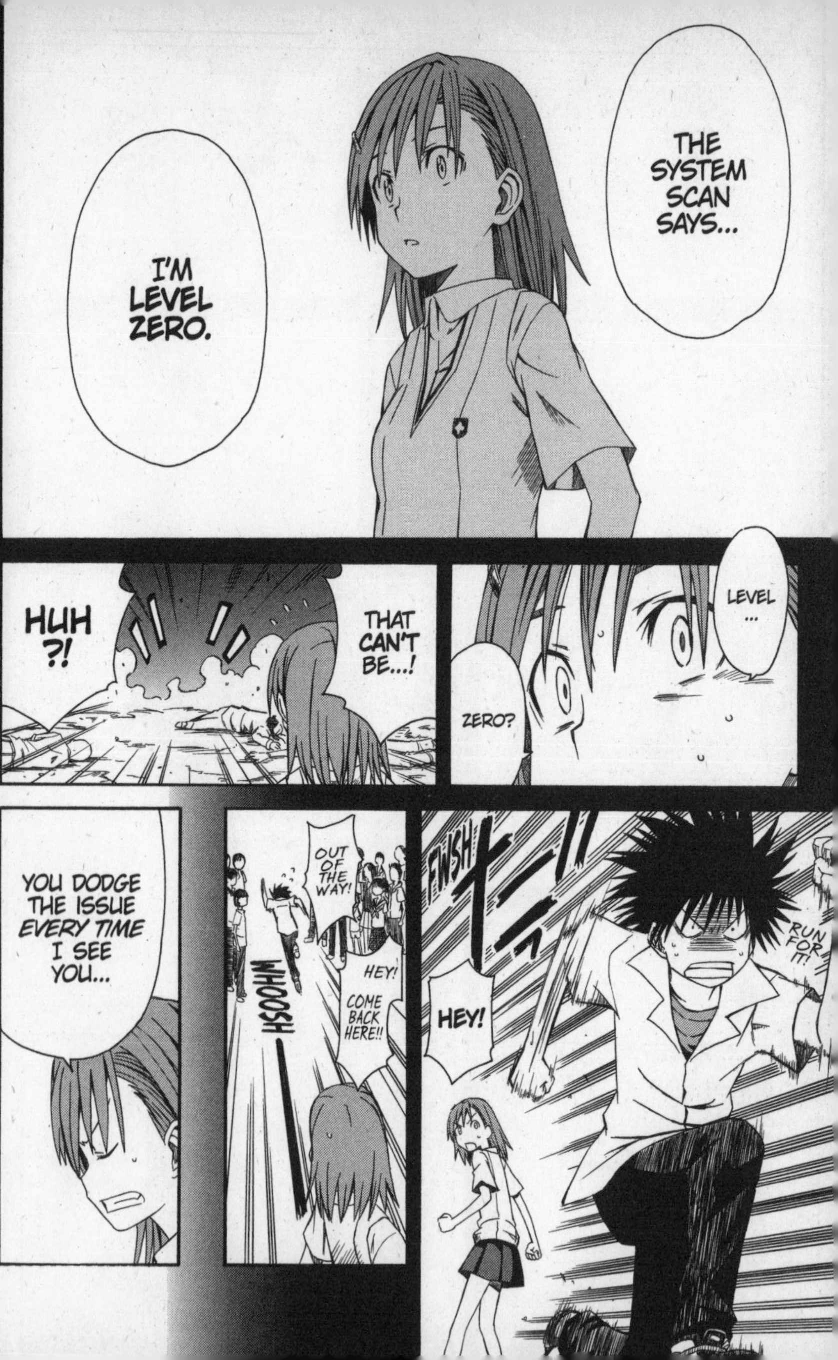
THE SYSTEM SCAN SAYS...
I'M LEVEL ZERO.
LEVEL ...
ZERO?
THAT CAN'T BE...!
HUH ?!
FWSH
RUN FOR IT!
HEY!
OUT OF THE WAY!
HEY! COME BACK HERE!!
WHOOSH
YOU DODGE THE ISSUE *EVERY TIME* I SEE YOU...

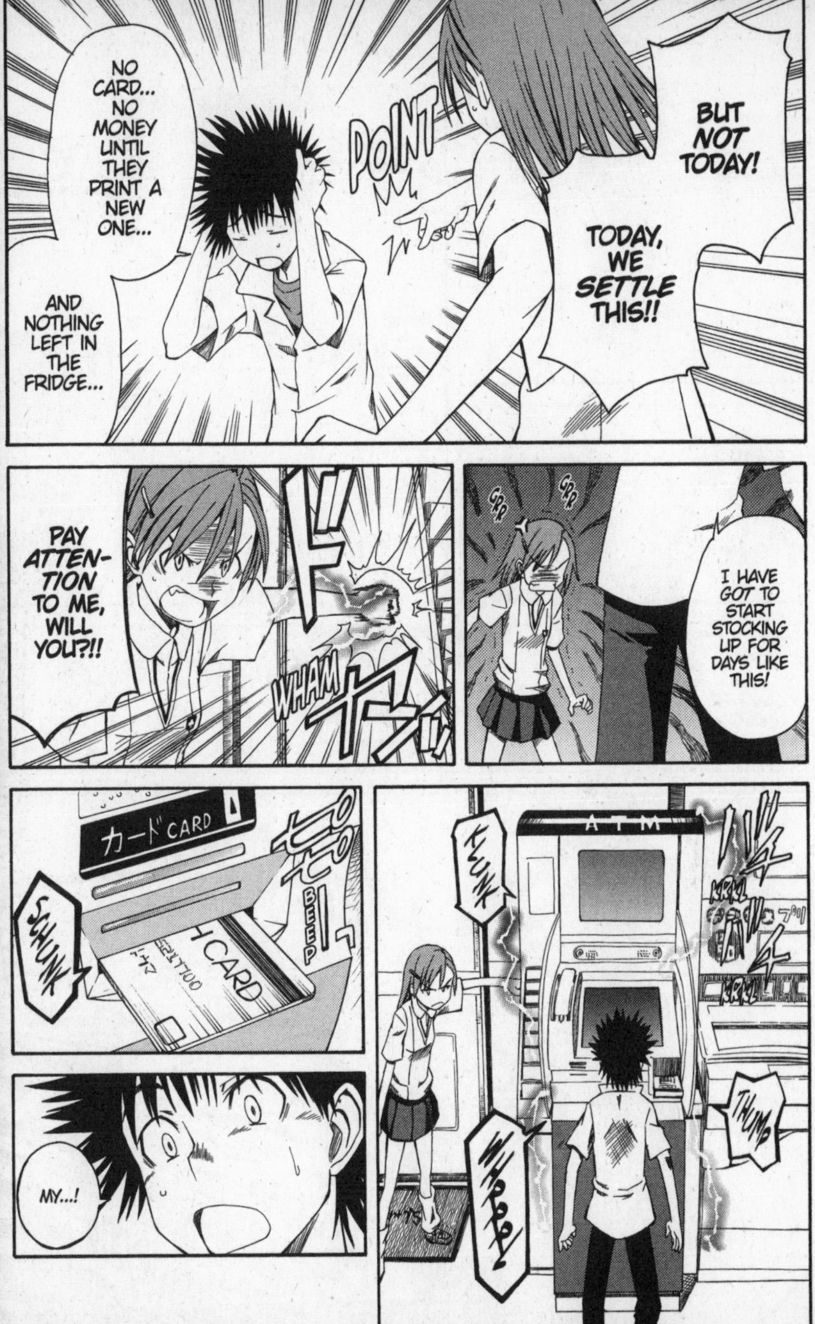
BUT NOT TODAY!
TODAY, WE SETTLE THIS!!
POINT
NO CARD... NO MONEY UNTIL THEY PRINT A NEW ONE...
AND NOTHING LEFT IN THE FRIDGE...
GRR
GRR
I HAVE GOT TO START STOCKING UP FOR DAYS LIKE THIS!
PAY ATTENTION TO ME, WILL YOU?!!
WHAM
ATM
KLUNK
KRRL
KRRL
THUMP
カード CARD
CARD
BEEP
SCHUNK
MY...!

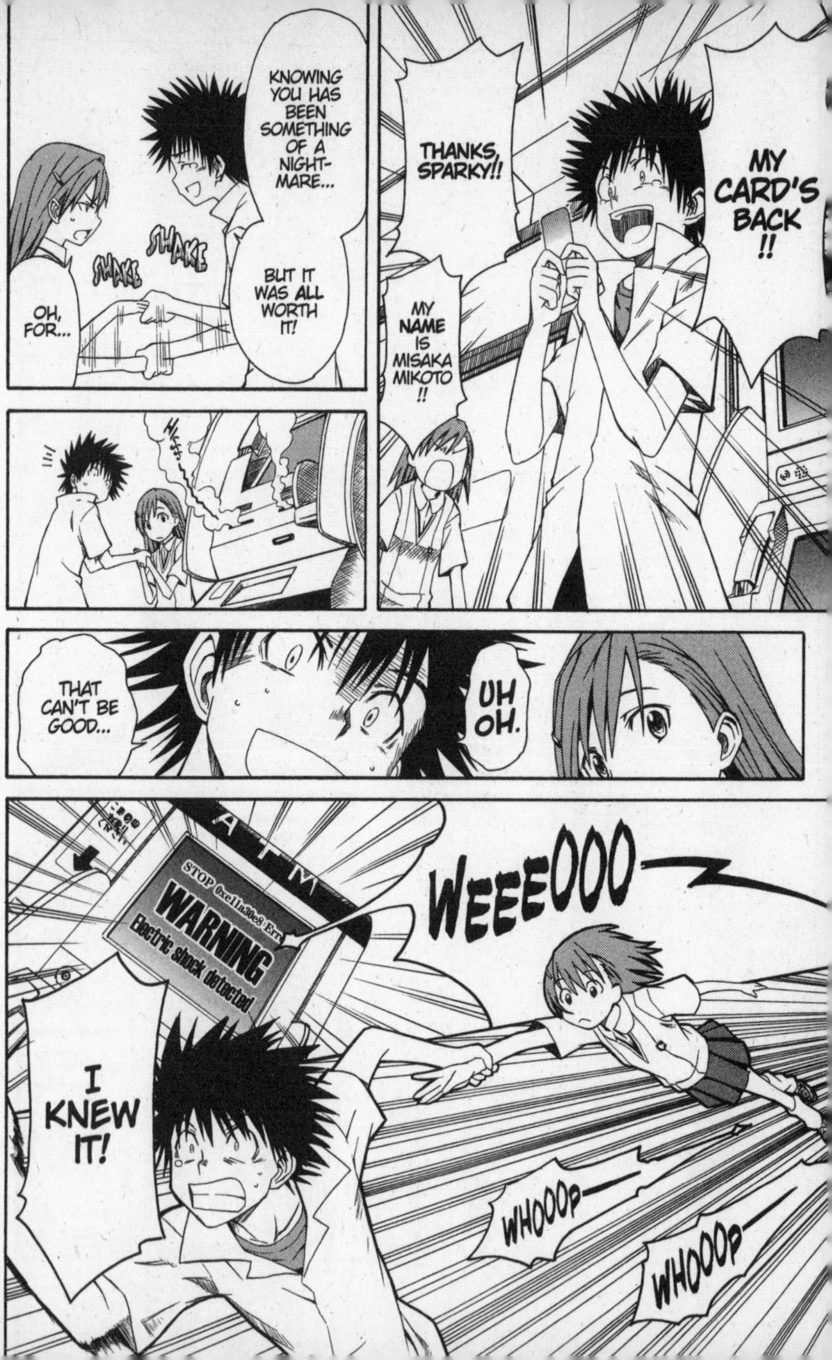
MY CARD'S BACK!!
THANKS, SPARKY!!
MY NAME IS MISAKA MIKOTO!!
KNOWING YOU HAS BEEN SOMETHING OF A NIGHT-MARE...
SHAKE
SHAKE
BUT IT WAS ALL WORTH IT!
OH, FOR...
UH OH.
THAT CAN'T BE GOOD...
WEEEOOO—
ATM
STOP 0xe11a30c8 Err
WARNING
Electric shock detected
I KNEW IT!
WHOOOP—
WHOOOP—

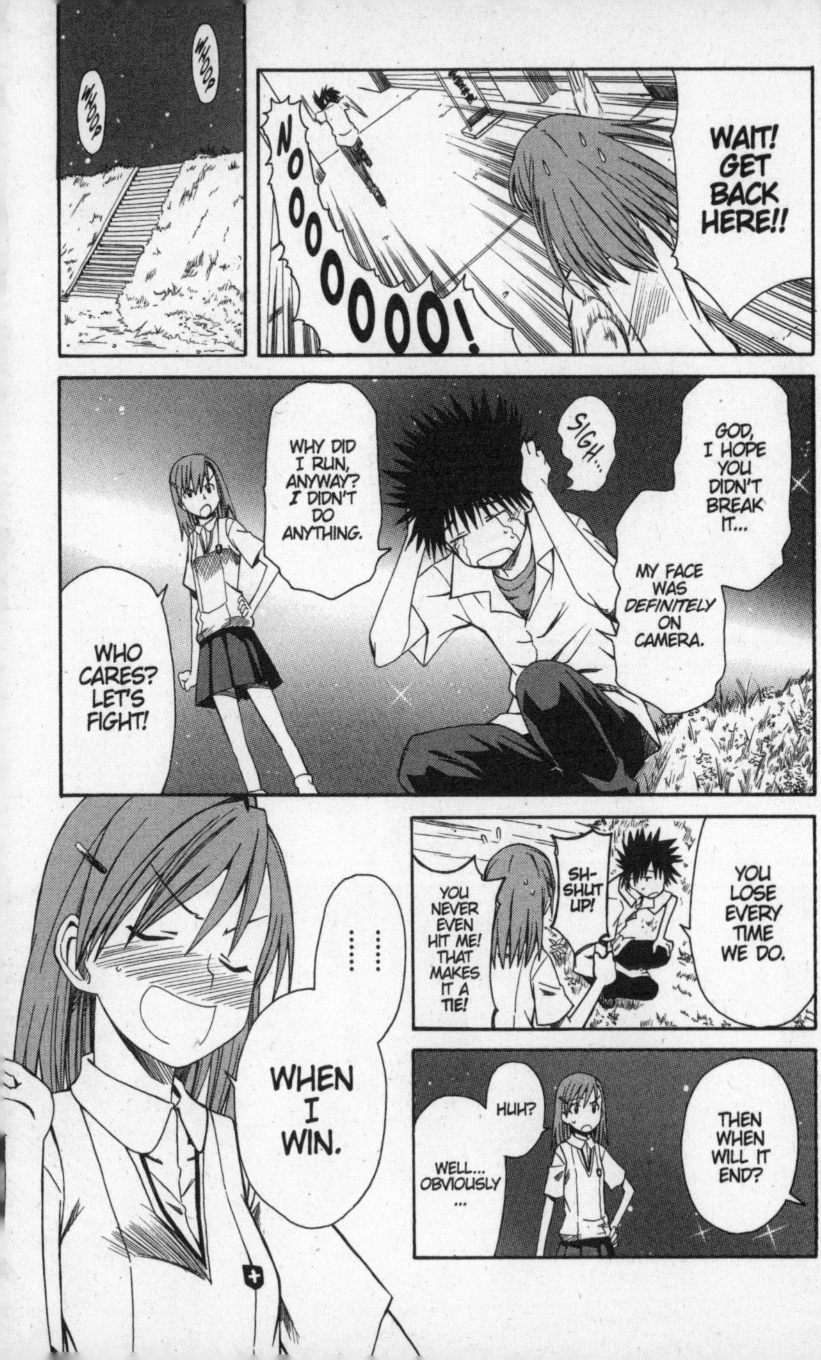
WAIT! GET BACK HERE!!
NOOOOOOOO!
WHOOP
WHOOP
GOD, I HOPE YOU DIDN'T BREAK IT...
SIGH...
MY FACE WAS DEFINITELY ON CAMERA.
WHY DID I RUN, ANYWAY? I DIDN'T DO ANYTHING.
WHO CARES? LET'S FIGHT!
YOU LOSE EVERY TIME WE DO.
SH-SHUT UP!
YOU NEVER EVEN HIT ME! THAT MAKES IT A TIE!
THEN WHEN WILL IT END?
HUH?
WELL... OBVIOUSLY ...
......
WHEN I WIN.

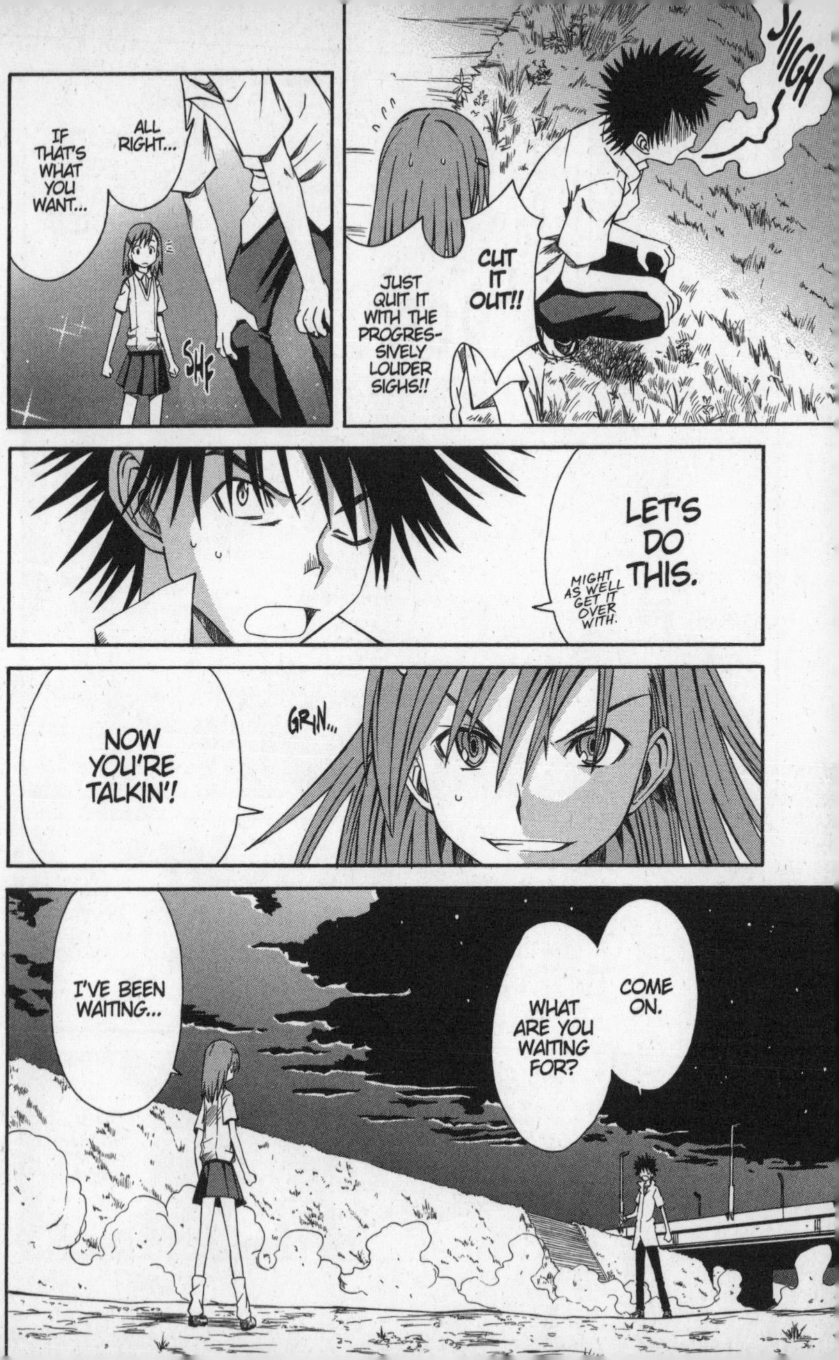
SIIIGH
CUT IT OUT!!
JUST QUIT IT WITH THE PROGRES-SIVELY LOUDER SIGHS!!
ALL RIGHT...
IF THAT'S WHAT YOU WANT...
SHF
LET'S DO THIS.
MIGHT AS WELL GET IT OVER WITH.
GRIN...
NOW YOU'RE TALKIN'!
COME ON.
WHAT ARE YOU WAITING FOR?
I'VE BEEN WAITING...

SHROOM

FZZKRSH

FOR YOU!

SHMM

SHMM

SHMM

SHMM

PSSHEET

IN THAT CASE...

KRKL

ELECTRICITY IS USELESS.

NOT EVEN A SCRATCH.

UH...

WHAT THE ...?

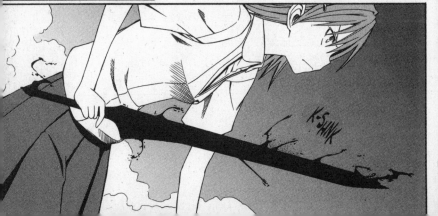

K-SHINK

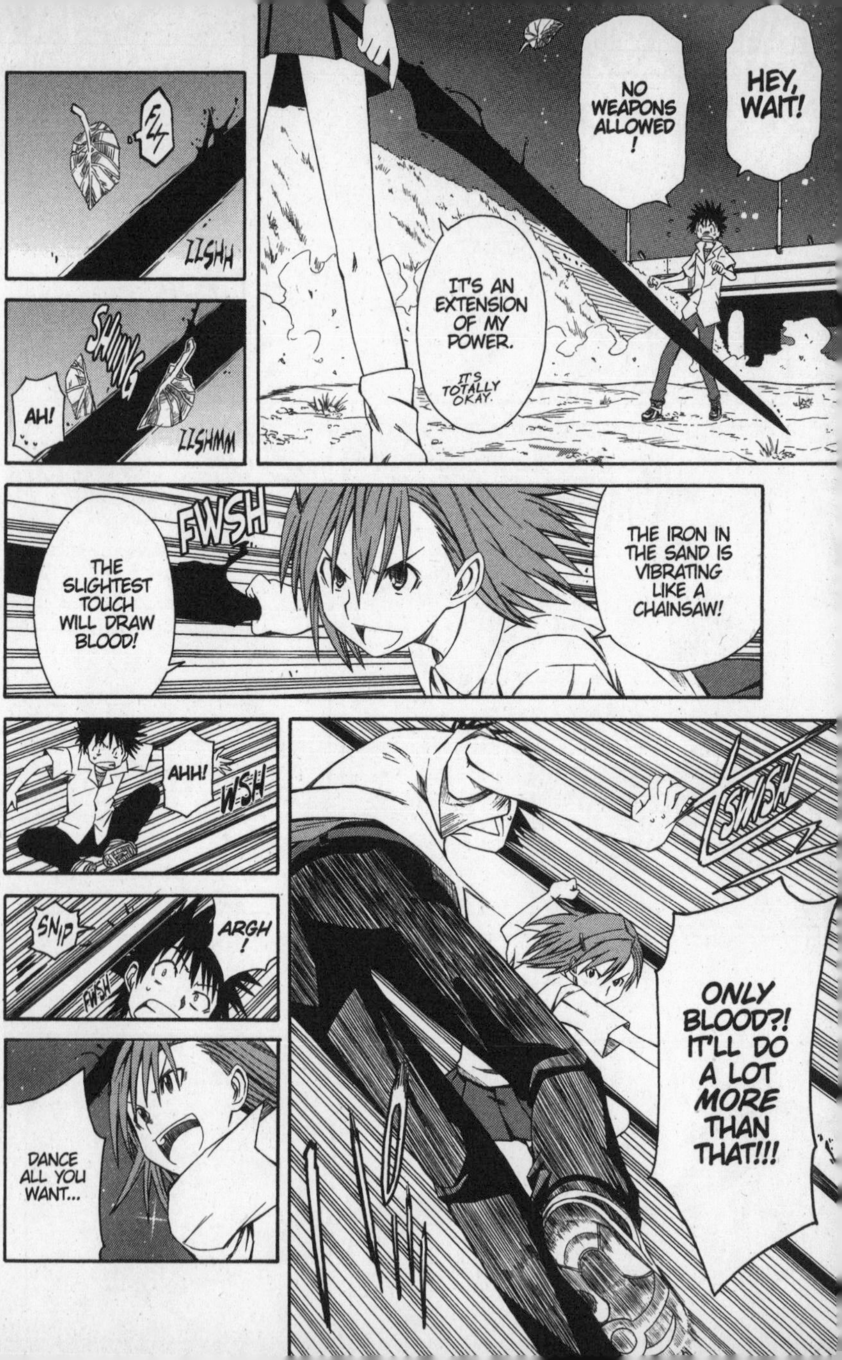
HEY, WAIT!
NO WEAPONS ALLOWED!
IT'S AN EXTENSION OF MY POWER.
IT'S TOTALLY OKAY.
SHING
AH!
THE IRON IN THE SAND IS VIBRATING LIKE A CHAINSAW!
FWSH
THE SLIGHTEST TOUCH WILL DRAW BLOOD!
ONLY BLOOD?! IT'LL DO A LOT MORE THAN THAT!!!
AHH!
WSH
ARGH!
SNIP
FWSH
DANCE ALL YOU WANT...

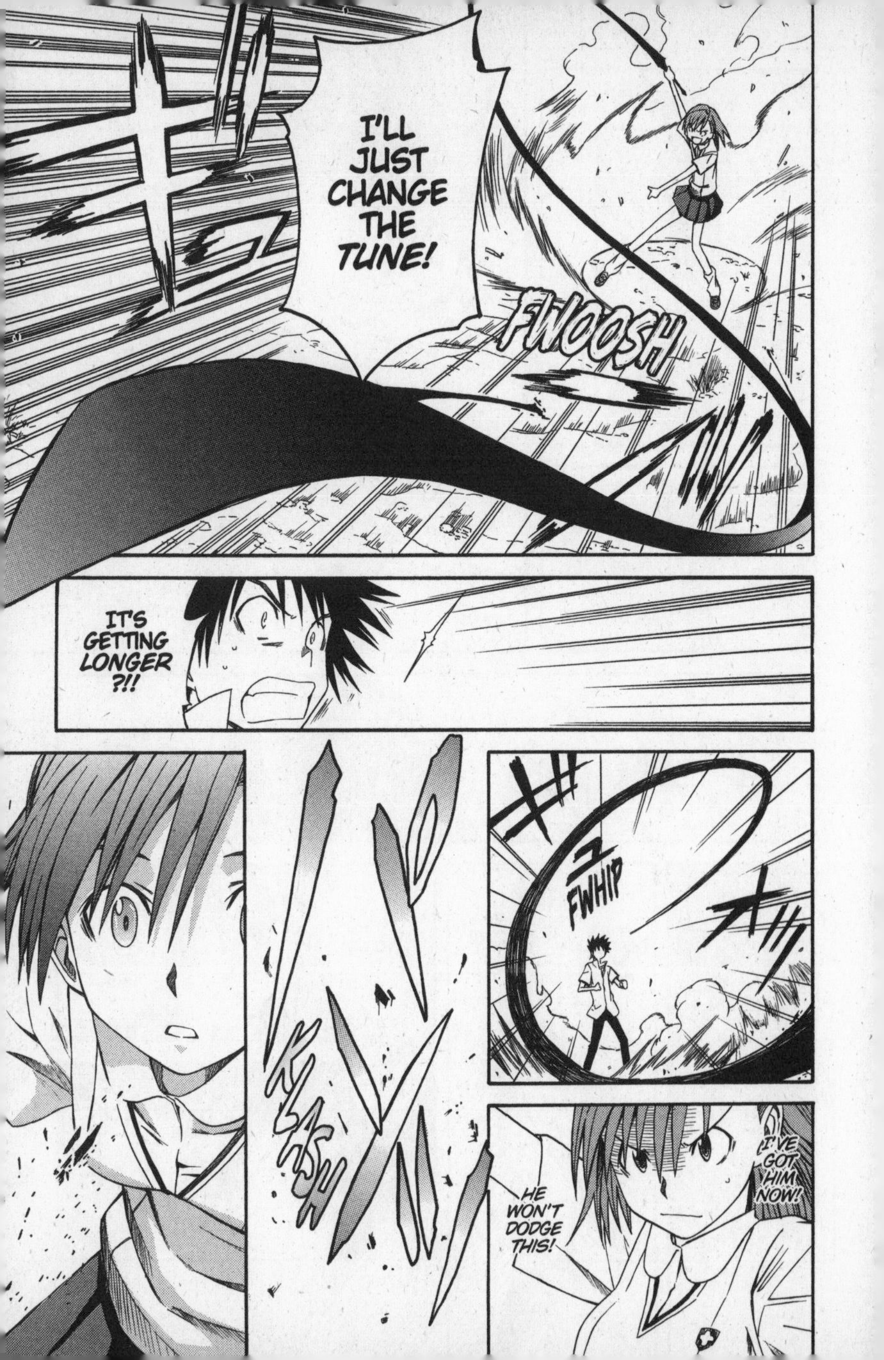
I'LL JUST CHANGE THE TUNE!
FWOOSH
IT'S GETTING LONGER ?!!
FWHIP
I'VE GOT HIM NOW!
HE WON'T DODGE THIS!
KLASH

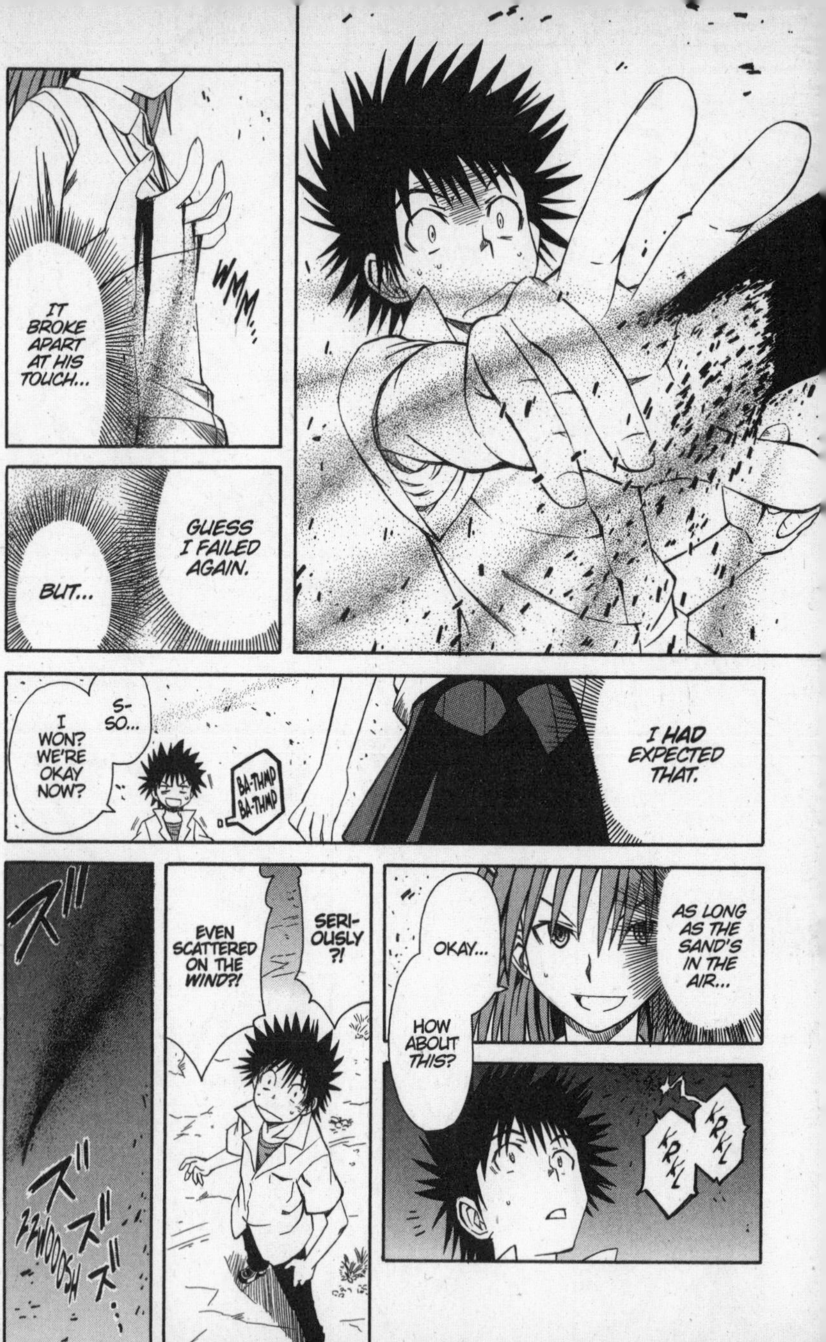

IT BROKE APART AT HIS TOUCH...
WMM...
GUESS I FAILED AGAIN.
BUT...
I HAD EXPECTED THAT.
S-SO...
I WON? WE'RE OKAY NOW?
BA-THMP BA-THMP
AS LONG AS THE SAND'S IN THE AIR...
OKAY...
HOW ABOUT THIS?
KRKL KRKL
SERI-OUSLY?!
EVEN SCATTERED ON THE WIND?!
ZZWOOOSH

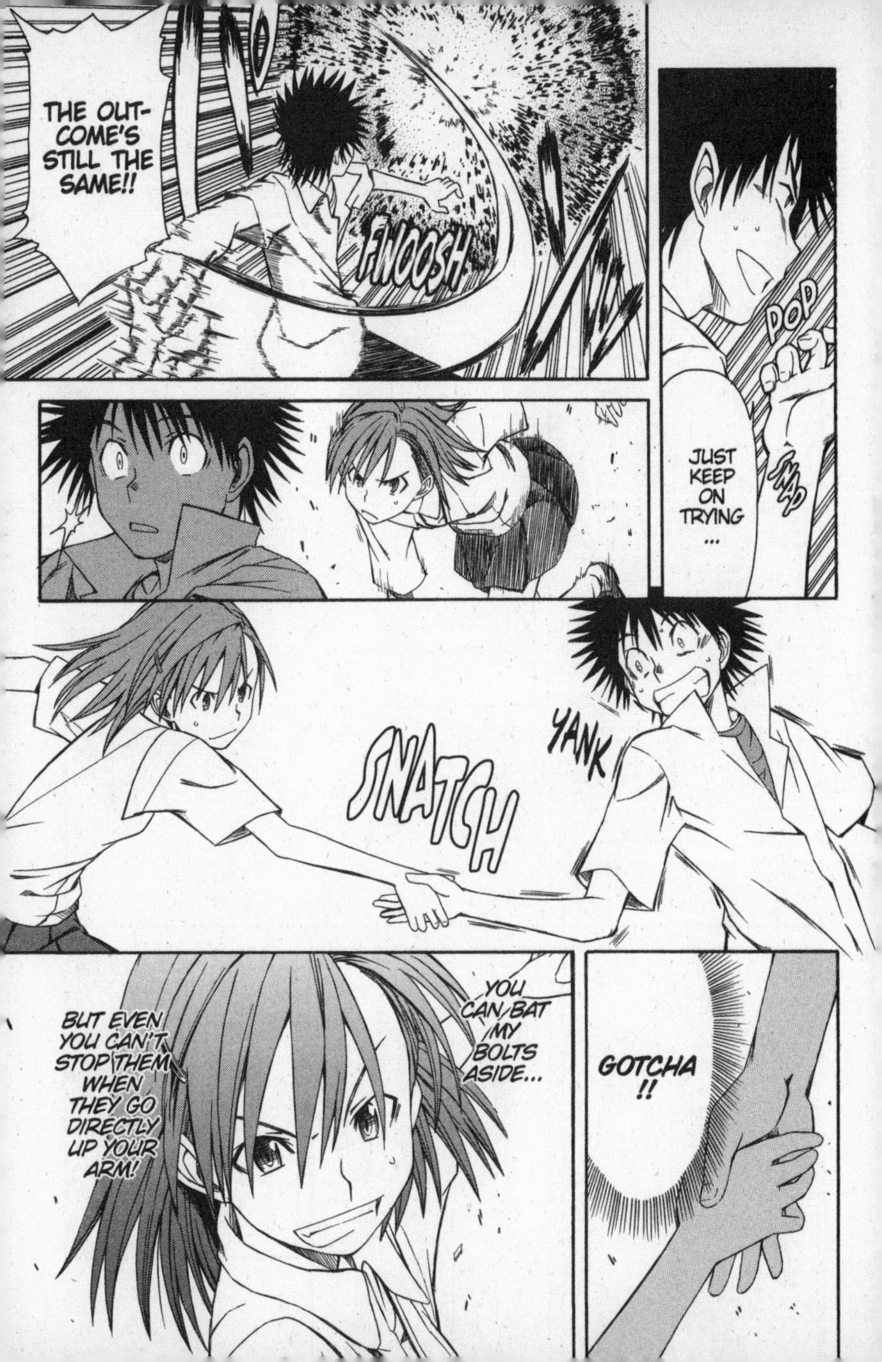
POP
SNAP
JUST KEEP ON TRYING...
THE OUT-COME'S STILL THE SAME!!
FWOOSH
YANK
SNATCH
GOTCHA!!
YOU CAN BAT MY BOLTS ASIDE...
BUT EVEN YOU CAN'T STOP THEM WHEN THEY GO DIRECTLY UP YOUR ARM!

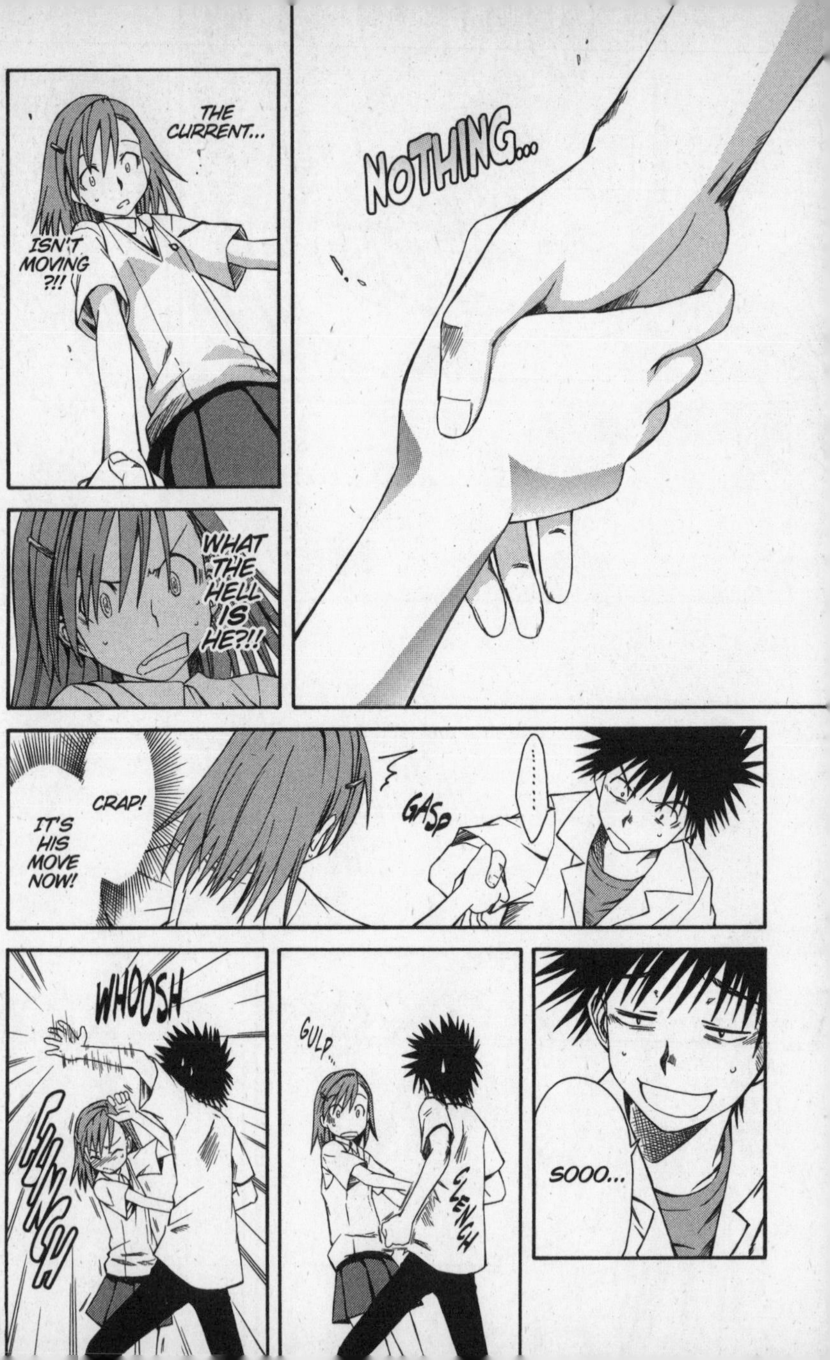
NOTHING...
THE CURRENT...
ISN'T MOVING ?!!
WHAT THE HELL IS HE?!!
......
GASP
CRAP!
IT'S HIS MOVE NOW!
SOOO...
GULP...
CLENCH
WHOOSH

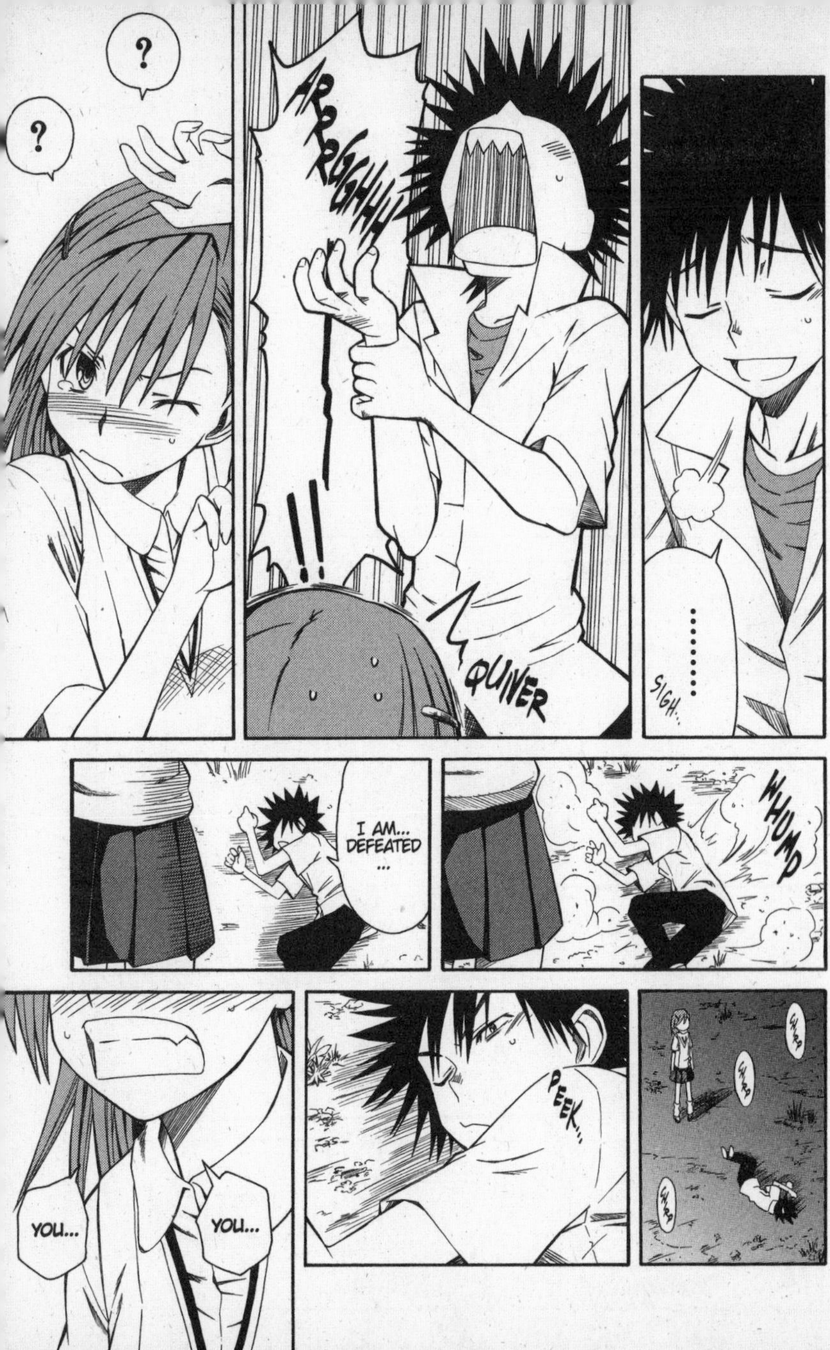

....
SIGH...
ARRRGHHH
!!
QUIVER
?
?
WHUMP
I AM... DEFEATED ...
CHIRP
CHIRP
CHIRP
PEEK...
YOU...
YOU...

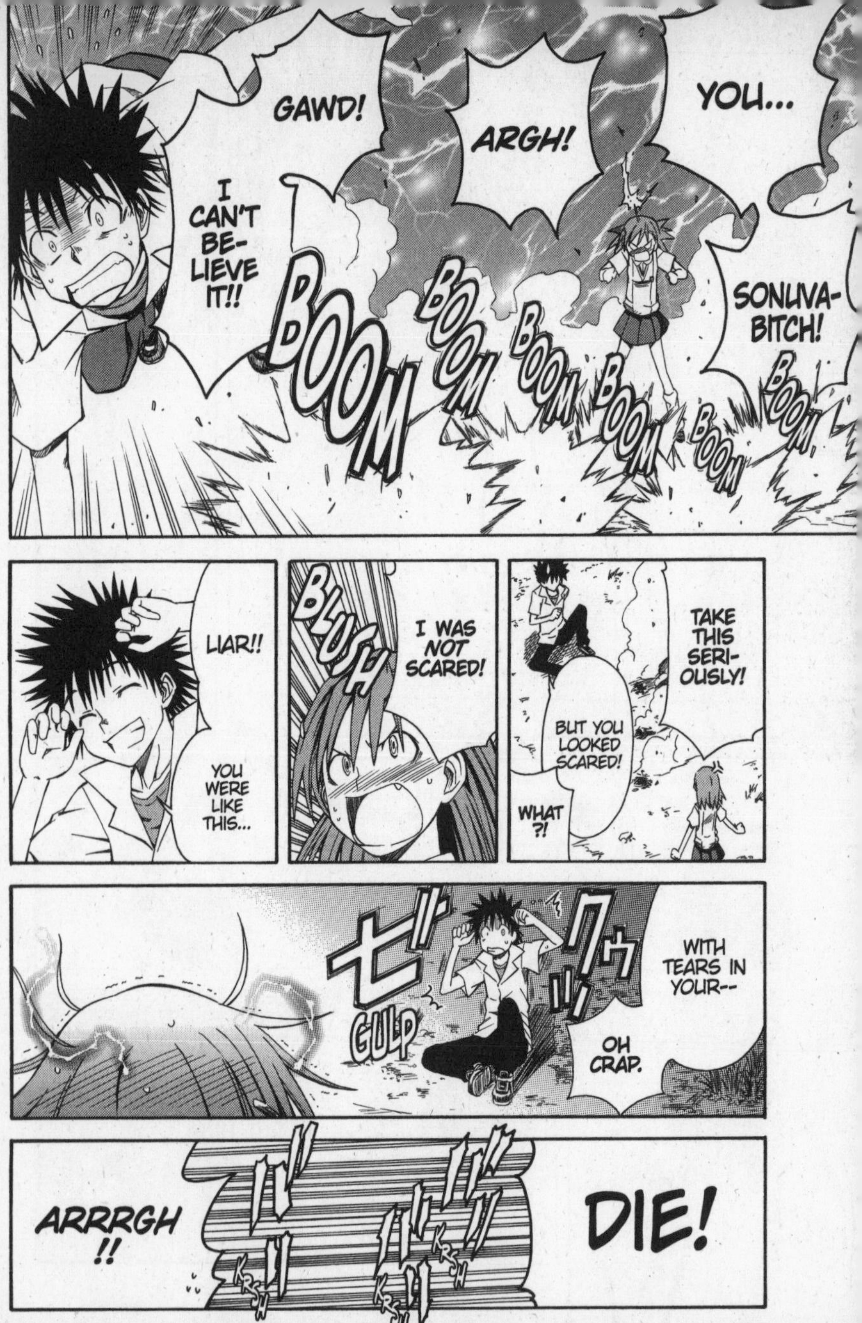
YOU...
SONUVA-BITCH!
ARGH!
GAWD!
I CAN'T BE-LIEVE IT!!
BOOM
BOOM
BOOM
BOOM
BOOM
BOOM
TAKE THIS SERI-OUSLY!
BUT YOU LOOKED SCARED!
WHAT ?!
BLUSH
I WAS NOT SCARED!
LIAR!!
YOU WERE LIKE THIS...
WITH TEARS IN YOUR--
OH CRAP.
GULP
DIE!
KRSH
KRSH
KRSH
KRSH
ARRRGH !!

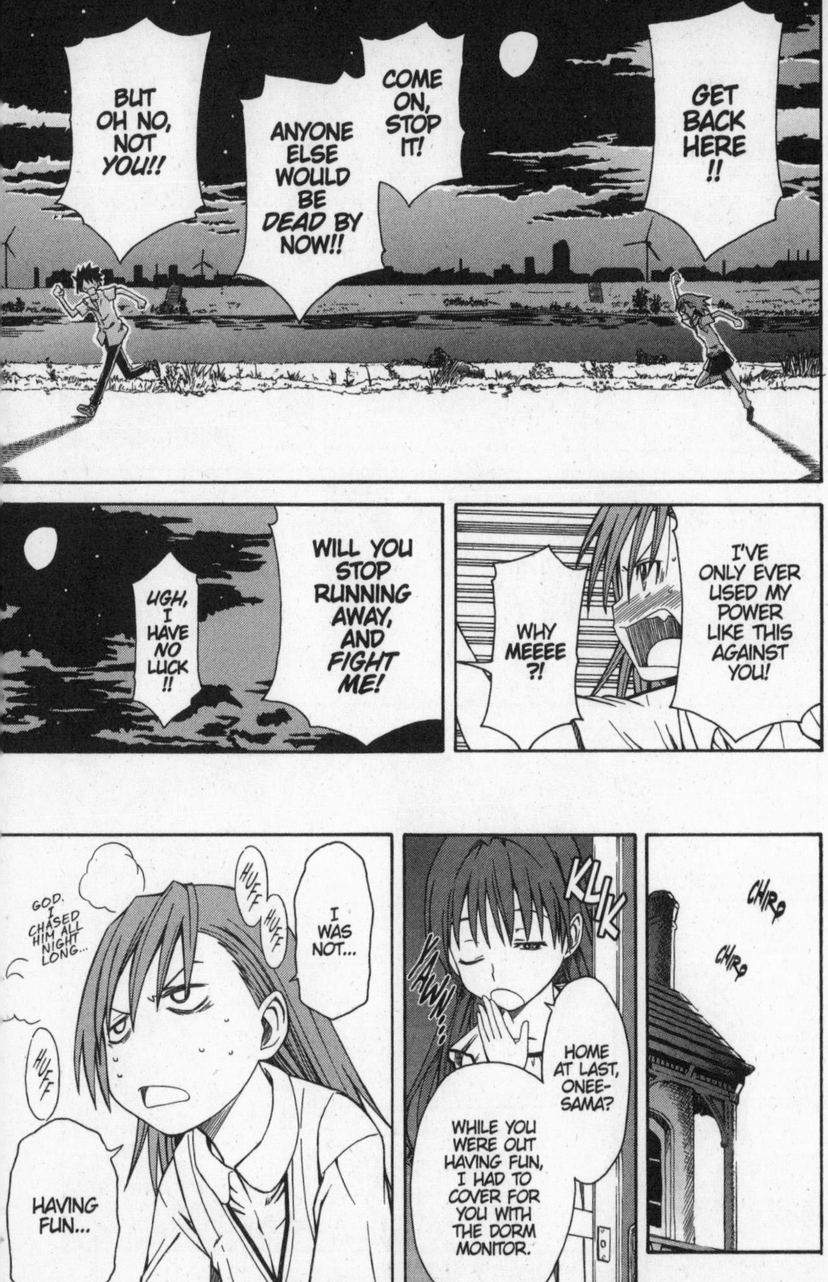

GET BACK HERE!!
COME ON, STOP IT!
ANYONE ELSE WOULD BE DEAD BY NOW!!
BUT OH NO, NOT YOU!!
I'VE ONLY EVER USED MY POWER LIKE THIS AGAINST YOU!
WHY MEEEE?!
WILL YOU STOP RUNNING AWAY, AND FIGHT ME!
UGH, I HAVE NO LUCK!!
CHIRP
CHIRP
KLIK
YAWN...
HOME AT LAST, ONEE-SAMA?
WHILE YOU WERE OUT HAVING FUN, I HAD TO COVER FOR YOU WITH THE DORM MONITOR.
HUFF HUFF
I WAS NOT...
GOD. I CHASED HIM ALL NIGHT LONG...
HUFF
HAVING FUN...

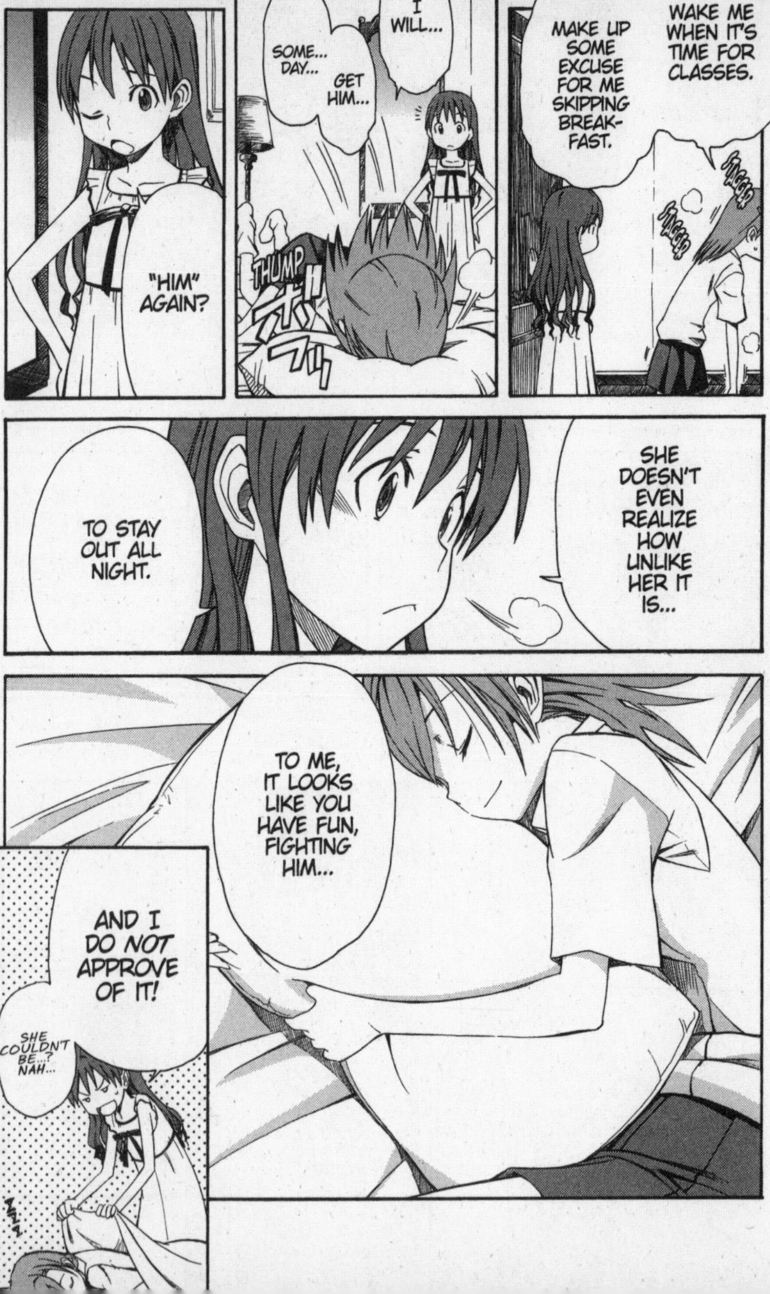
WAKE ME WHEN IT'S TIME FOR CLASSES.
MAKE UP SOME EXCUSE FOR ME SKIPPING BREAK-FAST.
STAGGER
STAGGER
I WILL...
SOME... DAY... GET HIM...
THUMP
"HIM" AGAIN?
SHE DOESN'T EVEN REALIZE HOW UNLIKE HER IT IS...
TO STAY OUT ALL NIGHT.
TO ME, IT LOOKS LIKE YOU HAVE FUN, FIGHTING HIM...
AND I DO NOT APPROVE OF IT!
SHE COULDN'T BE...? NAH...
ZZZ

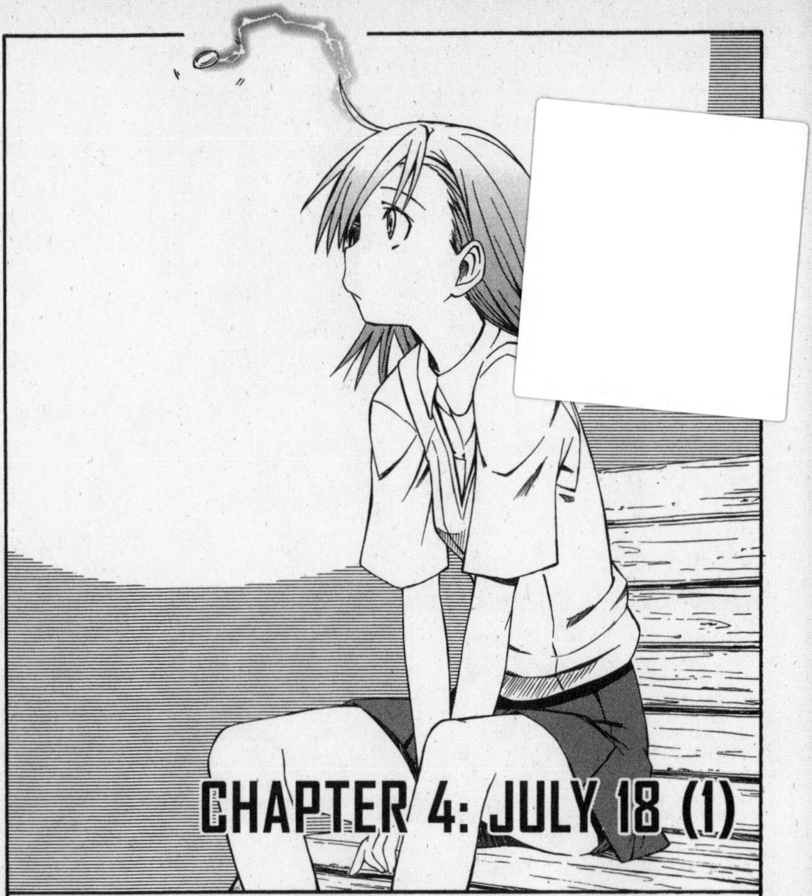

CHAPTER 4: JULY 18 (1)

MISAKA MIKOTO
(ELECTROMASTER)

* SHE IS ONE OF ONLY SEVEN LEVEL FIVE PSYCHICS IN ACADEMY CITY, AND THE STAR OF TOKIWADAI MIDDLE SCHOOL.
* HER SPECIAL MOVE INVOLVES CHARGING AN ARCADE TOKEN WITH ELECTRICITY, AND FIRING IT AT THREE TIMES THE SPEED OF SOUND, THUS EARNING HER THE NICKNAME "RAILGUN."
* HER ELECTRIC POWERS CAN BE AS STRONG AS A BILLION VOLTS. ADDITIONALLY, SHE CONTROLS NOT ONLY ELECTRIC CURRENT, BUT ALSO MAGNETIC WAVES. SHE IS ADAPTIVE IN USING HER POWERS, WITH TECHNIQUES SUCH AS THE RAILGUN OR THE IRONSAND SWORD. SHE IS FAR STRONGER THAN ANY OTHER ELECTROMASTER.
* SHE HAS AN AGGRESSIVE PERSONALITY, AND HATES TO LOSE. OCCASIONALLY, SHE IS FOUND TO BE SURPRISINGLY FOND OF GIRLISH THINGS, SUCH AS CUTE PAJAMAS.
* SHE READS MANGA AT THE CONVENIENCE STORE EVERY MONDAY AND WEDNESDAY, AND SHE ALWAYS HITS THE BOOKSTORE ON THE 10TH OF THE MONTH.

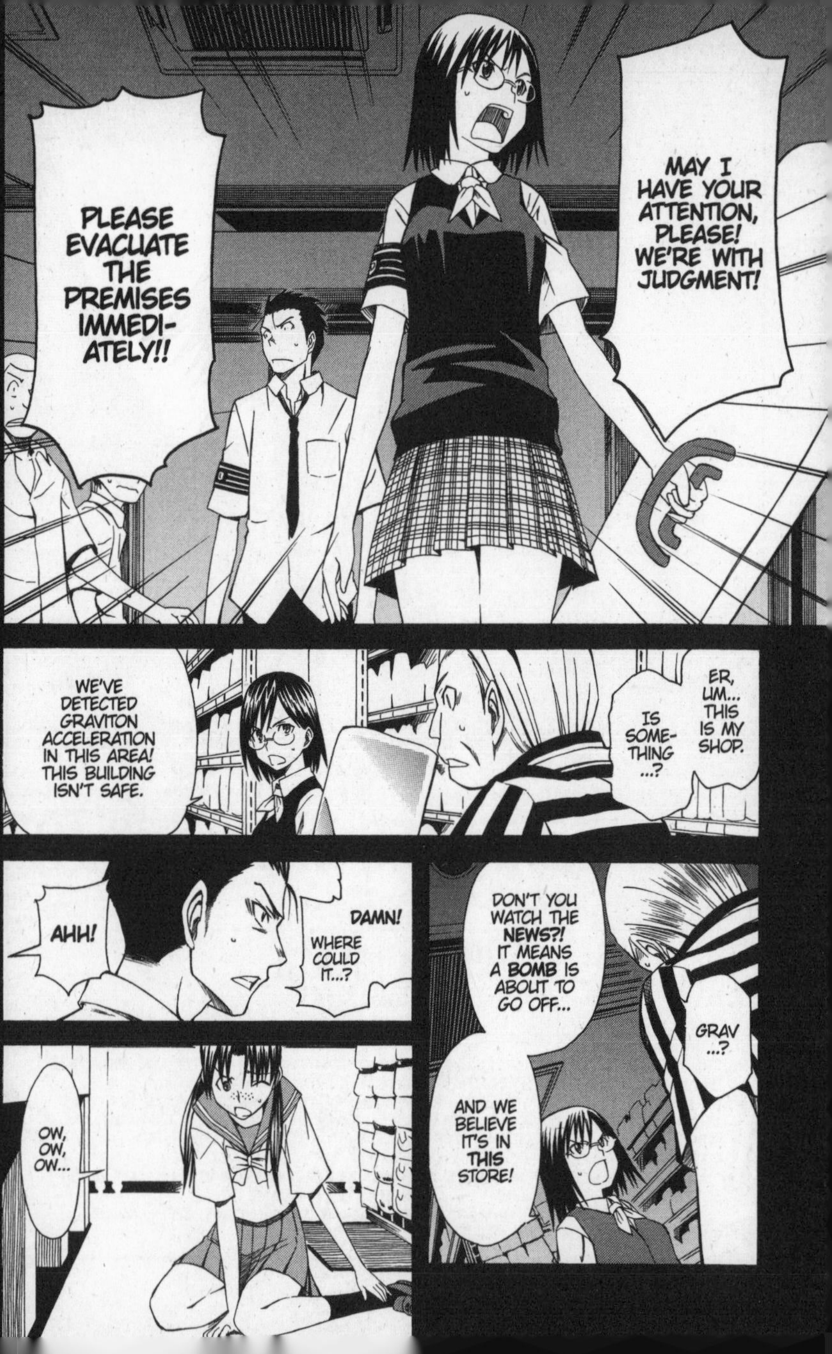
MAY I HAVE YOUR ATTENTION, PLEASE! WE'RE WITH JUDGMENT!
PLEASE EVACUATE THE PREMISES IMMEDI-ATELY!!
ER, UM... THIS IS MY SHOP.
IS SOMETHING ...?
WE'VE DETECTED GRAVITON ACCELERATION IN THIS AREA! THIS BUILDING ISN'T SAFE.
GRAV ...?
DON'T YOU WATCH THE NEWS?! IT MEANS A BOMB IS ABOUT TO GO OFF...
AND WE BELIEVE IT'S IN THIS STORE!
DAMN!
WHERE COULD IT...?
AHH!
OW, OW, OW...

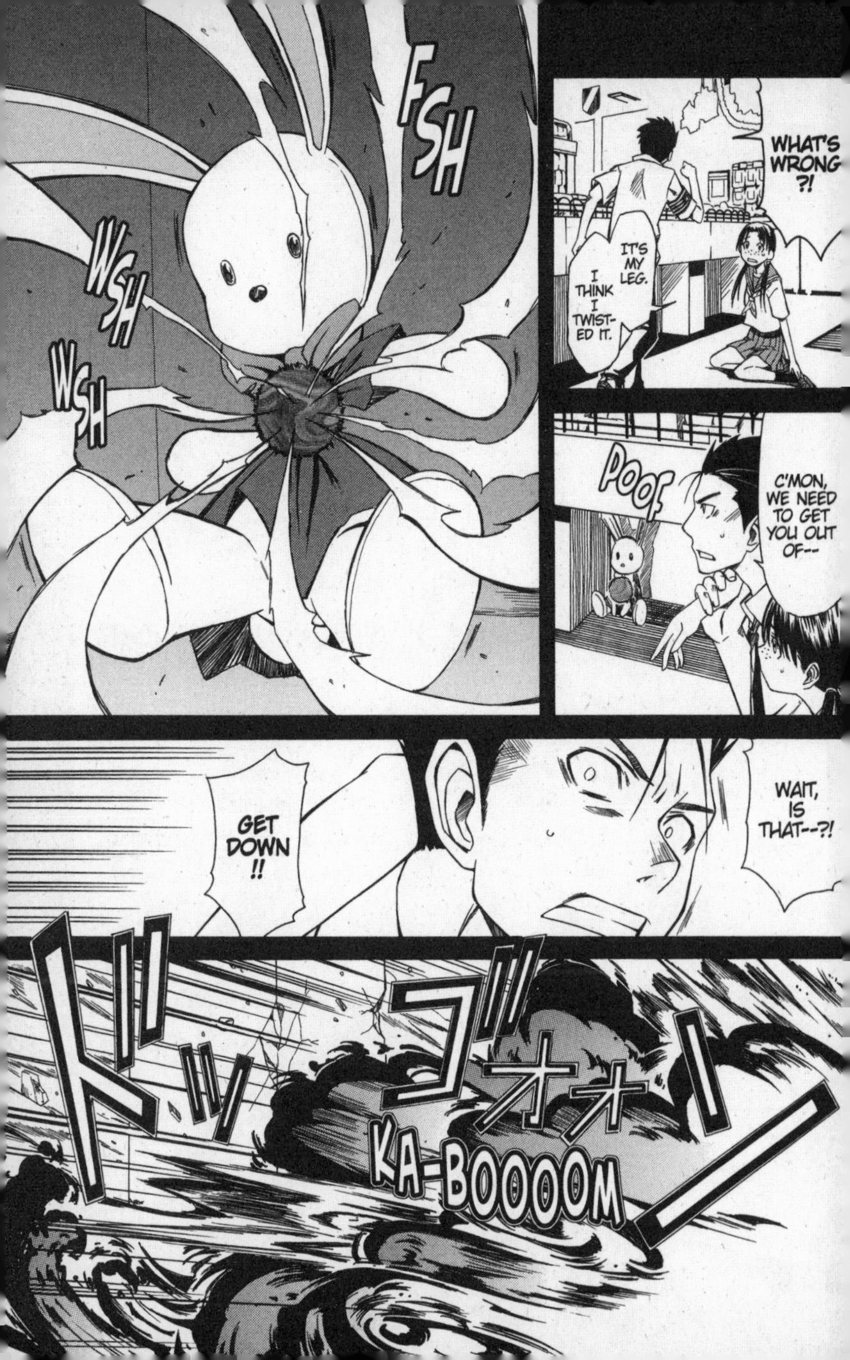
WHAT'S WRONG?!
IT'S MY LEG.
I THINK I TWISTED IT.
C'MON, WE NEED TO GET YOU OUT OF--
POOF
FSH
WSH
WSH
WAIT, IS THAT--?!
GET DOWN!!
KA-BOOOOM

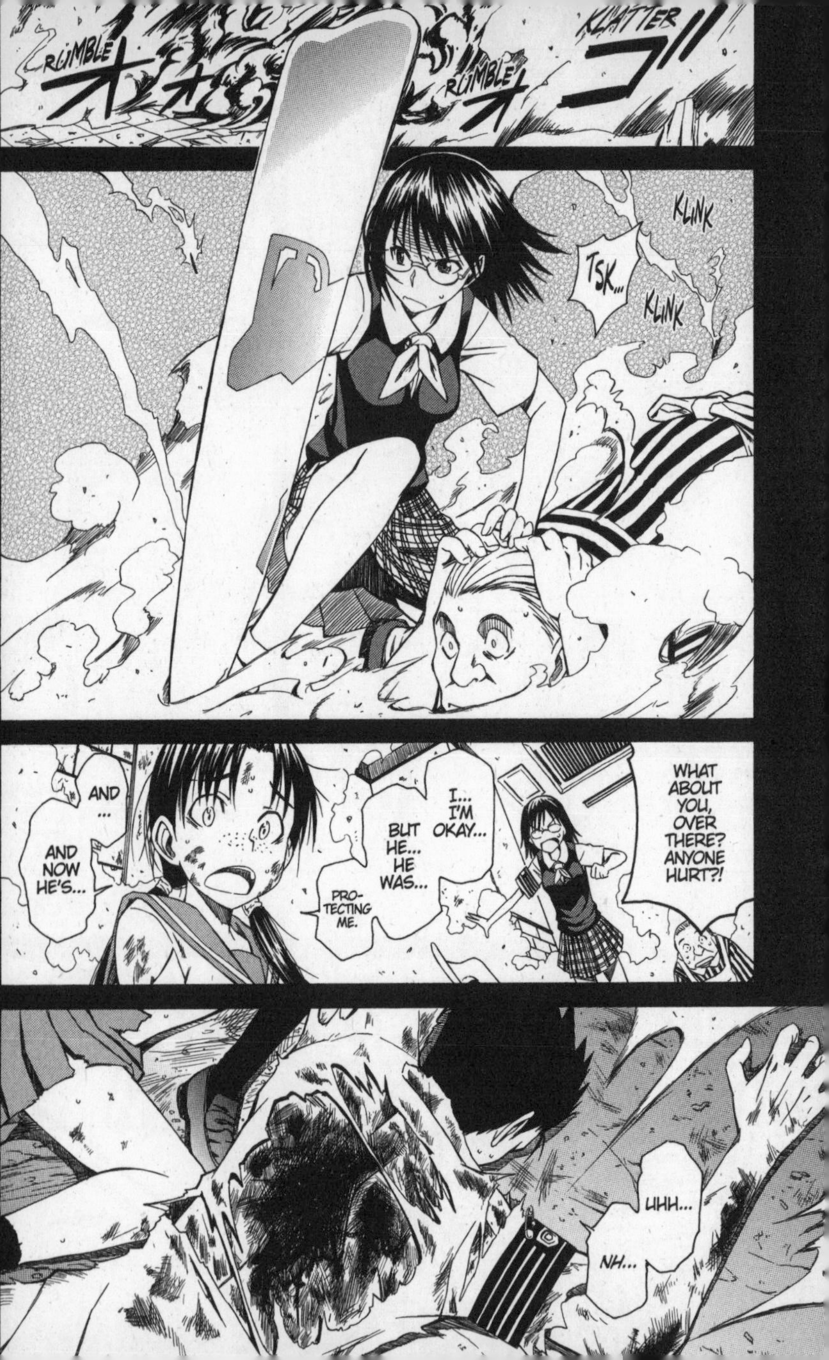
KLATTER
RUMBLE
RUMBLE
KLINK
TSK...
KLINK
WHAT ABOUT YOU, OVER THERE? ANYONE HURT?!
I... I'M OKAY...
BUT HE... HE WAS...
PROTECTING ME.
AND...
AND NOW HE'S...
UHH...
NH...

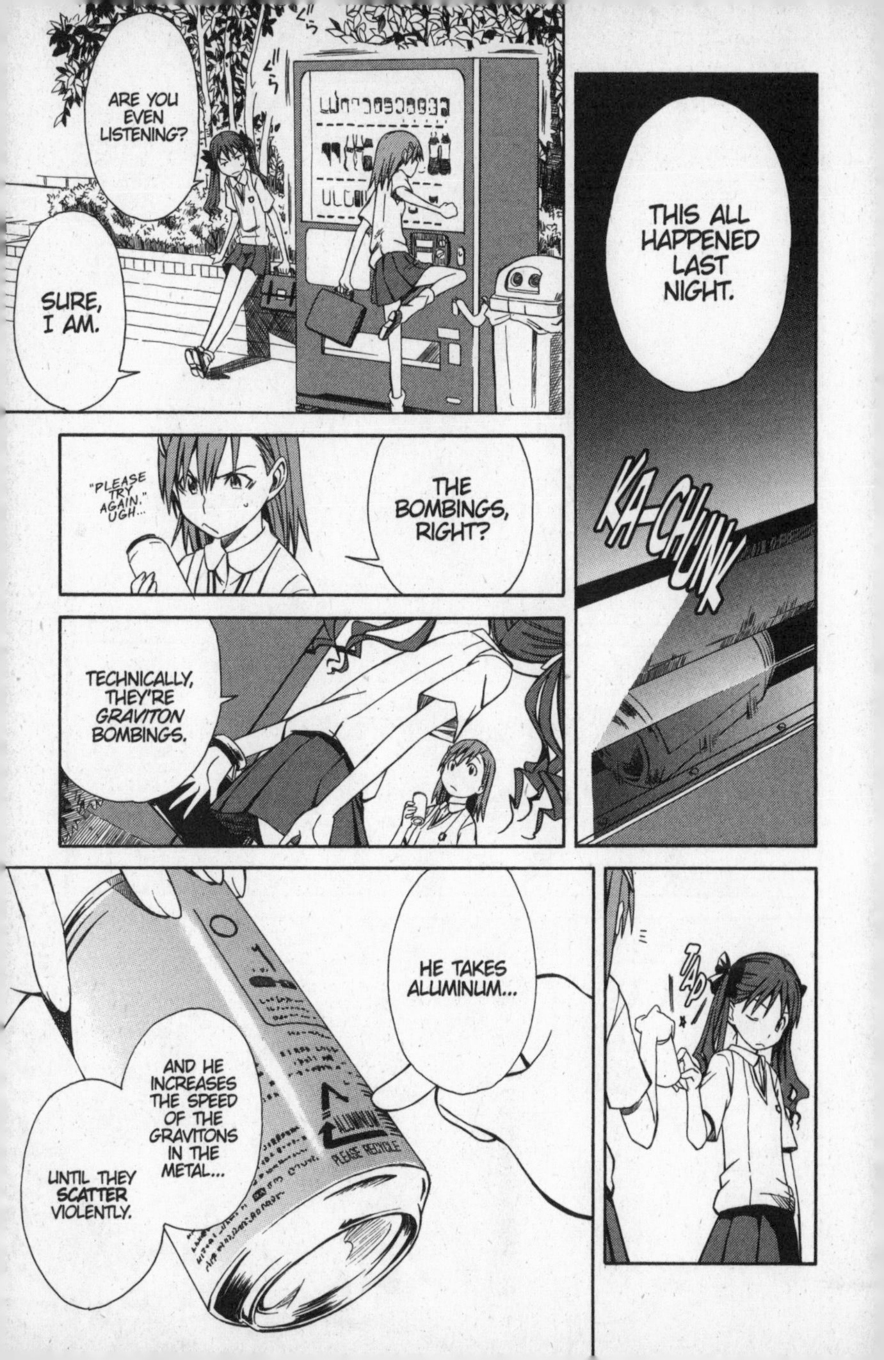
THIS ALL HAPPENED LAST NIGHT.
KA-CHUNK
ARE YOU EVEN LISTENING?
SURE, I AM.
THE BOMBINGS, RIGHT?
"PLEASE TRY AGAIN." UGH...
TECHNICALLY, THEY'RE *GRAVITON* BOMBINGS.
TAP
HE TAKES ALUMINUM...
AND HE INCREASES THE SPEED OF THE GRAVITONS IN THE METAL...
UNTIL THEY SCATTER VIOLENTLY.
ALUMINUM
PLEASE RECYCLE

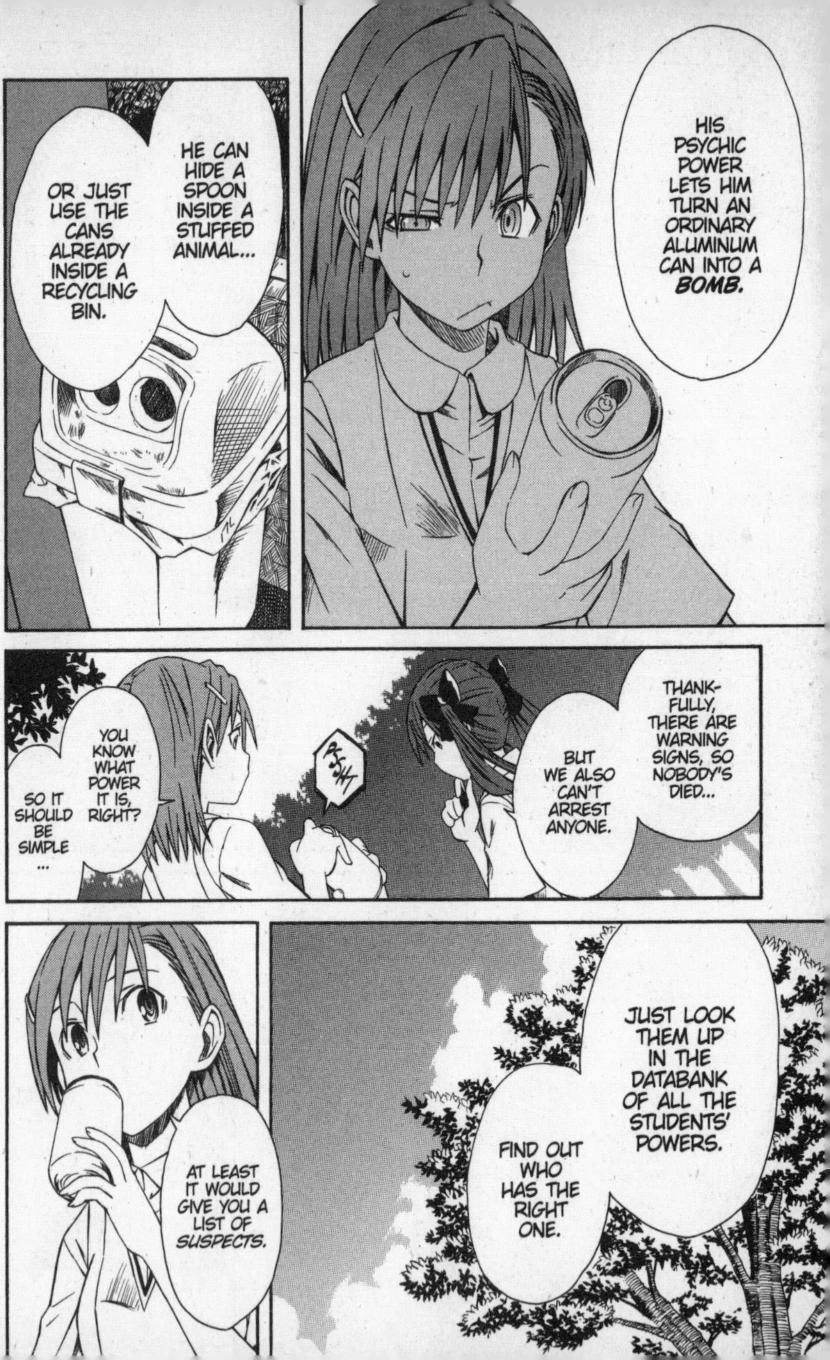
HIS PSYCHIC POWER LETS HIM TURN AN ORDINARY ALUMINUM CAN INTO A ***BOMB.***
HE CAN HIDE A SPOON INSIDE A STUFFED ANIMAL...
OR JUST USE THE CANS ALREADY INSIDE A RECYCLING BIN.
THANK-FULLY, THERE ARE WARNING SIGNS, SO NOBODY'S DIED...
BUT WE ALSO CAN'T ARREST ANYONE.
YOU KNOW WHAT POWER IT IS, RIGHT?
SO IT SHOULD BE SIMPLE ...
JUST LOOK THEM UP IN THE DATABANK OF ALL THE STUDENTS' POWERS.
FIND OUT WHO HAS THE RIGHT ONE.
AT LEAST IT WOULD GIVE YOU A LIST OF *SUSPECTS.*

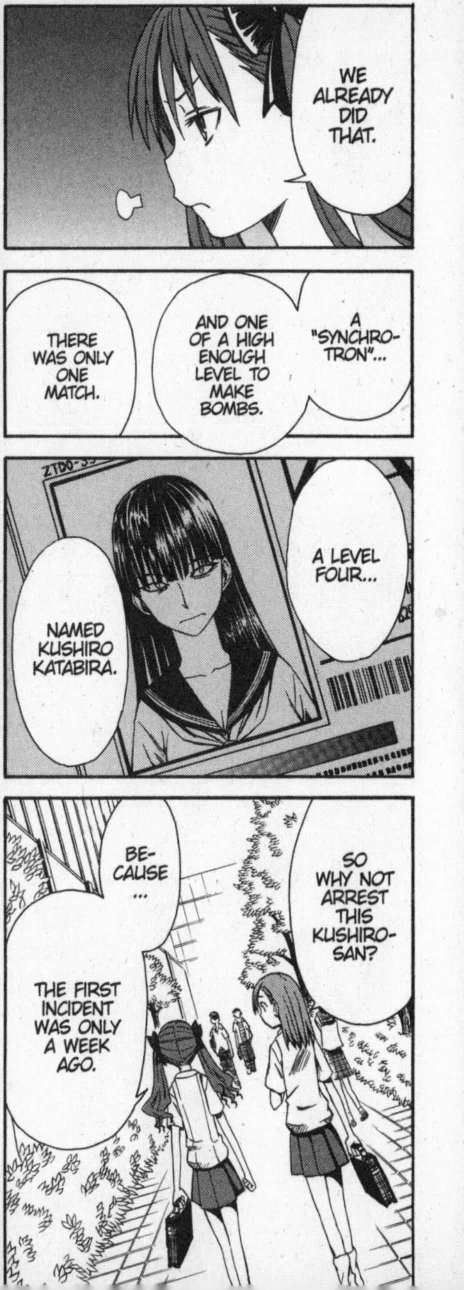
WE ALREADY DID THAT.
A "SYNCHRO-TRON"...
AND ONE OF A HIGH ENOUGH LEVEL TO MAKE BOMBS.
THERE WAS ONLY ONE MATCH.
A LEVEL FOUR...
NAMED KUSHIRO KATABIRA.
SO WHY NOT ARREST THIS KUSHIRO-SAN?
BE-CAUSE...
THE FIRST INCIDENT WAS ONLY A WEEK AGO.
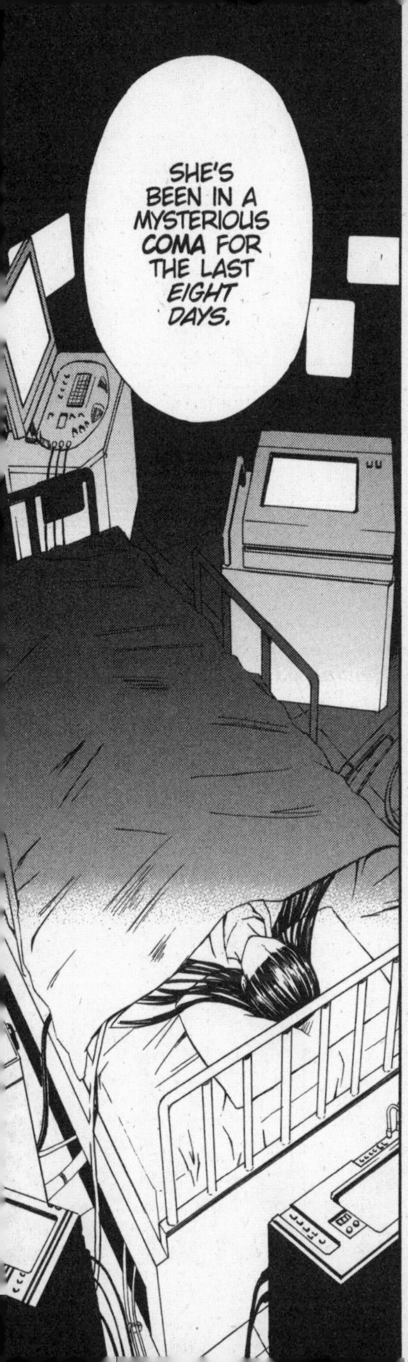
SHE'S BEEN IN A MYSTERIOUS COMA FOR THE LAST EIGHT DAYS.

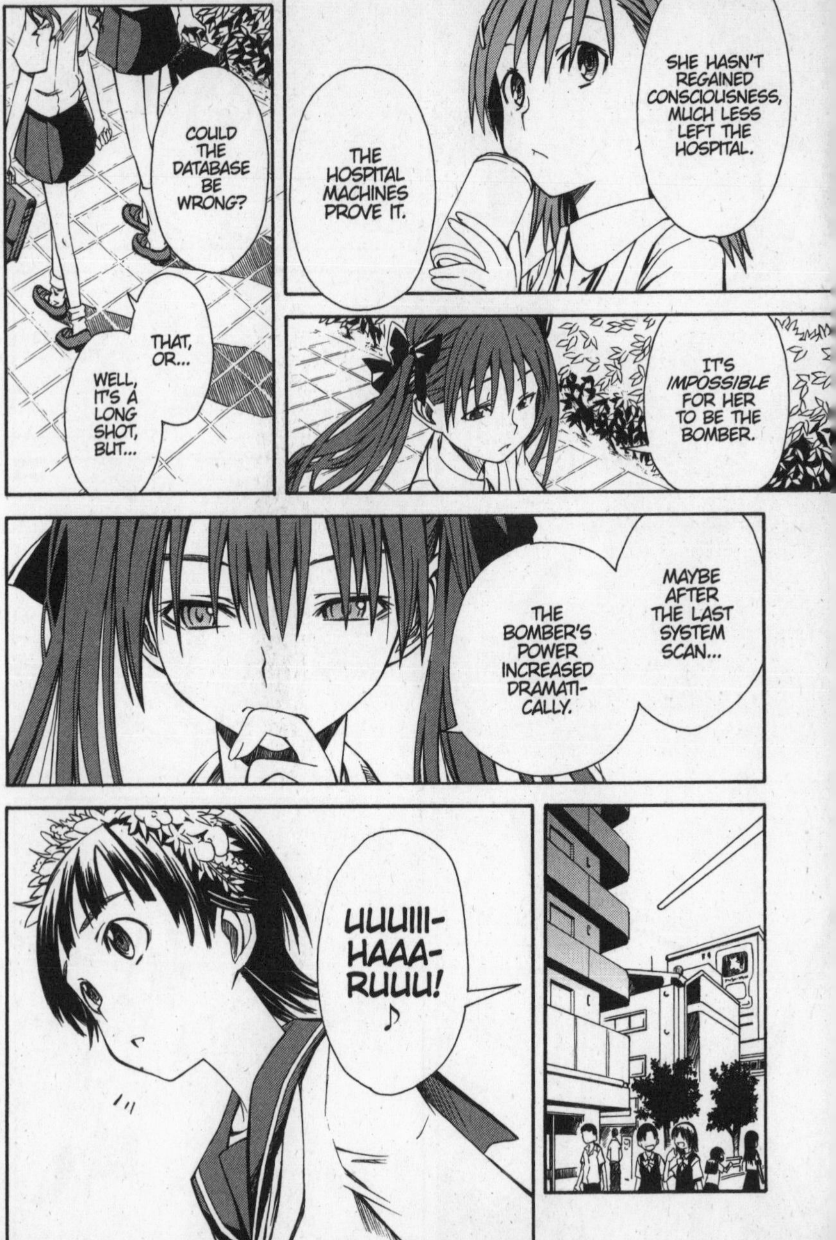
SHE HASN'T REGAINED CONSCIOUSNESS, MUCH LESS LEFT THE HOSPITAL.
THE HOSPITAL MACHINES PROVE IT.
IT'S *IMPOSSIBLE* FOR HER TO BE THE BOMBER.
COULD THE DATABASE BE WRONG?
THAT, OR...
WELL, IT'S A LONG SHOT, BUT...
MAYBE AFTER THE LAST SYSTEM SCAN...
THE BOMBER'S POWER INCREASED DRAMATI-CALLY.
UUUIII-HAAA-RUUU! ♪

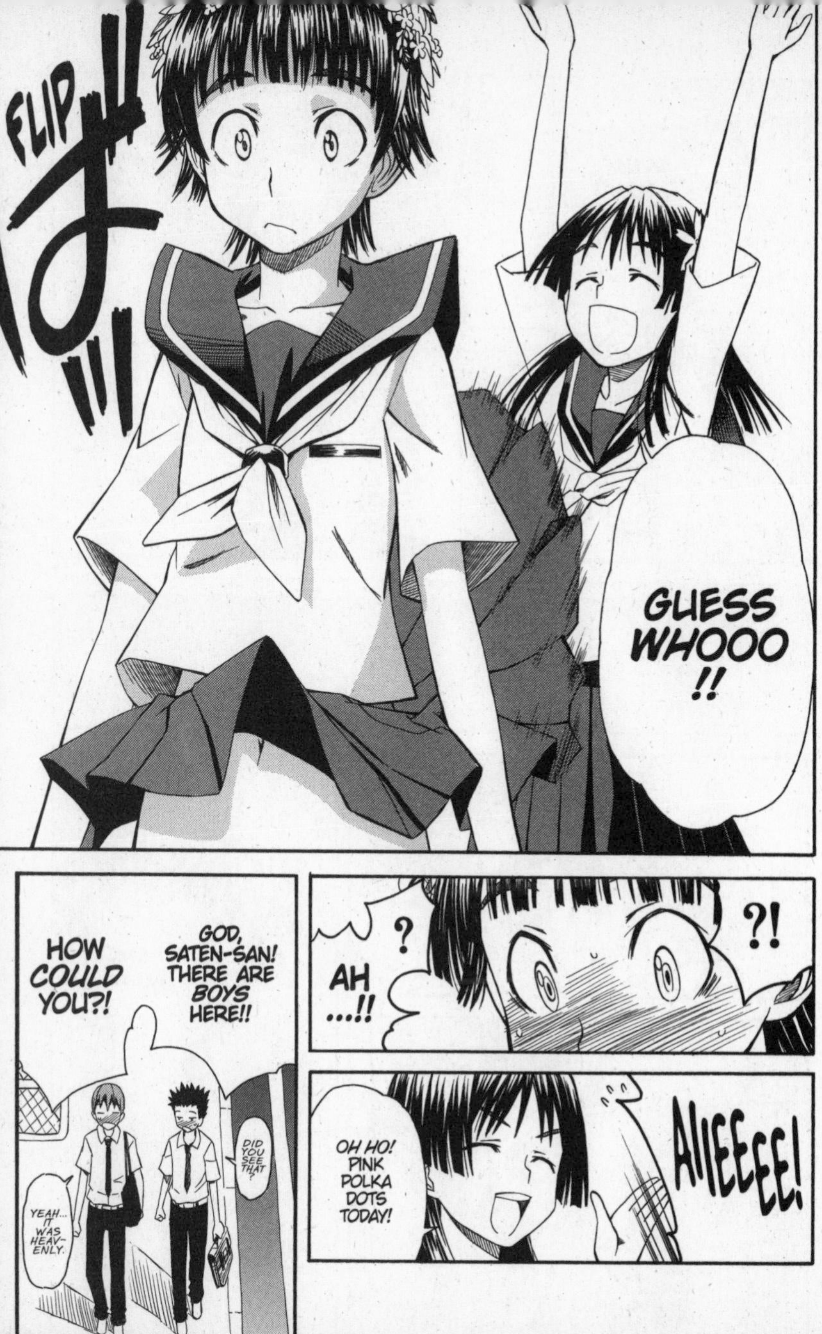
FLIP
GUESS WHOOO!!
?!
?
AH ...!!
AIIEEEEE!
OH HO! PINK POLKA DOTS TODAY!
GOD, SATEN-SAN! THERE ARE BOYS HERE!!
HOW COULD YOU?!
DID YOU SEE THAT?
YEAH... IT WAS HEAVENLY.

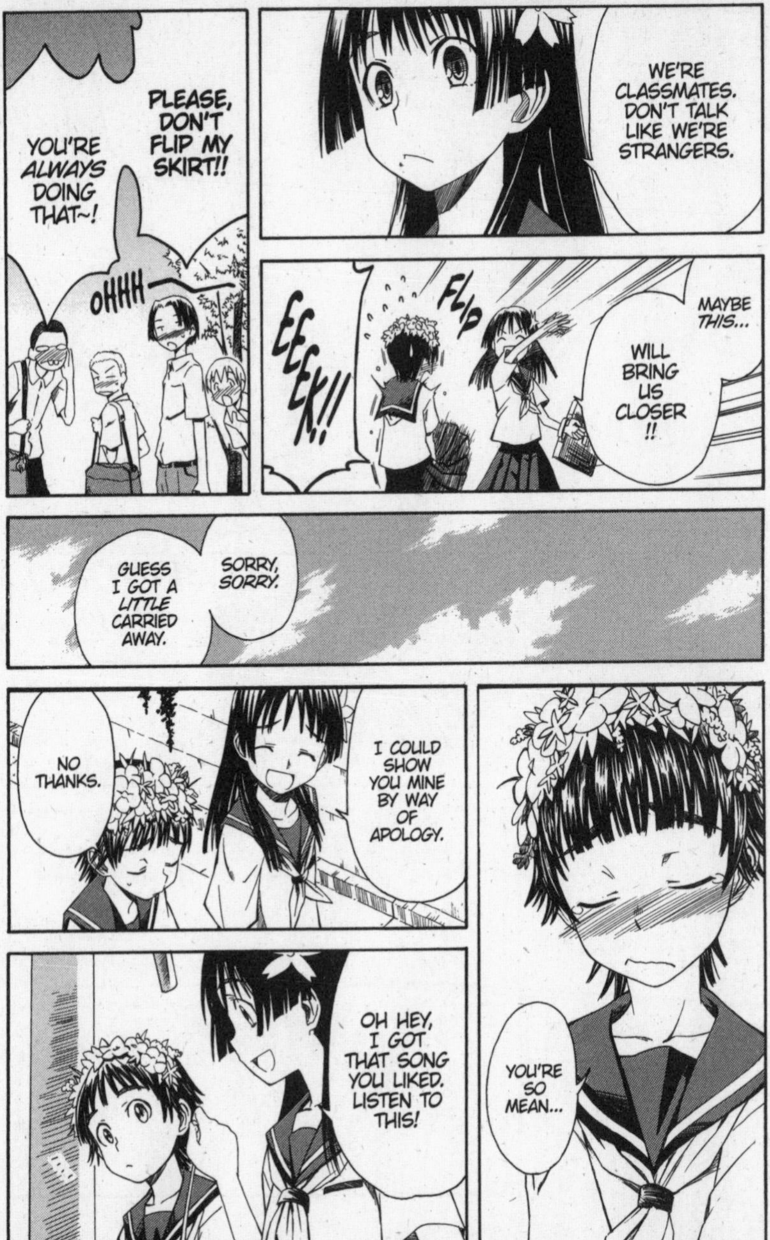
WE'RE CLASSMATES. DON'T TALK LIKE WE'RE STRANGERS.
MAYBE THIS...
WILL BRING US CLOSER !!
FLIP
EEEK!!
PLEASE, DON'T FLIP MY SKIRT!!
YOU'RE ALWAYS DOING THAT~!
OHHH—
SORRY, SORRY.
GUESS I GOT A LITTLE CARRIED AWAY.
YOU'RE SO MEAN...
I COULD SHOW YOU MINE BY WAY OF APOLOGY.
NO THANKS.
OH HEY, I GOT THAT SONG YOU LIKED. LISTEN TO THIS!

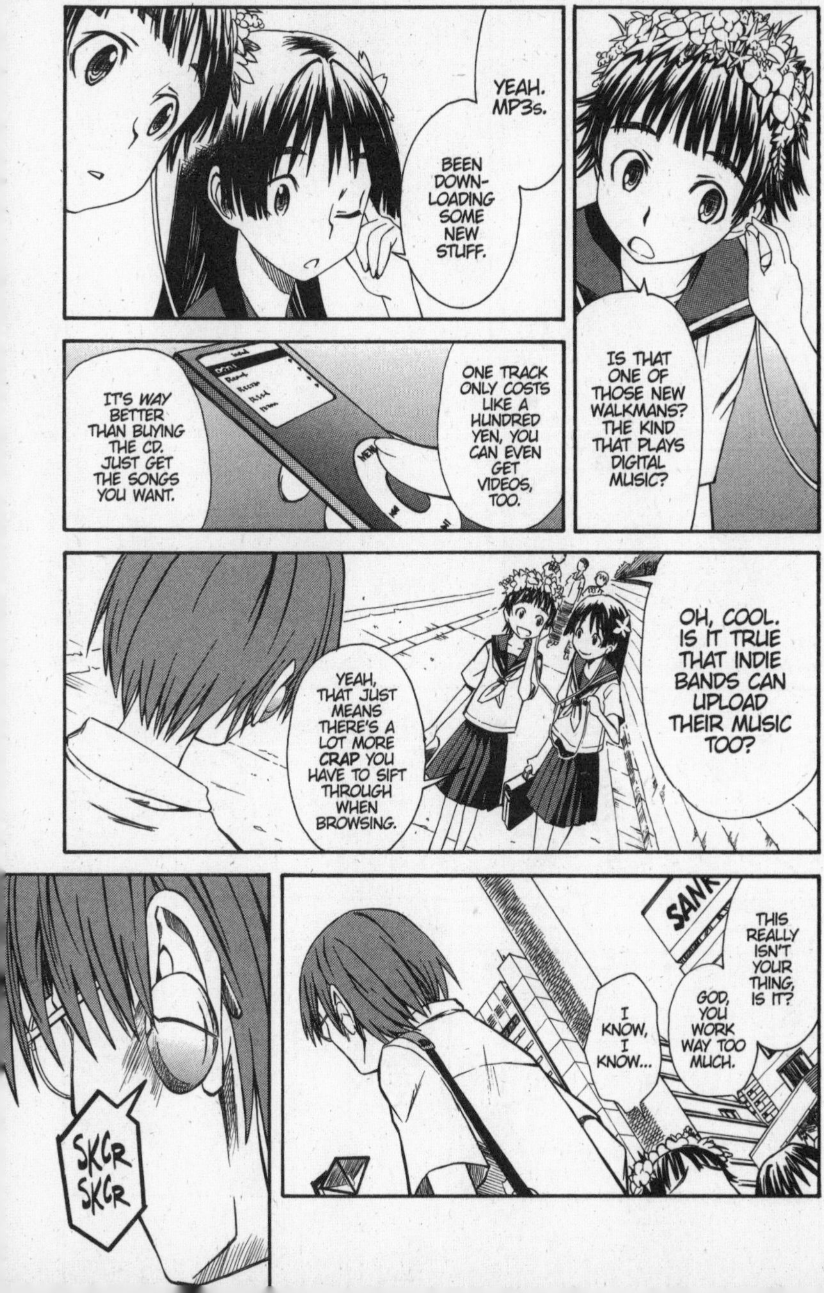

IS THAT ONE OF THOSE NEW WALKMANS? THE KIND THAT PLAYS DIGITAL MUSIC?
YEAH. MP3s.
BEEN DOWNLOADING SOME NEW STUFF.
ONE TRACK ONLY COSTS LIKE A HUNDRED YEN, YOU CAN EVEN GET VIDEOS, TOO.
IT'S *WAY* BETTER THAN BUYING THE CD. JUST GET THE SONGS YOU WANT.
OH, COOL. IS IT TRUE THAT INDIE BANDS CAN UPLOAD THEIR MUSIC TOO?
YEAH, THAT JUST MEANS THERE'S A LOT MORE CRAP YOU HAVE TO SIFT THROUGH WHEN BROWSING.
SANK
THIS REALLY ISN'T YOUR THING, IS IT?
GOD, YOU WORK WAY TOO MUCH.
I KNOW, I KNOW...
SKCR SKCR

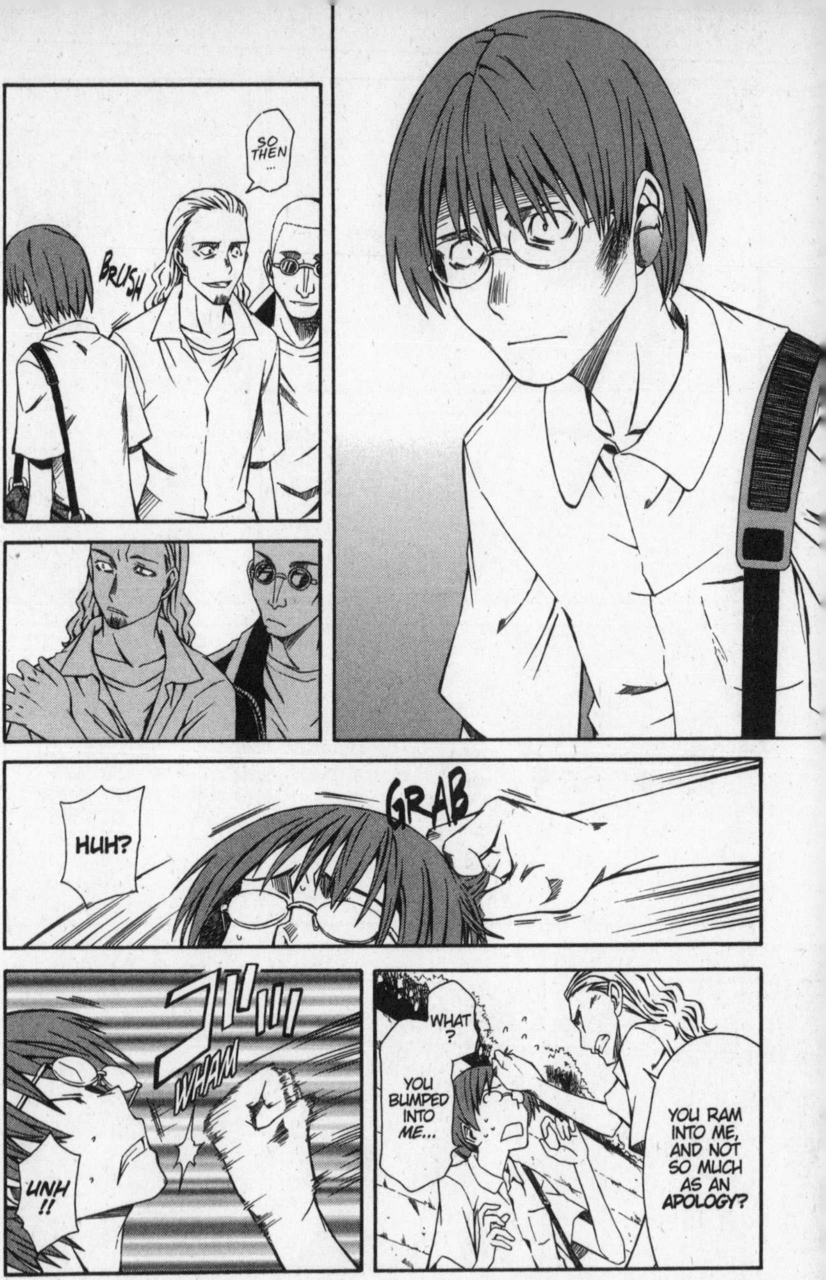
SO THEN ...
BRUSH
HUH?
GRAB
WHAT?
YOU RAM INTO ME, AND NOT SO MUCH AS AN APOLOGY?
YOU BUMPED INTO ME...
WHAM
UNH!!

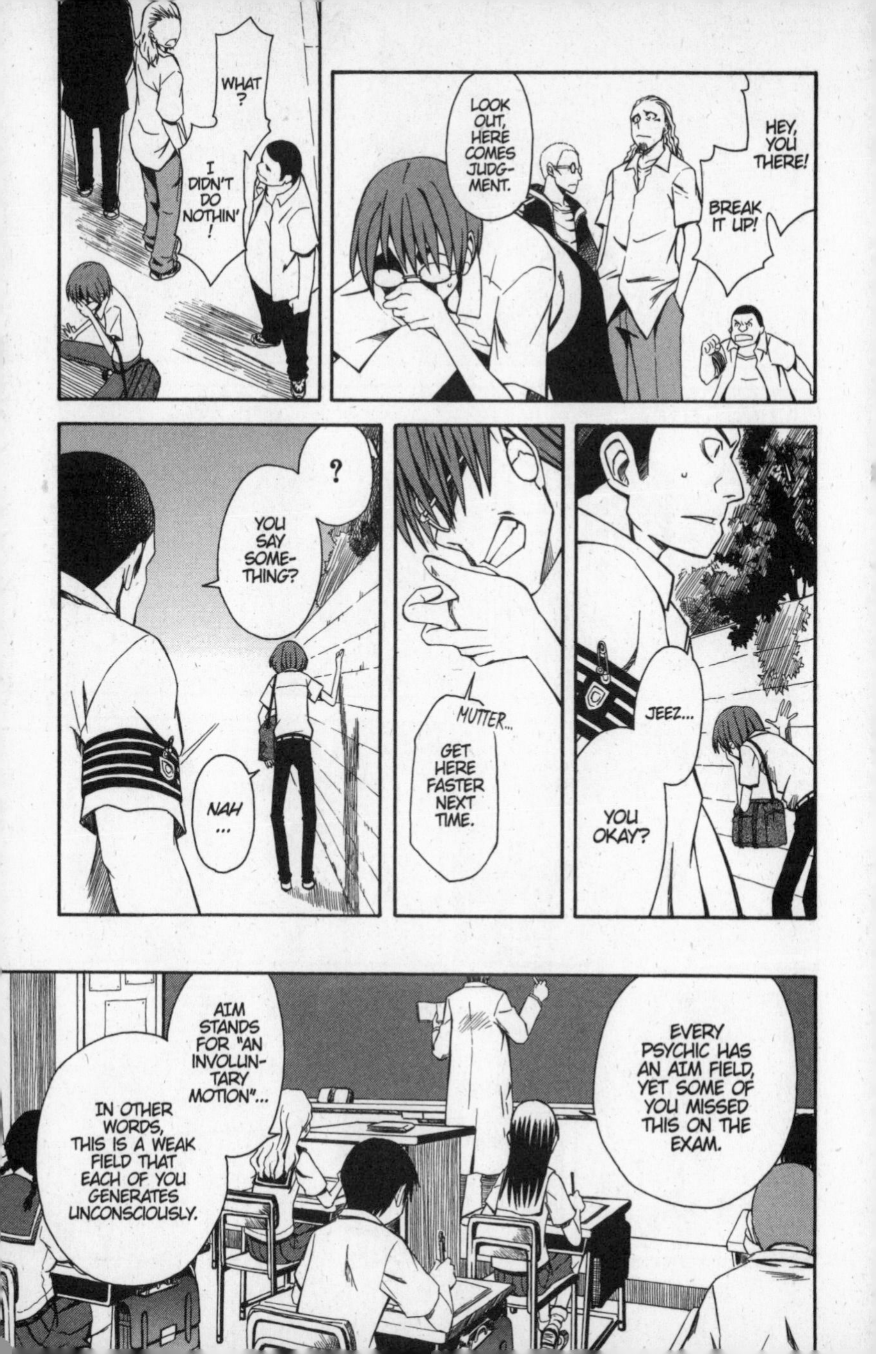
HEY, YOU THERE!
BREAK IT UP!
LOOK OUT, HERE COMES JUDGMENT.
WHAT?
I DIDN'T DO NOTHIN'!
JEEZ...
YOU OKAY?
MUTTER...
GET HERE FASTER NEXT TIME.
?
YOU SAY SOMETHING?
NAH...
EVERY PSYCHIC HAS AN AIM FIELD, YET SOME OF YOU MISSED THIS ON THE EXAM.
AIM STANDS FOR "AN INVOLUNTARY MOTION"...
IN OTHER WORDS, THIS IS A WEAK FIELD THAT EACH OF YOU GENERATES UNCONSCIOUSLY.

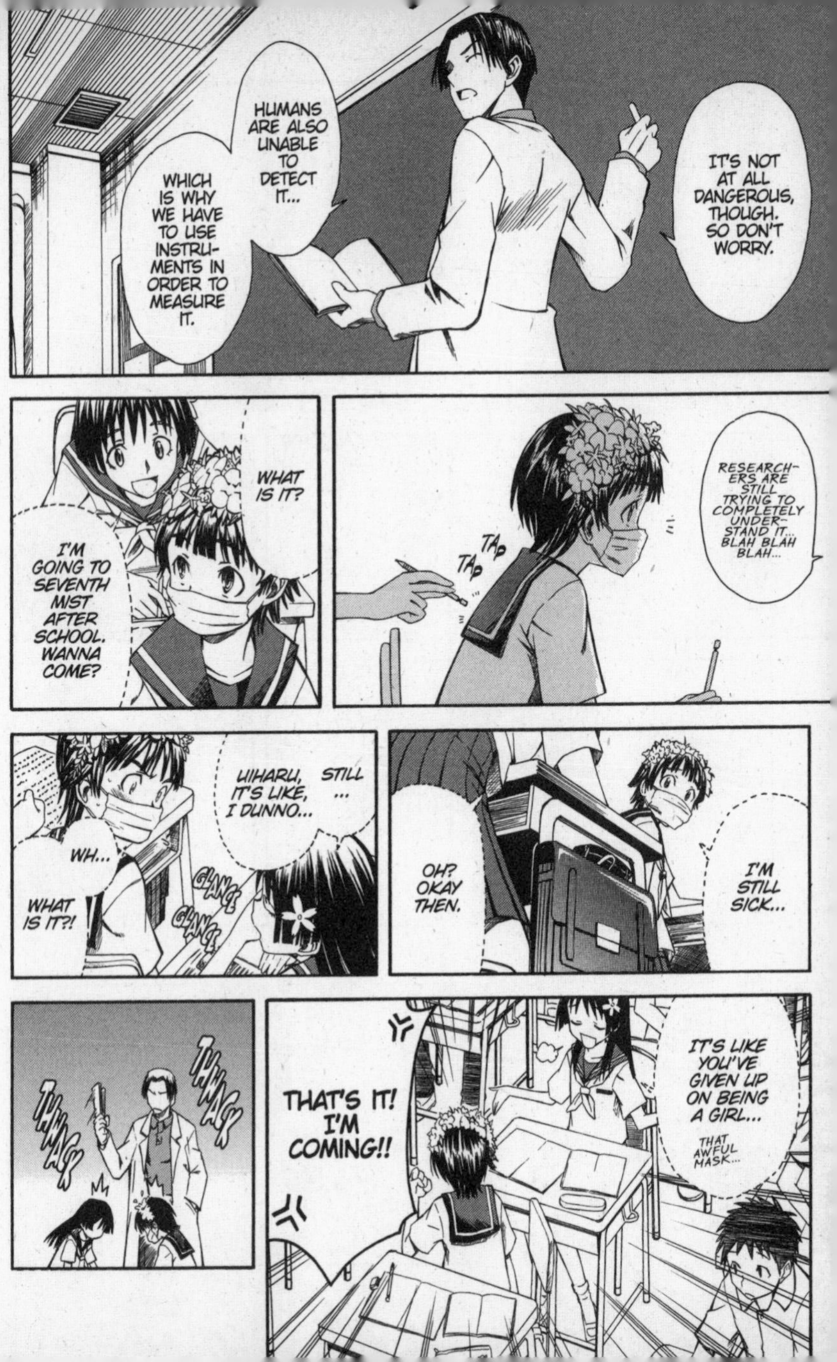
IT'S NOT AT ALL DANGEROUS, THOUGH. SO DON'T WORRY.
HUMANS ARE ALSO UNABLE TO DETECT IT...
WHICH IS WHY WE HAVE TO USE INSTRUMENTS IN ORDER TO MEASURE IT.
RESEARCHERS ARE STILL TRYING TO COMPLETELY UNDERSTAND IT... BLAH BLAH BLAH...
TAP TAP
WHAT IS IT?
I'M GOING TO SEVENTH MIST AFTER SCHOOL. WANNA COME?
I'M STILL SICK...
OH? OKAY THEN.
STILL ...
UIHARU, IT'S LIKE, I DUNNO...
GLANCE GLANCE
WH... WHAT IS IT?!
IT'S LIKE YOU'VE GIVEN UP ON BEING A GIRL...
THAT AWFUL MASK...
THAT'S IT! I'M COMING!!
THWACK THWACK THWACK

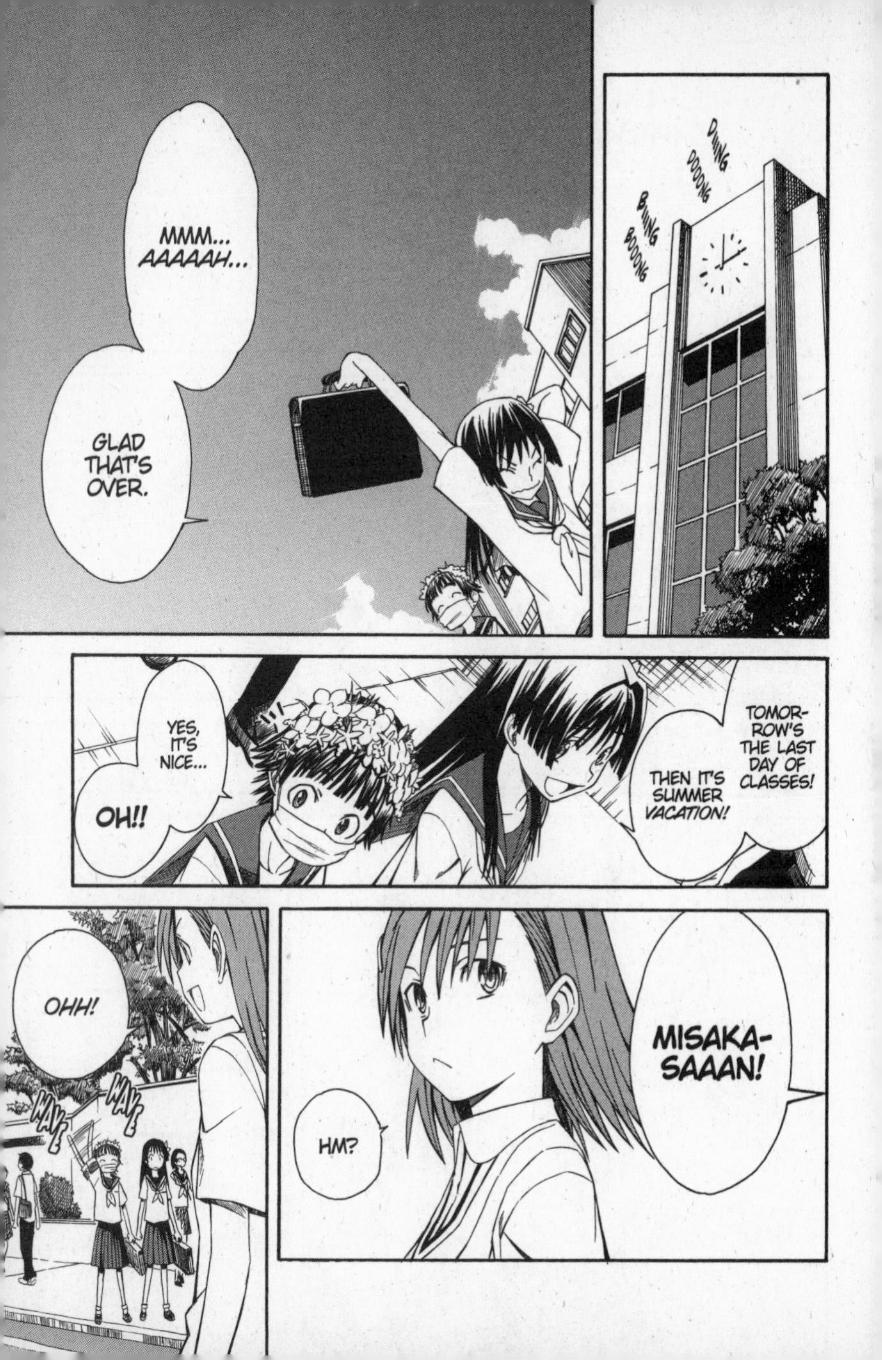
DIIING DOOONG
BIIING BOOONG
MMM... AAAAAH...
GLAD THAT'S OVER.
TOMORROW'S THE LAST DAY OF CLASSES!
THEN IT'S SUMMER VACATION!
YES, IT'S NICE...
OH!!
MISAKA-SAAAN!
HM?
OHH!
WAVE
WAVE

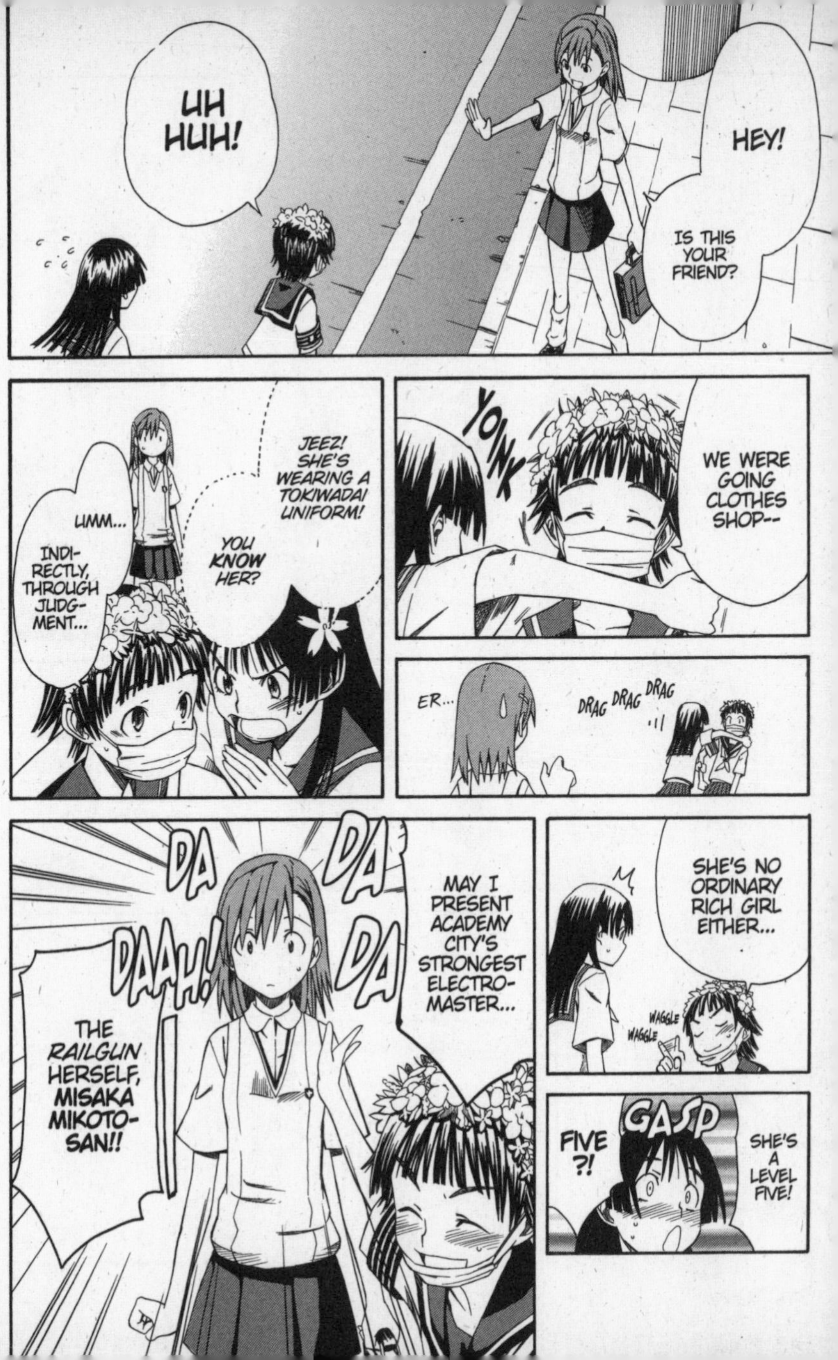
HEY!
IS THIS YOUR FRIEND?
UH HUH!
YOINK
WE WERE GOING CLOTHES SHOP--
DRAG DRAG DRAG
ER...
JEEZ! SHE'S WEARING A TOKIWADAI UNIFORM!
YOU KNOW HER?
UMM... INDIRECTLY, THROUGH JUDGMENT...
SHE'S NO ORDINARY RICH GIRL EITHER...
WAGGLE WAGGLE
SHE'S A LEVEL FIVE!
GASP
FIVE?!
DA DA DA
MAY I PRESENT ACADEMY CITY'S STRONGEST ELECTROMASTER...
DAAH!
THE RAILGUN HERSELF, MISAKA MIKOTO-SAN!!

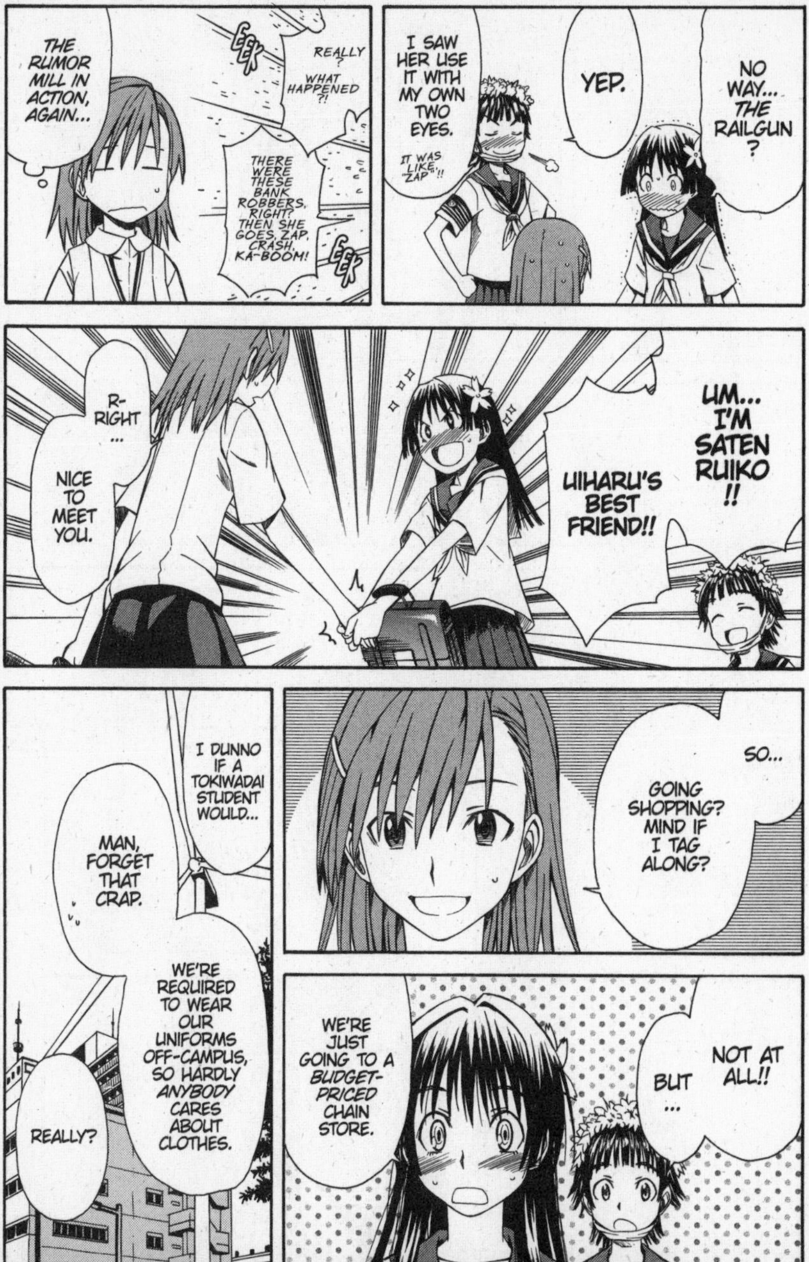
NO WAY... THE RAILGUN?
YEP.
I SAW HER USE IT WITH MY OWN TWO EYES.
IT WAS LIKE, "ZAP"!!
REALLY? WHAT HAPPENED?!
EEK
THERE WERE THESE BANK ROBBERS, RIGHT? THEN SHE GOES, ZAP, CRASH, KA-BOOM!
EEK
THE RUMOR MILL IN ACTION, AGAIN...
UM... I'M SATEN RUIKO!!
UIHARU'S BEST FRIEND!!
R-RIGHT...
NICE TO MEET YOU.
SO...
GOING SHOPPING? MIND IF I TAG ALONG?
NOT AT ALL!!
BUT...
WE'RE JUST GOING TO A BUDGET-PRICED CHAIN STORE.
I DUNNO IF A TOKIWADAI STUDENT WOULD...
MAN, FORGET THAT CRAP.
WE'RE REQUIRED TO WEAR OUR UNIFORMS OFF-CAMPUS, SO HARDLY ANYBODY CARES ABOUT CLOTHES.
REALLY?

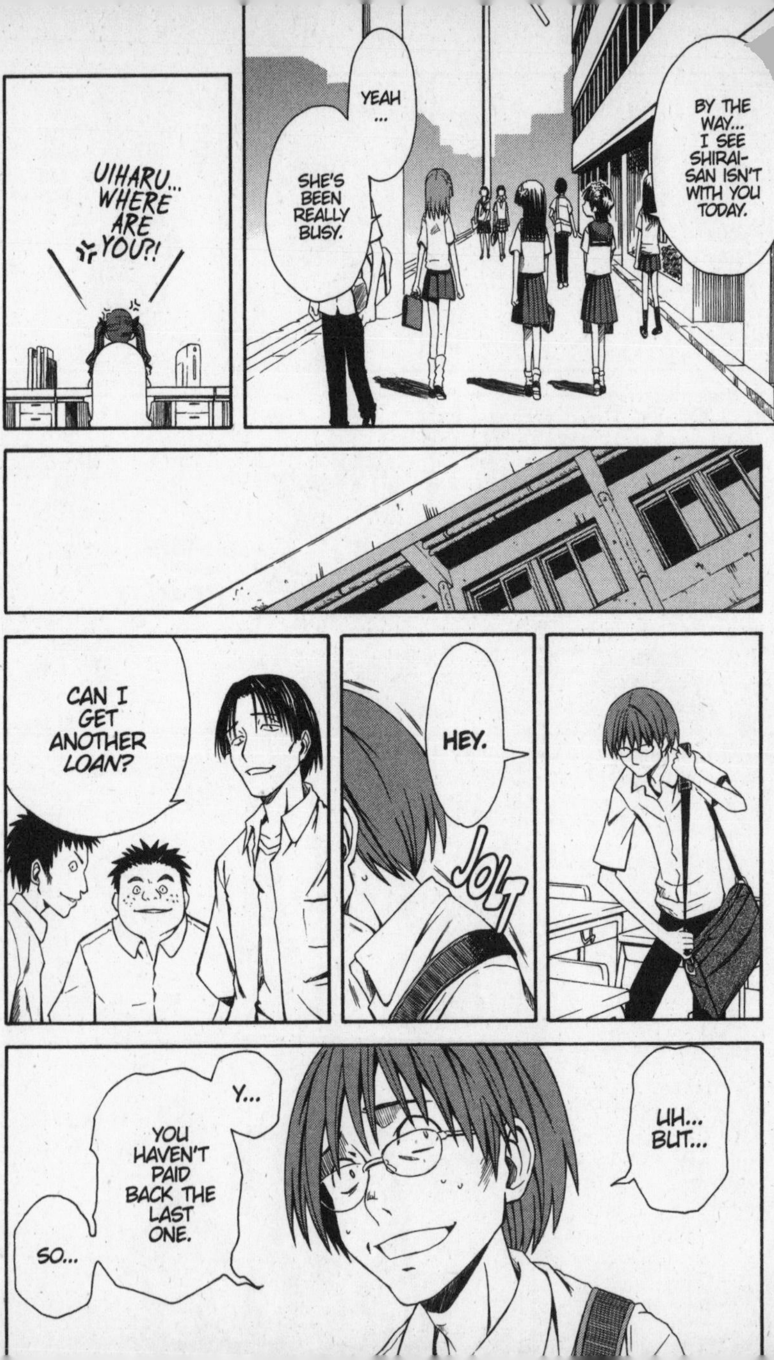
BY THE WAY... I SEE SHIRAI-SAN ISN'T WITH YOU TODAY.
YEAH ...
SHE'S BEEN REALLY BUSY.
UIHARU... WHERE ARE YOU?!
HEY.
JOLT
CAN I GET ANOTHER LOAN?
UH... BUT...
Y...
YOU HAVEN'T PAID BACK THE LAST ONE.
SO...

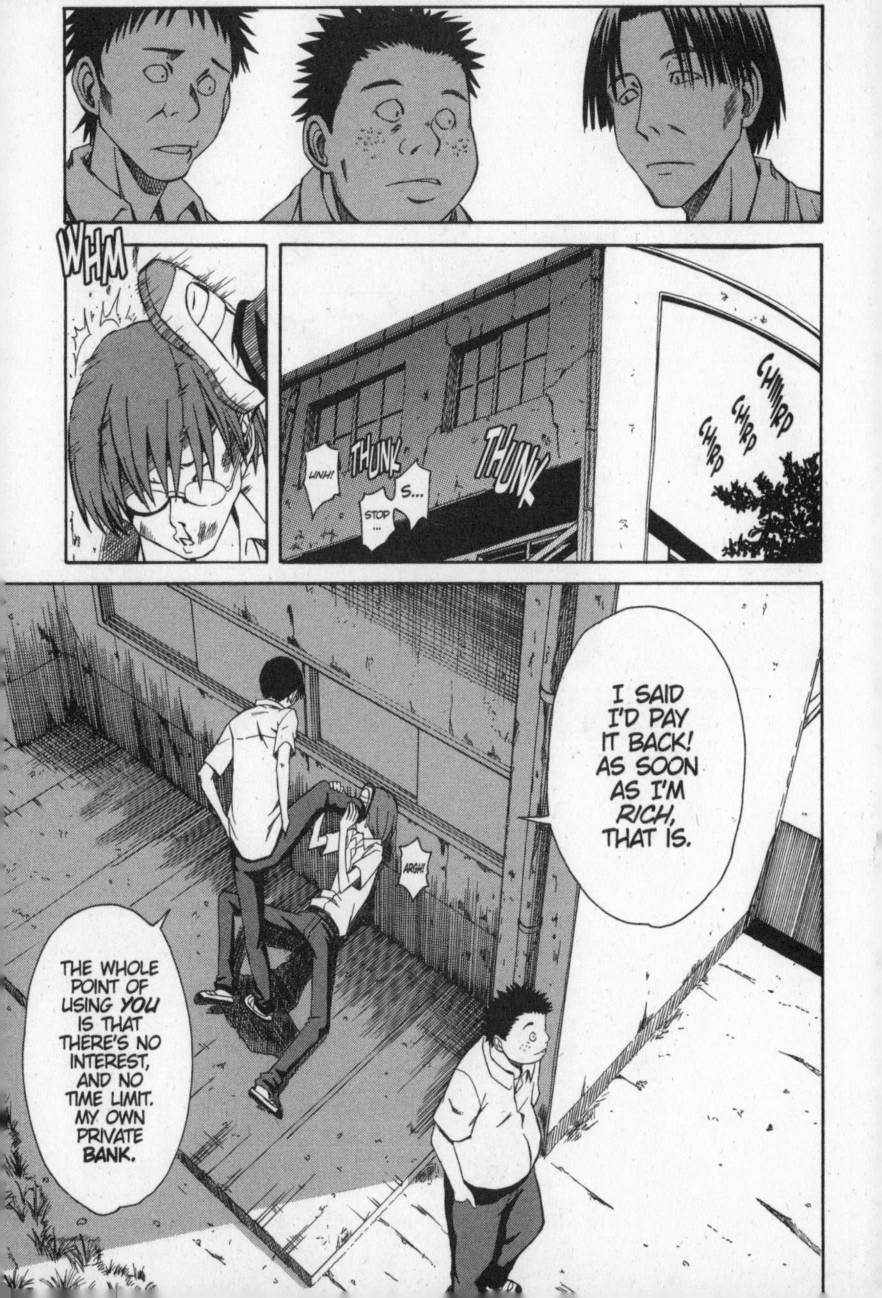
CHIRRP
CHIRP
CHIRP
THUNK
S...
THUNK
UNH!
STOP ...
WHM
I SAID I'D PAY IT BACK! AS SOON AS I'M *RICH*, THAT IS.
ARGH!
THE WHOLE POINT OF USING ***YOU*** IS THAT THERE'S NO INTEREST, AND NO TIME LIMIT. MY OWN PRIVATE BANK.

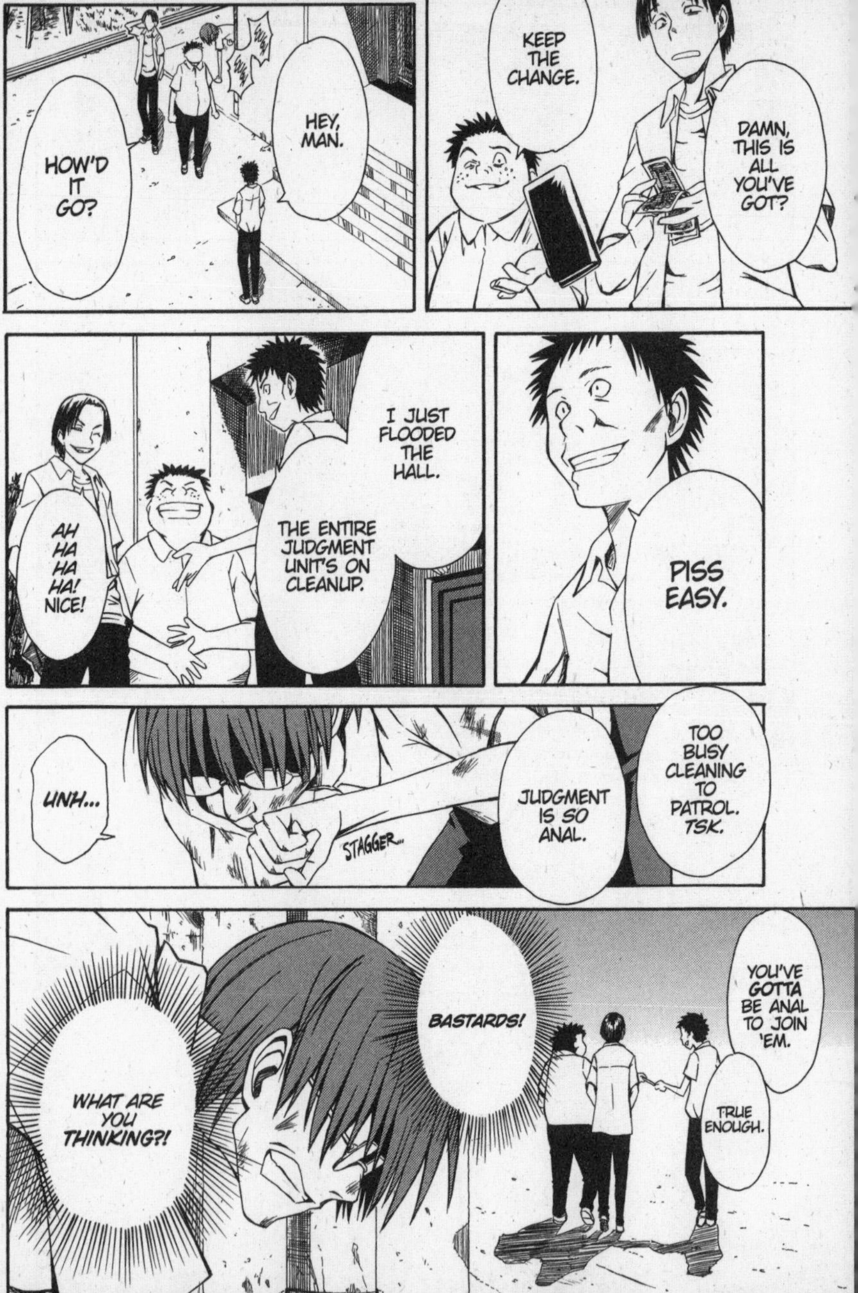
DAMN, THIS IS ALL YOU'VE GOT?
KEEP THE CHANGE.
HEY, MAN.
HOW'D IT GO?
PISS EASY.
I JUST FLOODED THE HALL.
THE ENTIRE JUDGMENT UNIT'S ON CLEANUP.
AH HA HA HA! NICE!
TOO BUSY CLEANING TO PATROL. TSK.
JUDGMENT IS SO ANAL.
STAGGER...
UNH...
YOU'VE GOTTA BE ANAL TO JOIN 'EM.
TRUE ENOUGH.
BASTARDS!
WHAT ARE YOU THINKING?!

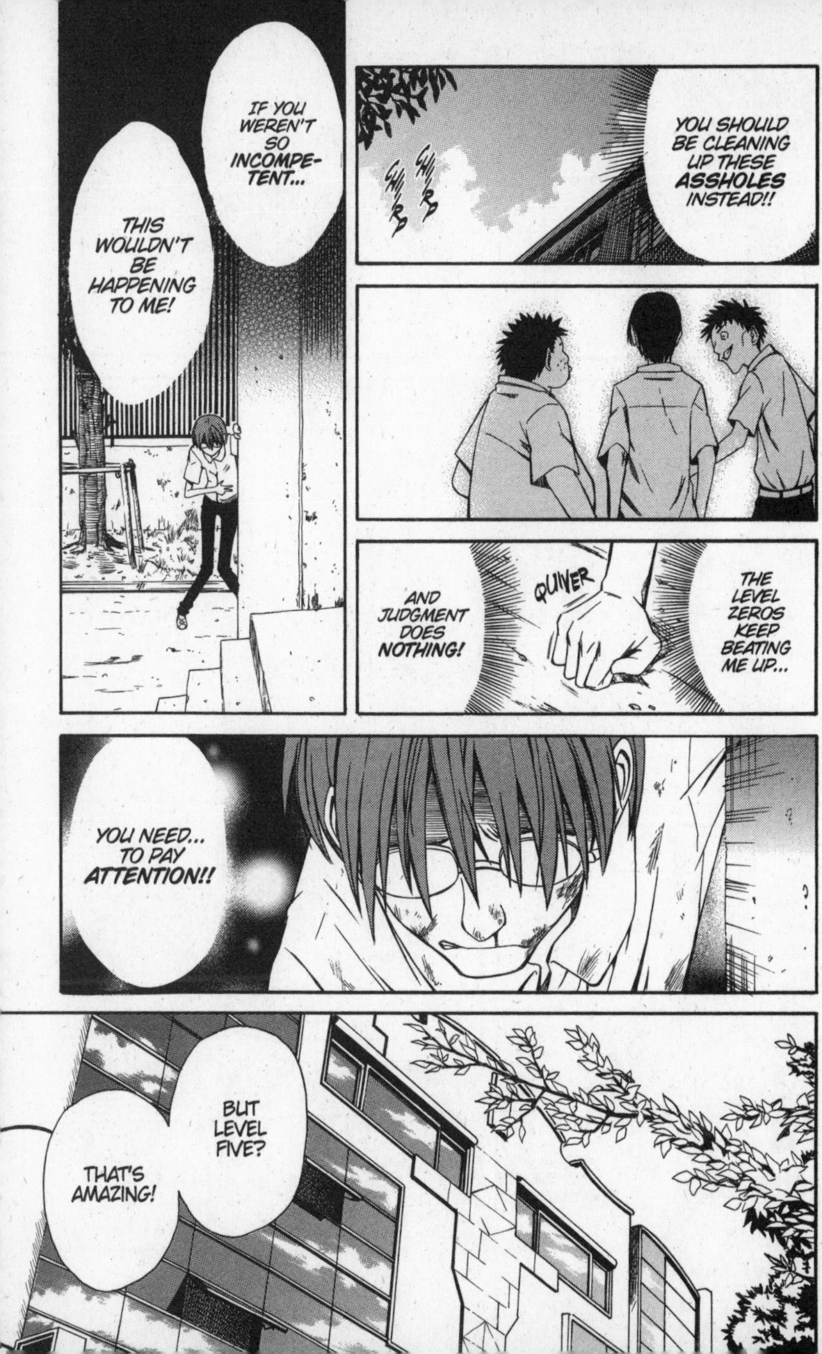
YOU SHOULD BE CLEANING UP THESE ASSHOLES INSTEAD!!
CHIRP
CHIRP
THE LEVEL ZEROS KEEP BEATING ME UP...
QUIVER
AND JUDGMENT DOES NOTHING!
IF YOU WEREN'T SO INCOMPETENT...
THIS WOULDN'T BE HAPPENING TO ME!
YOU NEED... TO PAY ATTENTION!!
BUT LEVEL FIVE?
THAT'S AMAZING!

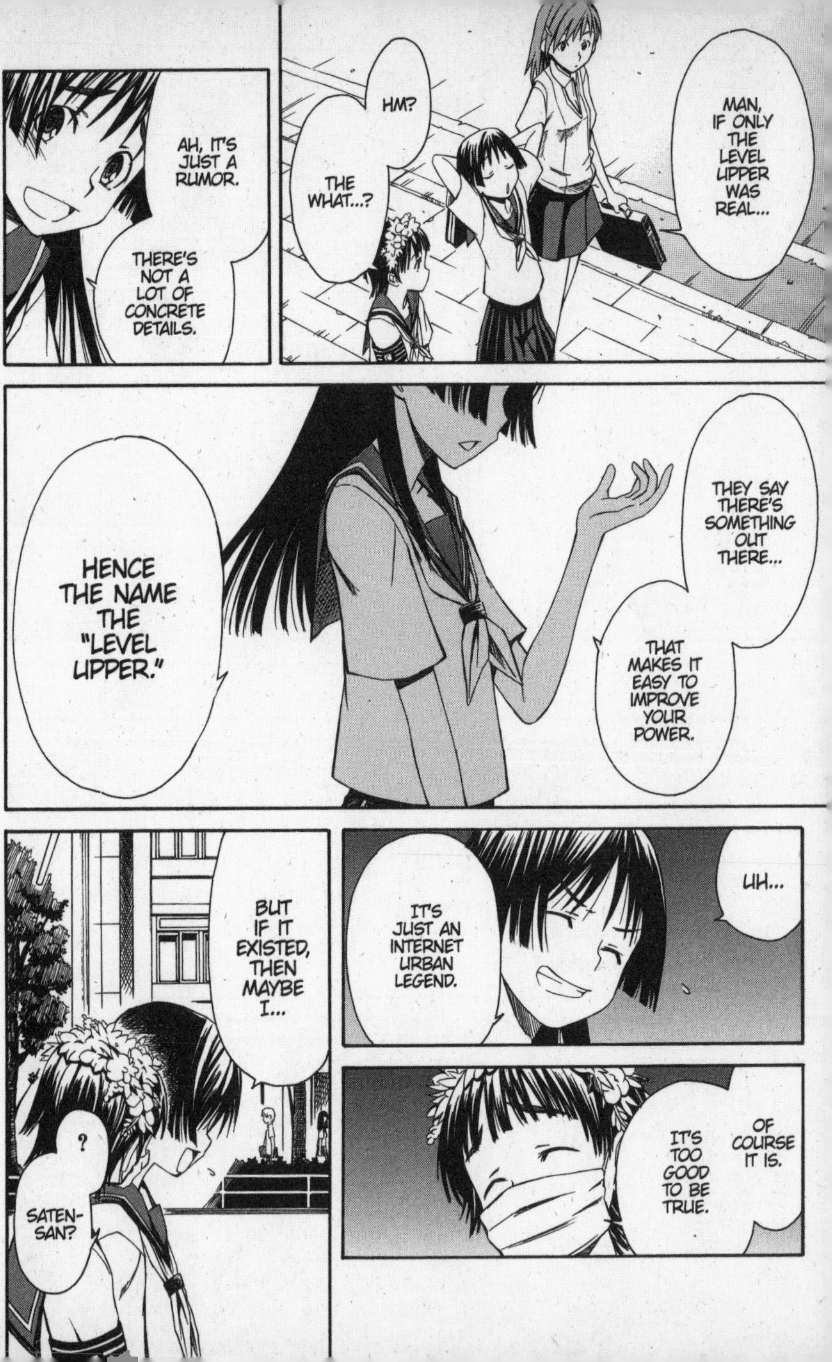
MAN, IF ONLY THE LEVEL UPPER WAS REAL...
HM?
THE WHAT...?
AH, IT'S JUST A RUMOR.
THERE'S NOT A LOT OF CONCRETE DETAILS.
THEY SAY THERE'S SOMETHING OUT THERE...
THAT MAKES IT EASY TO IMPROVE YOUR POWER.
HENCE THE NAME THE "LEVEL UPPER."
UH...
IT'S JUST AN INTERNET URBAN LEGEND.
OF COURSE IT IS.
IT'S TOO GOOD TO BE TRUE.
BUT IF IT EXISTED, THEN MAYBE I...
?
SATEN-SAN?

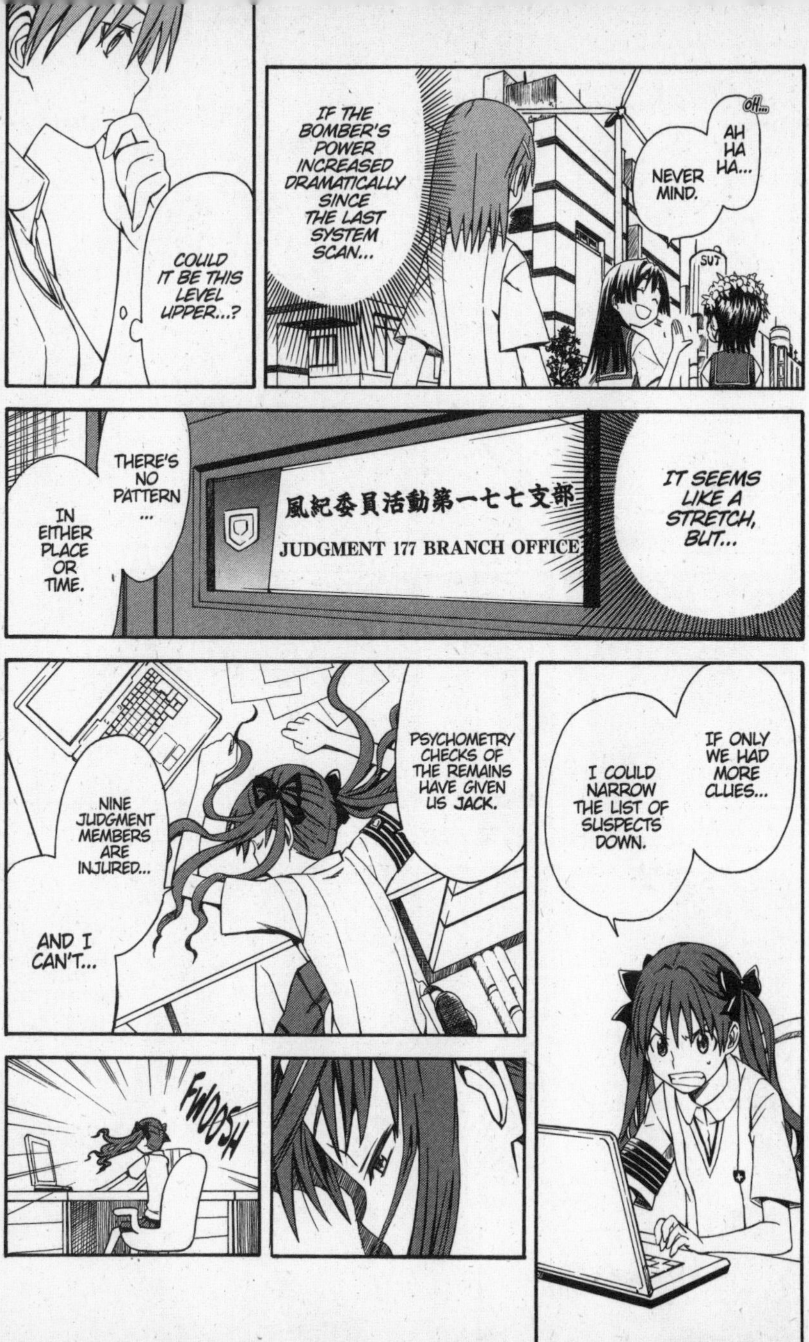
OH...
AH HA HA...
NEVER MIND.
IF THE BOMBER'S POWER INCREASED DRAMATICALLY SINCE THE LAST SYSTEM SCAN...
COULD IT BE THIS LEVEL UPPER...?
IT SEEMS LIKE A STRETCH, BUT...
風紀委員活動第一七七支部
JUDGMENT 177 BRANCH OFFICE
THERE'S NO PATTERN ...
IN EITHER PLACE OR TIME.
IF ONLY WE HAD MORE CLUES...
I COULD NARROW THE LIST OF SUSPECTS DOWN.
PSYCHOMETRY CHECKS OF THE REMAINS HAVE GIVEN US JACK.
NINE JUDGMENT MEMBERS ARE INJURED...
AND I CAN'T...
FWOOSH

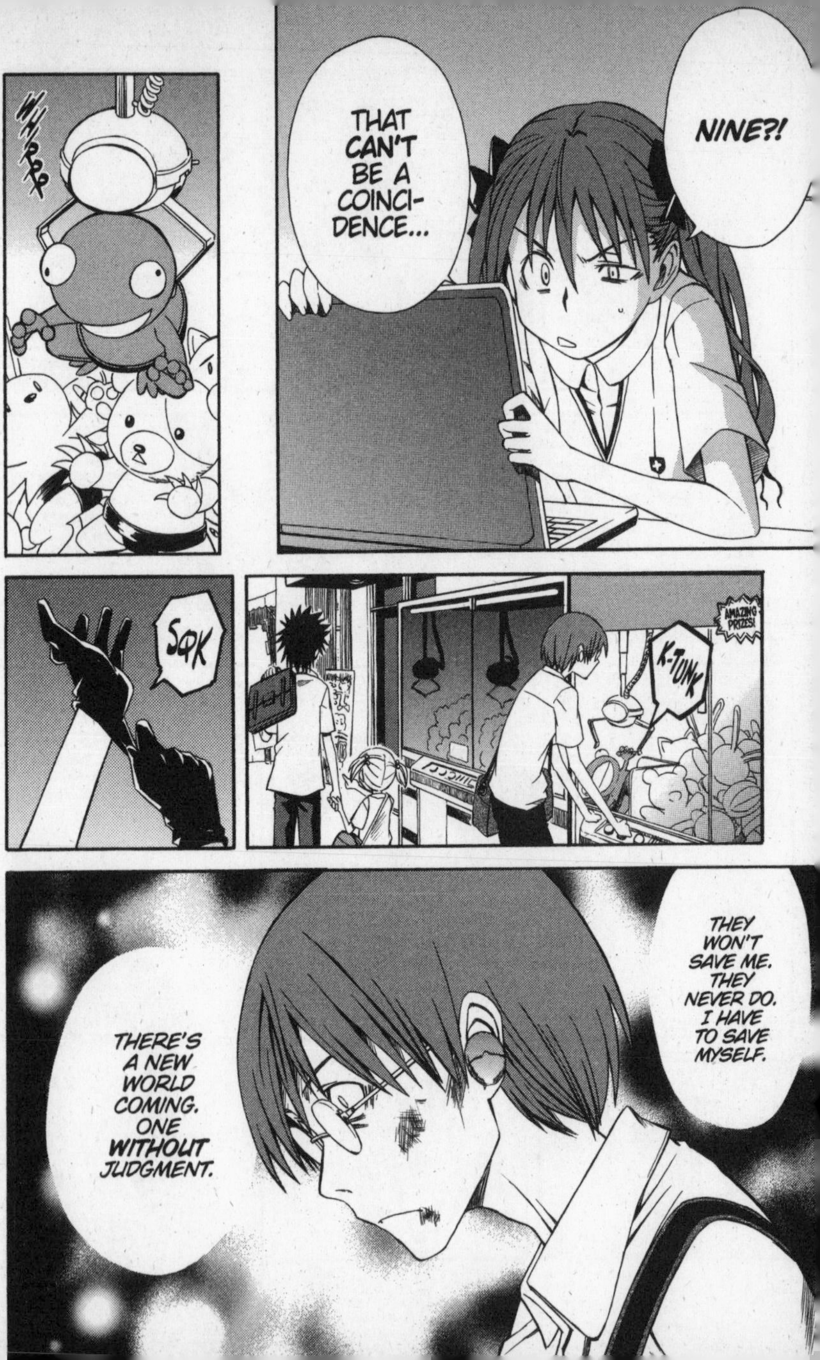
NINE?!
THAT CAN'T BE A COINCIDENCE...
WHIRRR
AMAZING PRIZES!
K-TUNK
SQK
THEY WON'T SAVE ME. THEY NEVER DO. I HAVE TO SAVE MYSELF.
THERE'S A NEW WORLD COMING. ONE WITHOUT JUDGMENT.

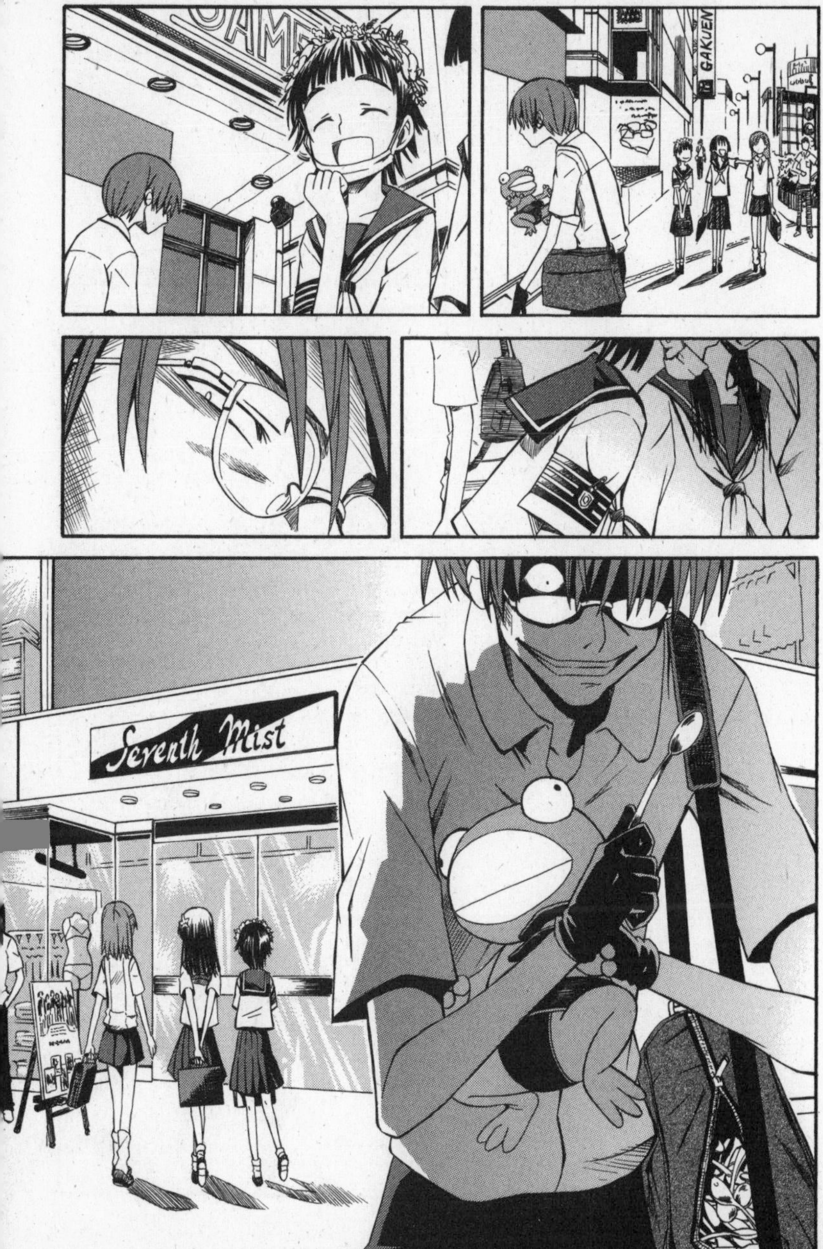
GAKUEN
Seventh Mist

THE WILL OF THE UNIVERSE

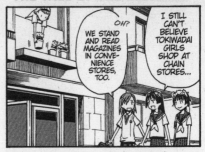

I STILL CAN'T BELIEVE TOKIWADAI GIRLS SHOP AT CHAIN STORES...
OH?
WE STAND AND READ MAGAZINES IN CONVENIENCE STORES, TOO.
REALLY?
YOU'RE RICH, THOUGH. WHY NOT JUST BUY THE MAGAZINE?
HMM...
THEY TAKE UP TOO MUCH SPACE.
AND THEY'RE HEAVY, AS WELL.
HEY!
HOP
TOPPLE
YOU KNOW WHAT? I HATE IT WHEN MAGAZINES ARE IN BAGS, AND YOU CAN'T JUST READ THEM.
UH...
BUT MAGAZINES THESE DAYS ARE SO WELL MADE!
Y-YEAH! WITH RARE ILLUSTRATIONS, AND TONS OF ARTICLES!

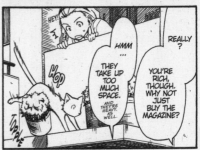

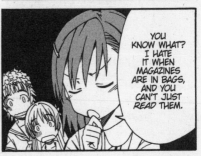

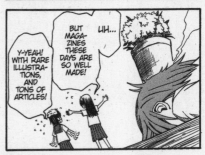

CHAPTER 5: JULY 18 (2)

KAMIJOU TOUMA
(LEVEL ZERO)

* THE MAIN CHARACTER OF *A CERTAIN MAGICAL INDEX*. HE'S A FIRST YEAR HIGH SCHOOL STUDENT IN ACADEMY CITY.
* HE IS OF AVERAGE HEIGHT AND WEIGHT. HE HAS SPIKY HAIR AND INCREDIBLE BAD LUCK; HE'S ALWAYS GETTING IN TROUBLE, OR GETTING MIXED UP IN SOME DISASTER OR OTHER.
* HIS RIGHT HAND CONTAINS A MYSTERIOUS POWER THAT HE CALLS THE "IMAGINE BREAKER," BUT ACADEMY CITY'S SYSTEM SCAN IS UNABLE TO DETECT IT, SO OFFICIALLY HE IS A LEVEL ZERO.
* HE'S UNABLE TO ABANDON PEOPLE WHEN THEY ARE IN TROUBLE, AND OFTEN JUMPS IN WITHOUT THINKING.
* HE HAS LIVED IN THE DORMS, FAR AWAY FROM HIS PARENTS, FOR QUITE SOME TIME, SO HE'S GETTING PRETTY GOOD AT COOKING.

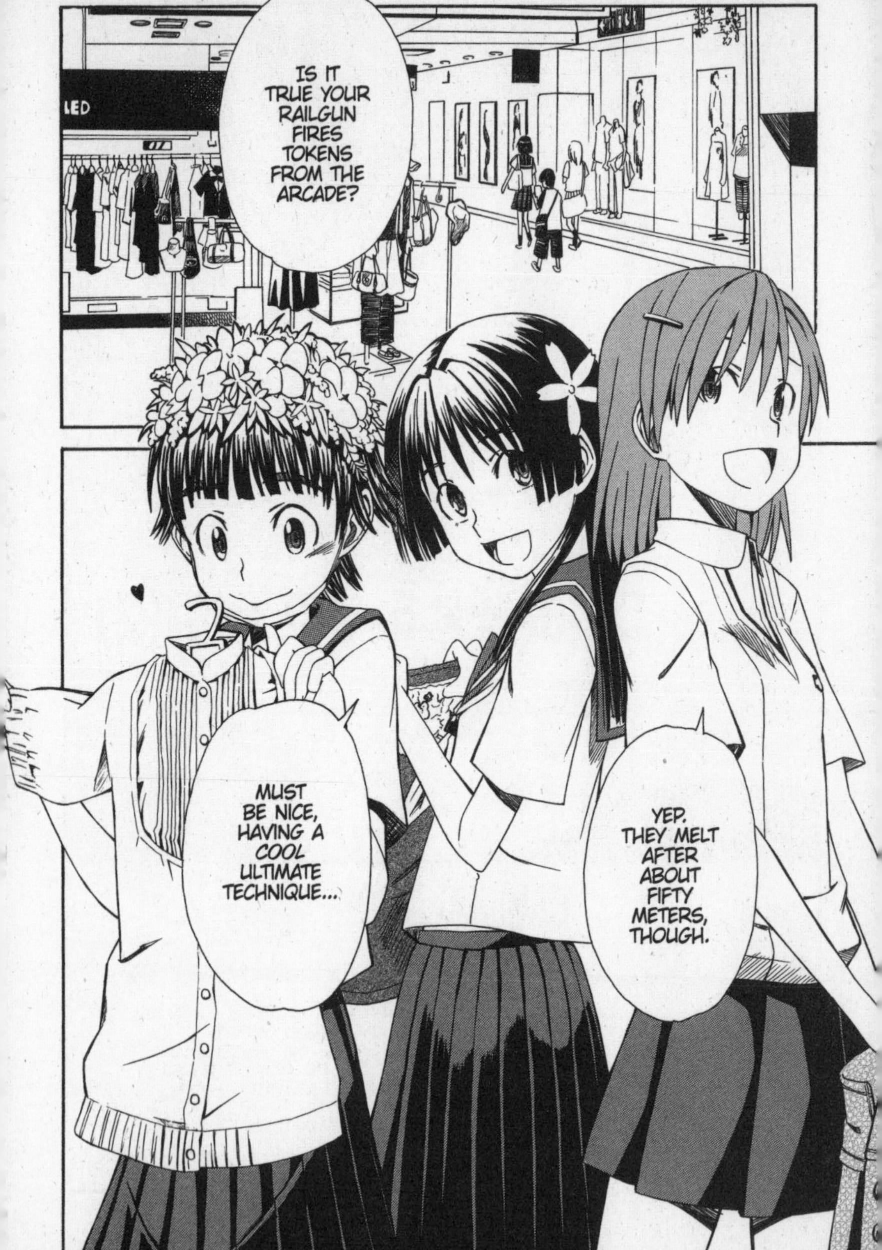
LED
IS IT TRUE YOUR RAILGUN FIRES TOKENS FROM THE ARCADE?
YEP. THEY MELT AFTER ABOUT FIFTY METERS, THOUGH.
MUST BE NICE, HAVING A COOL ULTIMATE TECHNIQUE...

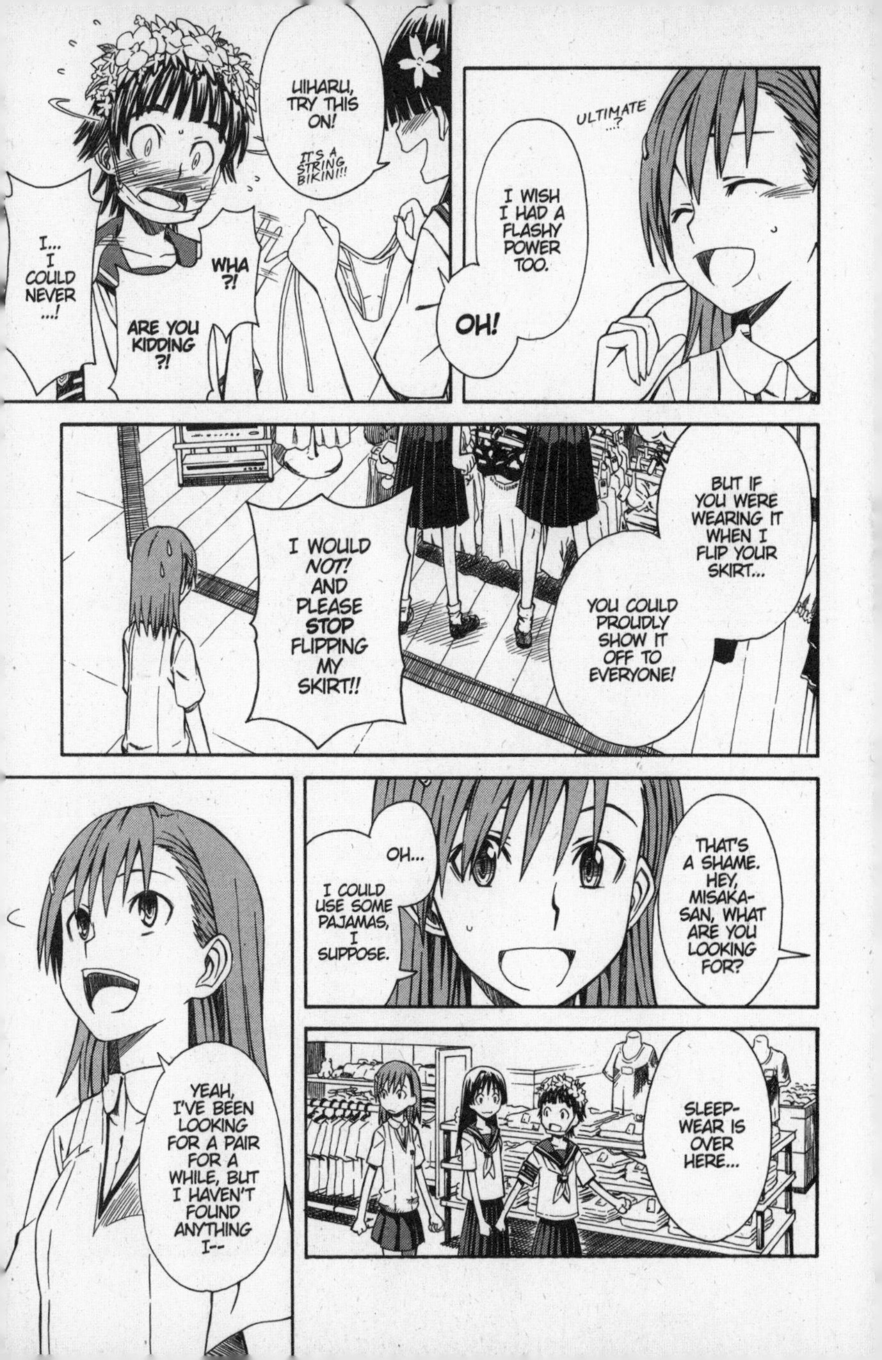
ULTIMATE ...?
I WISH I HAD A FLASHY POWER TOO.
OH!
UIHARU, TRY THIS ON!
IT'S A STRING BIKINI!!!
WHA ?!
ARE YOU KIDDING ?!
I... I COULD NEVER ...!
BUT IF YOU WERE WEARING IT WHEN I FLIP YOUR SKIRT...
YOU COULD PROUDLY SHOW IT OFF TO EVERYONE!
I WOULD *NOT!* AND PLEASE STOP FLIPPING MY SKIRT!!
THAT'S A SHAME. HEY, MISAKA-SAN, WHAT ARE YOU LOOKING FOR?
OH...
I COULD USE SOME PAJAMAS, I SUPPOSE.
SLEEP-WEAR IS OVER HERE...
YEAH, I'VE BEEN LOOKING FOR A PAIR FOR A WHILE, BUT I HAVEN'T FOUND ANYTHING I--

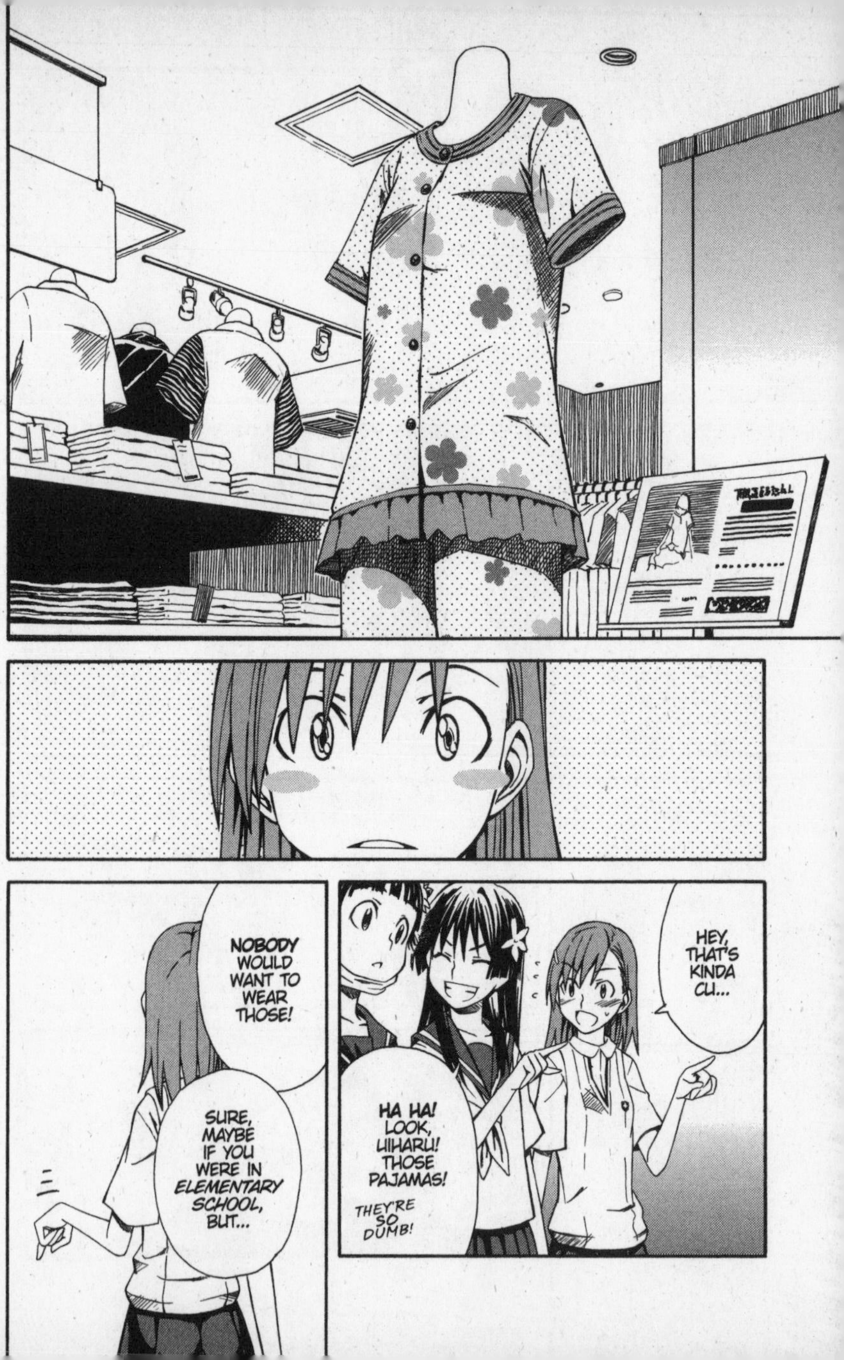
HEY, THAT'S KINDA CU...
HA HA! LOOK, UIHARU! THOSE PAJAMAS!
THEY'RE SO DUMB!
NOBODY WOULD WANT TO WEAR THOSE!
SURE, MAYBE IF YOU WERE IN ELEMENTARY SCHOOL, BUT...

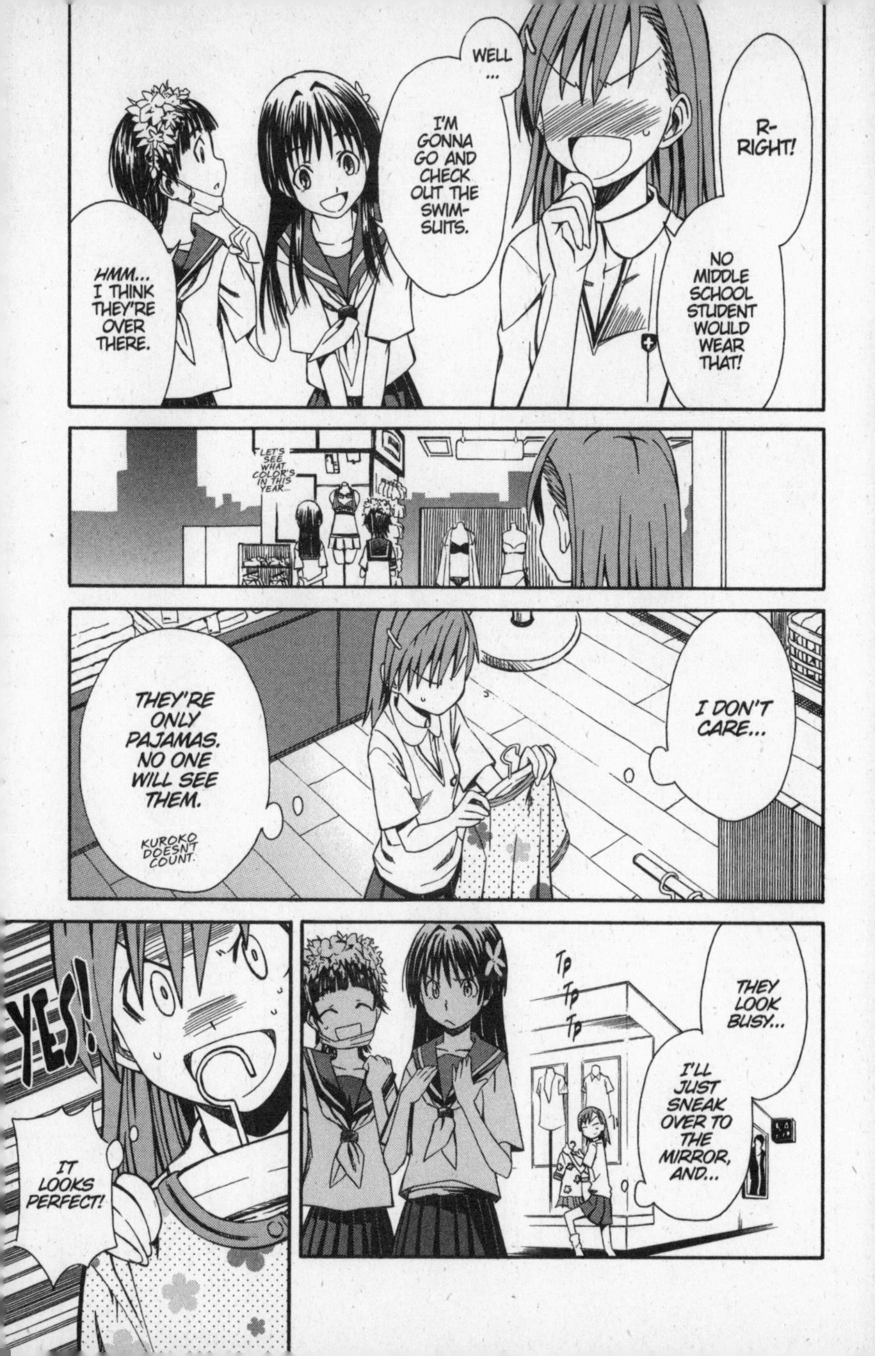
R-RIGHT!
NO MIDDLE SCHOOL STUDENT WOULD WEAR THAT!
WELL ...
I'M GONNA GO AND CHECK OUT THE SWIM-SUITS.
HMM... I THINK THEY'RE OVER THERE.
LET'S SEE WHAT COLOR'S IN THIS YEAR...
I DON'T CARE...
THEY'RE ONLY PAJAMAS. NO ONE WILL SEE THEM.
KUROKO DOESN'T COUNT.
THEY LOOK BUSY...
I'LL JUST SNEAK OVER TO THE MIRROR, AND...
Tp Tp Tp
YES!
IT LOOKS PERFECT!

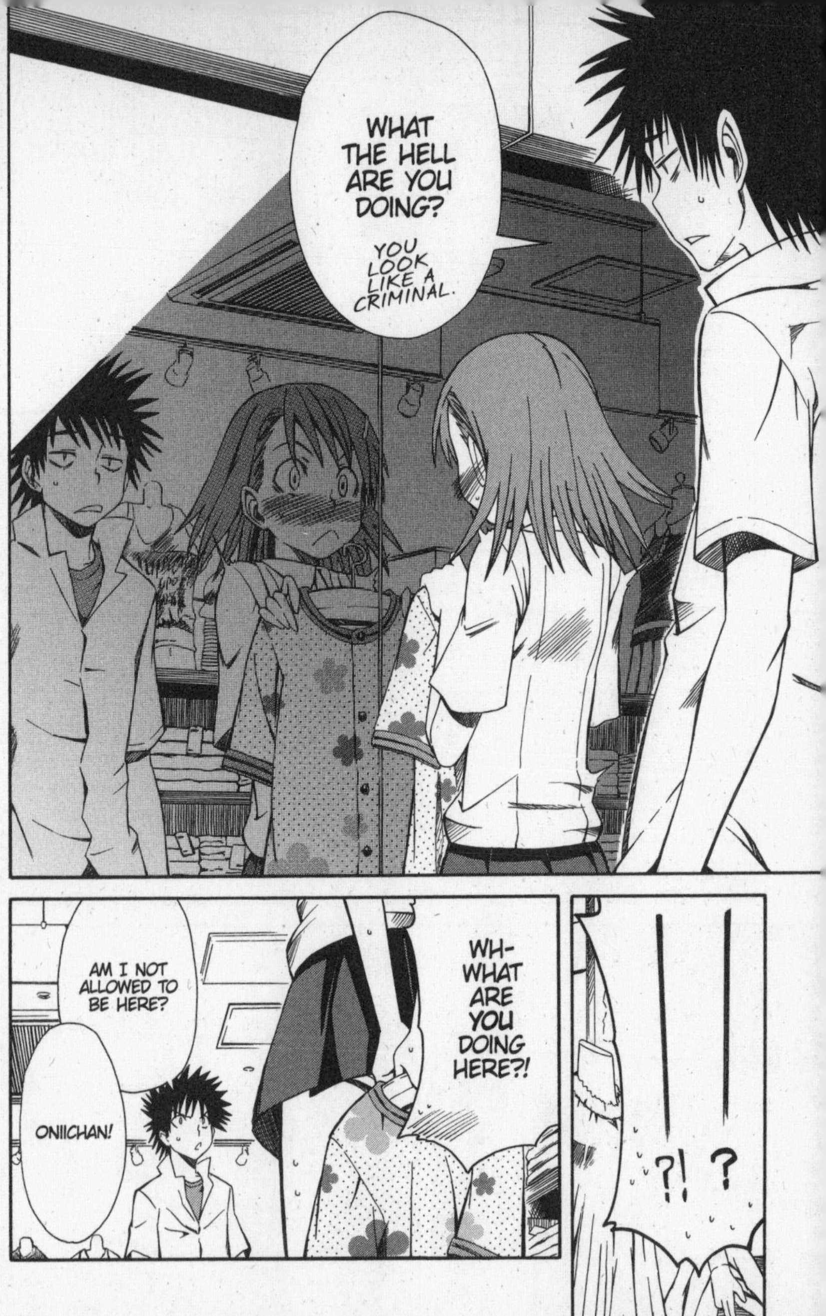
WHAT THE HELL ARE YOU DOING?
YOU LOOK LIKE A CRIMINAL.
?! ?
WH-WHAT ARE YOU DOING HERE?!
AM I NOT ALLOWED TO BE HERE?
ONIICHAN!

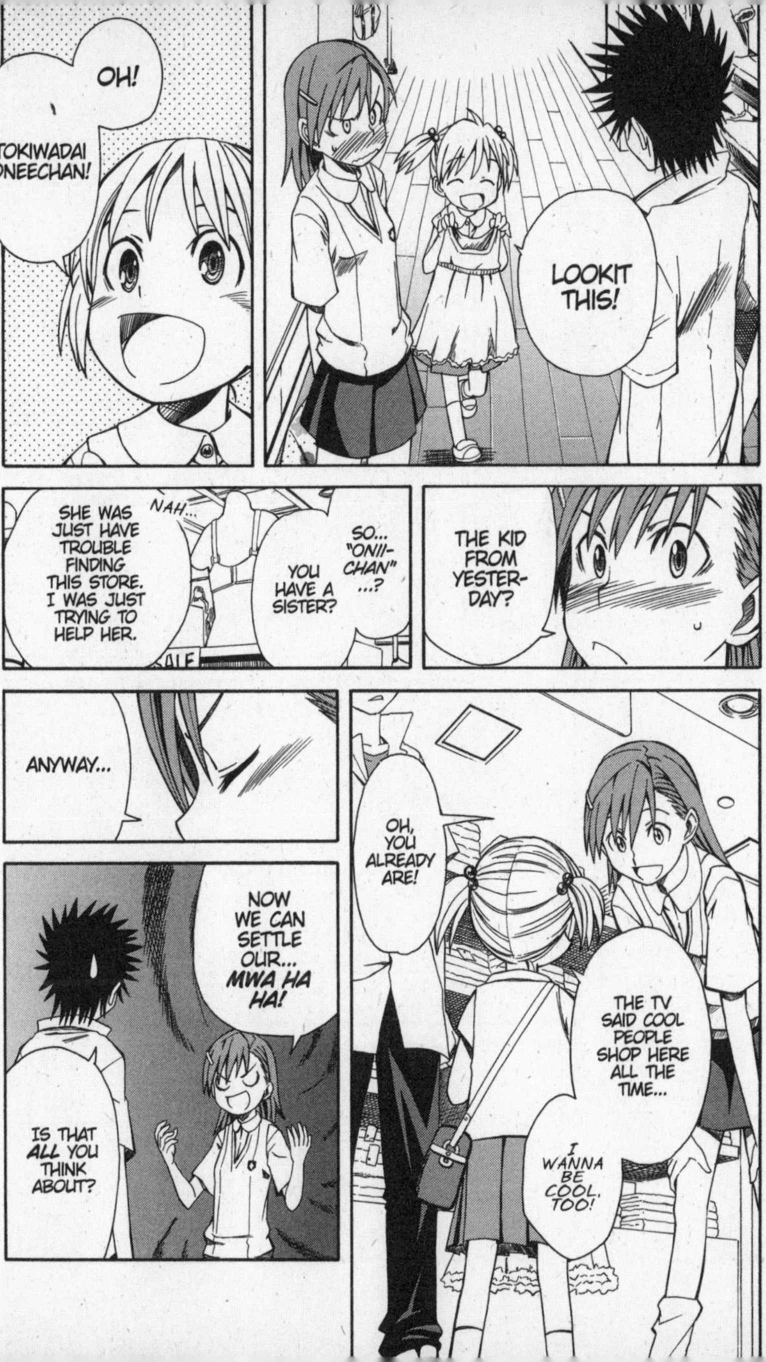
LOOKIT THIS!
OH!
TOKIWADAI ONEECHAN!
THE KID FROM YESTER-DAY?
SO... "ONII-CHAN" ...?
YOU HAVE A SISTER?
NAH...
SHE WAS JUST HAVE TROUBLE FINDING THIS STORE. I WAS JUST TRYING TO HELP HER.
THE TV SAID COOL PEOPLE SHOP HERE ALL THE TIME...
I WANNA BE COOL, TOO!
OH, YOU ALREADY ARE!
ANYWAY...
NOW WE CAN SETTLE OUR... *MWA HA HA!*
IS THAT *ALL* YOU THINK ABOUT?

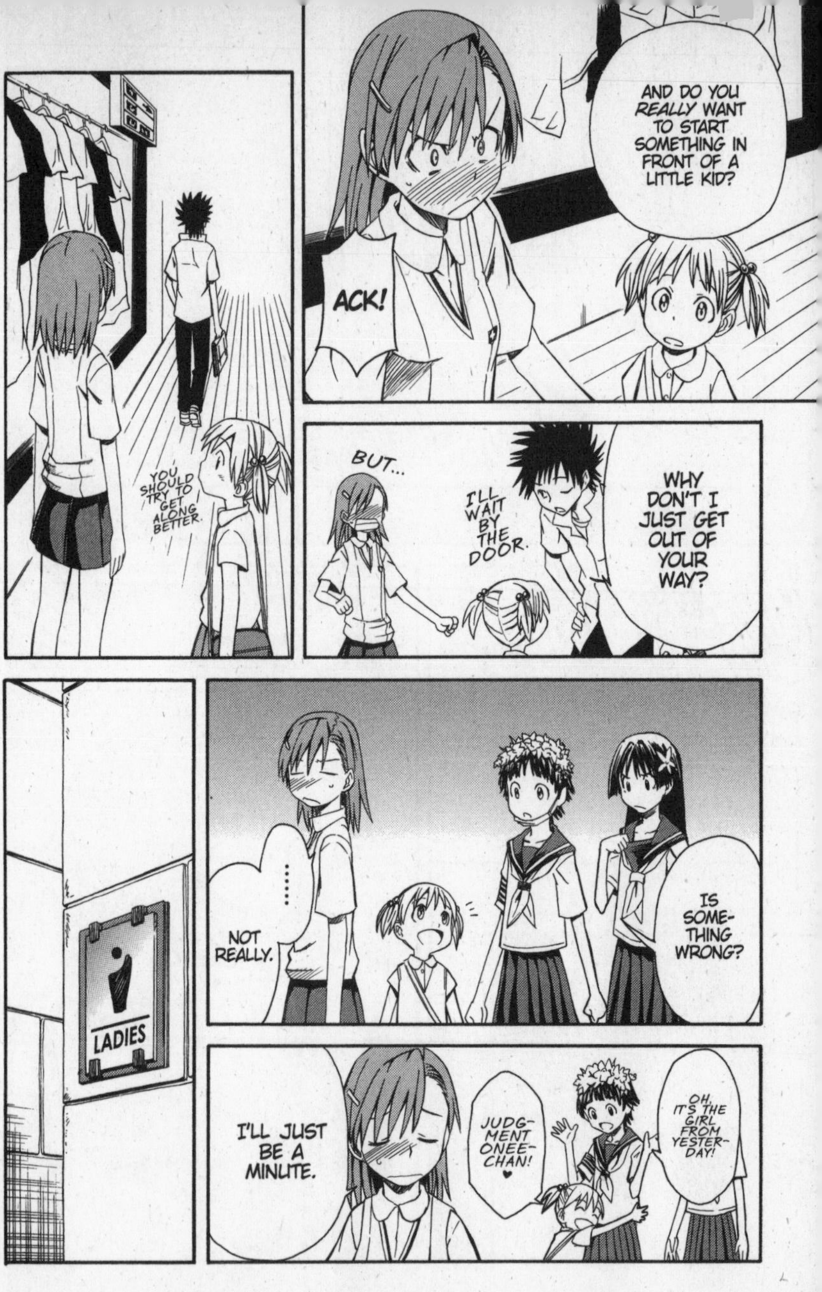
AND DO YOU *REALLY* WANT TO START SOMETHING IN FRONT OF A LITTLE KID?
ACK!
WHY DON'T I JUST GET OUT OF YOUR WAY?
I'LL WAIT BY THE DOOR.
BUT...
YOU SHOULD TRY TO GET ALONG BETTER.
IS SOME-THING WRONG?
......
NOT REALLY.
OH, IT'S THE GIRL FROM YESTER-DAY!
JUDG-MENT ONEE-CHAN! ♥
I'LL JUST BE A MINUTE.
LADIES

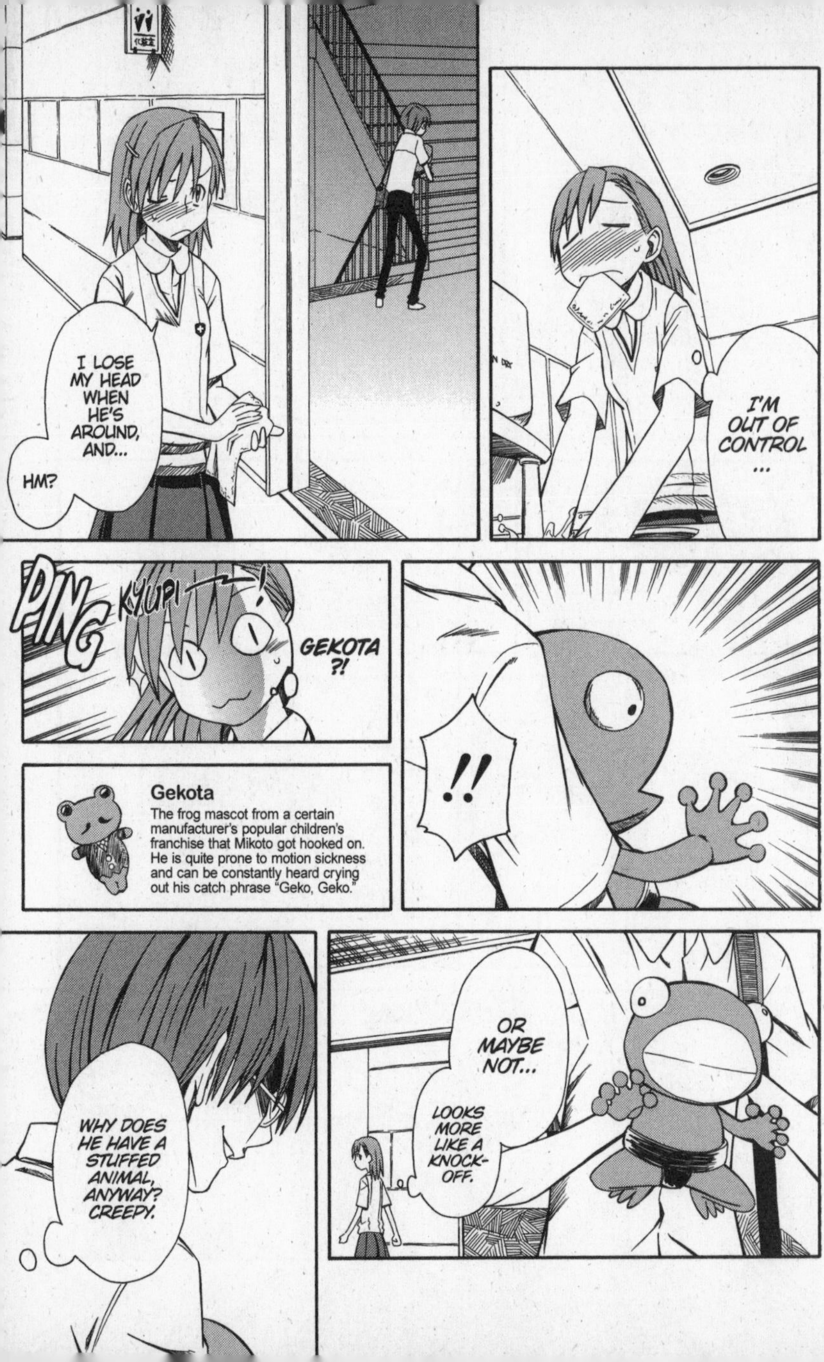
I'M OUT OF CONTROL ...
I LOSE MY HEAD WHEN HE'S AROUND, AND...
HM?
!!
PING
KYUPI
GEKOTA?!
Gekota
The frog mascot from a certain manufacturer's popular children's franchise that Mikoto got hooked on. He is quite prone to motion sickness and can be constantly heard crying out his catch phrase "Geko, Geko."
OR MAYBE NOT...
LOOKS MORE LIKE A KNOCK-OFF.
WHY DOES HE HAVE A STUFFED ANIMAL, ANYWAY? CREEPY.

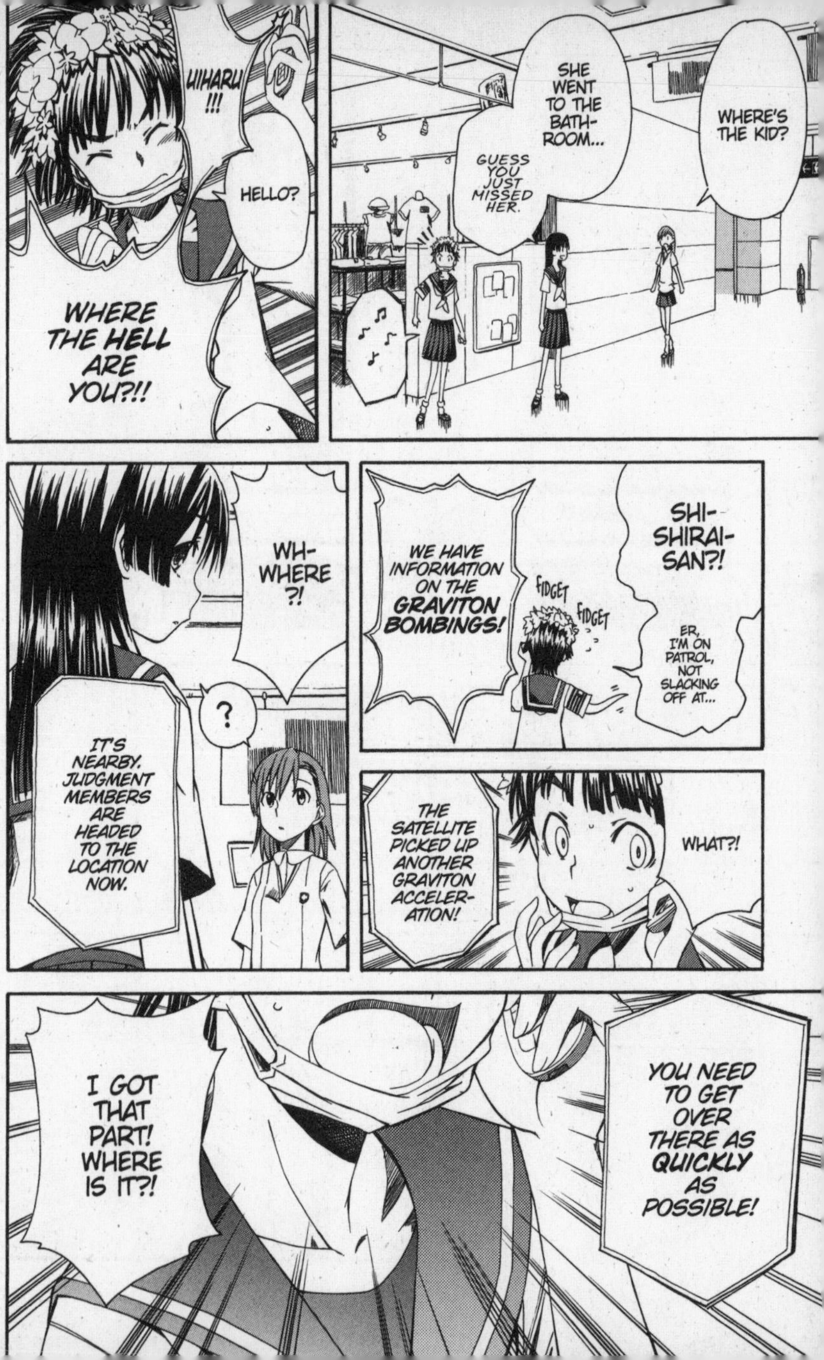
WHERE'S THE KID?
SHE WENT TO THE BATH-ROOM...
GUESS YOU JUST MISSED HER.
UIHARU !!!
HELLO?
WHERE THE HELL ARE YOU?!!
SHI-SHIRAI-SAN?!
ER, I'M ON PATROL, NOT SLACKING OFF AT...
FIDGET FIDGET
WE HAVE INFORMATION ON THE GRAVITON BOMBINGS!
WHAT?!
THE SATELLITE PICKED UP ANOTHER GRAVITON ACCELER-ATION!
WH-WHERE?!
?
IT'S NEARBY. JUDGMENT MEMBERS ARE HEADED TO THE LOCATION NOW.
YOU NEED TO GET OVER THERE AS QUICKLY AS POSSIBLE!
I GOT THAT PART! WHERE IS IT?!

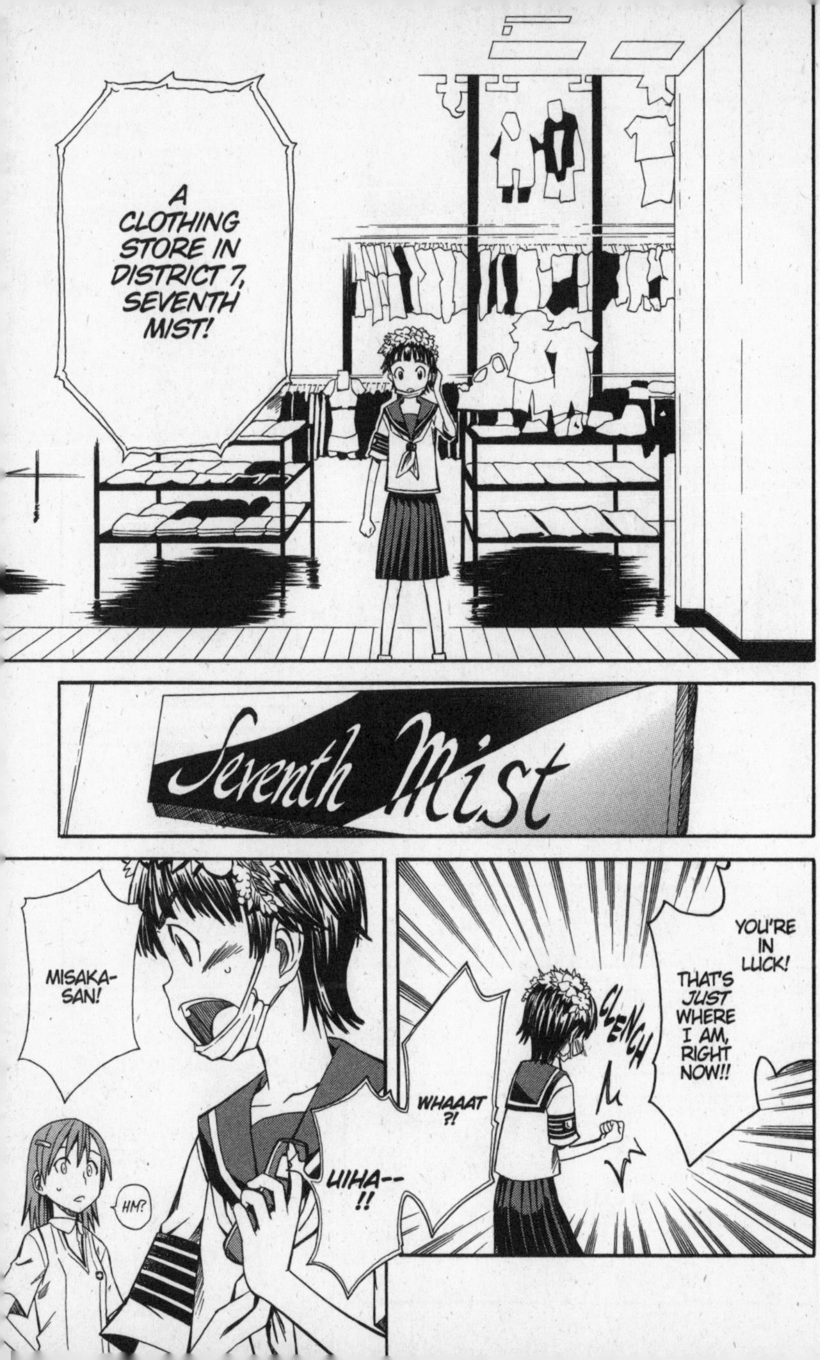
A CLOTHING STORE IN DISTRICT 7, SEVENTH MIST!
Seventh Mist
YOU'RE IN LUCK!
THAT'S JUST WHERE I AM, RIGHT NOW!!
CLENCH
WHAAAT?!
MISAKA-SAN!
UIHA--!!
HM?

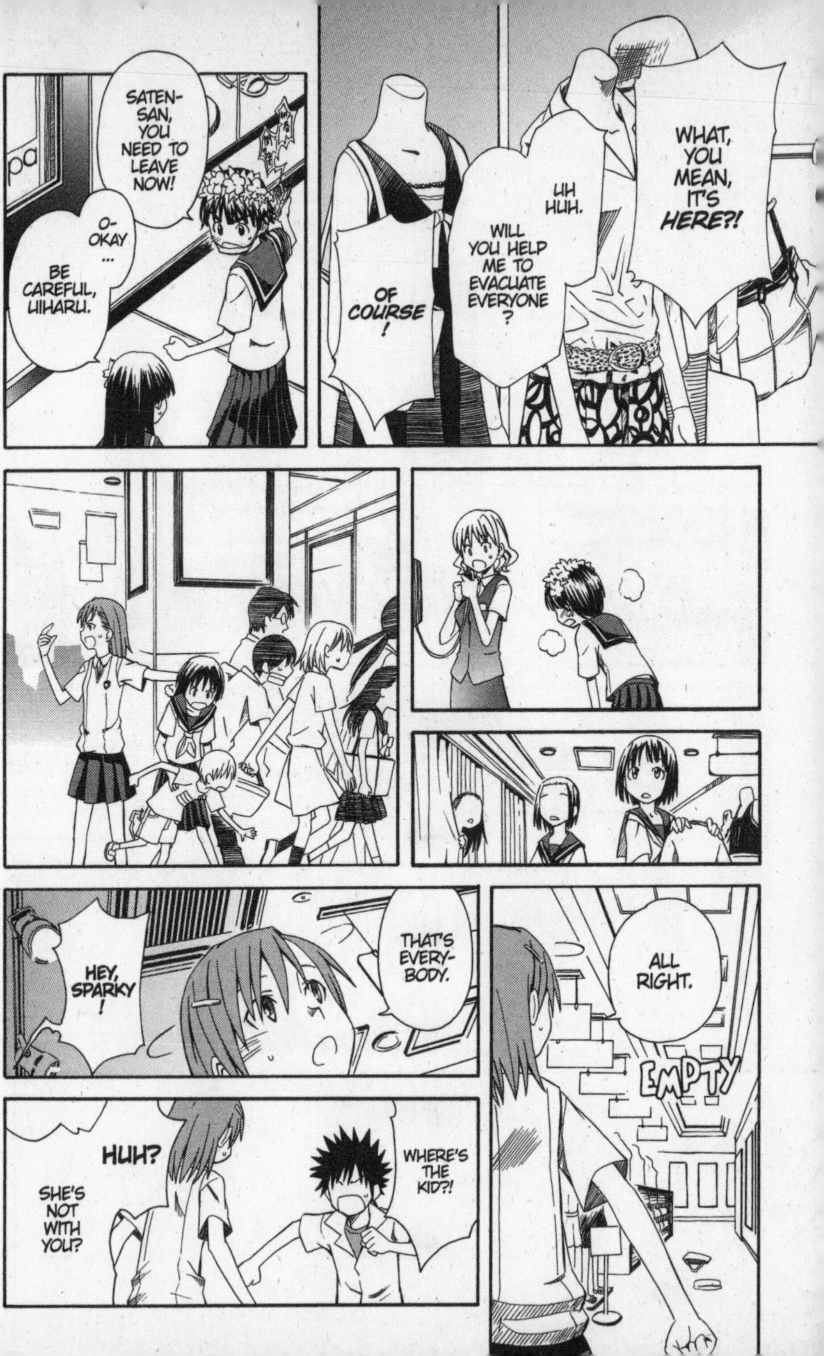
WHAT, YOU MEAN, IT'S HERE?!
UH HUH.
WILL YOU HELP ME TO EVACUATE EVERYONE?
OF COURSE!
SATEN-SAN, YOU NEED TO LEAVE NOW!
O-OKAY...
BE CAREFUL, UIHARU.
ALL RIGHT.
EMPTY
THAT'S EVERY-BODY.
HEY, SPARKY!
WHERE'S THE KID?!
HUH?
SHE'S NOT WITH YOU?

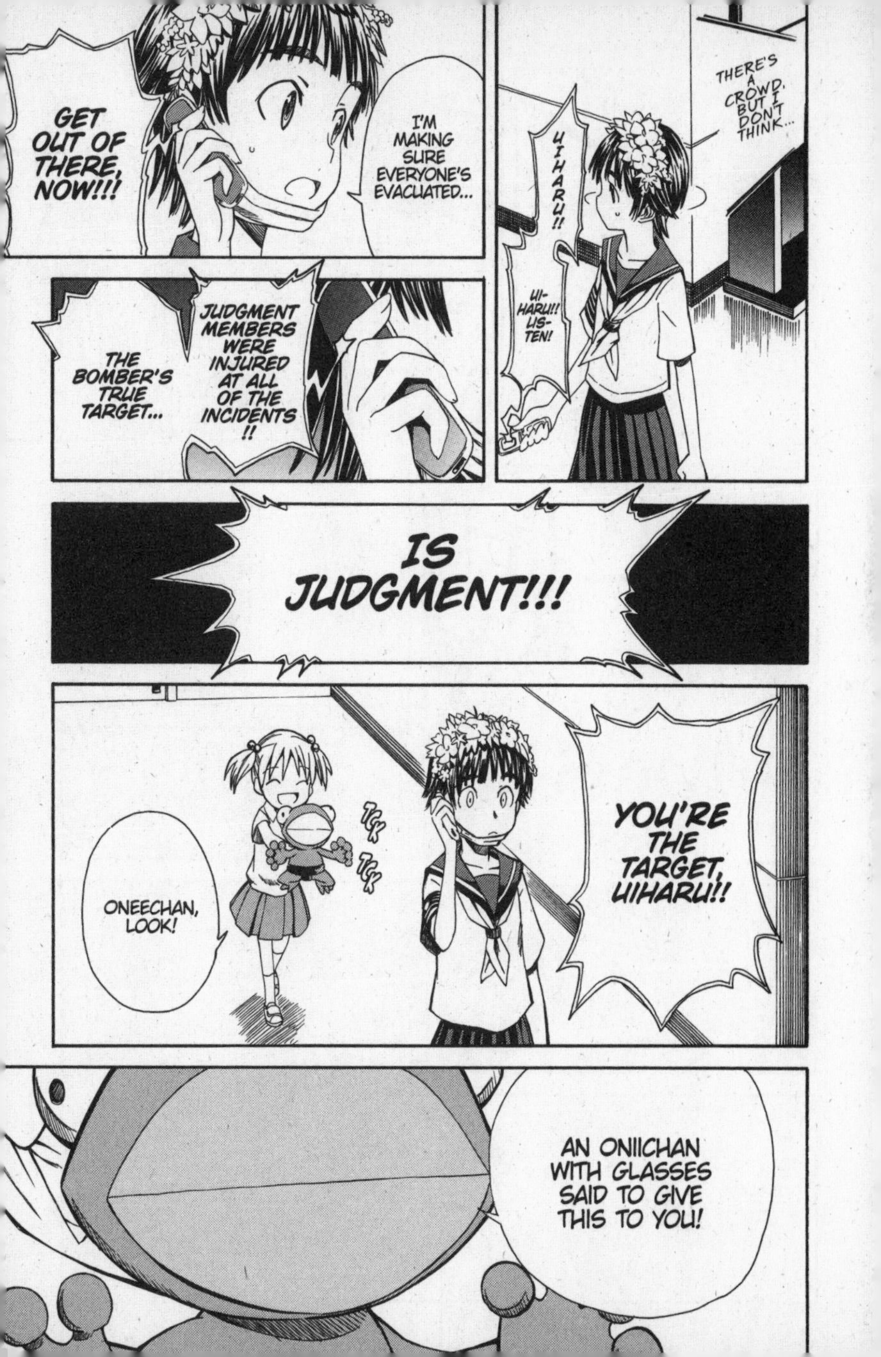
THERE'S A CROWD, BUT I DON'T THINK...
UIHARU!!
UI-HARU!! LIS-TEN!
I'M MAKING SURE EVERYONE'S EVACUATED...
GET OUT OF THERE, NOW!!!
JUDGMENT MEMBERS WERE INJURED AT ALL OF THE INCIDENTS!!
THE BOMBER'S TRUE TARGET...
IS JUDGMENT!!!
YOU'RE THE TARGET, UIHARU!!
TCK TCK
ONEECHAN, LOOK!
AN ONIICHAN WITH GLASSES SAID TO GIVE THIS TO YOU!

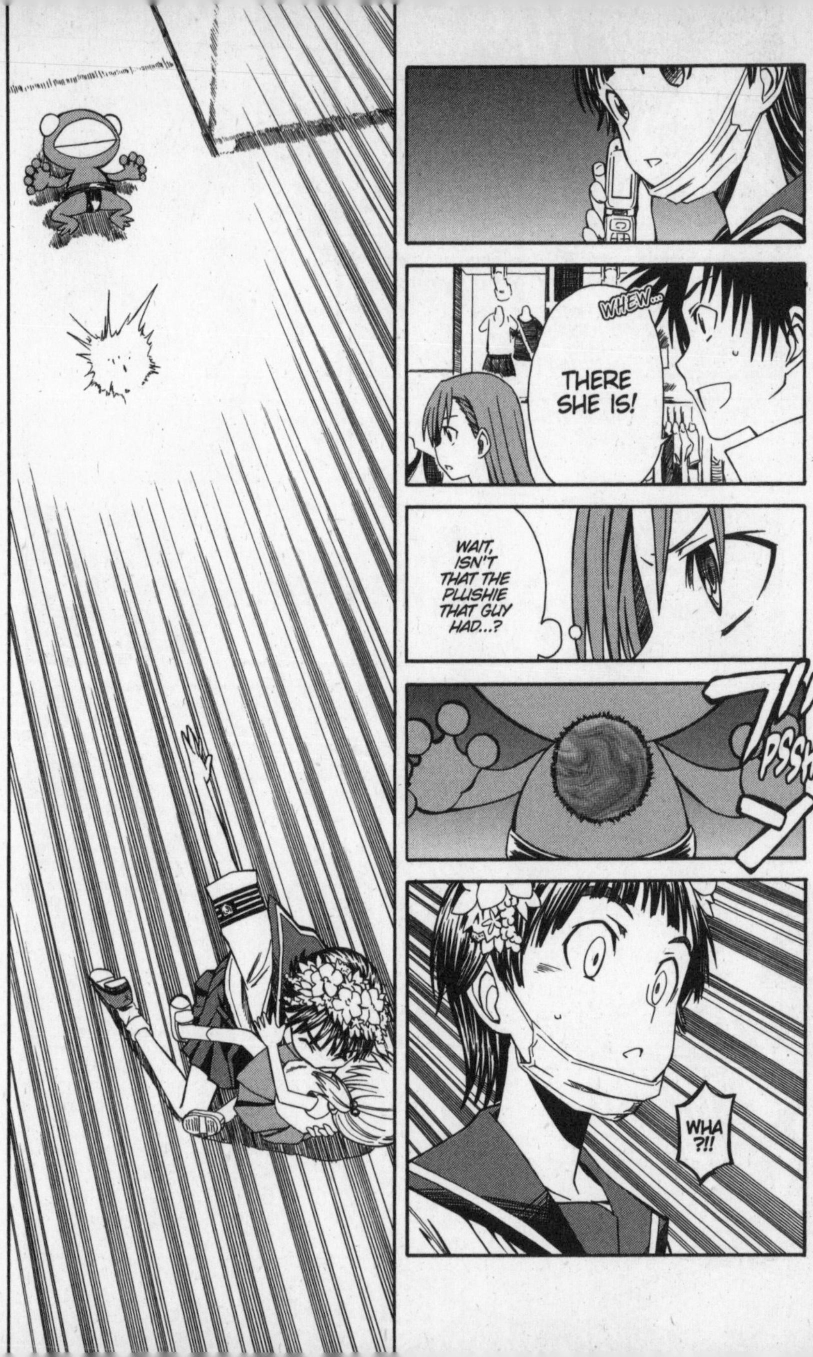
WHEW...
THERE SHE IS!
WAIT, ISN'T THAT THE PLUSHIE THAT GUY HAD...?
PSSHT
WHA?!!

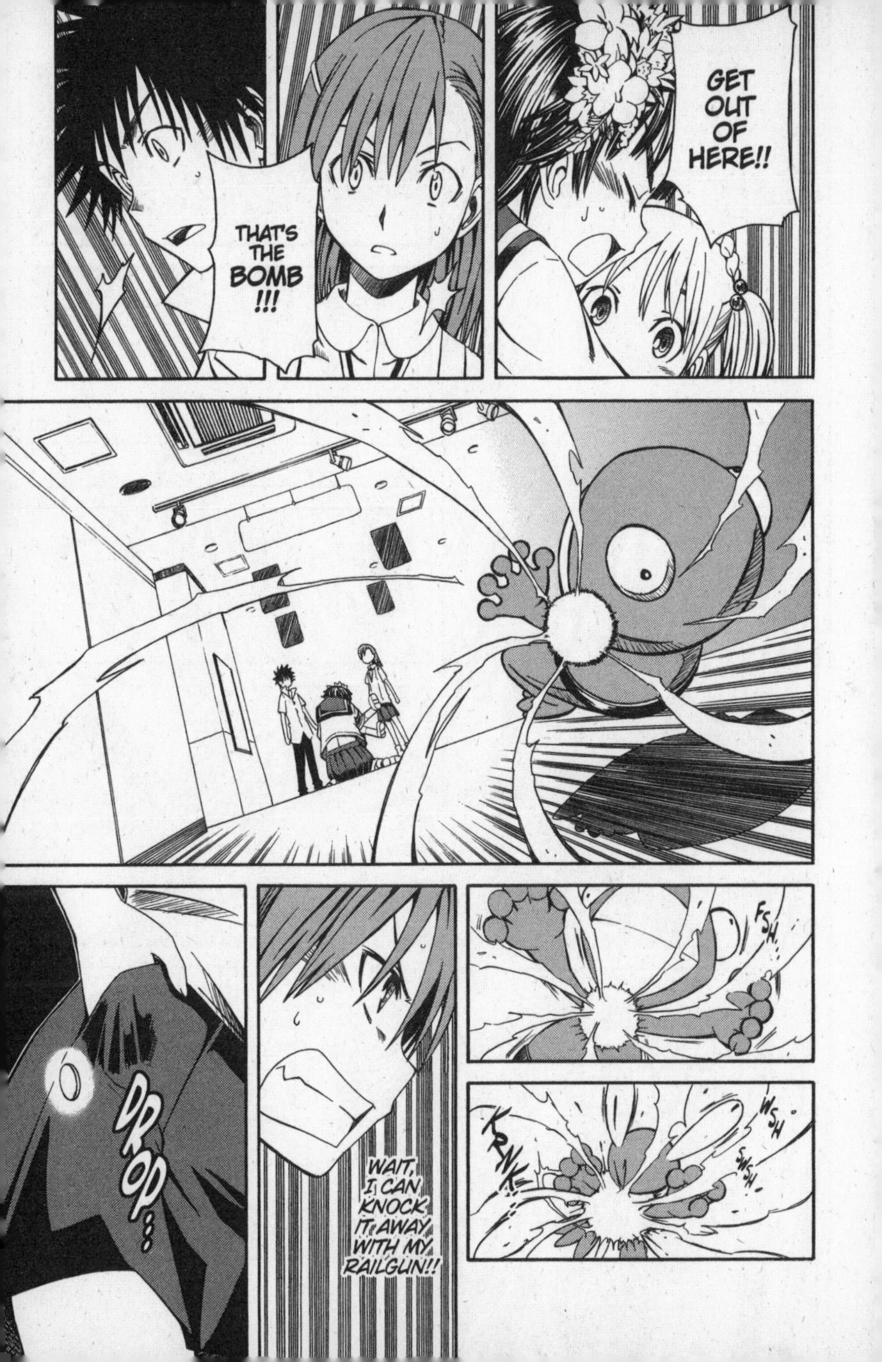
GET OUT OF HERE!!
THAT'S THE BOMB !!!
FSH..
WSH
SWSH..
KRNK..
WAIT, I CAN KNOCK IT AWAY WITH MY RAILGUN!!
DROP..

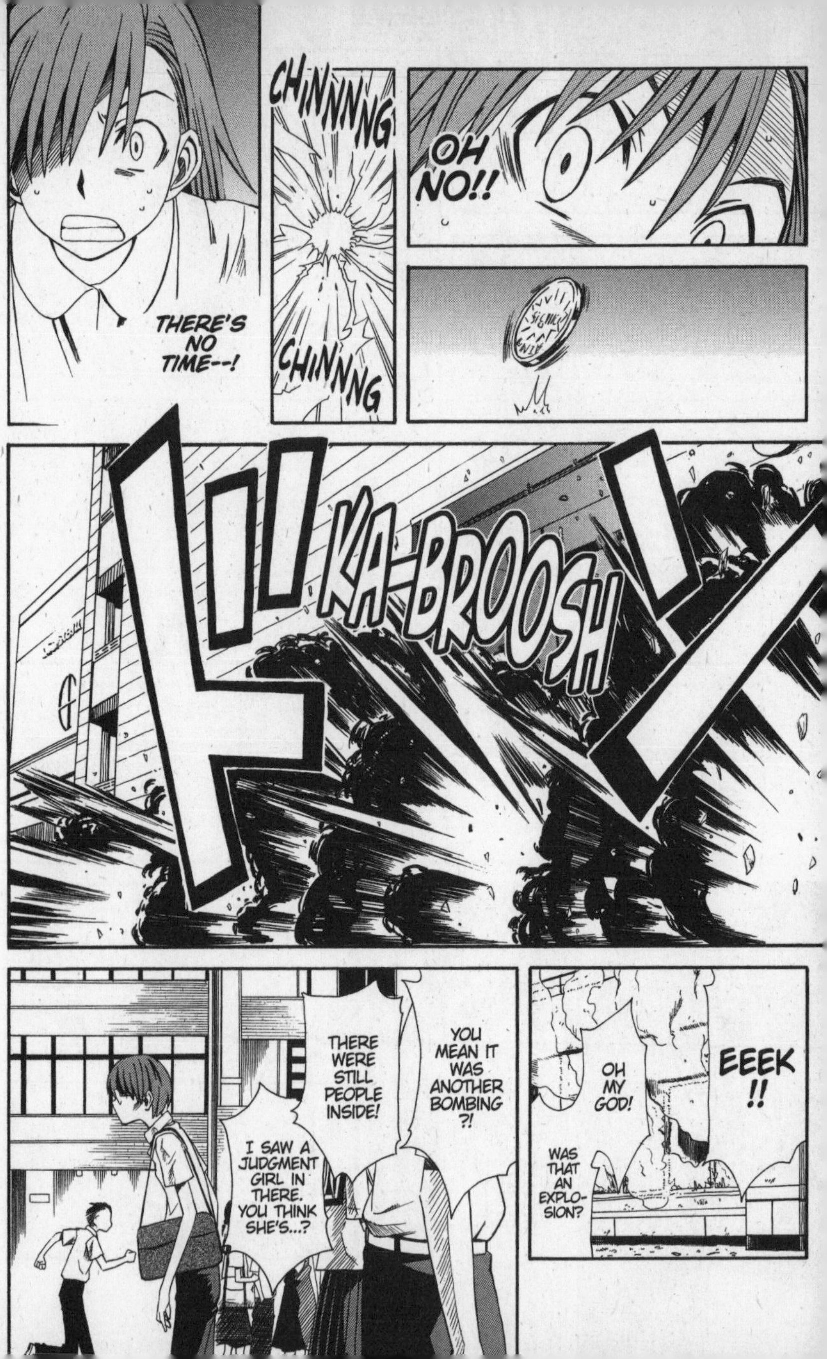
OH NO!!
CHINNNNG
CHINNNG
THERE'S NO TIME--!
KA-BROOSH
EEEK!!
OH MY GOD!
WAS THAT AN EXPLOSION?
YOU MEAN IT WAS ANOTHER BOMBING?!
THERE WERE STILL PEOPLE INSIDE!
I SAW A JUDGMENT GIRL IN THERE. YOU THINK SHE'S...?

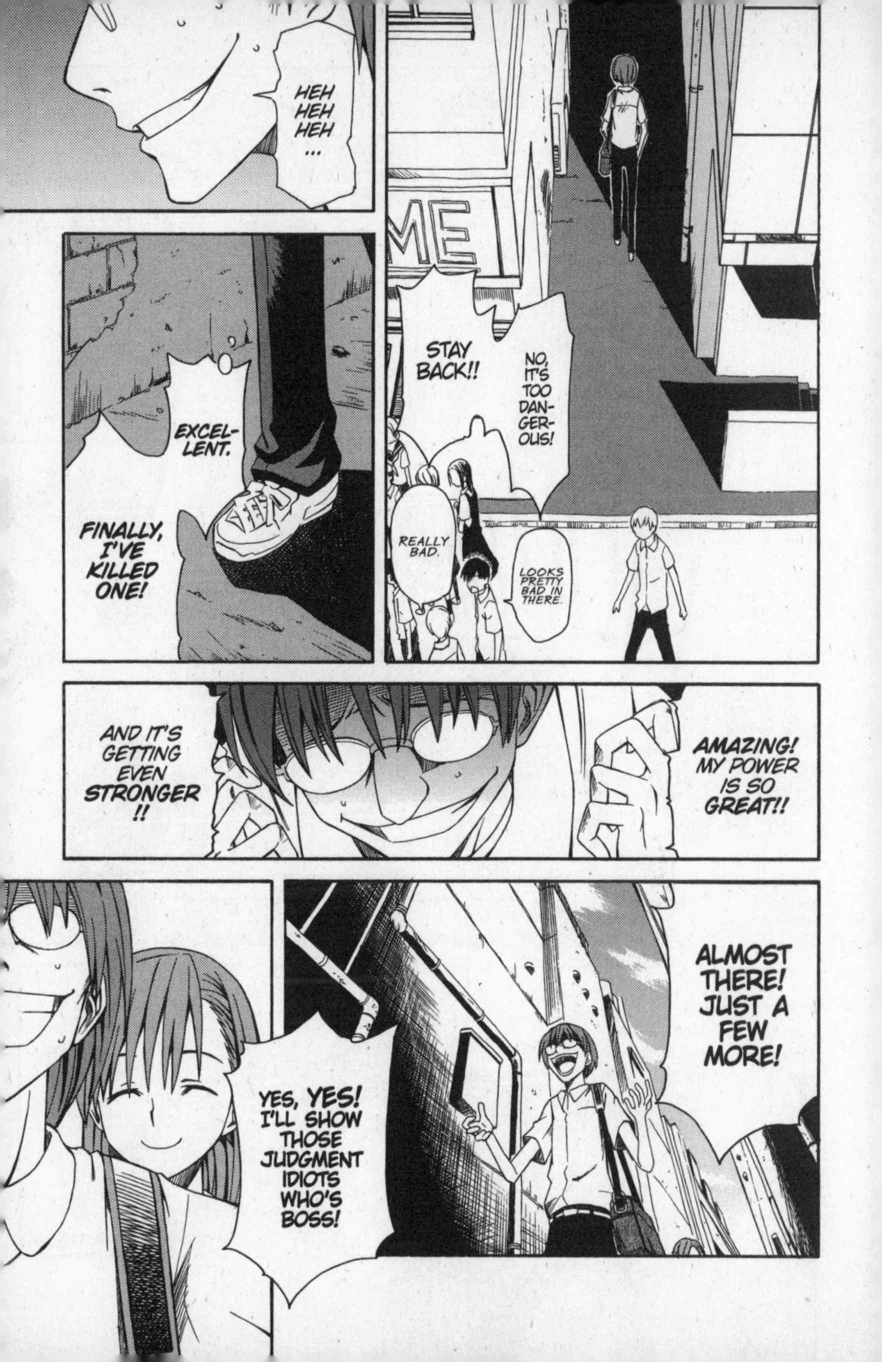

STAY BACK!! NO, IT'S TOO DAN-GER-OUS!
LOOKS PRETTY BAD IN THERE.
REALLY BAD.
HEH HEH HEH ...
EXCEL-LENT.
FINALLY, I'VE KILLED ONE!
AMAZING! MY POWER IS SO GREAT!!
AND IT'S GETTING EVEN STRONGER !!
ALMOST THERE! JUST A FEW MORE!
YES, YES! I'LL SHOW THOSE JUDGMENT IDIOTS WHO'S BOSS!

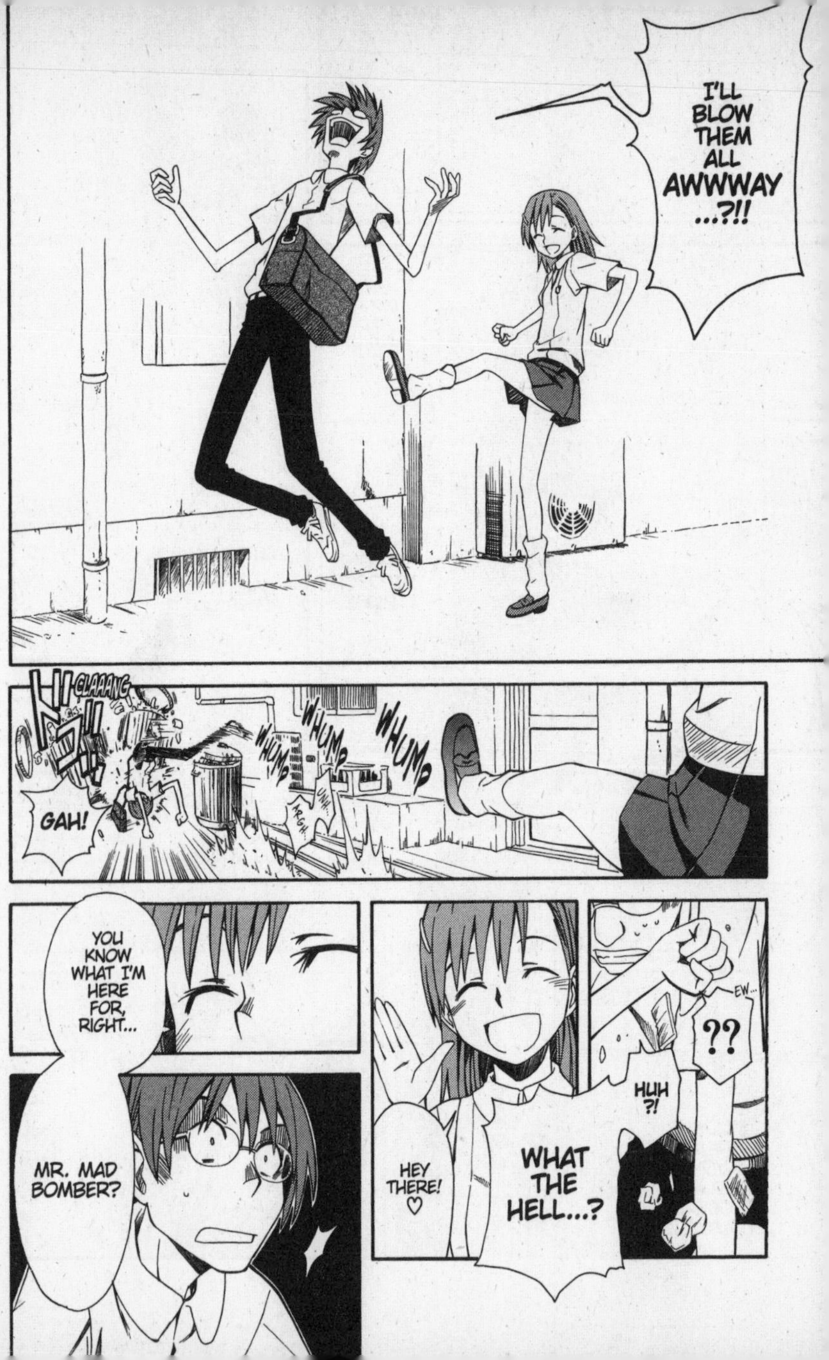
I'LL BLOW THEM ALL AWWWAY ...?!!
WHUMP
WHUMP
WHUMP
UNH...
ARGH...
CLAAANG
GAH!
EW...
??
HUH ?!
WHAT THE HELL...?
HEY THERE! ♡
YOU KNOW WHAT I'M HERE FOR, RIGHT...
MR. MAD BOMBER?

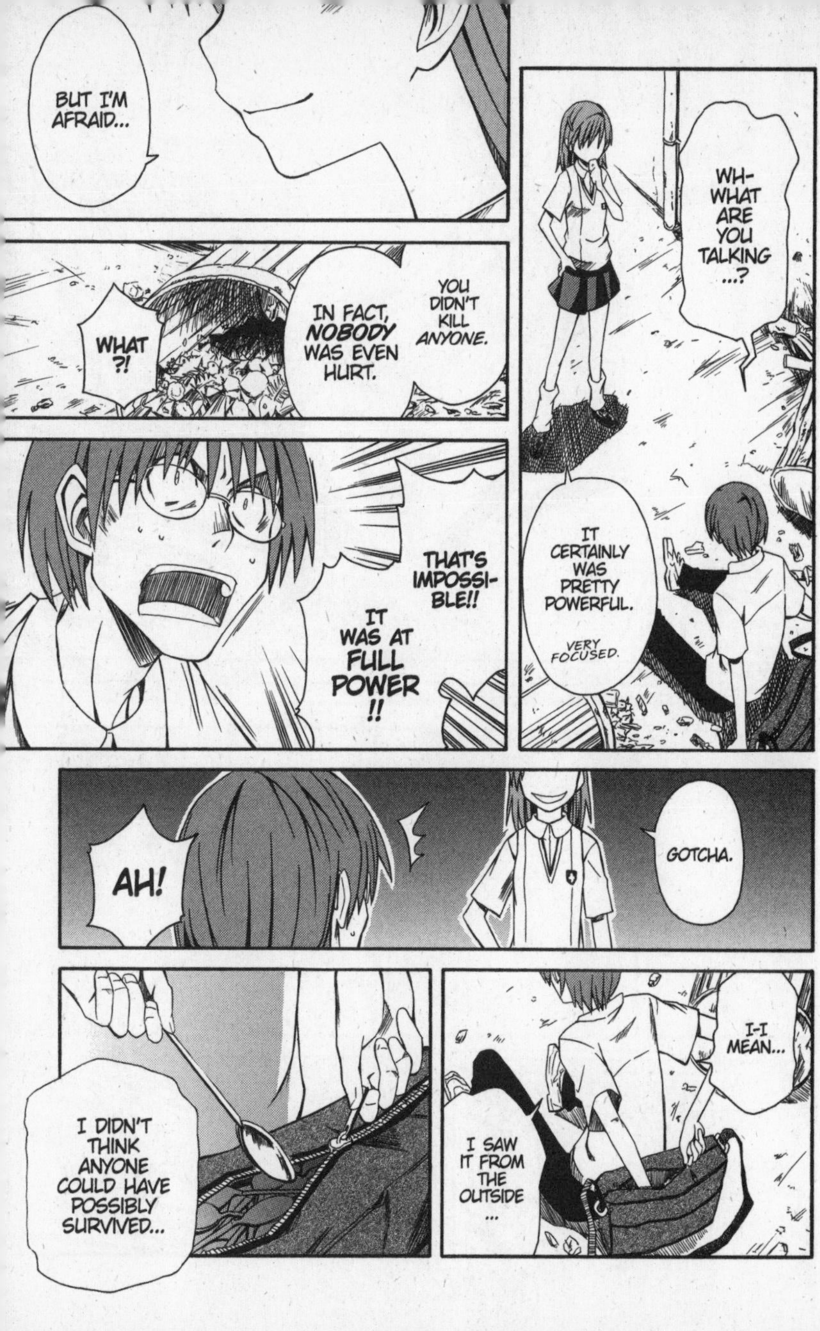
BUT I'M AFRAID...
WH- WHAT ARE YOU TALKING ...?
IT CERTAINLY WAS PRETTY POWERFUL.
VERY FOCUSED.
YOU DIDN'T KILL *ANYONE.*
IN FACT, ***NOBODY*** WAS EVEN HURT.
WHAT ?!
THAT'S IMPOSSI- BLE!!
IT WAS AT **FULL POWER** !!
GOTCHA.
AH!
I-I MEAN...
I SAW IT FROM THE OUTSIDE ...
I DIDN'T THINK ANYONE COULD HAVE POSSIBLY SURVIVED...

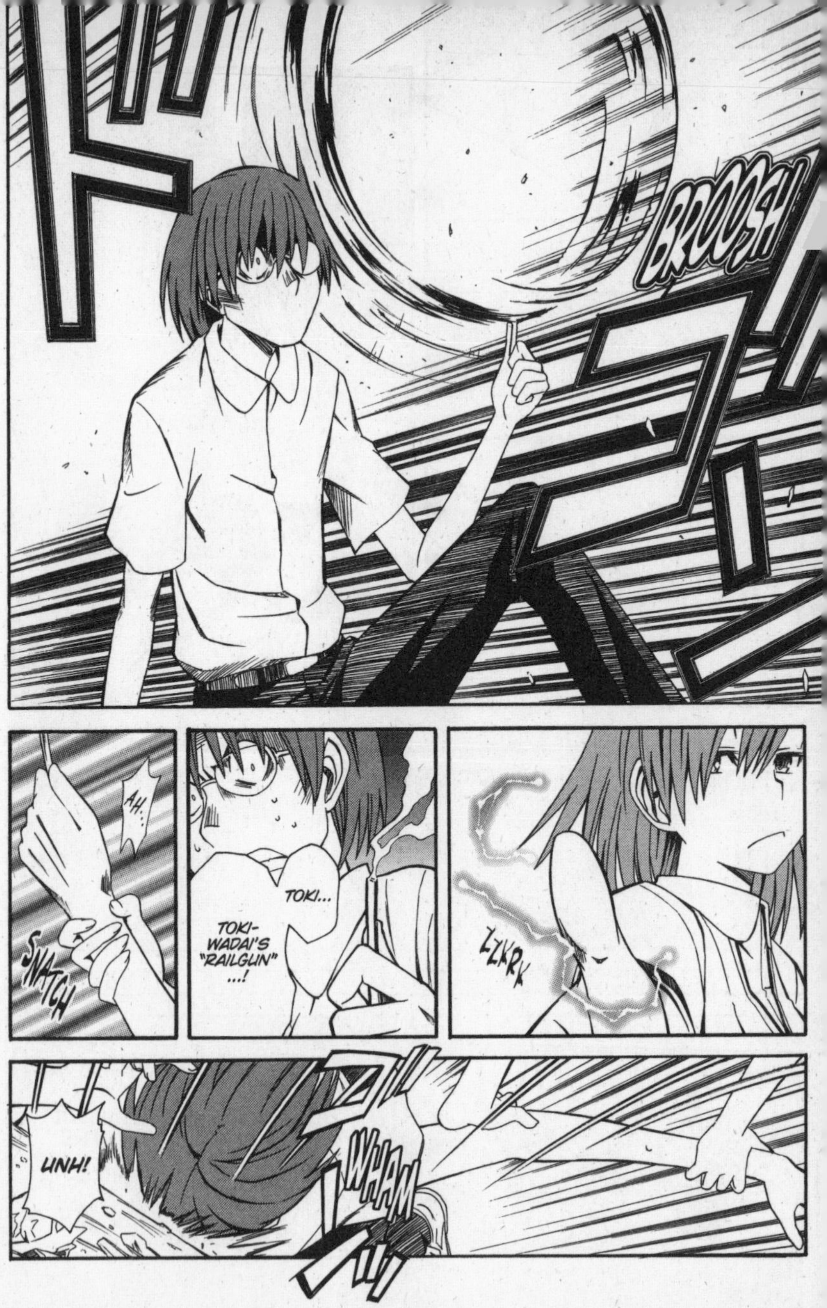
BROOSH
ZZKRK
TOKI...
TOKI-WADAI'S "RAILGUN" ...!
AH...
SNATCH
WHAM
UNH!

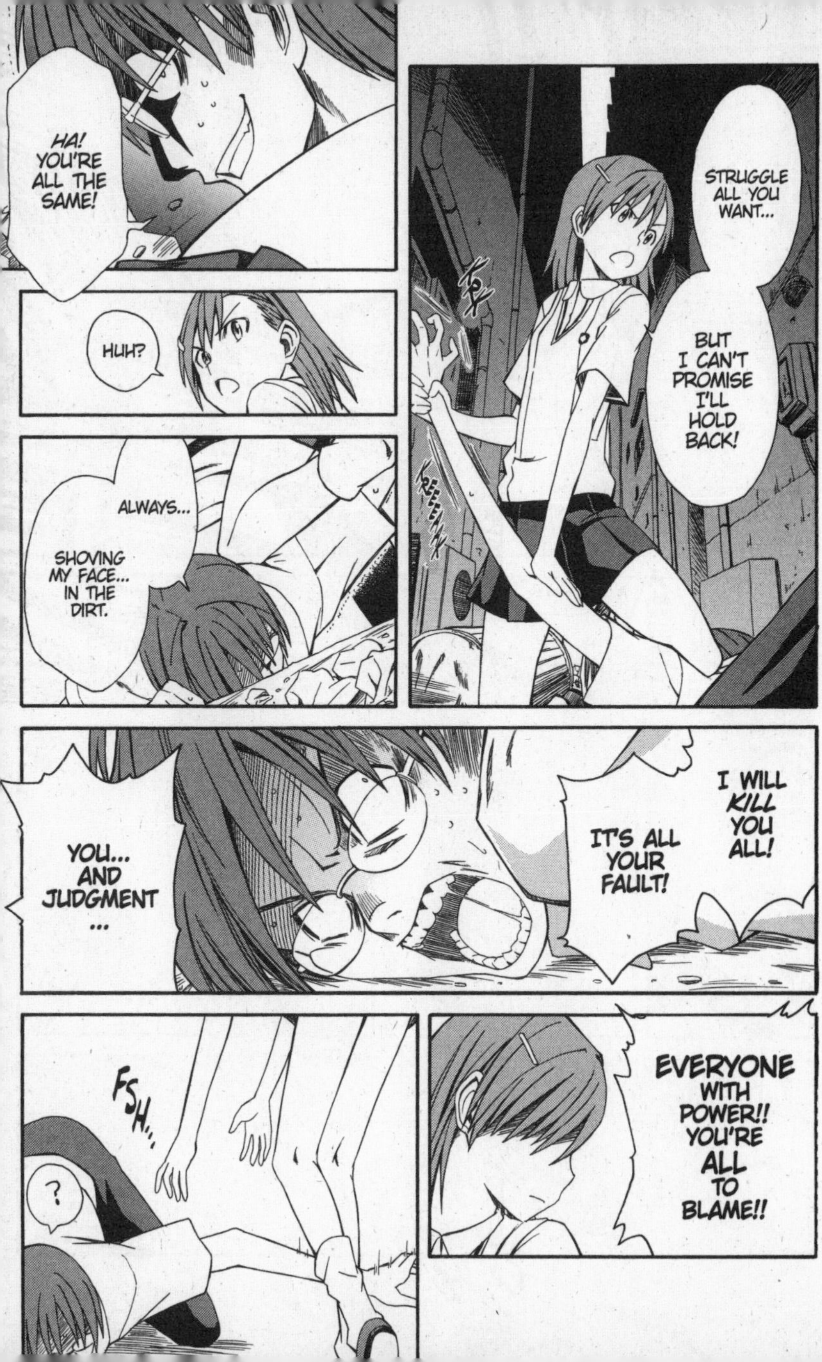
STRUGGLE ALL YOU WANT...
BUT I CAN'T PROMISE I'LL HOLD BACK!
HA! YOU'RE ALL THE SAME!
HUH?
ALWAYS...
SHOVING MY FACE... IN THE DIRT.
I WILL *KILL* YOU ALL!
IT'S ALL YOUR FAULT!
YOU... AND JUDGMENT ...
EVERYONE WITH POWER!! YOU'RE ALL TO BLAME!!
FSH...
?

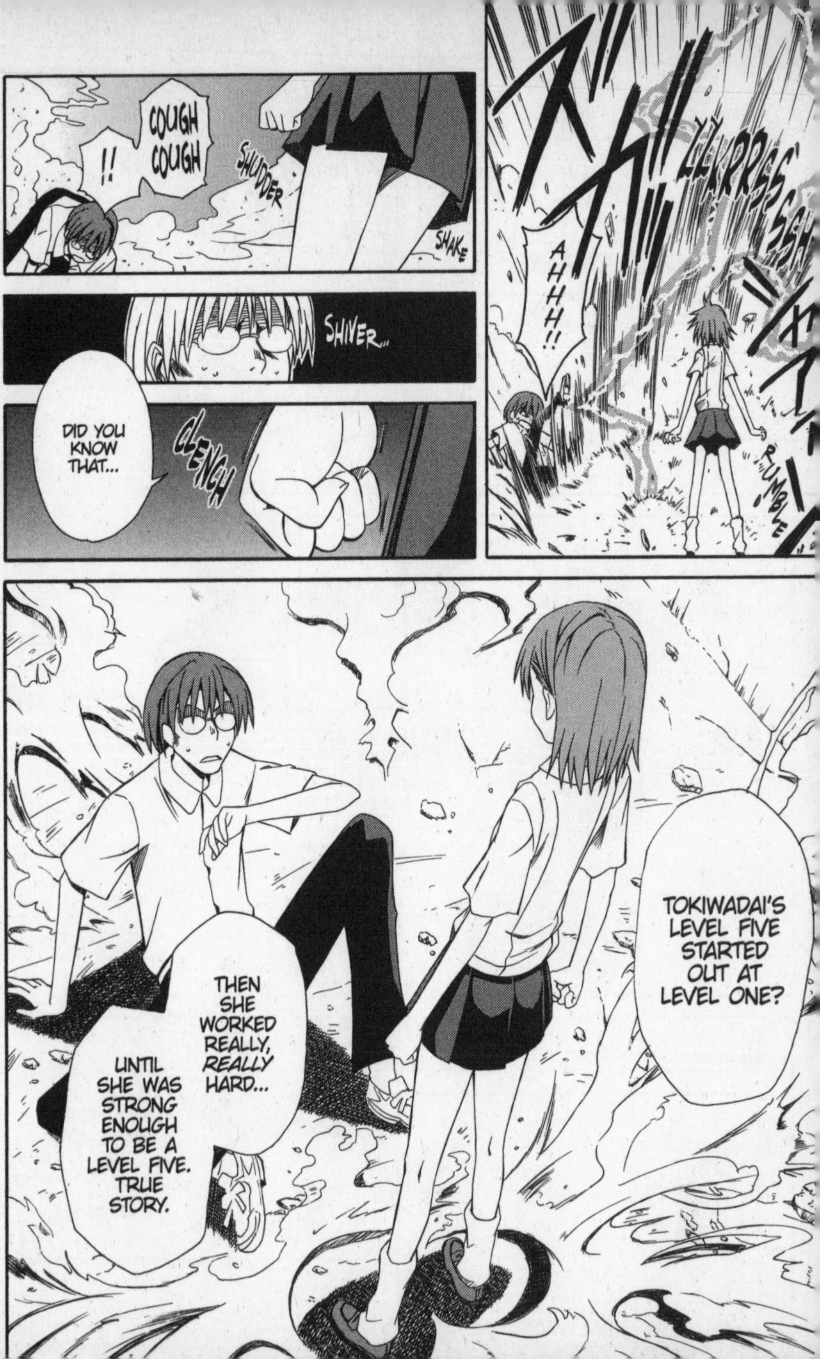
AHHH!!
RUMBLE
!!
COUGH COUGH
SHUDDER
SHAKE
SHIVER...
DID YOU KNOW THAT...
CLENCH
TOKIWADAI'S LEVEL FIVE STARTED OUT AT LEVEL ONE?
THEN SHE WORKED REALLY, REALLY HARD...
UNTIL SHE WAS STRONG ENOUGH TO BE A LEVEL FIVE. TRUE STORY.

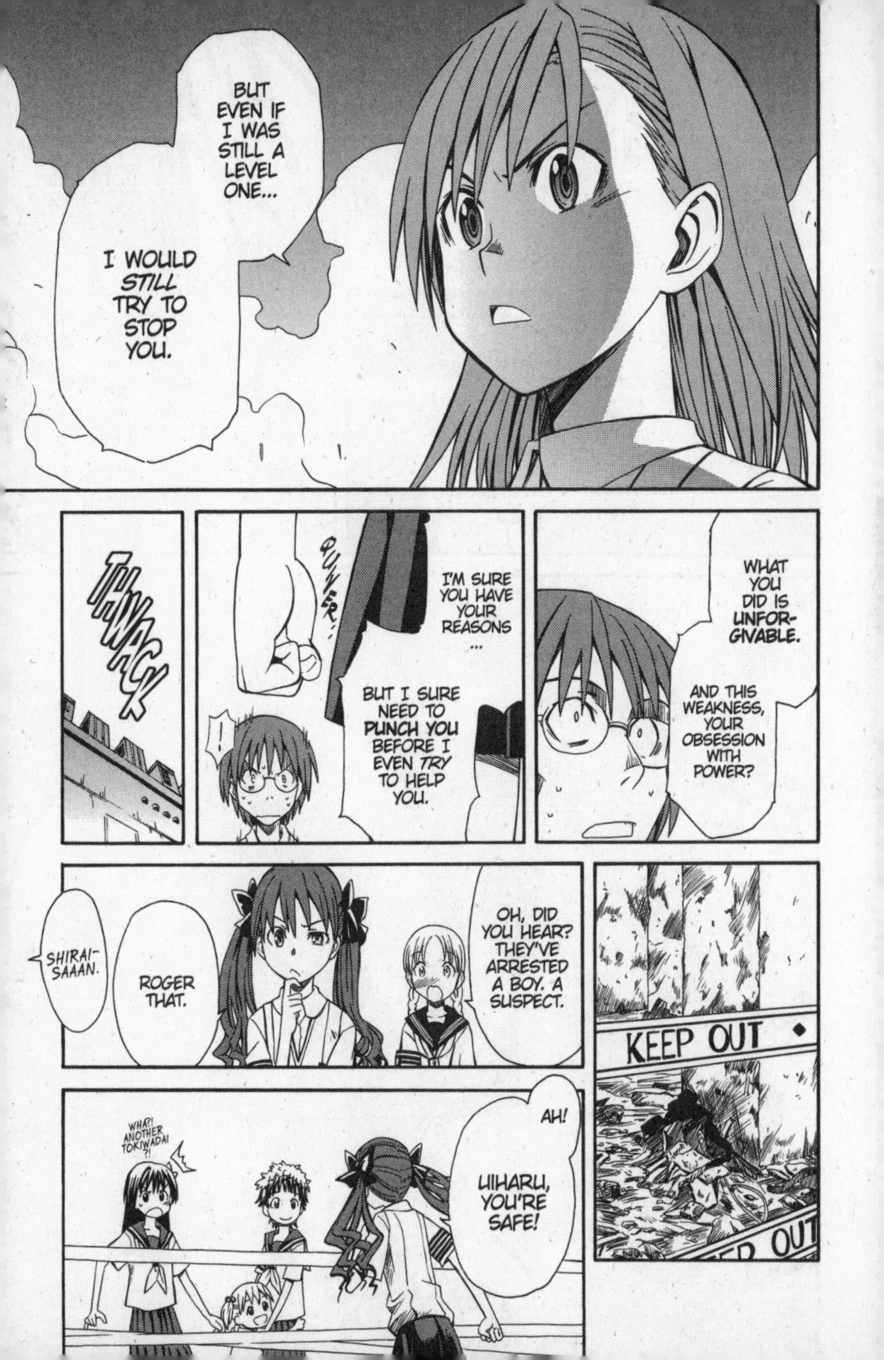
BUT EVEN IF I WAS STILL A LEVEL ONE...
I WOULD *STILL* TRY TO STOP YOU.
WHAT YOU DID IS UNFORGIVABLE.
AND THIS WEAKNESS, YOUR OBSESSION WITH POWER?
QUIVER
I'M SURE YOU HAVE YOUR REASONS ...
BUT I SURE NEED TO **PUNCH YOU** BEFORE I EVEN *TRY* TO HELP YOU.
!
THWACK
KEEP OUT
OH, DID YOU HEAR? THEY'VE ARRESTED A BOY. A SUSPECT.
ROGER THAT.
SHIRAI-SAAAN.
AH!
UIHARU, YOU'RE SAFE!
WHA?! ANOTHER TOKIWADAI ?!

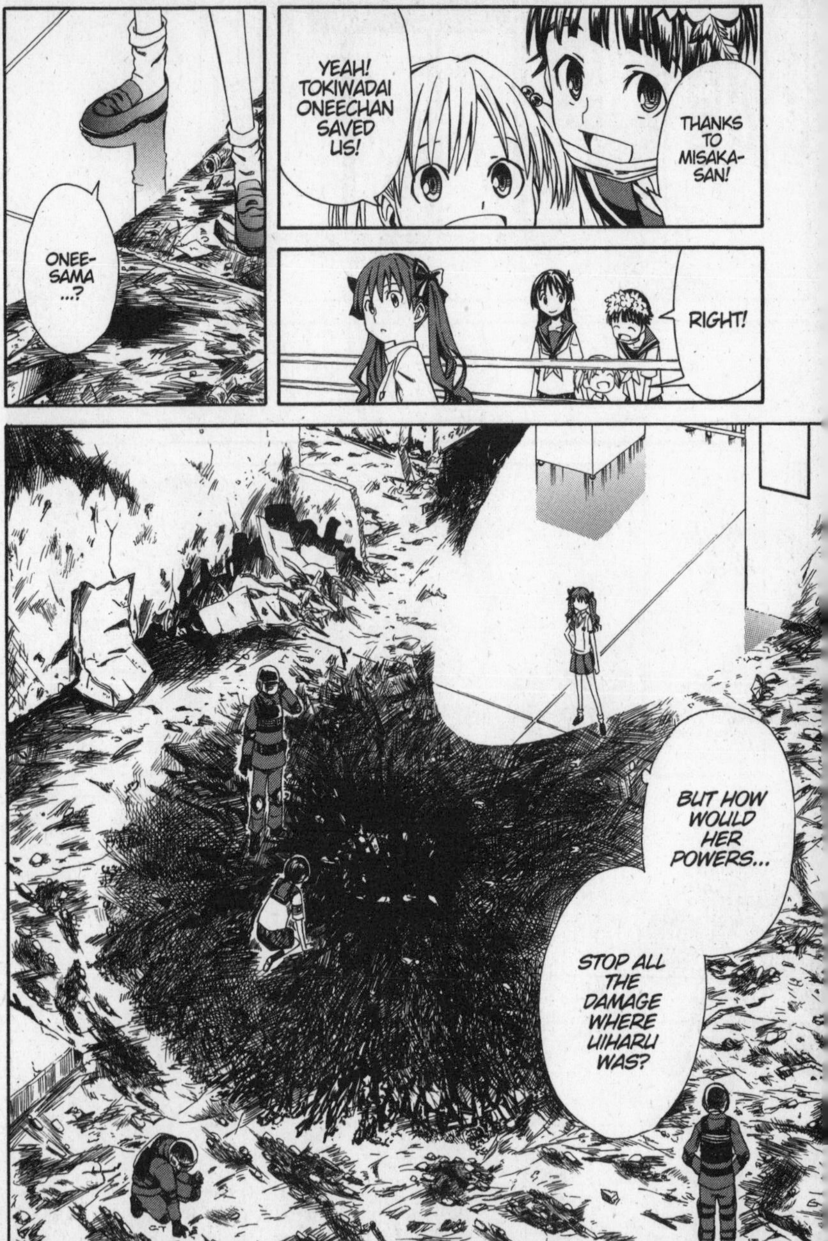
THANKS TO MISAKA-SAN!
YEAH! TOKIWADAI ONEECHAN SAVED US!
RIGHT!
ONEE-SAMA ...?
BUT HOW WOULD HER POWERS...
STOP ALL THE DAMAGE WHERE UIHARU WAS?

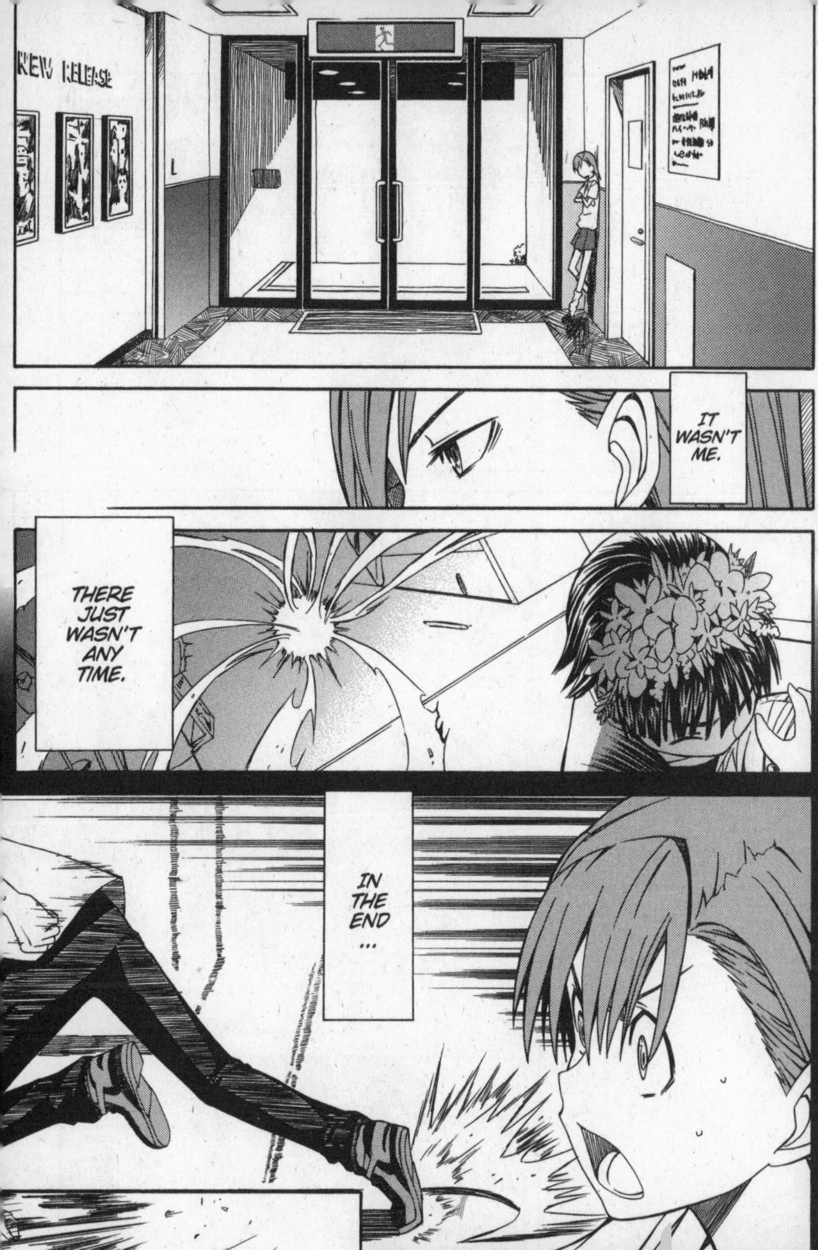
NEW RELEASE
IT WASN'T ME.
THERE JUST WASN'T ANY TIME.
IN THE END ...

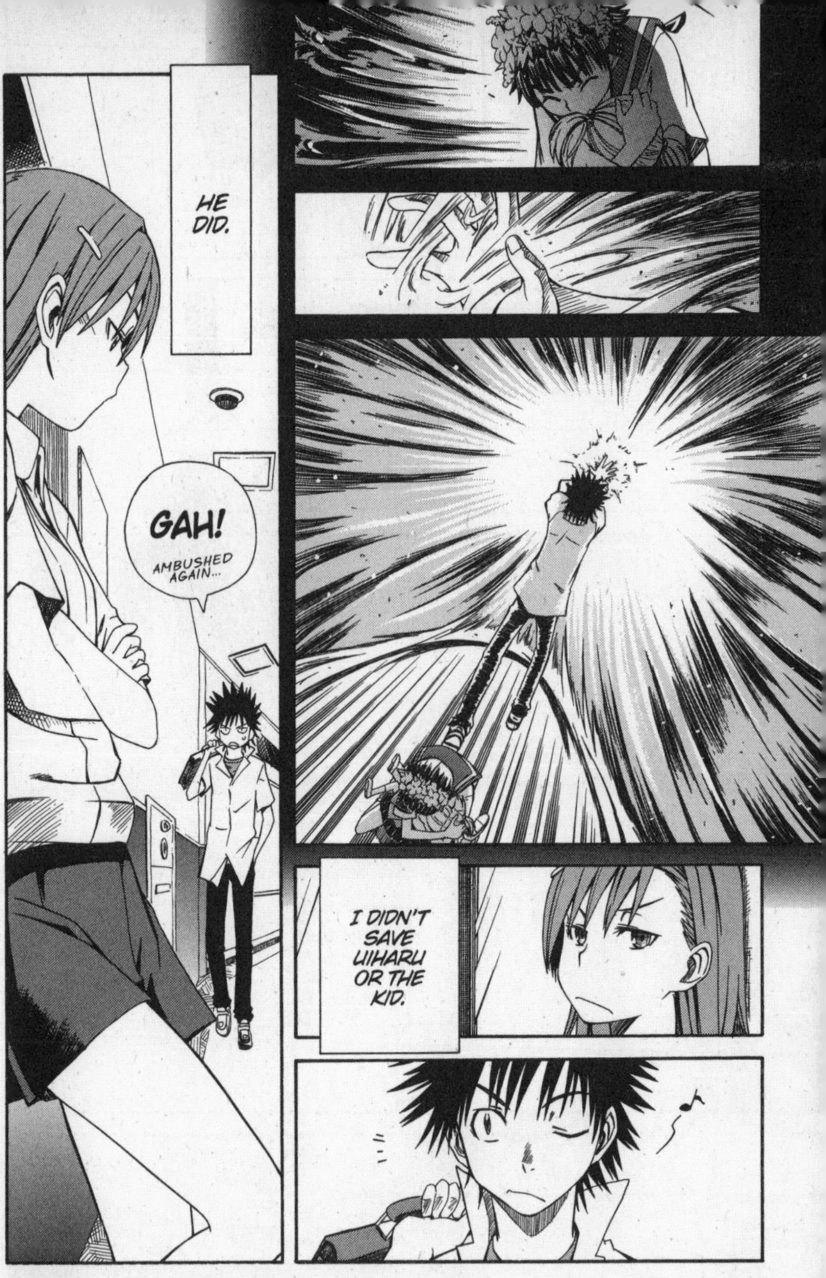
I DIDN'T SAVE UIHARU OR THE KID.
HE DID.
GAH!
AMBUSHED AGAIN...

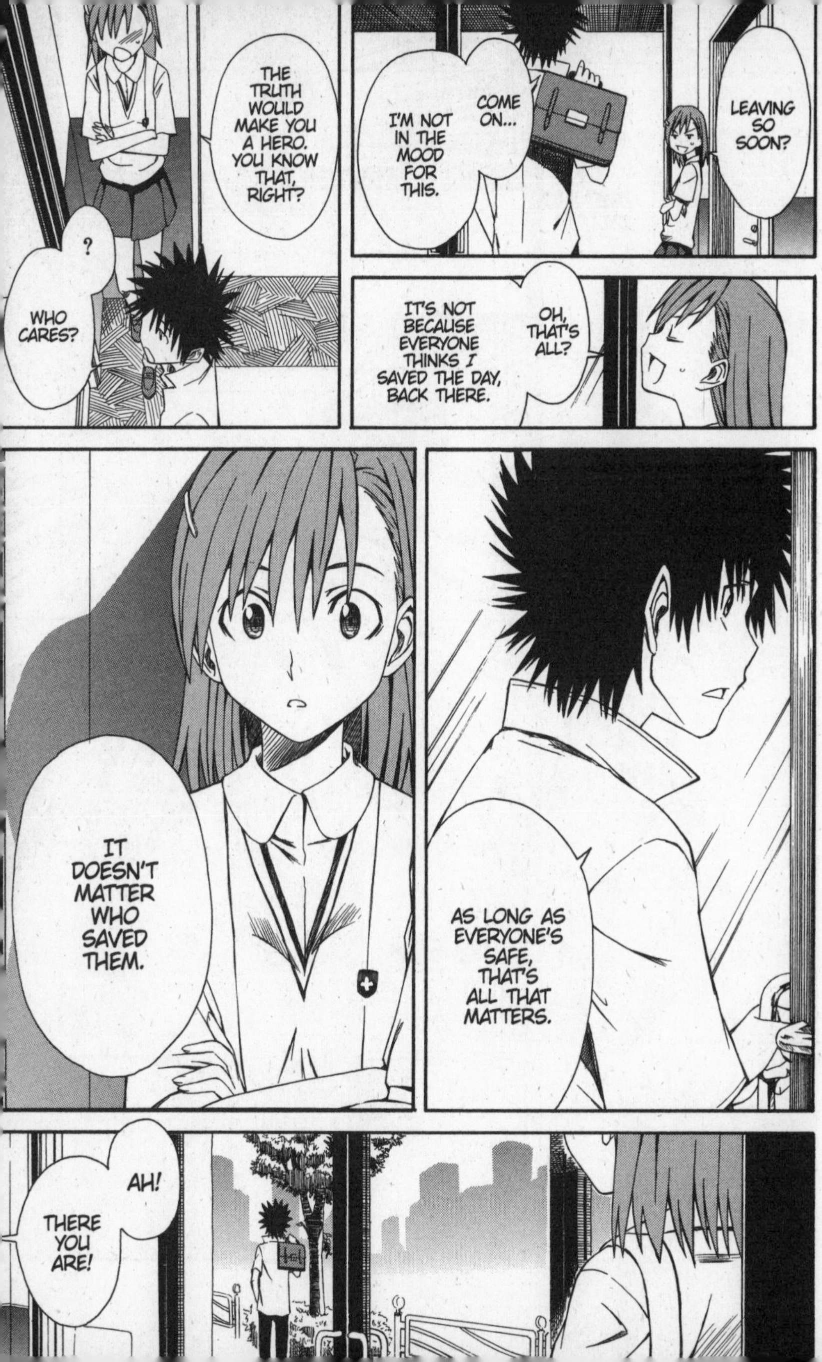
LEAVING SO SOON?
COME ON...
I'M NOT IN THE MOOD FOR THIS.
OH, THAT'S ALL?
IT'S NOT BECAUSE EVERYONE THINKS *I* SAVED THE DAY, BACK THERE.
THE TRUTH WOULD MAKE YOU A HERO. YOU KNOW THAT, RIGHT?
?
WHO CARES?
AS LONG AS EVERYONE'S SAFE, THAT'S ALL THAT MATTERS.
IT DOESN'T MATTER WHO SAVED THEM.
AH!
THERE YOU ARE!

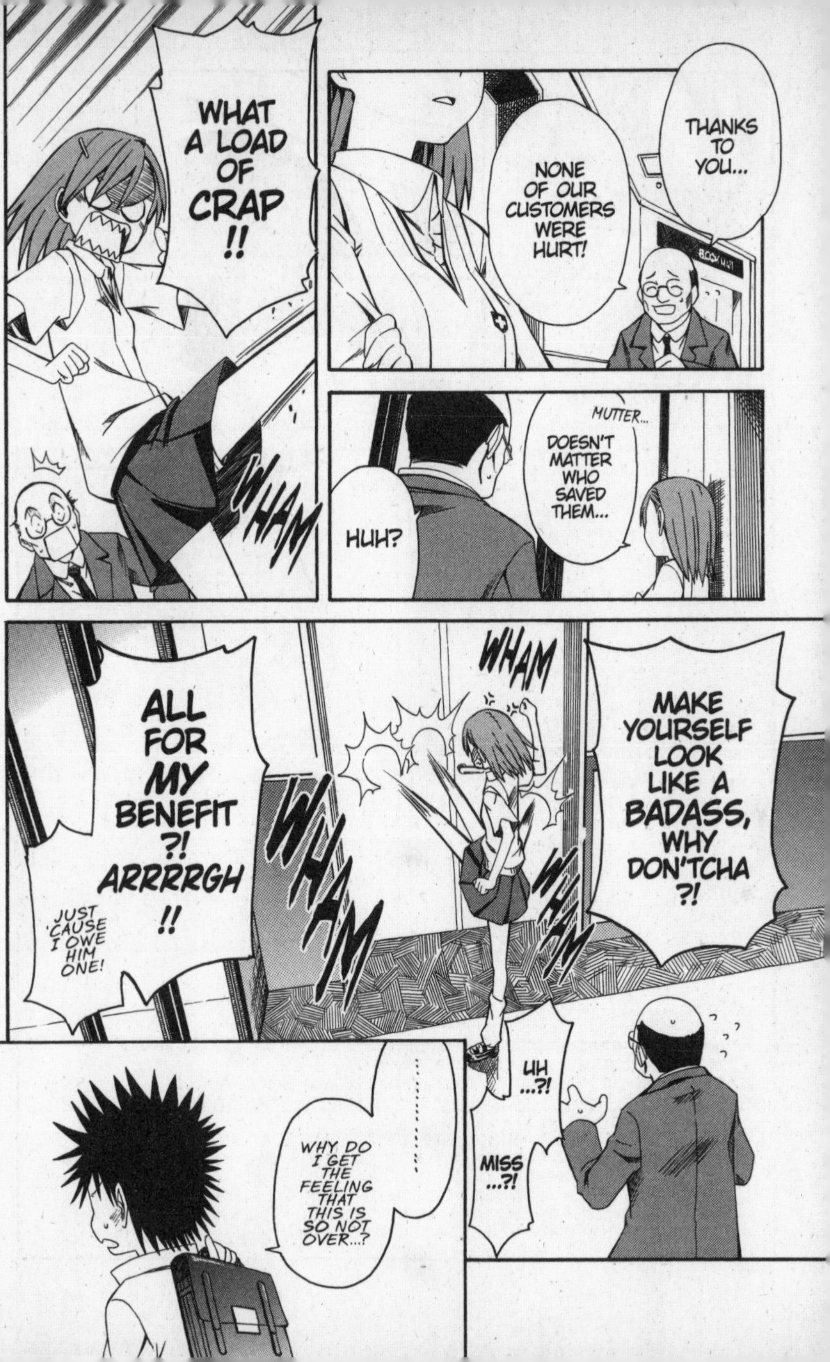
THANKS TO YOU...
NONE OF OUR CUSTOMERS WERE HURT!
MUTTER... DOESN'T MATTER WHO SAVED THEM...
HUH?
WHAT A LOAD OF CRAP!!
WHAM
MAKE YOURSELF LOOK LIKE A BADASS, WHY DON'TCHA?!
WHAM
WHAM
WHAM
ALL FOR MY BENEFIT?! ARRRRGH!!
JUST CAUSE I OWE HIM ONE!
UH...?!
MISS...?!
......
WHY DO I GET THE FEELING THAT THIS IS SO NOT OVER...?

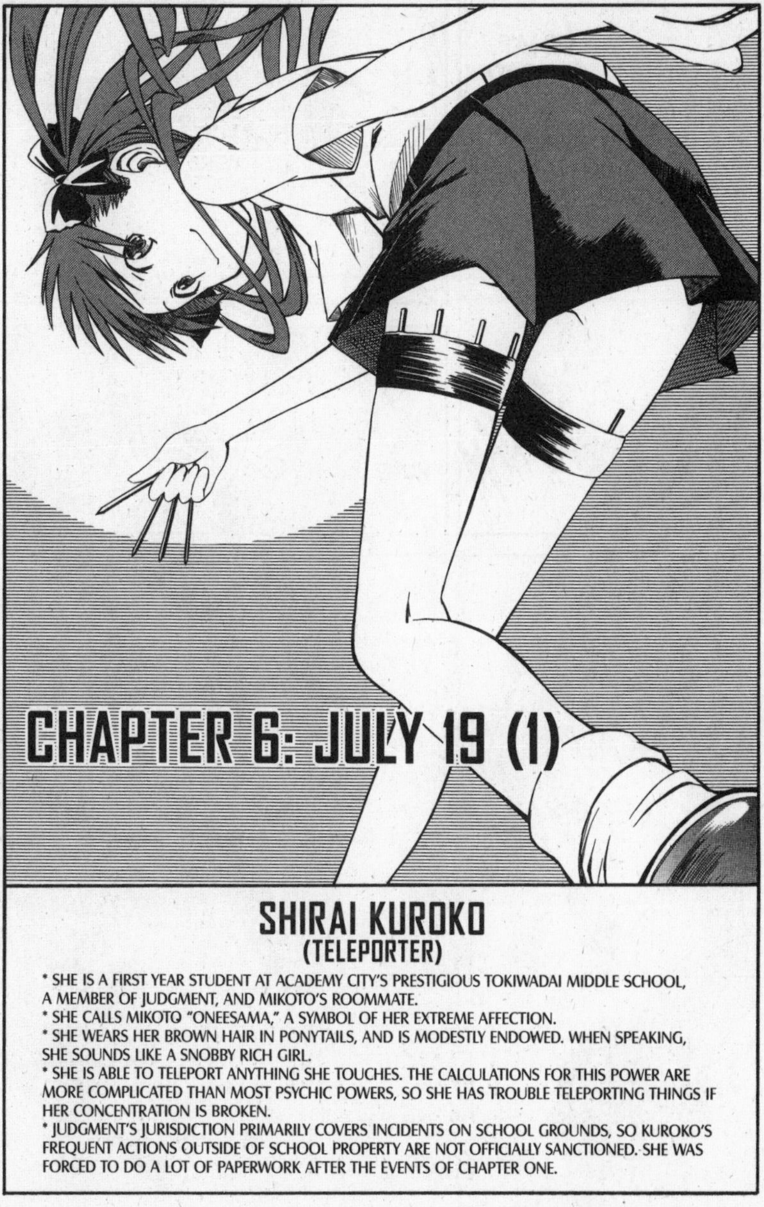
CHAPTER 6: JULY 19 (1)

SHIRAI KUROKO
(TELEPORTER)

* SHE IS A FIRST YEAR STUDENT AT ACADEMY CITY'S PRESTIGIOUS TOKIWADAI MIDDLE SCHOOL, A MEMBER OF JUDGMENT, AND MIKOTO'S ROOMMATE.
* SHE CALLS MIKOTO "ONEESAMA," A SYMBOL OF HER EXTREME AFFECTION.
* SHE WEARS HER BROWN HAIR IN PONYTAILS, AND IS MODESTLY ENDOWED. WHEN SPEAKING, SHE SOUNDS LIKE A SNOBBY RICH GIRL.
* SHE IS ABLE TO TELEPORT ANYTHING SHE TOUCHES. THE CALCULATIONS FOR THIS POWER ARE MORE COMPLICATED THAN MOST PSYCHIC POWERS, SO SHE HAS TROUBLE TELEPORTING THINGS IF HER CONCENTRATION IS BROKEN.
* JUDGMENT'S JURISDICTION PRIMARILY COVERS INCIDENTS ON SCHOOL GROUNDS, SO KUROKO'S FREQUENT ACTIONS OUTSIDE OF SCHOOL PROPERTY ARE NOT OFFICIALLY SANCTIONED. SHE WAS FORCED TO DO A LOT OF PAPERWORK AFTER THE EVENTS OF CHAPTER ONE.

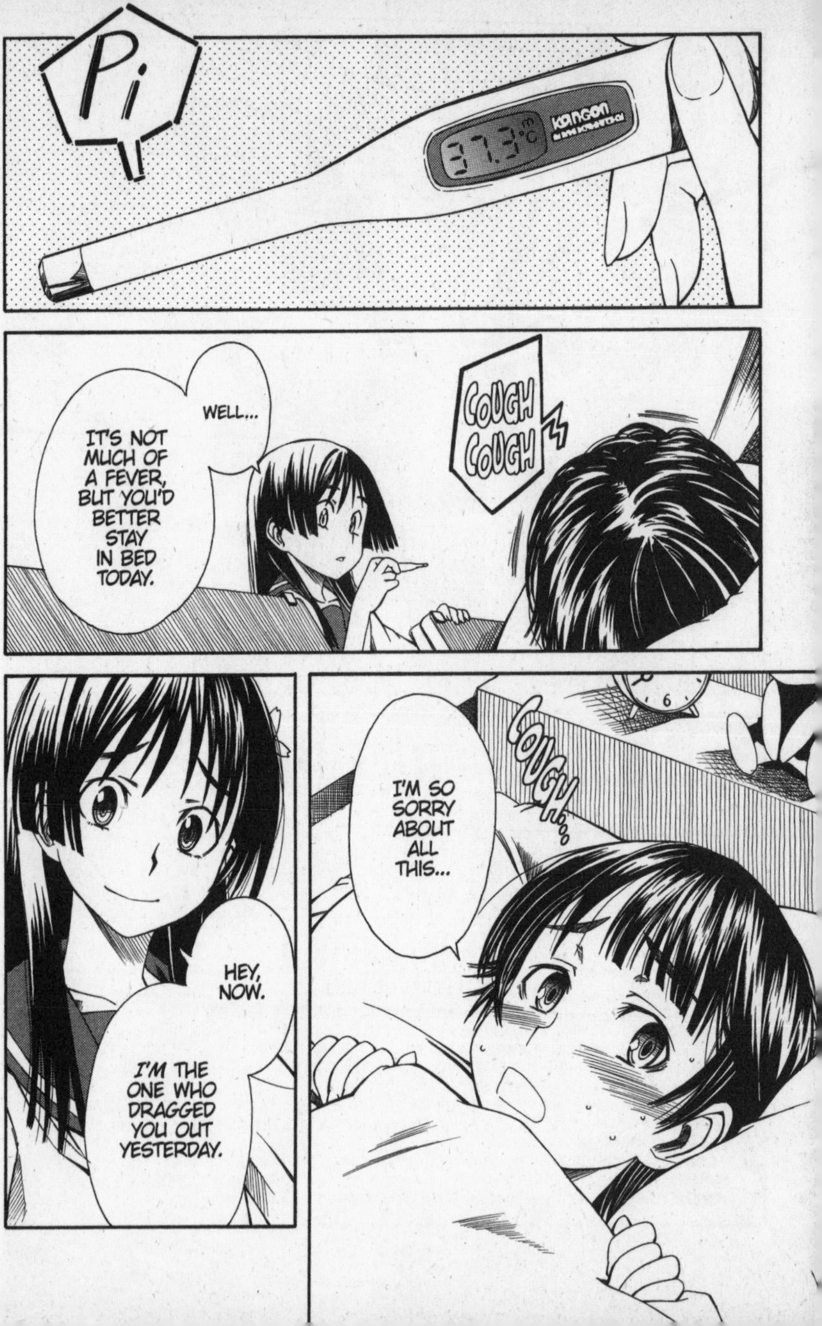
Pi
37.3°C
COUGH COUGH
WELL...
IT'S NOT MUCH OF A FEVER, BUT YOU'D BETTER STAY IN BED TODAY.
COUGH...
I'M SO SORRY ABOUT ALL THIS...
HEY, NOW.
I'M THE ONE WHO DRAGGED YOU OUT YESTERDAY.

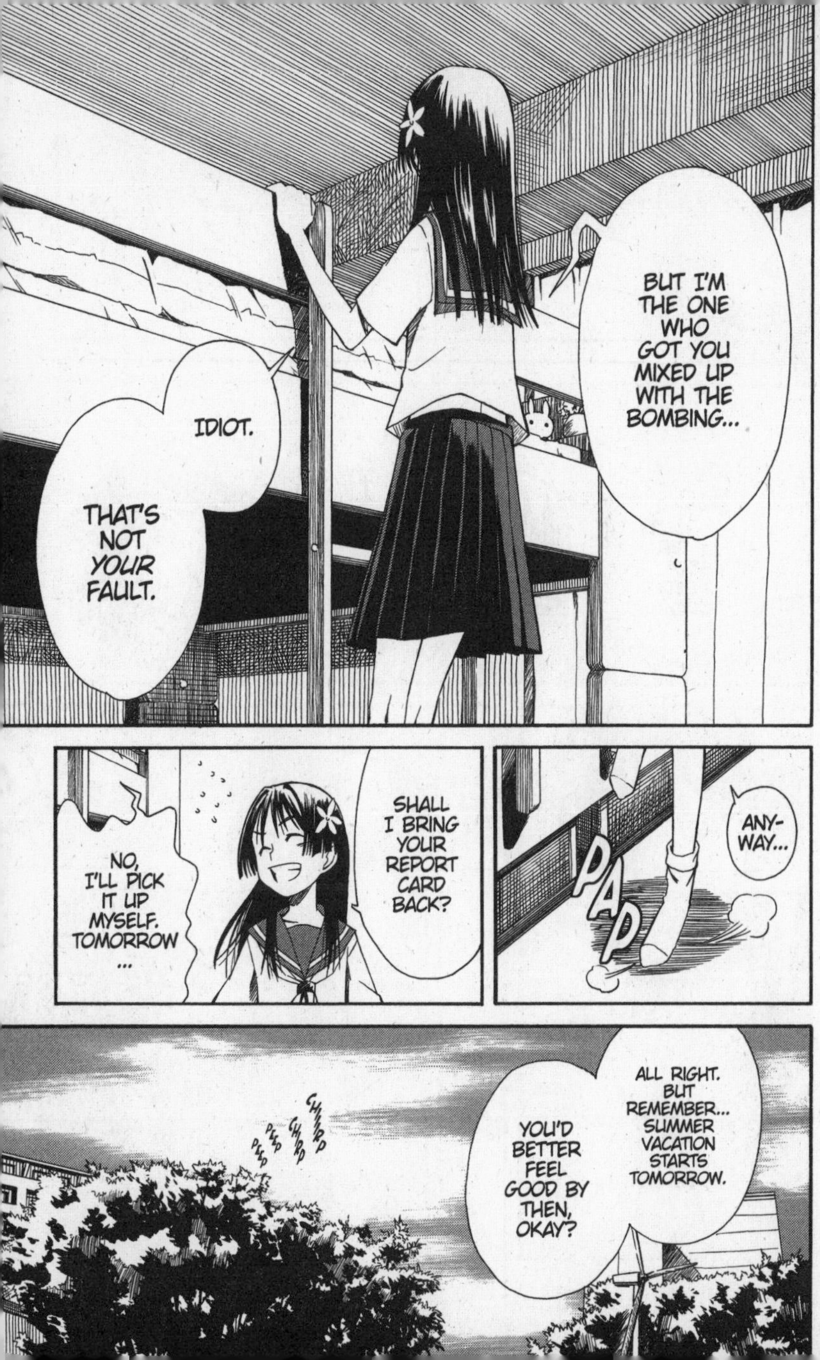
BUT I'M THE ONE WHO GOT YOU MIXED UP WITH THE BOMBING...
IDIOT.
THAT'S NOT *YOUR* FAULT.
ANY-WAY...
PAP
SHALL I BRING YOUR REPORT CARD BACK?
NO, I'LL PICK IT UP MYSELF. TOMORROW ...
ALL RIGHT. BUT REMEMBER... SUMMER VACATION STARTS TOMORROW.
YOU'D BETTER FEEL GOOD BY THEN, OKAY?
CHIRP
CHIRP
PEEP
PEEP

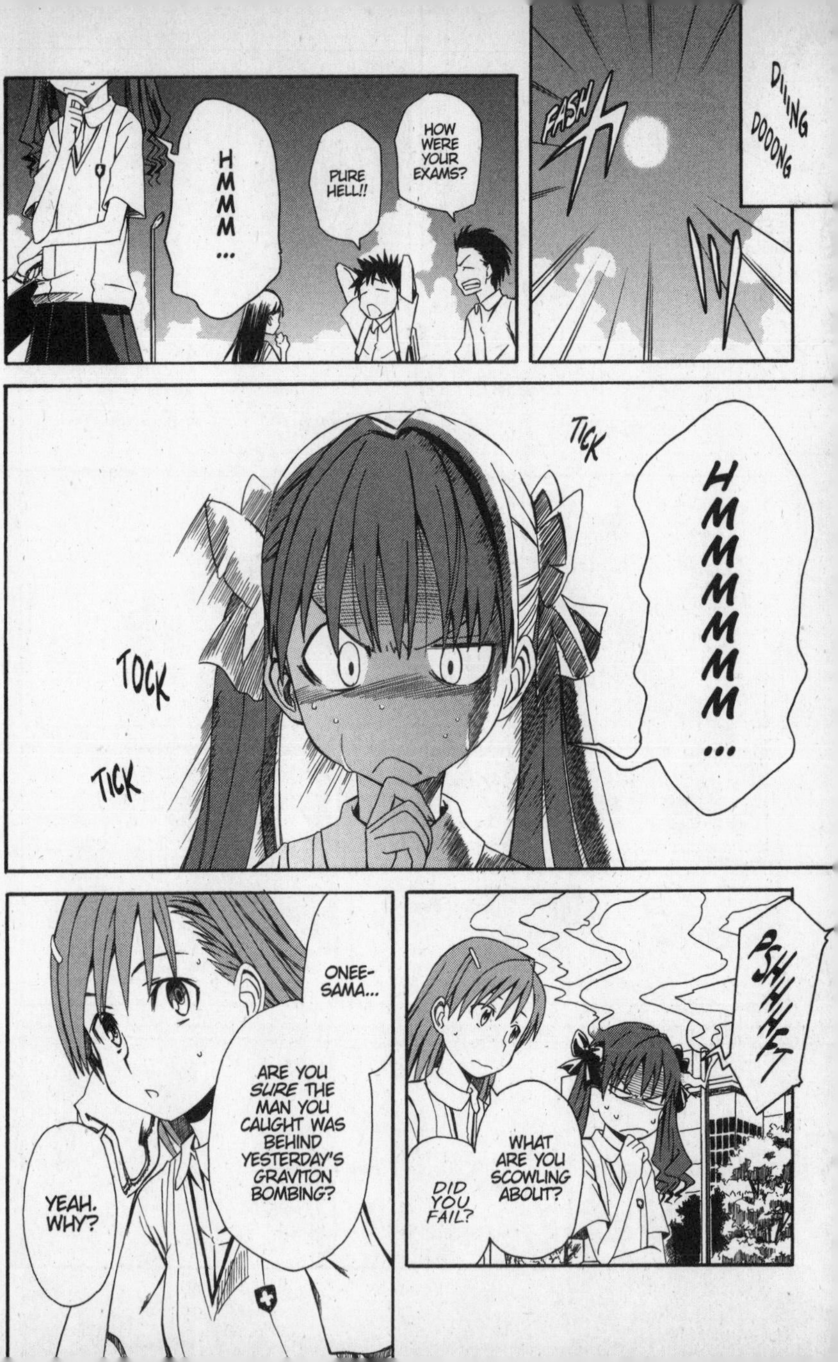
FASH
DIIIING DOOONG
HOW WERE YOUR EXAMS?
PURE HELL!!
HMMM...
TICK
HMMMMMMM...
TOCK
TICK
PSHHHFT
WHAT ARE YOU SCOWLING ABOUT?
DID YOU FAIL?
ONEE-SAMA...
ARE YOU SURE THE MAN YOU CAUGHT WAS BEHIND YESTERDAY'S GRAVITON BOMBING?
YEAH. WHY?

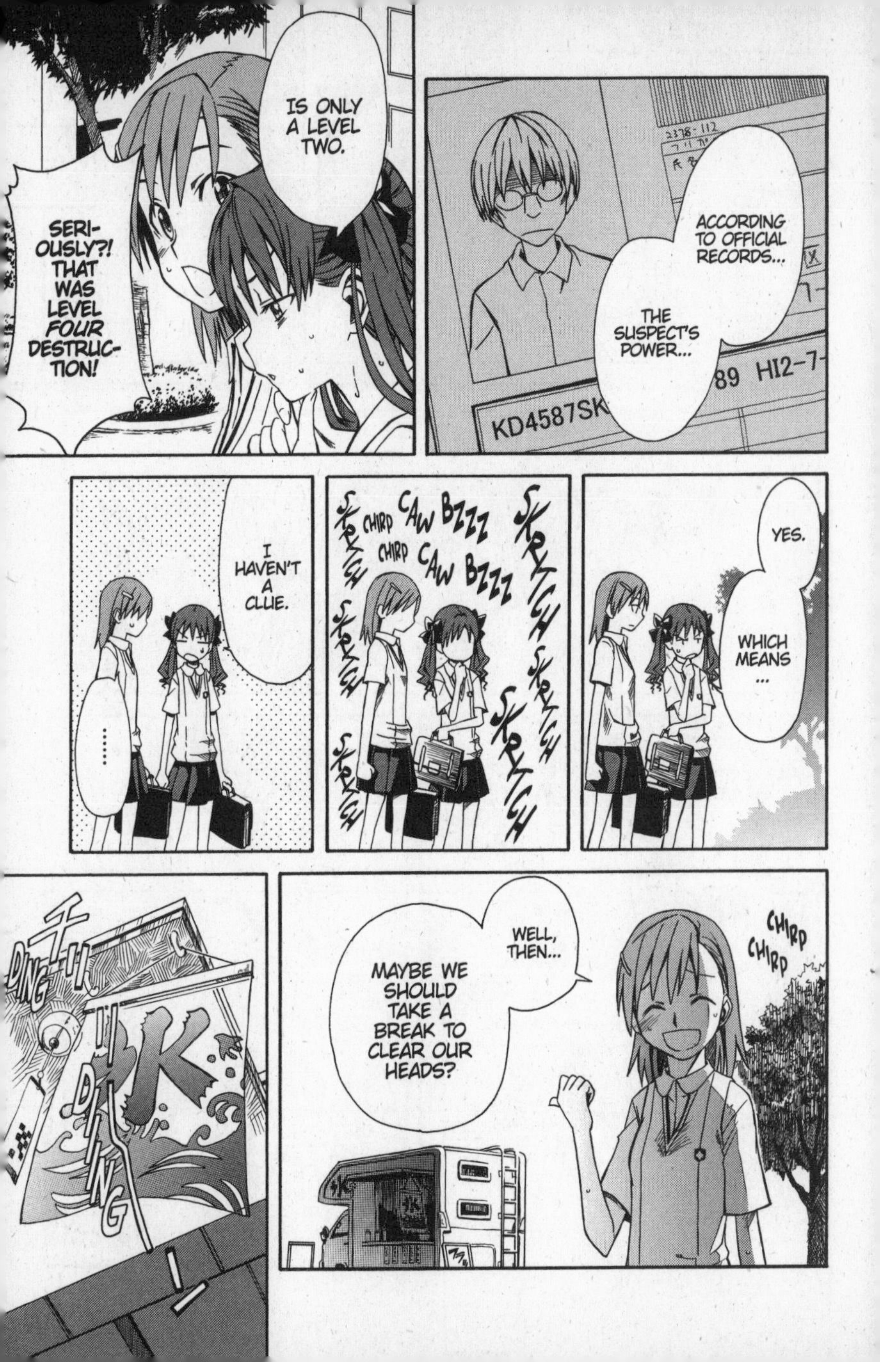
ACCORDING TO OFFICIAL RECORDS...
THE SUSPECT'S POWER...
KD4587SK
89 HI2-7-
IS ONLY A LEVEL TWO.
SERI-OUSLY?! THAT WAS LEVEL FOUR DESTRUC-TION!
YES.
WHICH MEANS ...
SKRYTCH SKRYTCH CHIRP CHIRP CAW CAW BZZZ BZZZ SKRYTCH SKRYTCH SKRYTCH SKRYTCH
I HAVEN'T A CLUE.
......
WELL, THEN...
MAYBE WE SHOULD TAKE A BREAK TO CLEAR OUR HEADS?
CHIRP CHIRP
DING DING DING

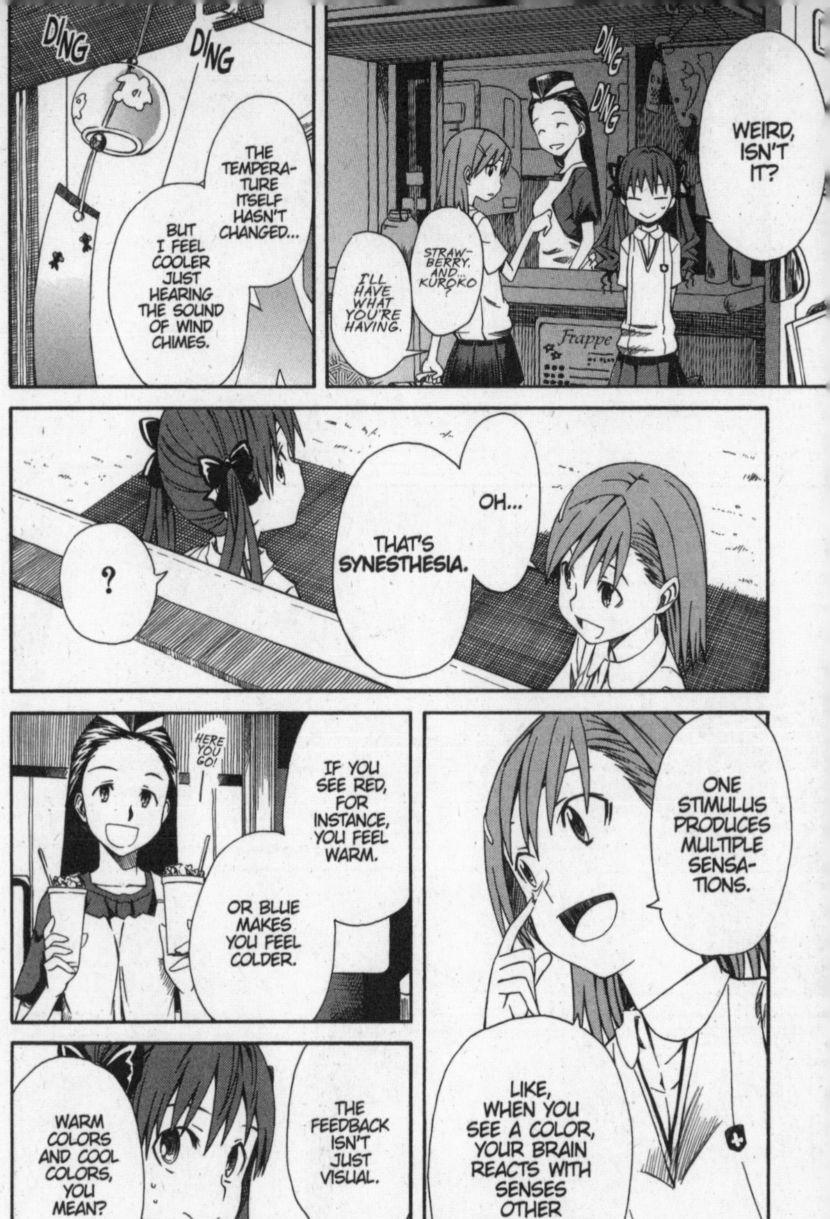
DING
DING
WEIRD, ISN'T IT?
STRAWBERRY. AND... KUROKO?
I'LL HAVE WHAT YOU'RE HAVING.
Frappe
DING
DING
THE TEMPERATURE ITSELF HASN'T CHANGED...
BUT I FEEL COOLER JUST HEARING THE SOUND OF WIND CHIMES.
OH...
THAT'S SYNESTHESIA.
?
ONE STIMULUS PRODUCES MULTIPLE SENSATIONS.
LIKE, WHEN YOU SEE A COLOR, YOUR BRAIN REACTS WITH SENSES OTHER THAN SIGHT ALONE.
IF YOU SEE RED, FOR INSTANCE, YOU FEEL WARM.
OR BLUE MAKES YOU FEEL COLDER.
HERE YOU GO!
THE FEEDBACK ISN'T JUST VISUAL.
WARM COLORS AND COOL COLORS, YOU MEAN?

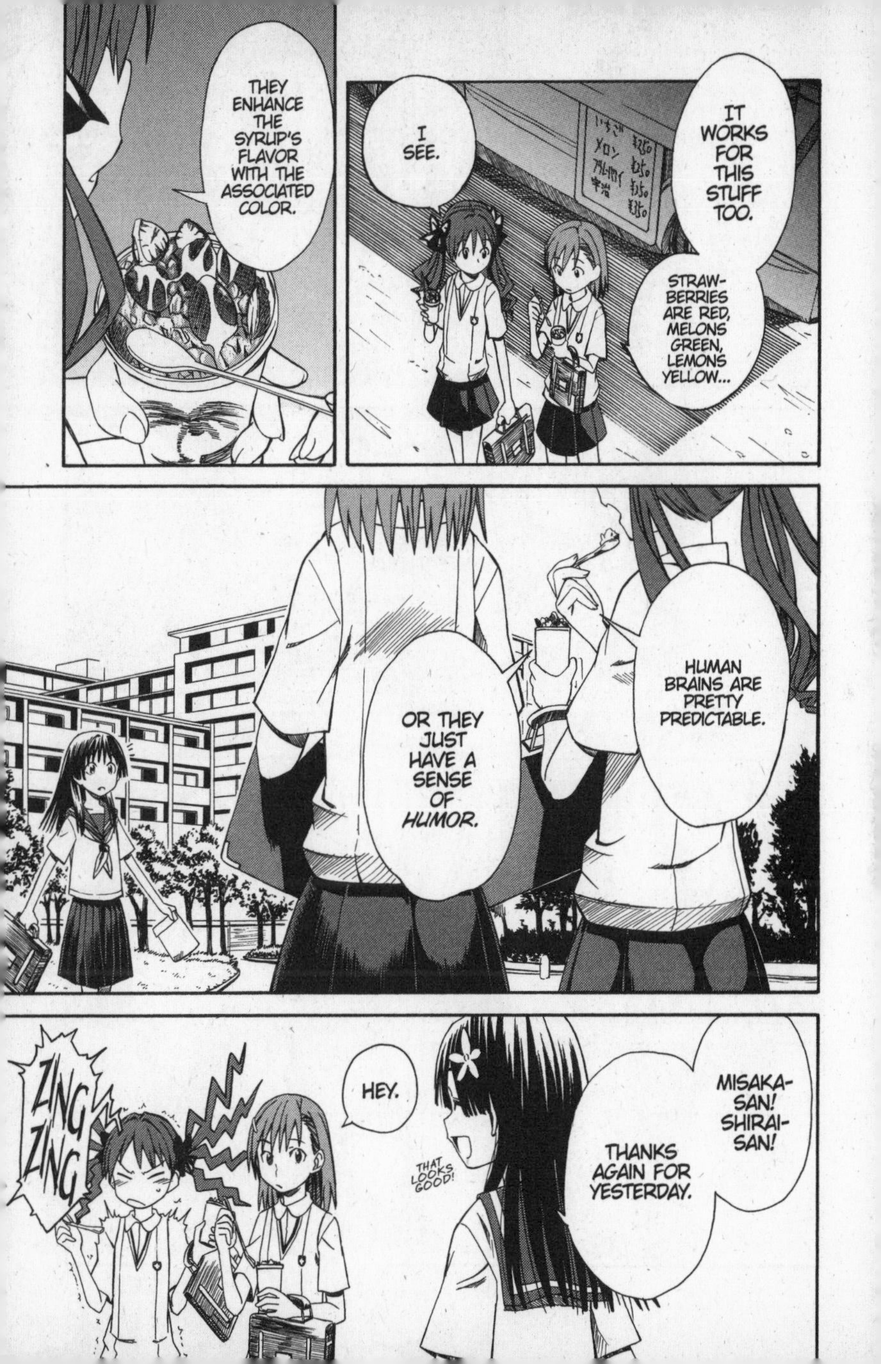
IT WORKS FOR THIS STUFF TOO.
STRAW-BERRIES ARE RED, MELONS GREEN, LEMONS YELLOW...
I SEE.
THEY ENHANCE THE SYRUP'S FLAVOR WITH THE ASSOCIATED COLOR.
HUMAN BRAINS ARE PRETTY PREDICTABLE.
OR THEY JUST HAVE A SENSE OF *HUMOR.*
MISAKA-SAN! SHIRAI-SAN!
THANKS AGAIN FOR YESTERDAY.
THAT LOOKS GOOD!
HEY.
ZING ZING

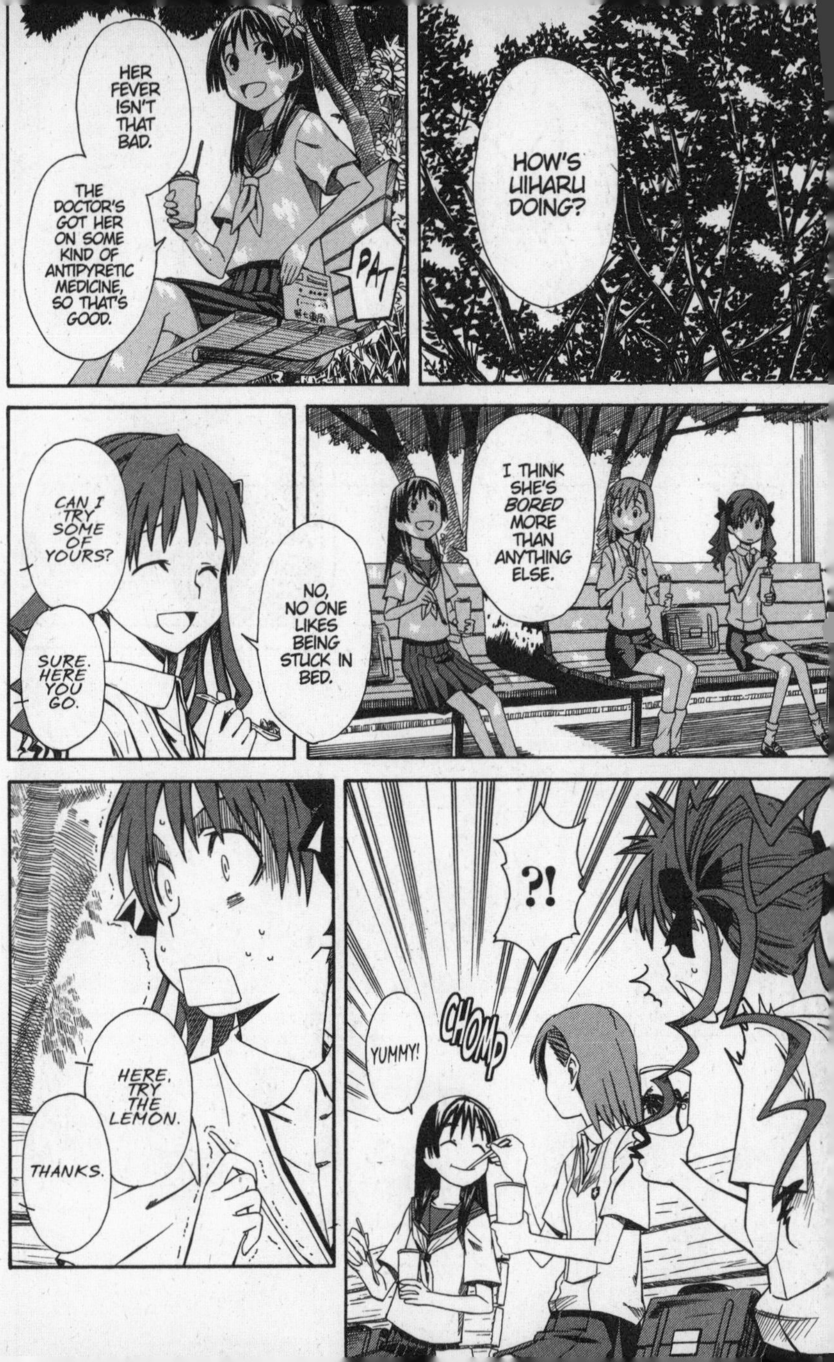
HOW'S UIHARU DOING?
HER FEVER ISN'T THAT BAD.
THE DOCTOR'S GOT HER ON SOME KIND OF ANTIPYRETIC MEDICINE, SO THAT'S GOOD.
PAT
I THINK SHE'S BORED MORE THAN ANYTHING ELSE.
NO, NO ONE LIKES BEING STUCK IN BED.
CAN I TRY SOME OF YOURS?
SURE. HERE YOU GO.
?!
CHOMP
YUMMY!
HERE, TRY THE LEMON.
THANKS.

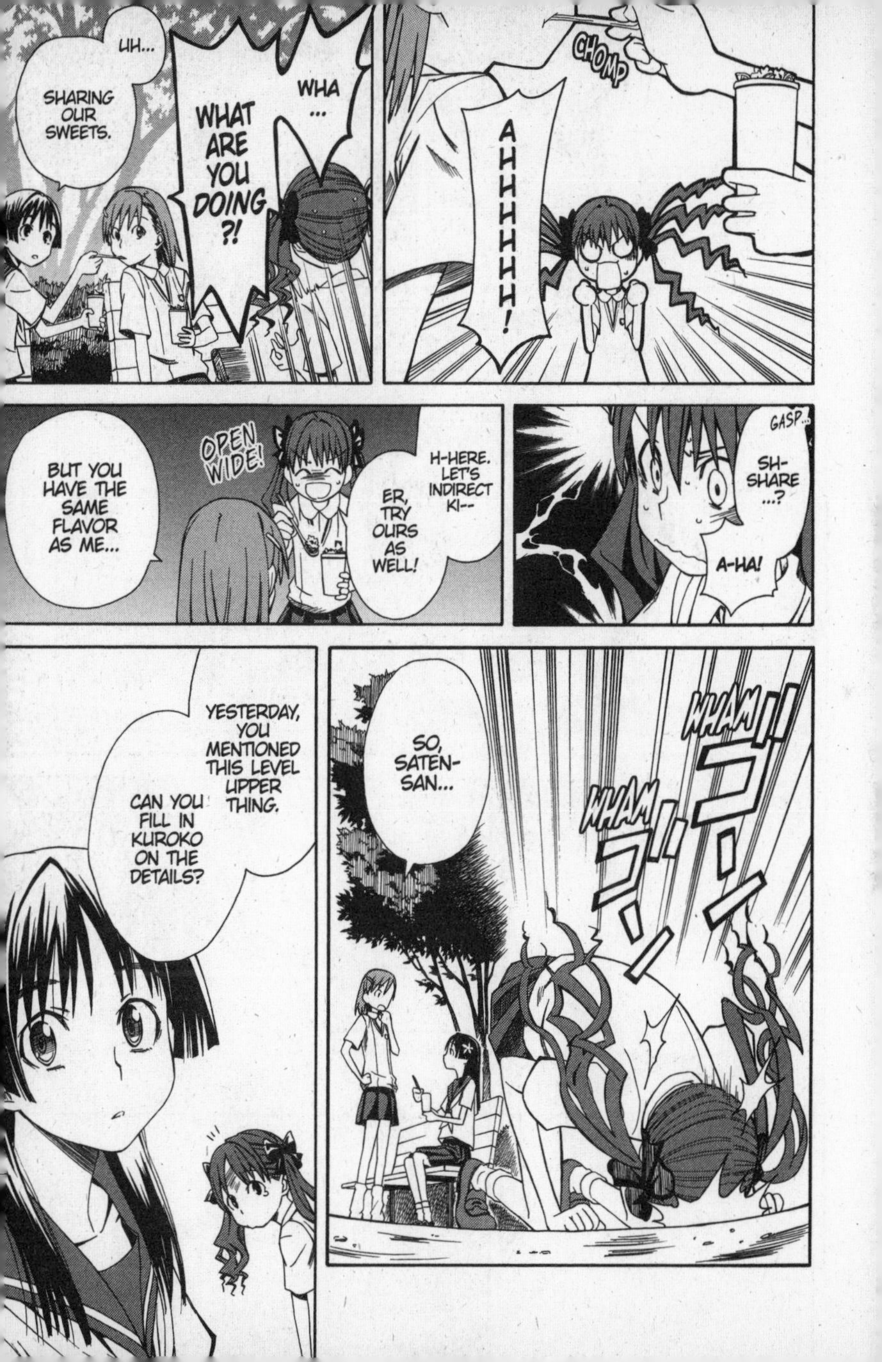
CHOMP
AHHHHHH!
WHA...
WHAT ARE YOU DOING?!
UH...
SHARING OUR SWEETS.
GASP...
SH-SHARE...?
A-HA!
H-HERE. LET'S INDIRECT KI--
ER, TRY OURS AS WELL!
OPEN WIDE!
BUT YOU HAVE THE SAME FLAVOR AS ME...
WHAM!!
WHAM!!
SO, SATEN-SAN...
YESTERDAY, YOU MENTIONED THIS LEVEL UPPER THING.
CAN YOU FILL IN KUROKO ON THE DETAILS?

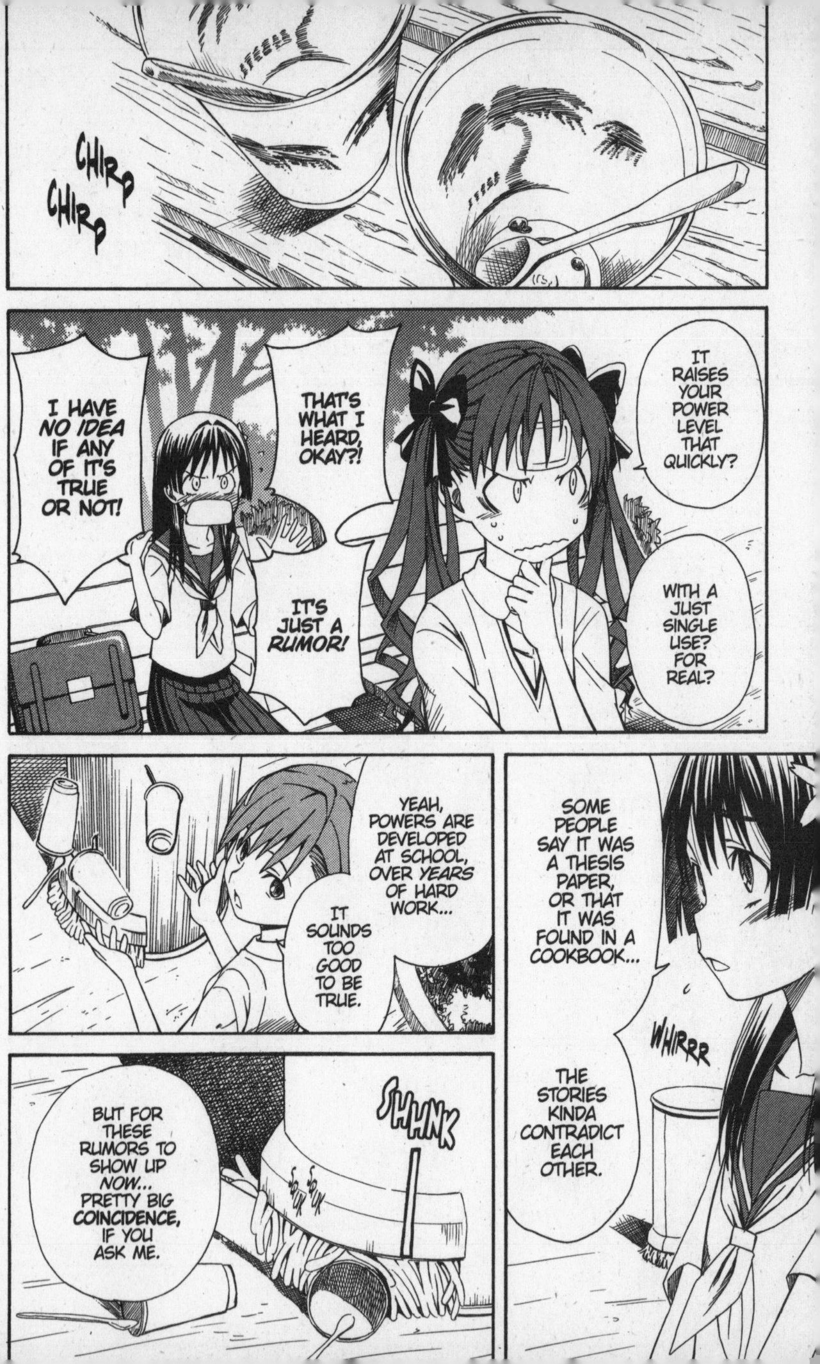
CHIRP
CHIRP
IT RAISES YOUR POWER LEVEL THAT QUICKLY?
WITH A JUST SINGLE USE? FOR REAL?
THAT'S WHAT I HEARD, OKAY?!
IT'S JUST A RUMOR!
I HAVE NO IDEA IF ANY OF IT'S TRUE OR NOT!
SOME PEOPLE SAY IT WAS A THESIS PAPER, OR THAT IT WAS FOUND IN A COOKBOOK...
WHIRRR
THE STORIES KINDA CONTRADICT EACH OTHER.
YEAH, POWERS ARE DEVELOPED AT SCHOOL, OVER YEARS OF HARD WORK...
IT SOUNDS TOO GOOD TO BE TRUE.
SHHUNK
BUT FOR THESE RUMORS TO SHOW UP NOW... PRETTY BIG COINCIDENCE, IF YOU ASK ME.

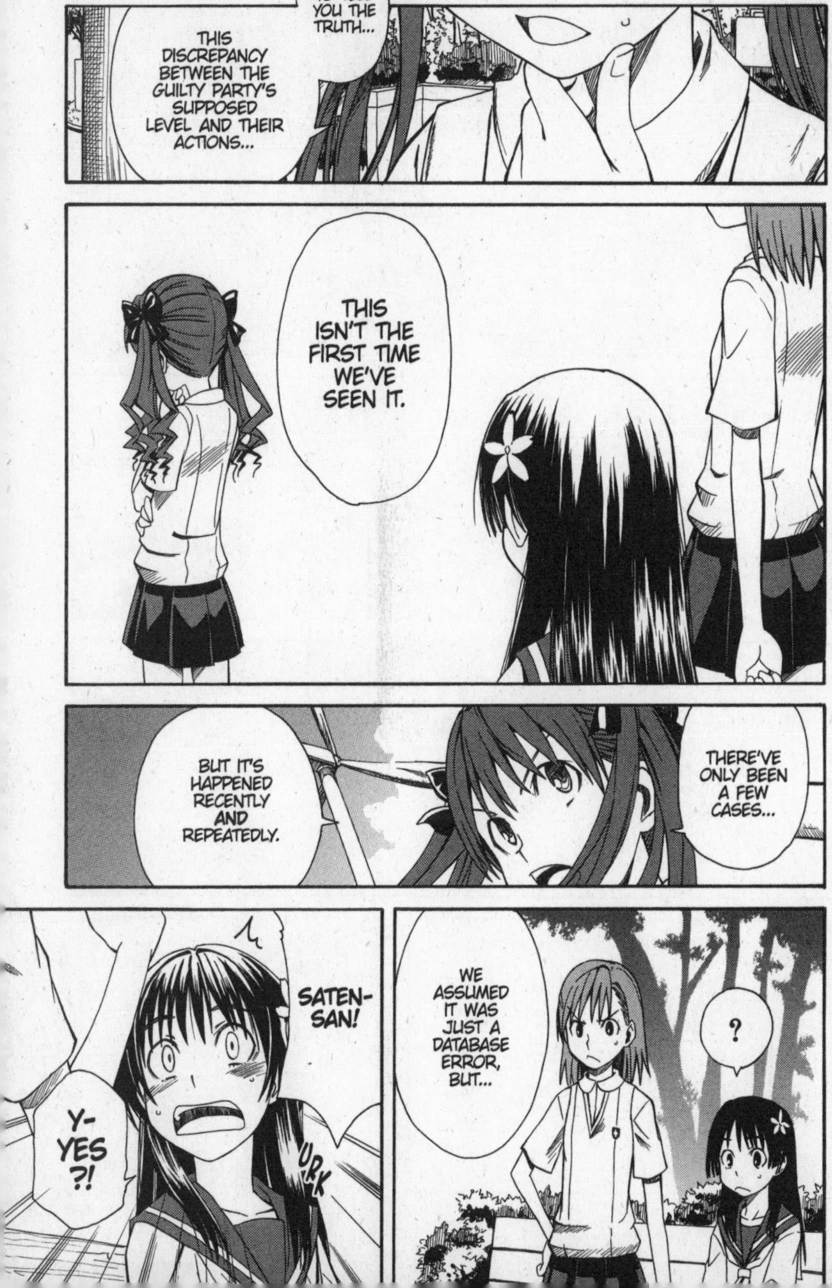
TO TELL YOU THE TRUTH...
THIS DISCREPANCY BETWEEN THE GUILTY PARTY'S SUPPOSED LEVEL AND THEIR ACTIONS...
THIS ISN'T THE FIRST TIME WE'VE SEEN IT.
THERE'VE ONLY BEEN A FEW CASES...
BUT IT'S HAPPENED RECENTLY AND REPEATEDLY.
WE ASSUMED IT WAS JUST A DATABASE ERROR, BUT...
?
SATEN-SAN!
Y-YES?!
URK

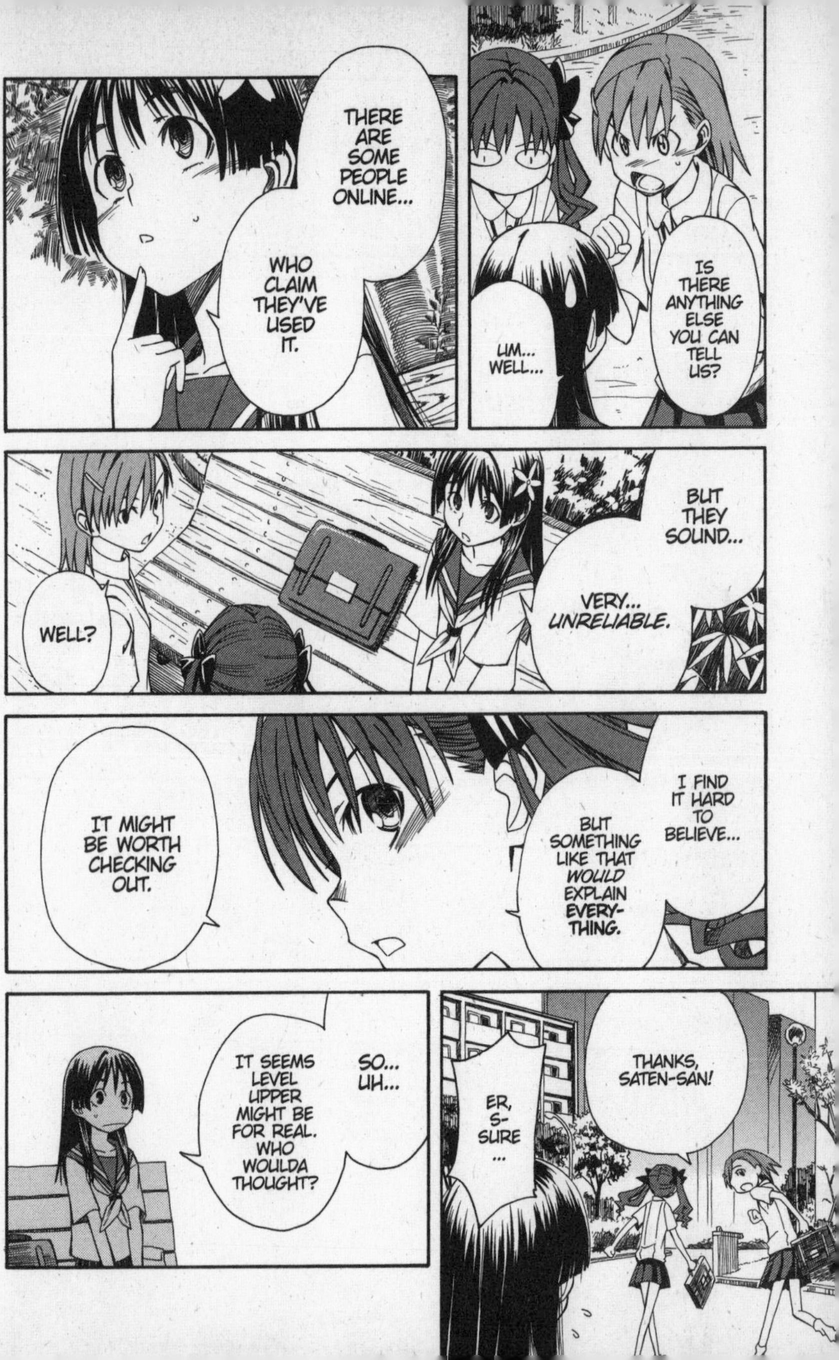
IS THERE ANYTHING ELSE YOU CAN TELL US?
UM... WELL...
THERE ARE SOME PEOPLE ONLINE...
WHO CLAIM THEY'VE USED IT.
BUT THEY SOUND...
VERY... UNRELIABLE.
WELL?
I FIND IT HARD TO BELIEVE...
BUT SOMETHING LIKE THAT WOULD EXPLAIN EVERYTHING.
IT MIGHT BE WORTH CHECKING OUT.
THANKS, SATEN-SAN!
ER, S-SURE ...
SO... UH...
IT SEEMS LEVEL UPPER MIGHT BE FOR REAL. WHO WOULDA THOUGHT?

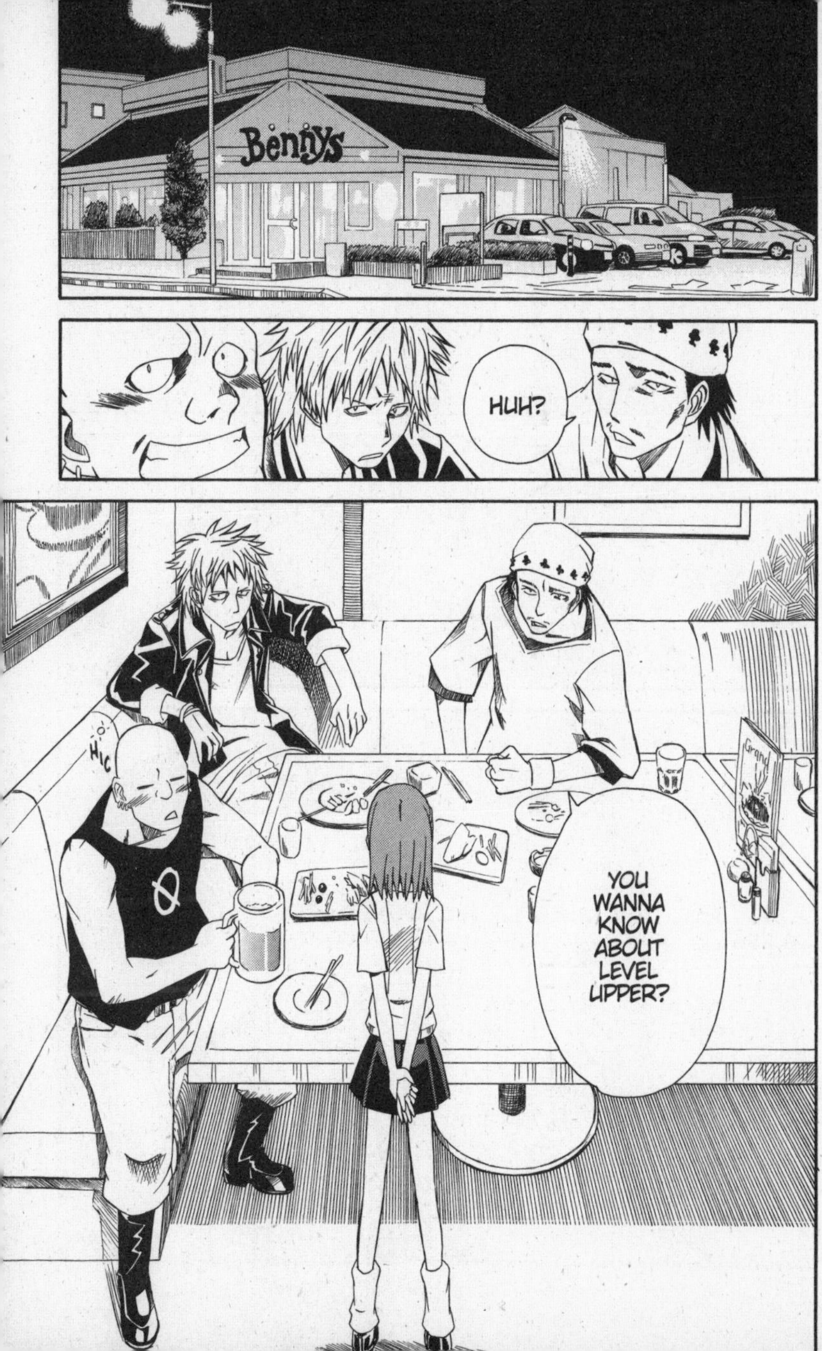
Bennys
HUH?
Grand
YOU WANNA KNOW ABOUT LEVEL UPPER?
HIC

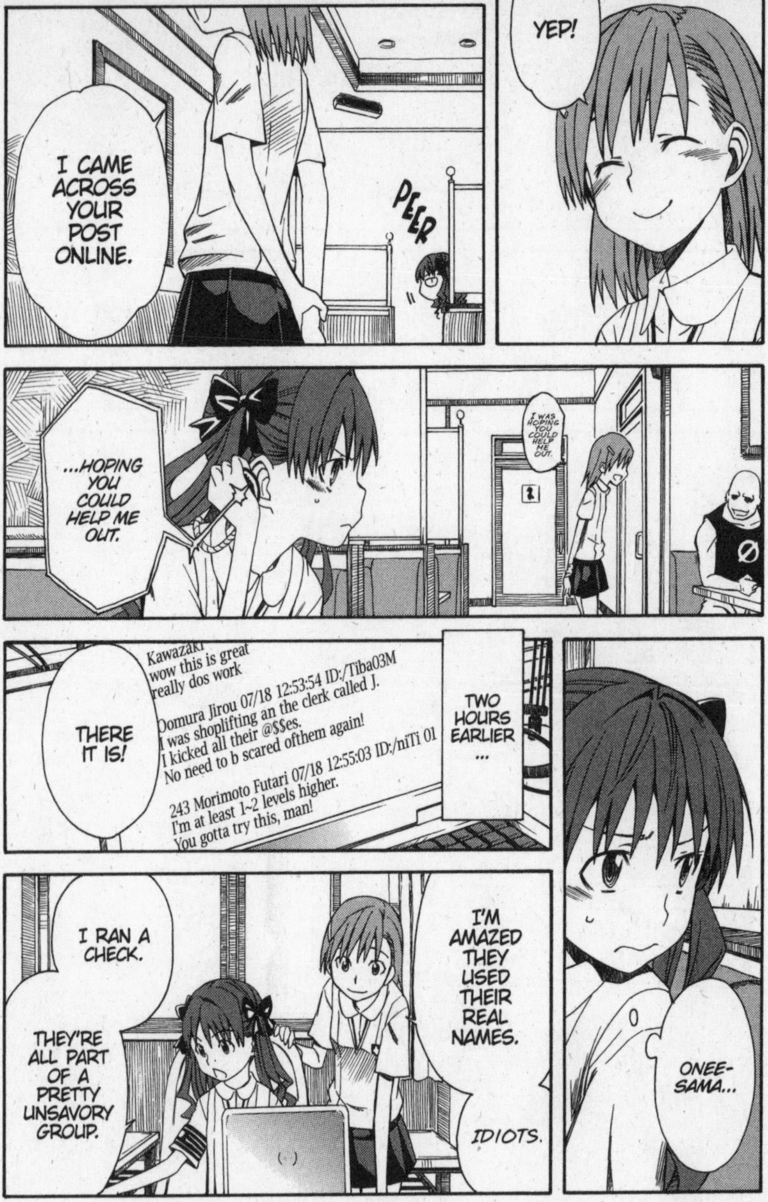
YEP!
I CAME ACROSS YOUR POST ONLINE.
PEER
I WAS HOPING YOU COULD HELP ME OUT.
...HOPING YOU COULD HELP ME OUT.
ONEE-SAMA...
TWO HOURS EARLIER ...
Kawazaki
wow this is great
really dos work
Oomura Jirou 07/18 12:53:54 ID:/Tiba03M
I was shoplifting an the clerk called J.
I kicked all their @$$es.
No need to b scared ofthem again!
Morimoto Futari 07/18 12:55:03 ID:/niTi 01
243 Morimoto Futari 07/18 12:55:03 ID:/niTi 01
I'm at least 1~2 levels higher.
You gotta try this, man!
THERE IT IS!
I'M AMAZED THEY USED THEIR REAL NAMES.
IDIOTS.
I RAN A CHECK.
THEY'RE ALL PART OF A PRETTY UNSAVORY GROUP.

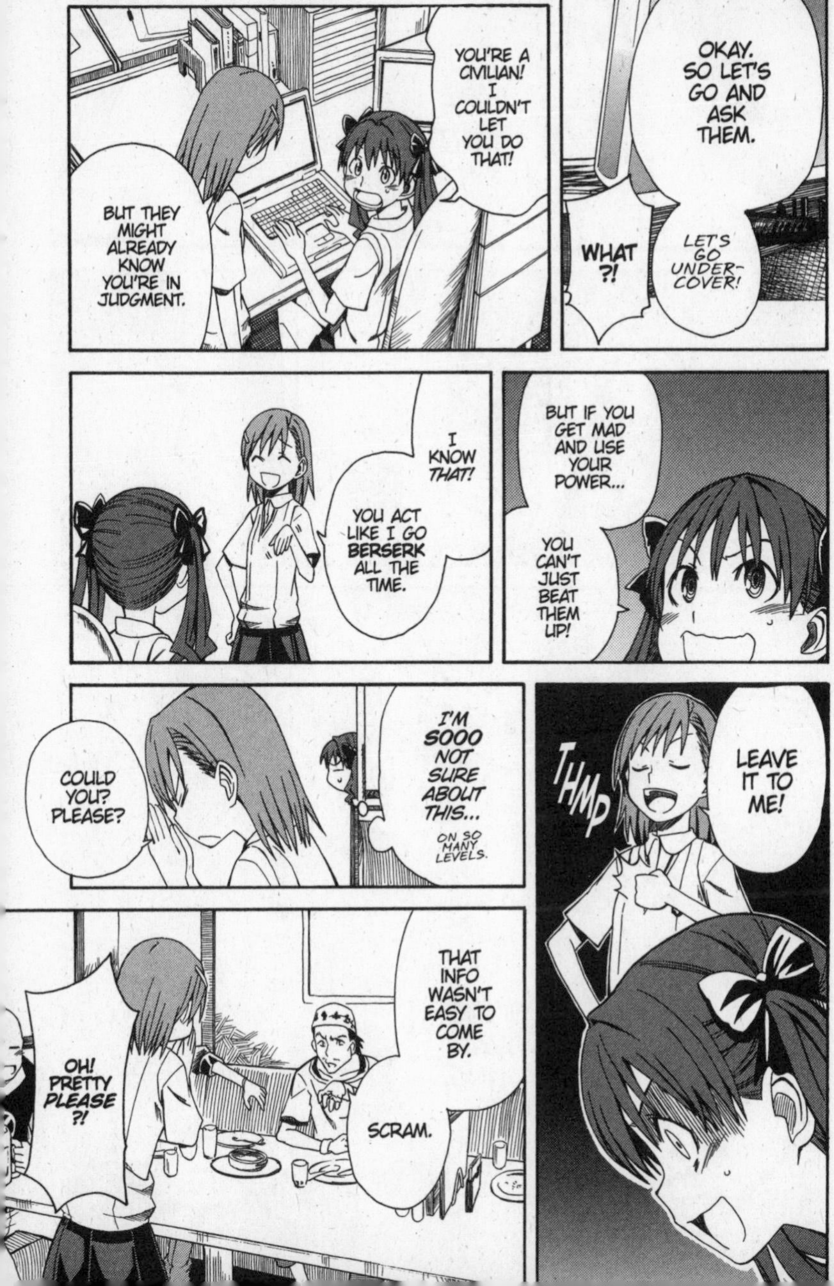
OKAY. SO LET'S GO AND ASK THEM.
LET'S GO UNDER-COVER!
WHAT?!
YOU'RE A CIVILIAN! I COULDN'T LET YOU DO THAT!
BUT THEY MIGHT ALREADY KNOW YOU'RE IN JUDGMENT.
BUT IF YOU GET MAD AND USE YOUR POWER...
YOU CAN'T JUST BEAT THEM UP!
I KNOW THAT!
YOU ACT LIKE I GO BERSERK ALL THE TIME.
LEAVE IT TO ME!
THMP
I'M SOOO NOT SURE ABOUT THIS...
ON SO MANY LEVELS.
COULD YOU? PLEASE?
THAT INFO WASN'T EASY TO COME BY.
SCRAM.
OH! PRETTY PLEASE?!

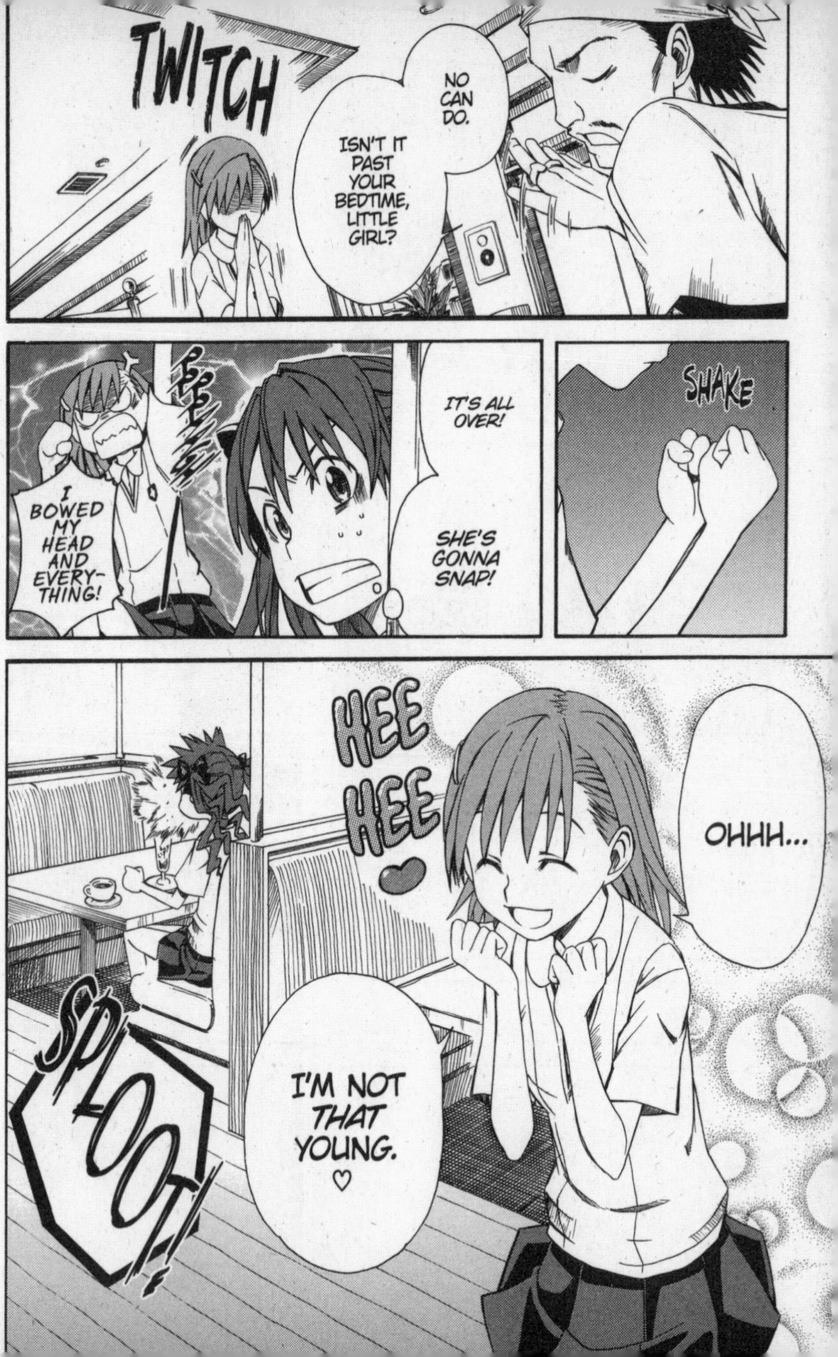
NO CAN DO.
ISN'T IT PAST YOUR BEDTIME, LITTLE GIRL?
TWITCH
SHAKE
IT'S ALL OVER!
SHE'S GONNA SNAP!
I BOWED MY HEAD AND EVERY-THING!
OHHH...
HEE HEE
I'M NOT *THAT* YOUNG. ♡
SPLOOT!

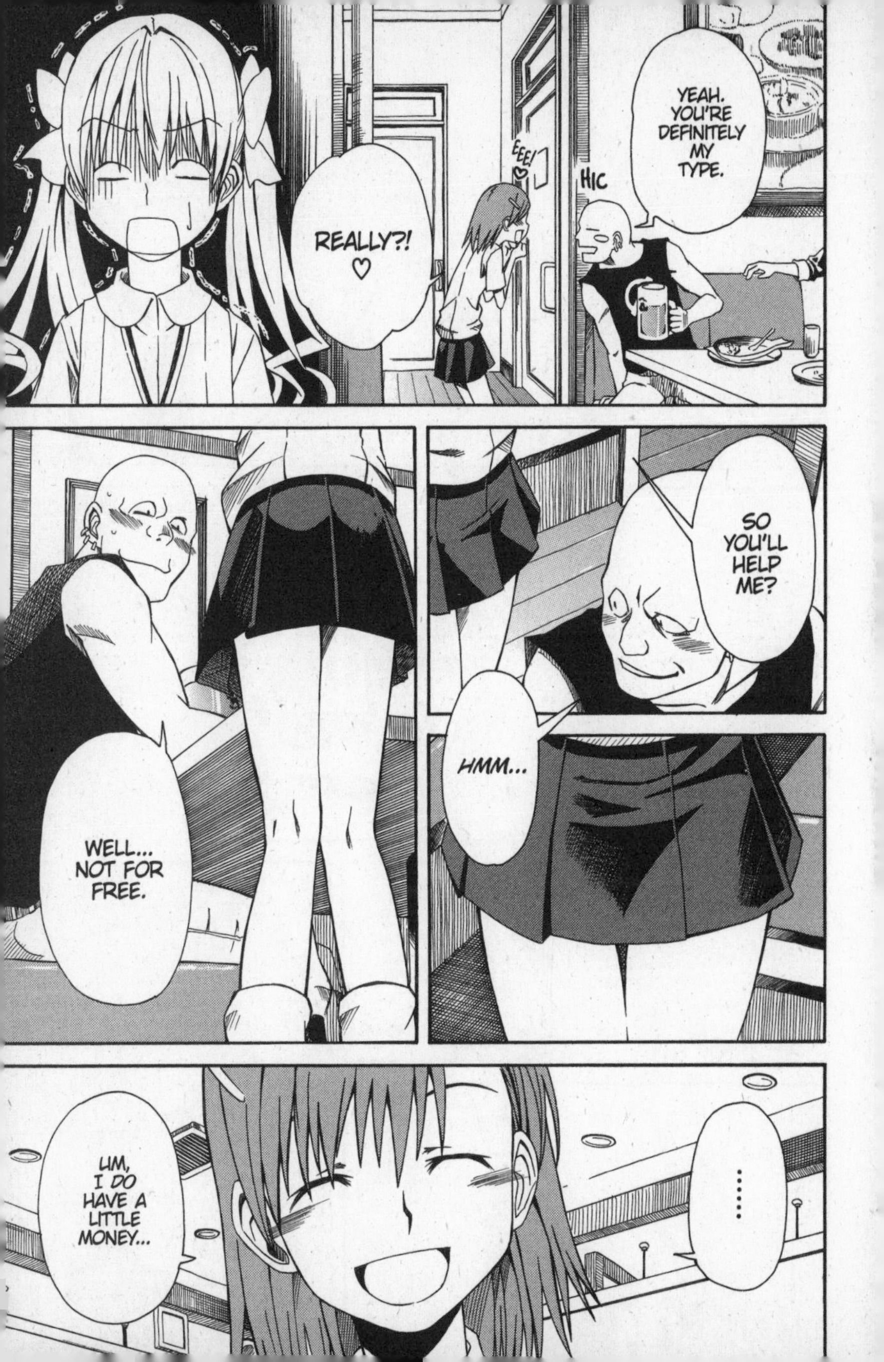
YEAH. YOU'RE DEFINITELY MY TYPE.
HIC
EEE! ♡
REALLY?! ♡
SO YOU'LL HELP ME?
HMM...
WELL... NOT FOR FREE.
......
UM, I DO HAVE A LITTLE MONEY...

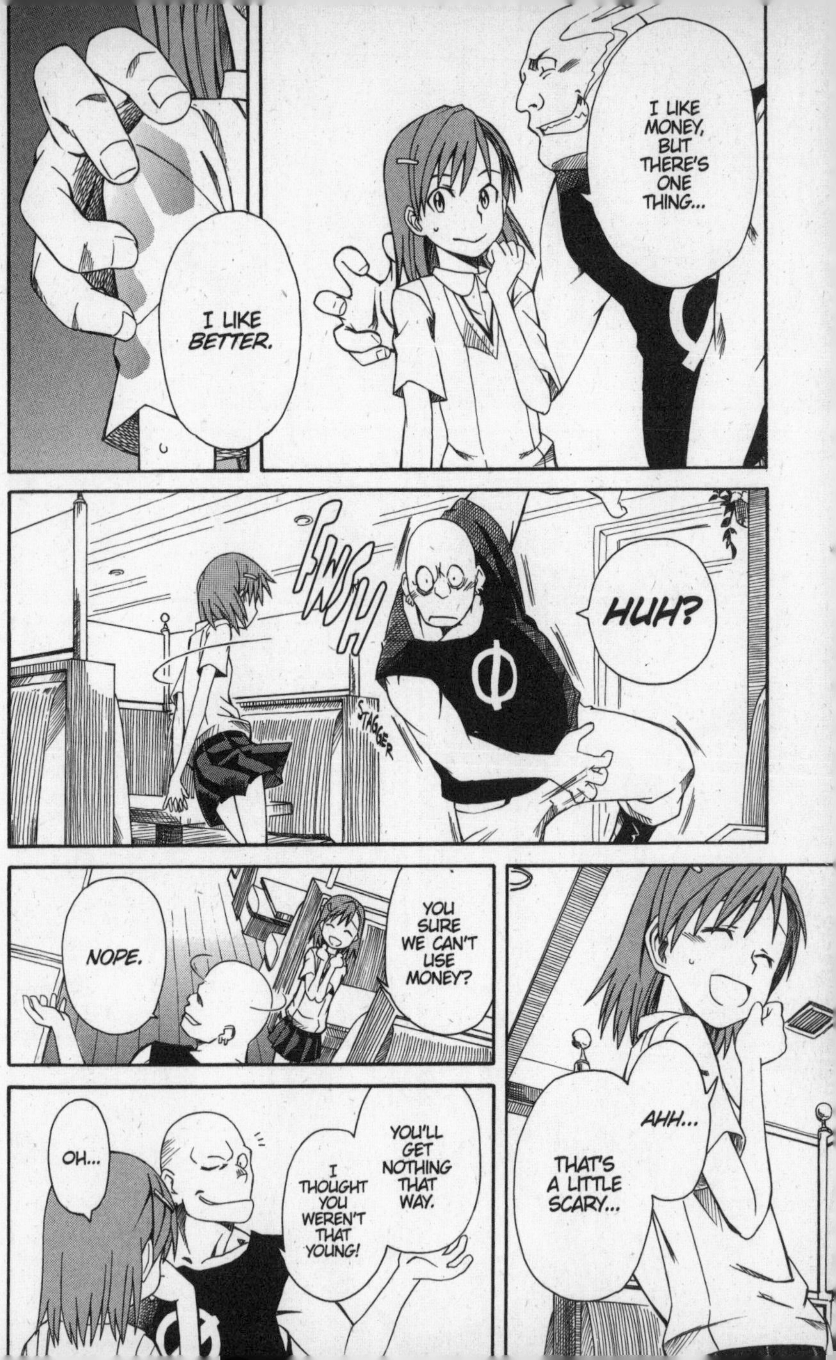
I LIKE MONEY, BUT THERE'S ONE THING...
I LIKE BETTER.
HUH?
FWISH
STAGGER
AHH...
THAT'S A LITTLE SCARY...
YOU SURE WE CAN'T USE MONEY?
NOPE.
YOU'LL GET NOTHING THAT WAY.
I THOUGHT YOU WEREN'T THAT YOUNG!
OH...

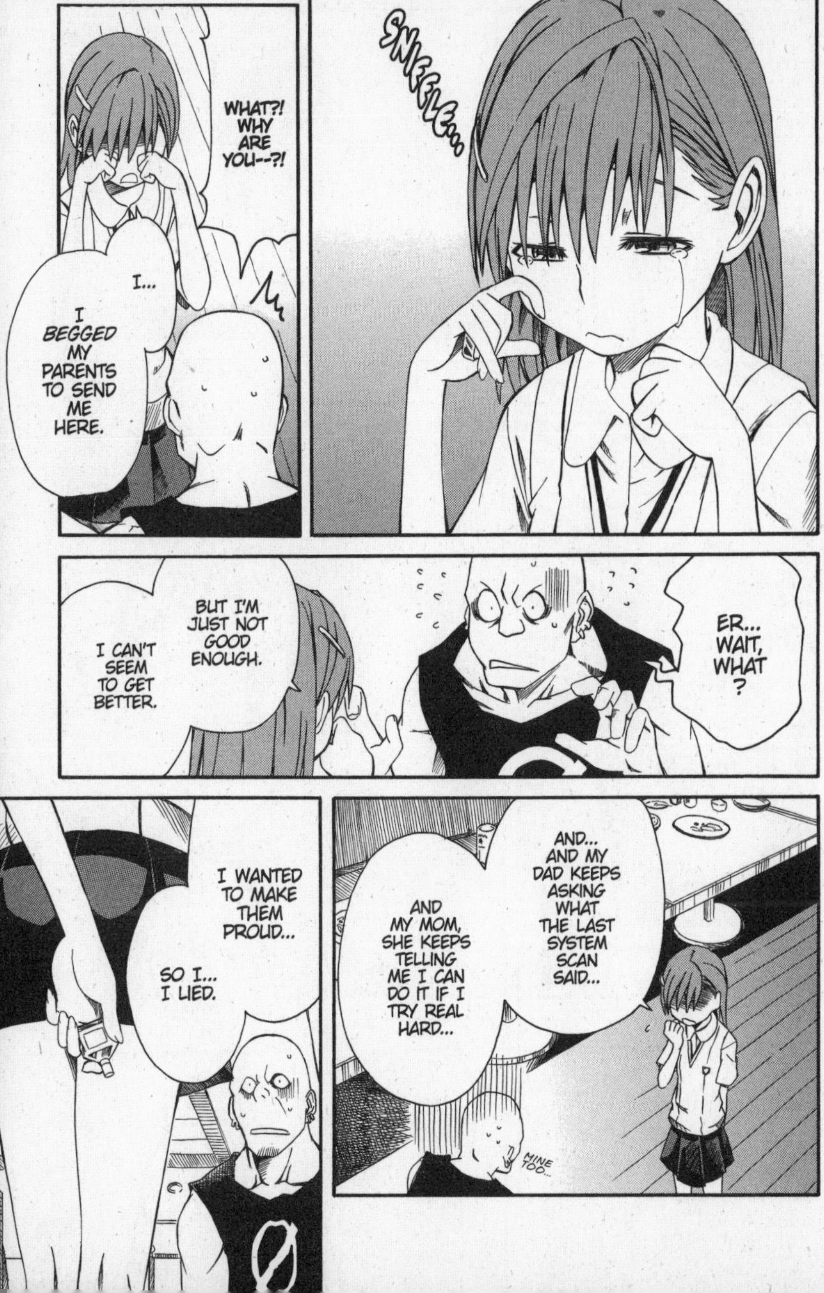
SNIFFLE...
WHAT?! WHY ARE YOU--?!
I... I BEGGED MY PARENTS TO SEND ME HERE.
ER... WAIT, WHAT?
BUT I'M JUST NOT GOOD ENOUGH.
I CAN'T SEEM TO GET BETTER.
AND... AND MY DAD KEEPS ASKING WHAT THE LAST SYSTEM SCAN SAID...
AND MY MOM, SHE KEEPS TELLING ME I CAN DO IT IF I TRY REAL HARD...
MINE TOO...
I WANTED TO MAKE THEM PROUD...
SO I... I LIED.

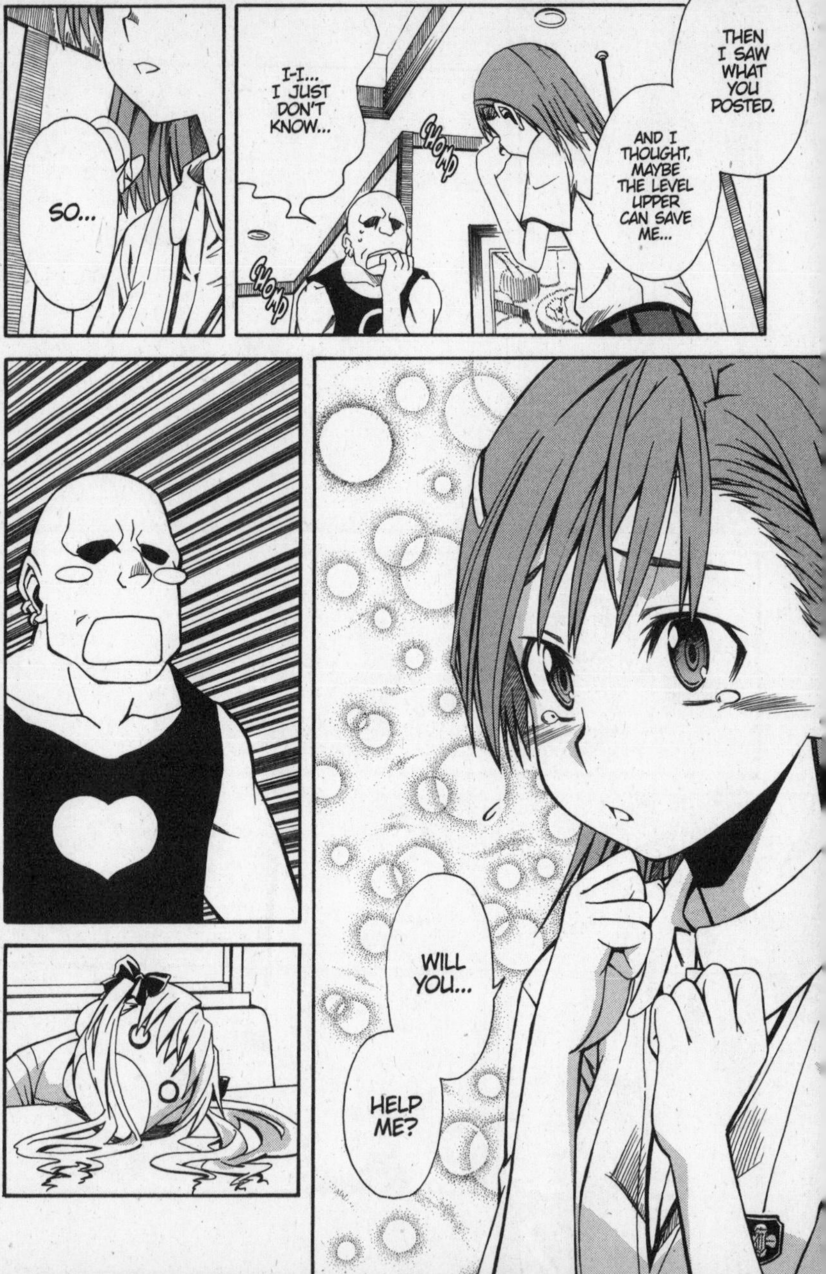
THEN I SAW WHAT YOU POSTED.
AND I THOUGHT, MAYBE THE LEVEL UPPER CAN SAVE ME...
I-I... I JUST DON'T KNOW...
CHOMP
CHOMP
SO...
WILL YOU...
HELP ME?

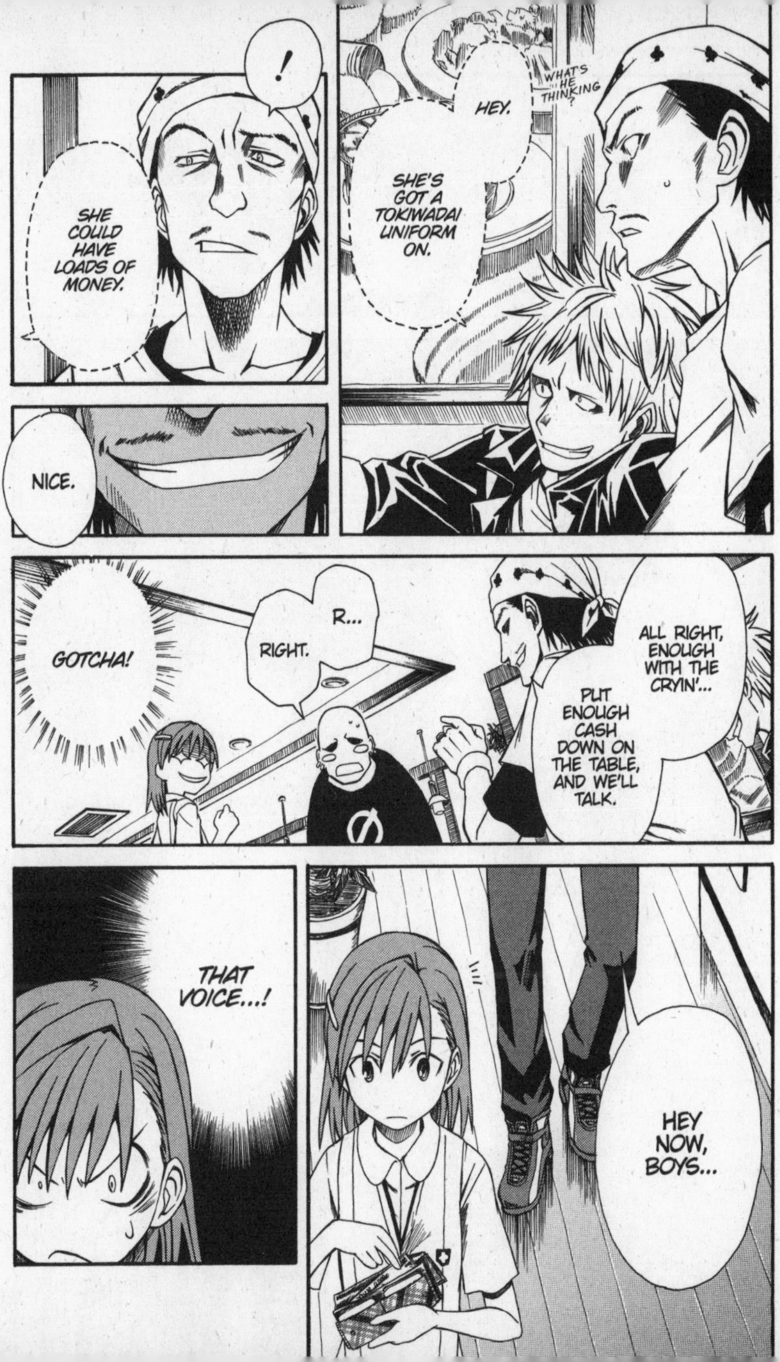

WHAT'S HE THINKING?
HEY.
SHE'S GOT A TOKIWADAI UNIFORM ON.
!
SHE COULD HAVE LOADS OF MONEY.
NICE.
ALL RIGHT, ENOUGH WITH THE CRYIN'...
PUT ENOUGH CASH DOWN ON THE TABLE, AND WE'LL TALK.
R... RIGHT.
GOTCHA!
HEY NOW, BOYS...
THAT VOICE...!

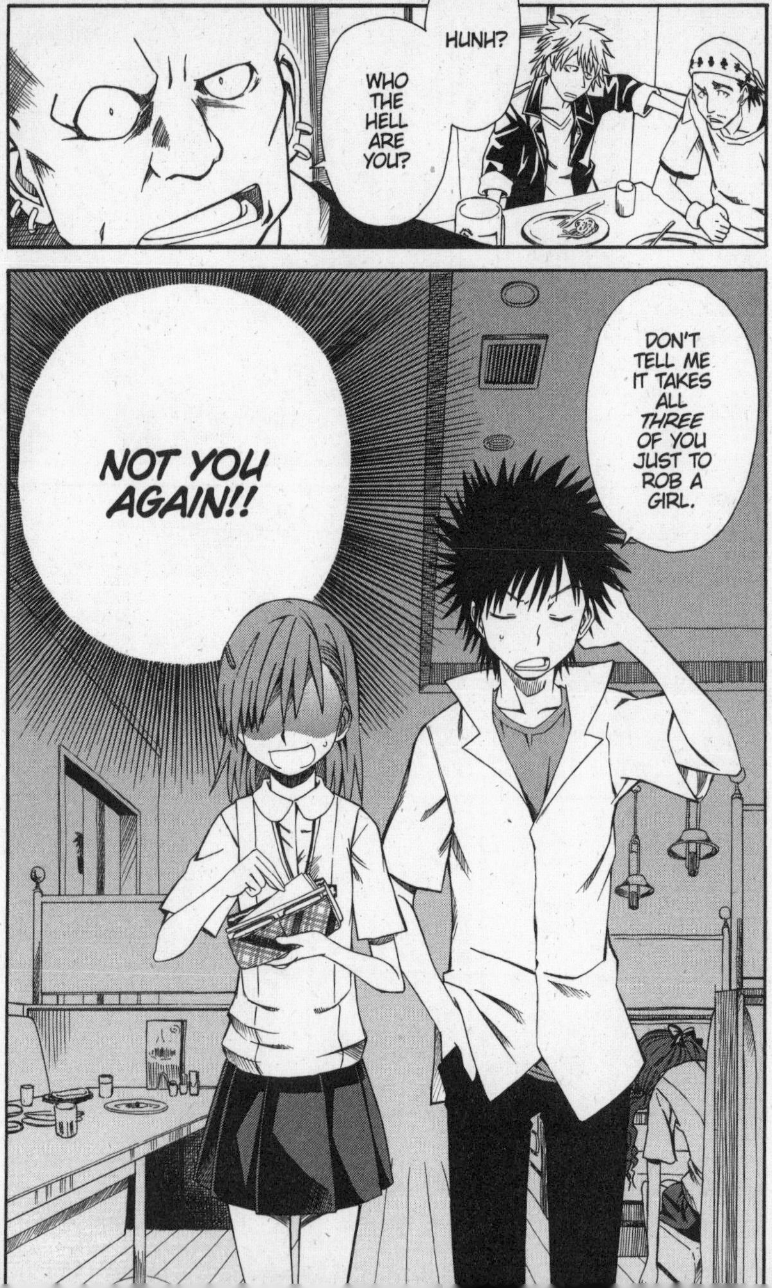
HUNH?
WHO THE HELL ARE YOU?
DON'T TELL ME IT TAKES ALL *THREE* OF YOU JUST TO ROB A GIRL.
NOT YOU AGAIN!!

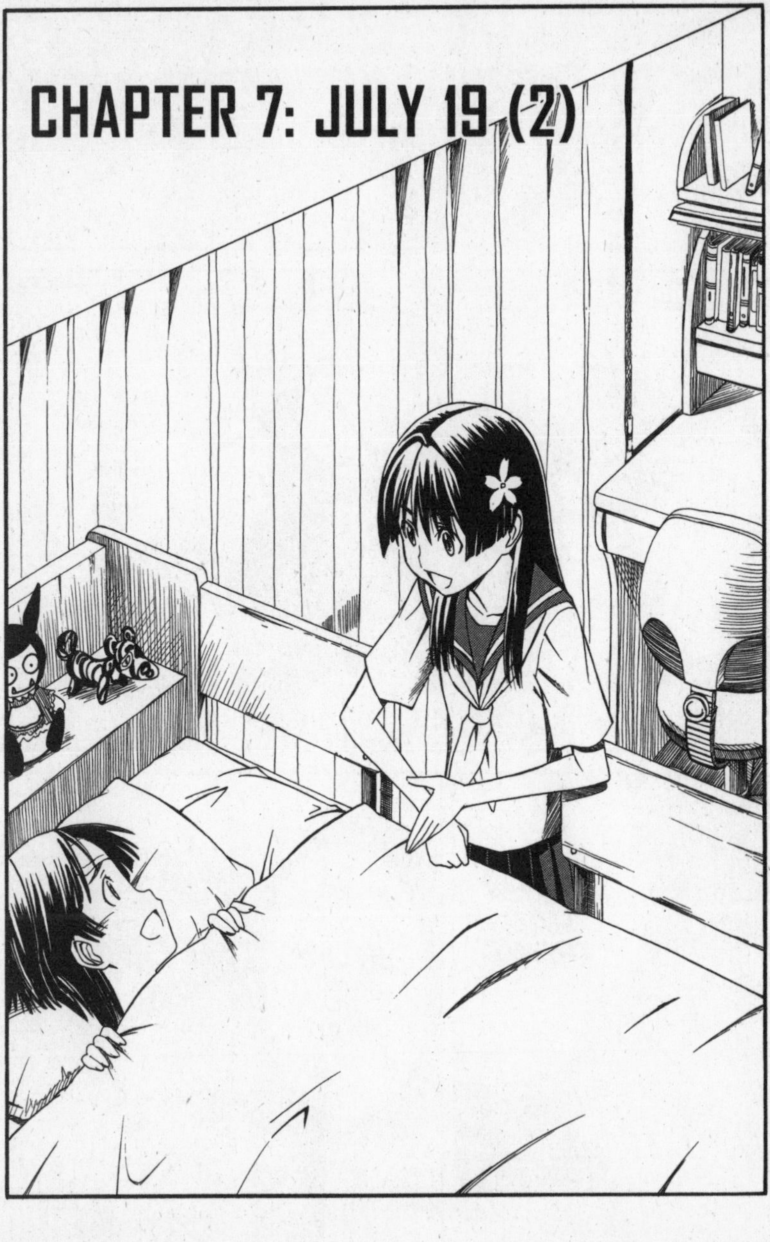
CHAPTER 7: JULY 19 (2)

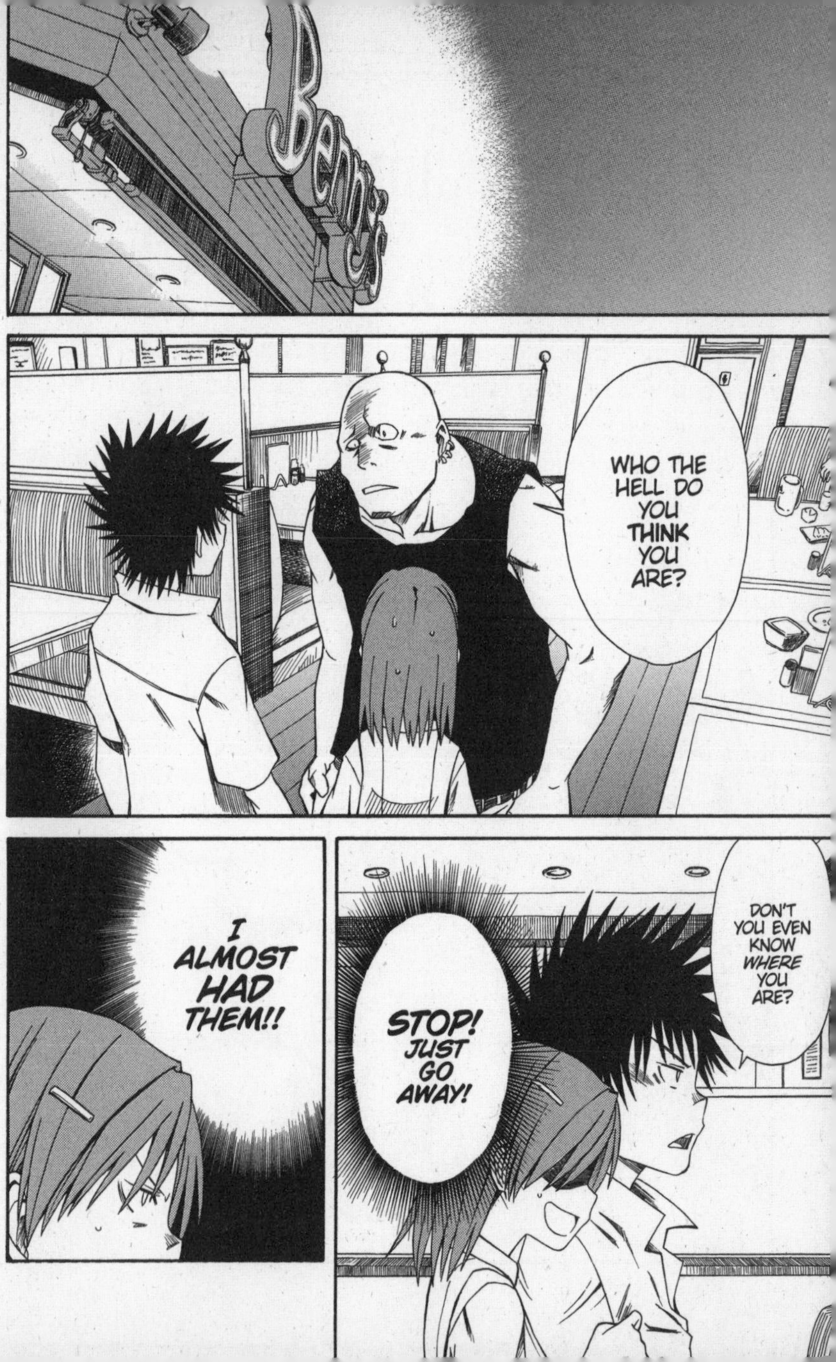
Benny's
WHO THE HELL DO YOU THINK YOU ARE?
DON'T YOU EVEN KNOW *WHERE* YOU ARE?
STOP! JUST GO AWAY!
I ALMOST HAD THEM!!

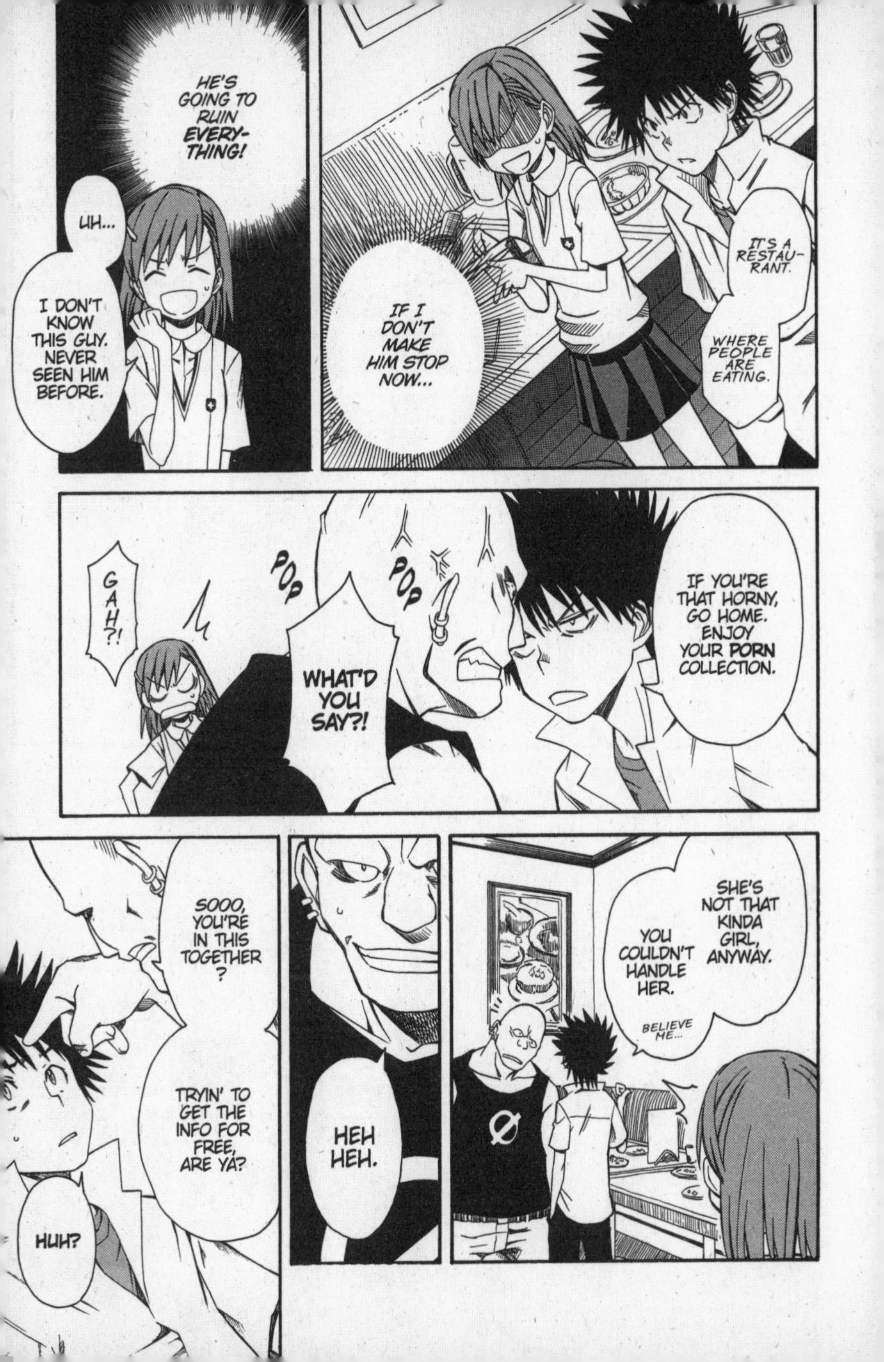
IT'S A RESTAURANT.
WHERE PEOPLE ARE EATING.
IF I DON'T MAKE HIM STOP NOW...
HE'S GOING TO RUIN EVERYTHING!
UH...
I DON'T KNOW THIS GUY. NEVER SEEN HIM BEFORE.
IF YOU'RE THAT HORNY, GO HOME. ENJOY YOUR PORN COLLECTION.
POP
POP
WHAT'D YOU SAY?!
GAH?!
SHE'S NOT THAT KINDA GIRL, ANYWAY.
YOU COULDN'T HANDLE HER.
BELIEVE ME...
HEH HEH.
SOOO, YOU'RE IN THIS TOGETHER?
TRYIN' TO GET THE INFO FOR FREE, ARE YA?
HUH?

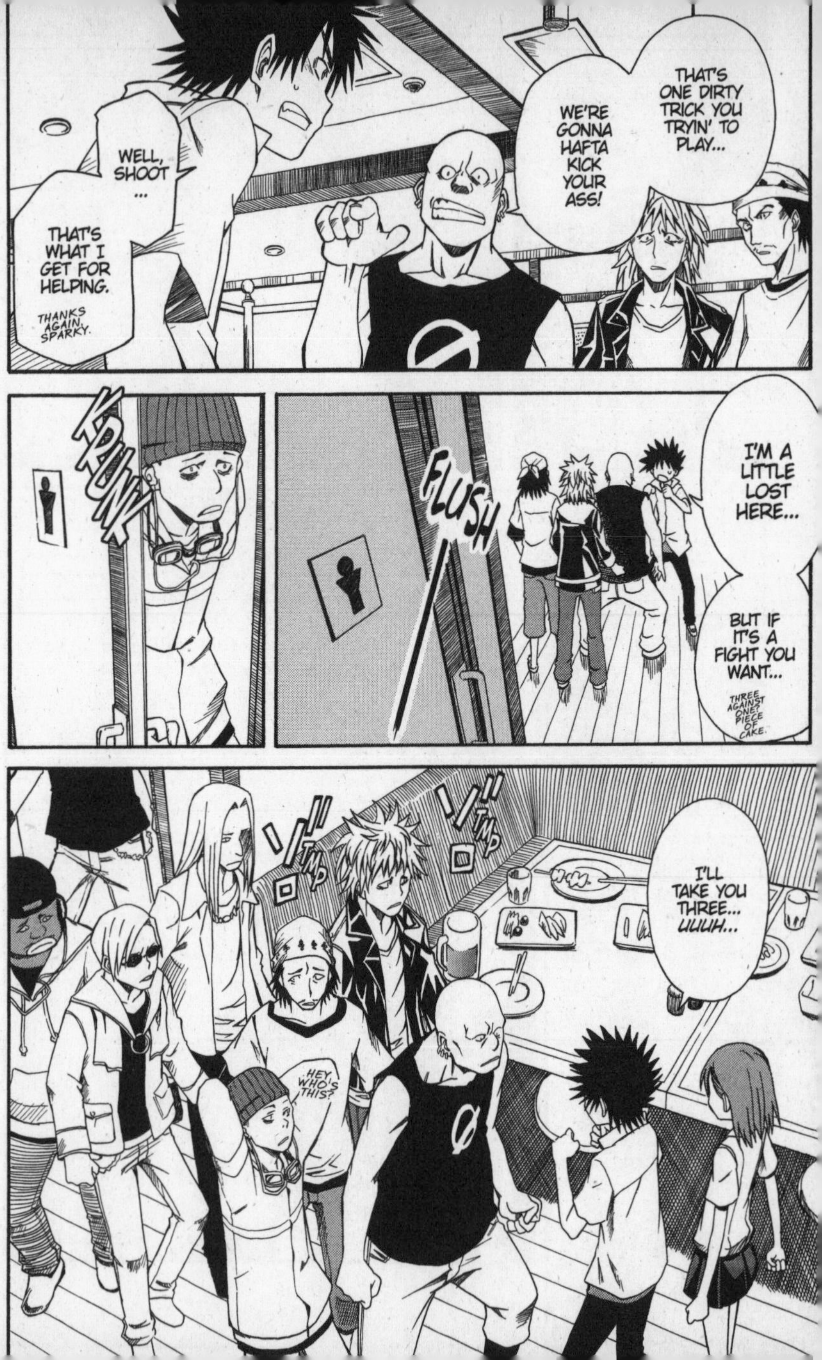
THAT'S ONE DIRTY TRICK YOU TRYIN' TO PLAY...
WE'RE GONNA HAFTA KICK YOUR ASS!
WELL, SHOOT ...
THAT'S WHAT I GET FOR HELPING.
THANKS AGAIN, SPARKY.
I'M A LITTLE LOST HERE...
BUT IF IT'S A FIGHT YOU WANT...
THREE AGAINST ONE? PIECE OF CAKE.
FLUSH
KRUNK
I'LL TAKE YOU THREE... UUUH...
HEY, WHO'S THIS?

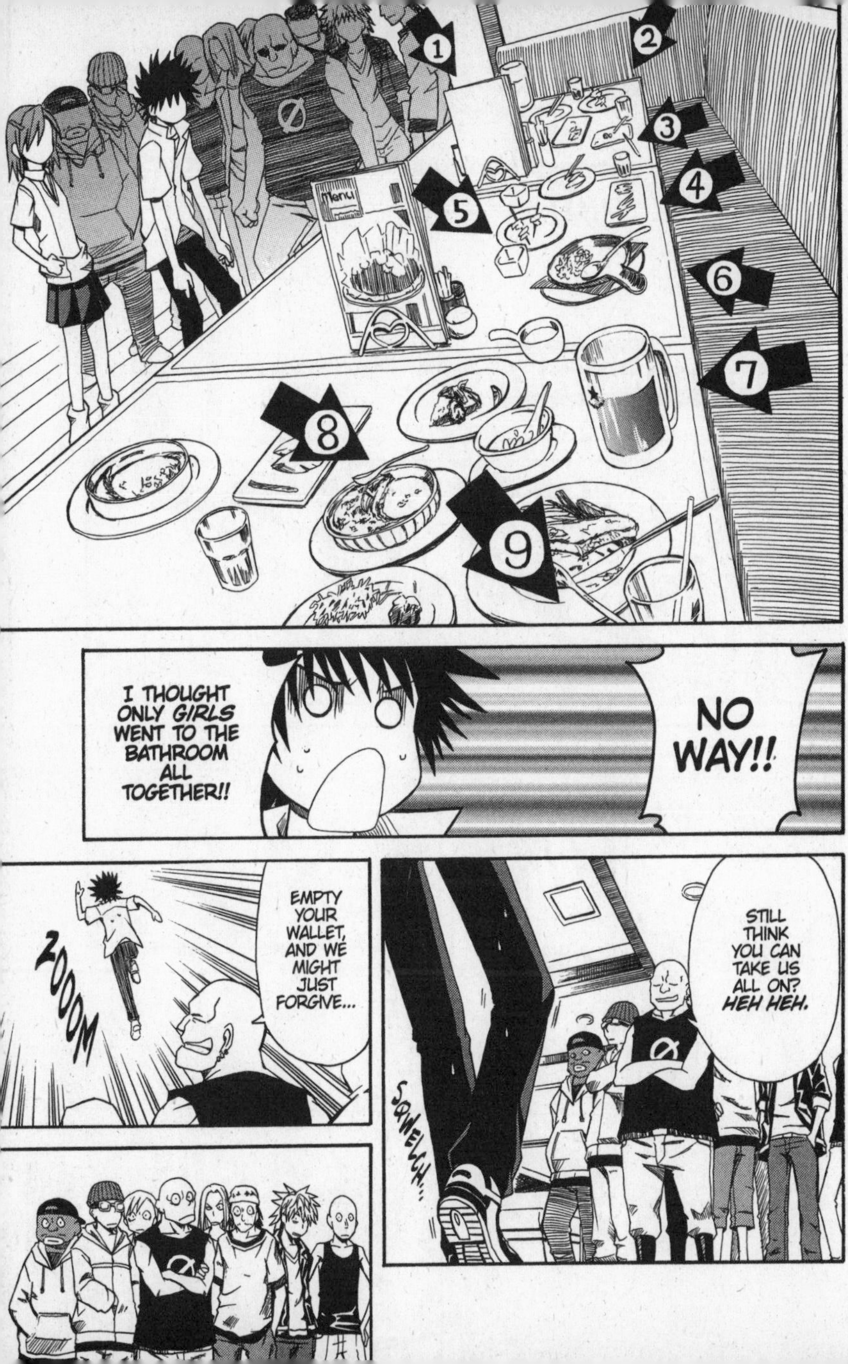

1
2
3
4
5
6
7
8
9
NO WAY!!
I THOUGHT ONLY *GIRLS* WENT TO THE BATHROOM ALL TOGETHER!!
STILL THINK YOU CAN TAKE US ALL ON? *HEH HEH.*
SQWELCH...
EMPTY YOUR WALLET, AND WE MIGHT JUST FORGIVE...
ZOOOM

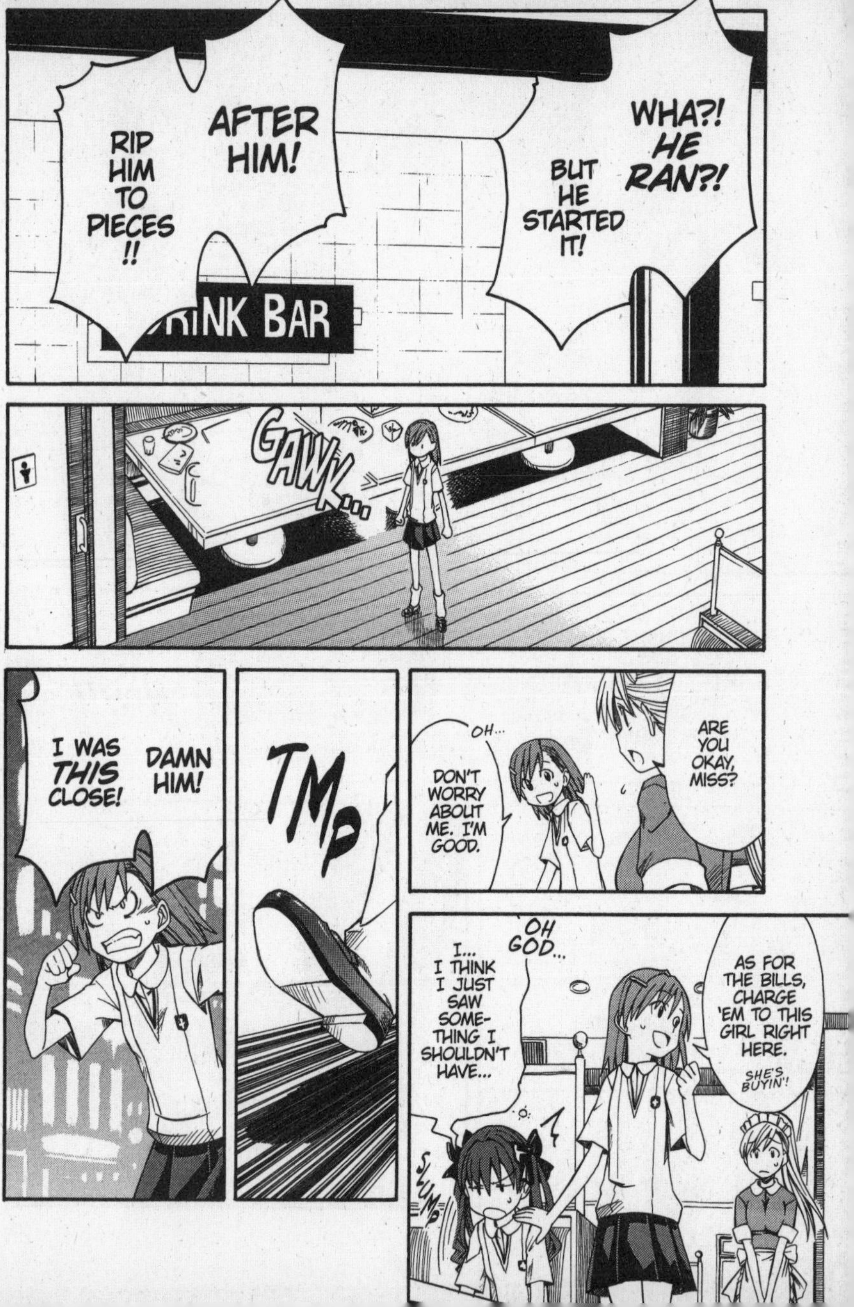
WHA?! HE RAN?!
BUT HE STARTED IT!
AFTER HIM!
RIP HIM TO PIECES!!
RINK BAR
GAWK...
ARE YOU OKAY, MISS?
OH...
DON'T WORRY ABOUT ME. I'M GOOD.
AS FOR THE BILLS, CHARGE 'EM TO THIS GIRL RIGHT HERE.
SHE'S BUYIN'!
OH GOD...
I... I THINK I JUST SAW SOME-THING I SHOULDN'T HAVE...
SLUMP
TMP
DAMN HIM!
I WAS THIS CLOSE!

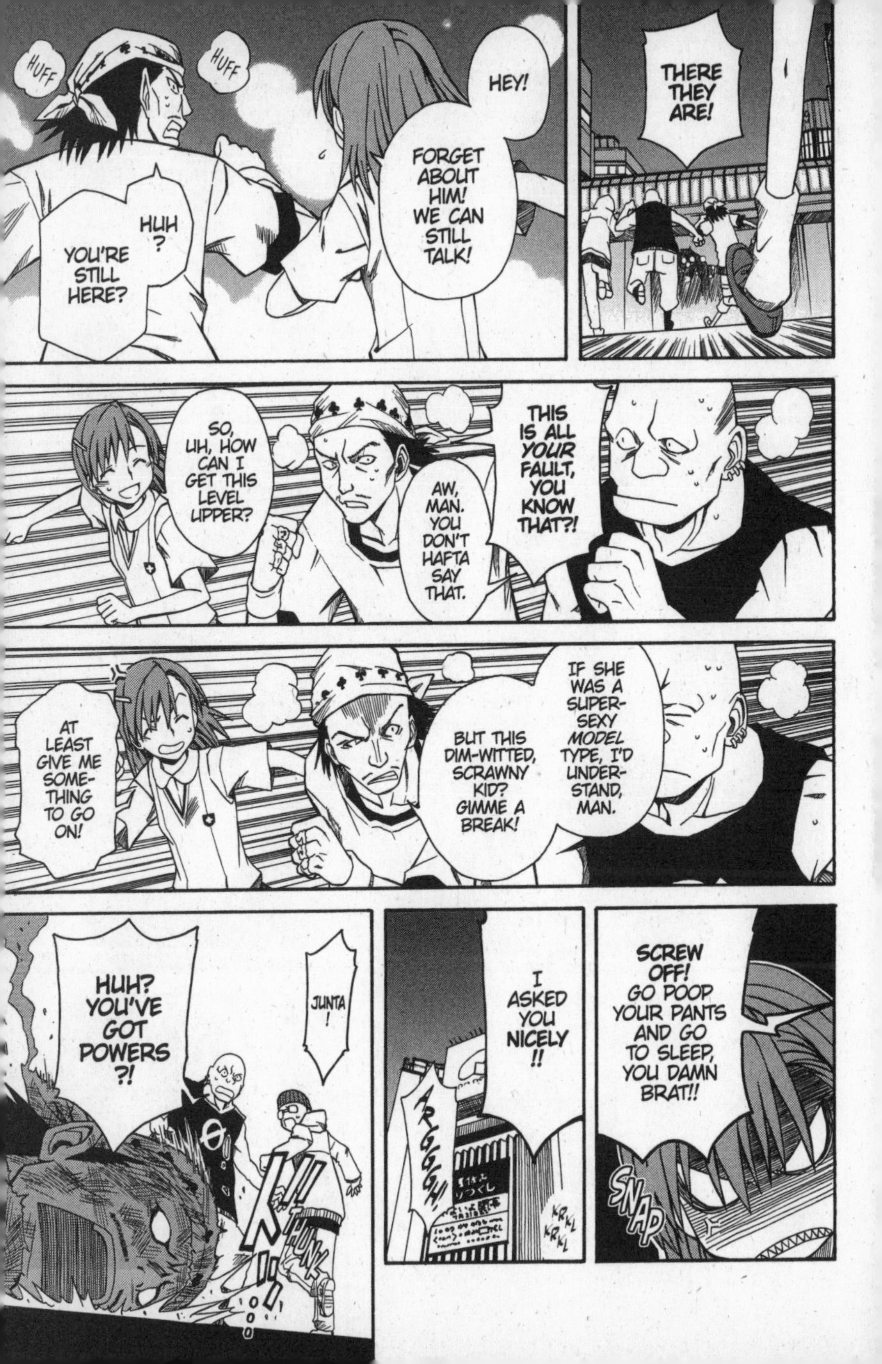
THERE THEY ARE!
HEY!
HUFF
HUFF
FORGET ABOUT HIM! WE CAN STILL TALK!
HUH?
YOU'RE STILL HERE?
THIS IS ALL *YOUR* FAULT, YOU KNOW THAT?!
AW, MAN. YOU DON'T HAFTA SAY THAT.
SO, UH, HOW CAN I GET THIS LEVEL UPPER?
IF SHE WAS A SUPER-SEXY *MODEL* TYPE, I'D UNDERSTAND, MAN.
BUT THIS DIM-WITTED, SCRAWNY KID? GIMME A BREAK!
AT LEAST GIVE ME SOMETHING TO GO ON!
SCREW OFF! GO POOP YOUR PANTS AND GO TO SLEEP, YOU DAMN BRAT!!
SNAP
I ASKED YOU NICELY!!
ARGGGH!
KRKL KRKL
JUNTA!
HUH? YOU'VE GOT POWERS?!
THUNK

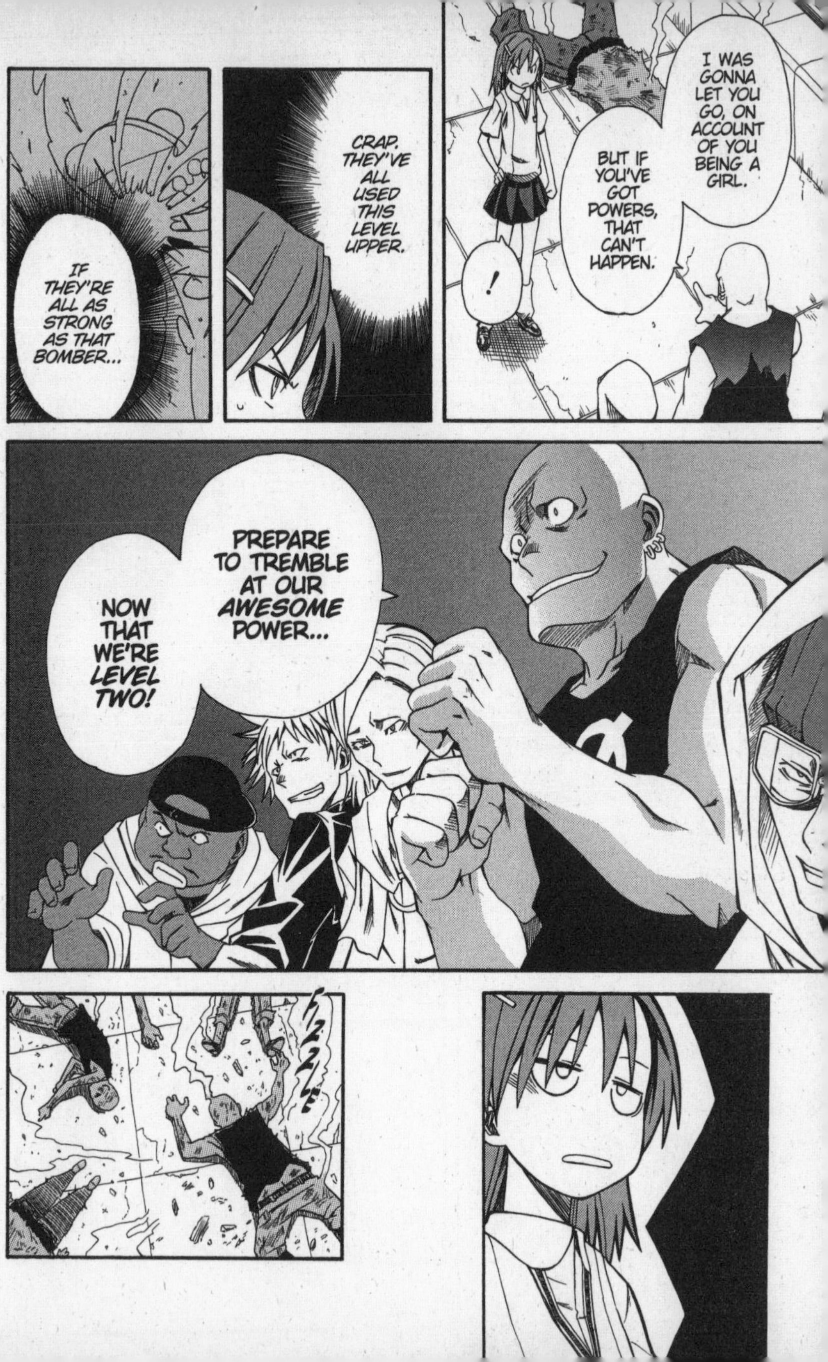
I WAS GONNA LET YOU GO, ON ACCOUNT OF YOU BEING A GIRL.
BUT IF YOU'VE GOT POWERS, THAT CAN'T HAPPEN.
!
CRAP. THEY'VE ALL USED THIS LEVEL UPPER.
IF THEY'RE ALL AS STRONG AS THAT BOMBER...
PREPARE TO TREMBLE AT OUR AWESOME POWER...
NOW THAT WE'RE LEVEL TWO!
FZZLE

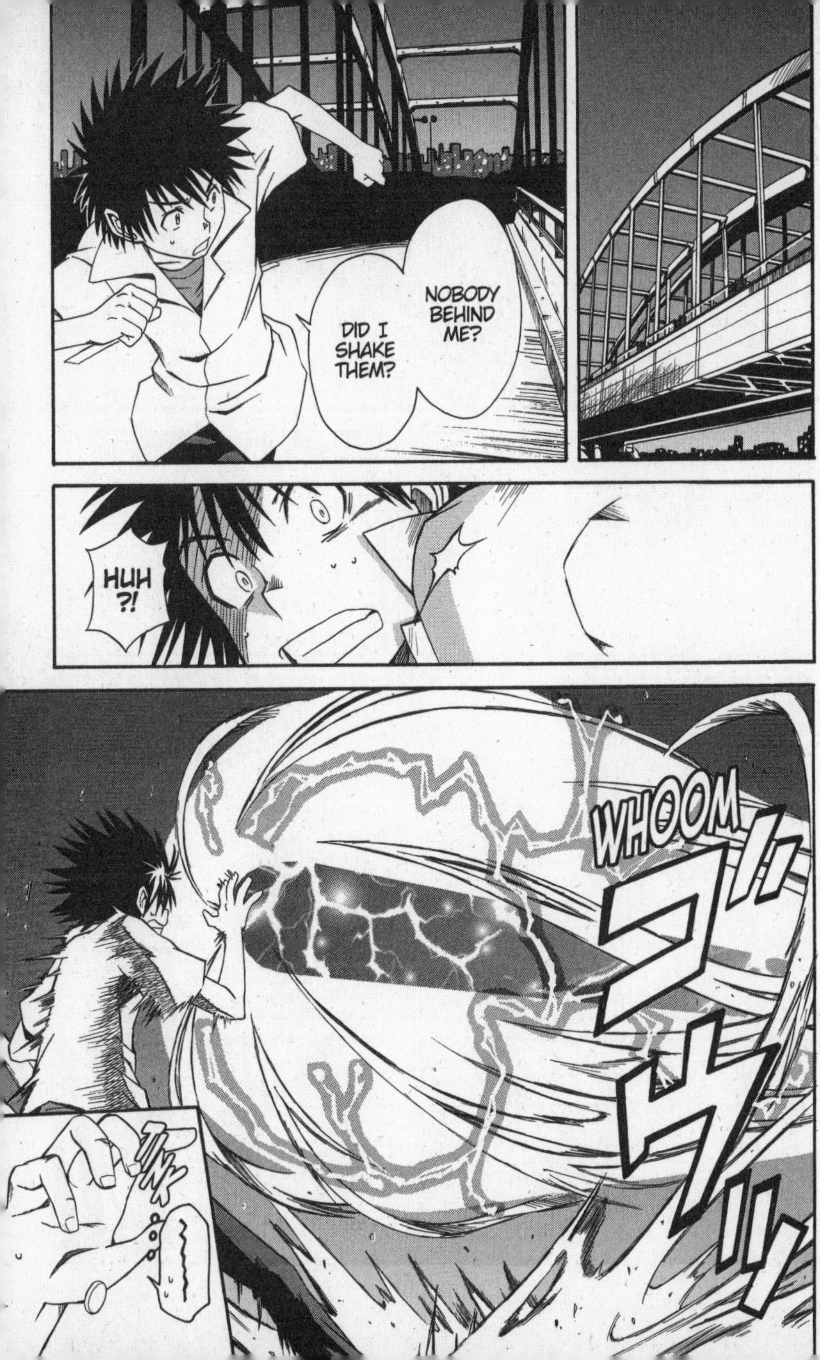
NOBODY BEHIND ME?
DID I SHAKE THEM?
HUH ?!
WHOOM
TINK

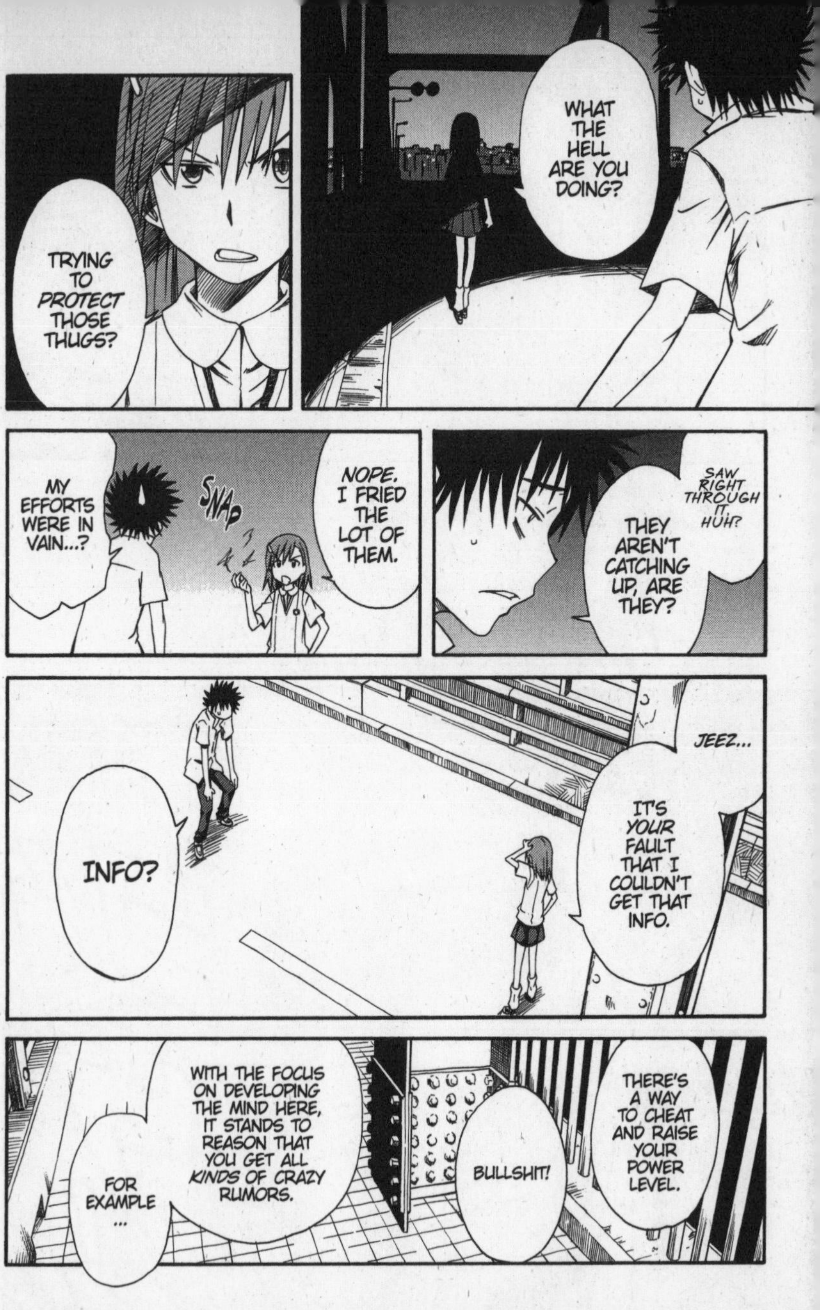
WHAT THE HELL ARE YOU DOING?
TRYING TO PROTECT THOSE THUGS?
SAW RIGHT THROUGH IT, HUH?
THEY AREN'T CATCHING UP, ARE THEY?
NOPE. I FRIED THE LOT OF THEM.
SNAP
MY EFFORTS WERE IN VAIN...?
JEEZ...
IT'S YOUR FAULT THAT I COULDN'T GET THAT INFO.
INFO?
THERE'S A WAY TO CHEAT AND RAISE YOUR POWER LEVEL.
BULLSHIT!
WITH THE FOCUS ON DEVELOPING THE MIND HERE, IT STANDS TO REASON THAT YOU GET ALL KINDS OF CRAZY RUMORS.
FOR EXAMPLE ...

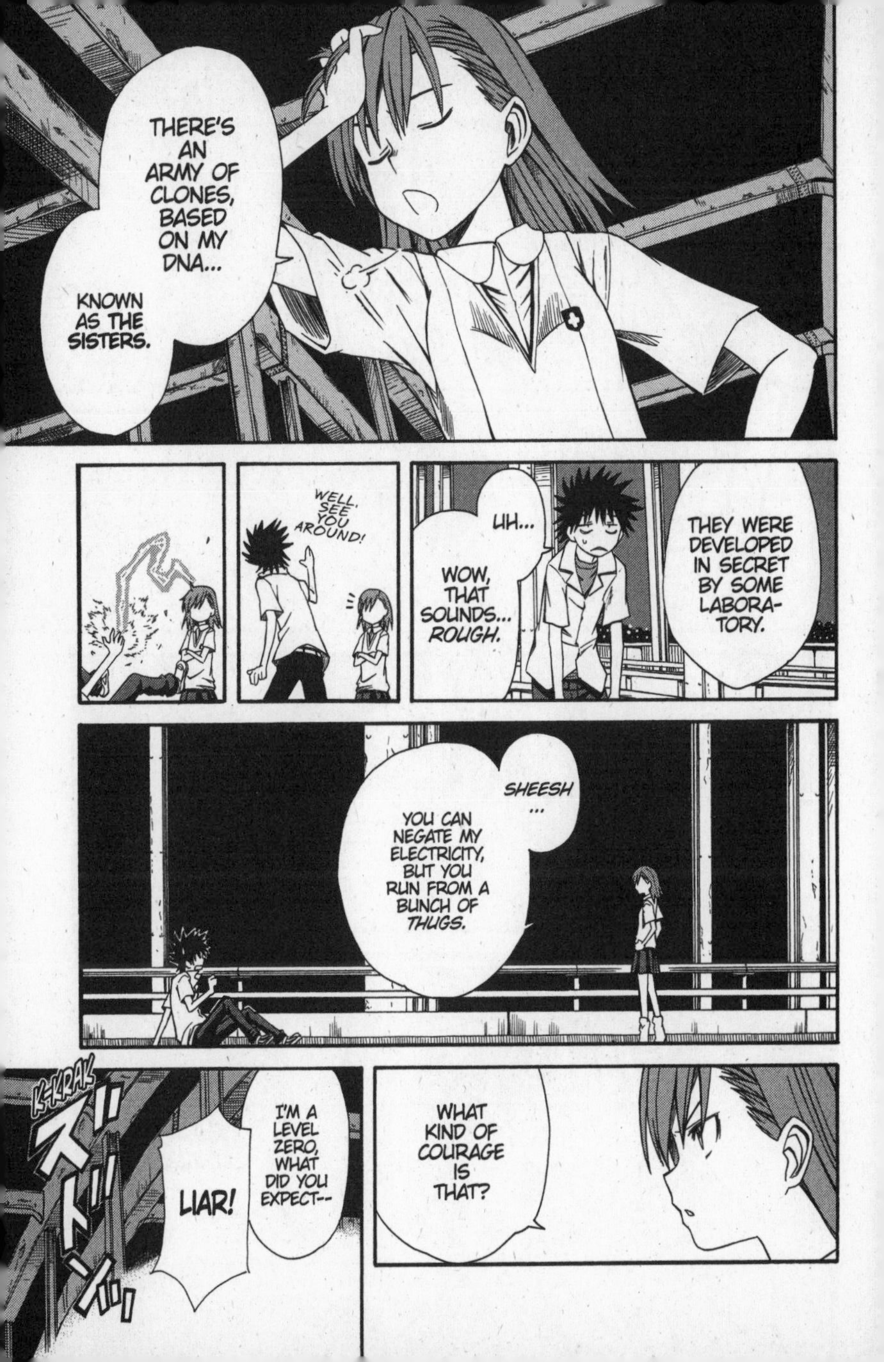
THERE'S AN ARMY OF CLONES, BASED ON MY DNA...
KNOWN AS THE SISTERS.
THEY WERE DEVELOPED IN SECRET BY SOME LABORATORY.
UH...
WOW, THAT SOUNDS... *ROUGH.*
WELL, SEE YOU AROUND!
SHEESH...
YOU CAN NEGATE MY ELECTRICITY, BUT YOU RUN FROM A BUNCH OF *THUGS.*
WHAT KIND OF COURAGE IS THAT?
I'M A LEVEL ZERO, WHAT DID YOU EXPECT--
LIAR!
K-KRAK

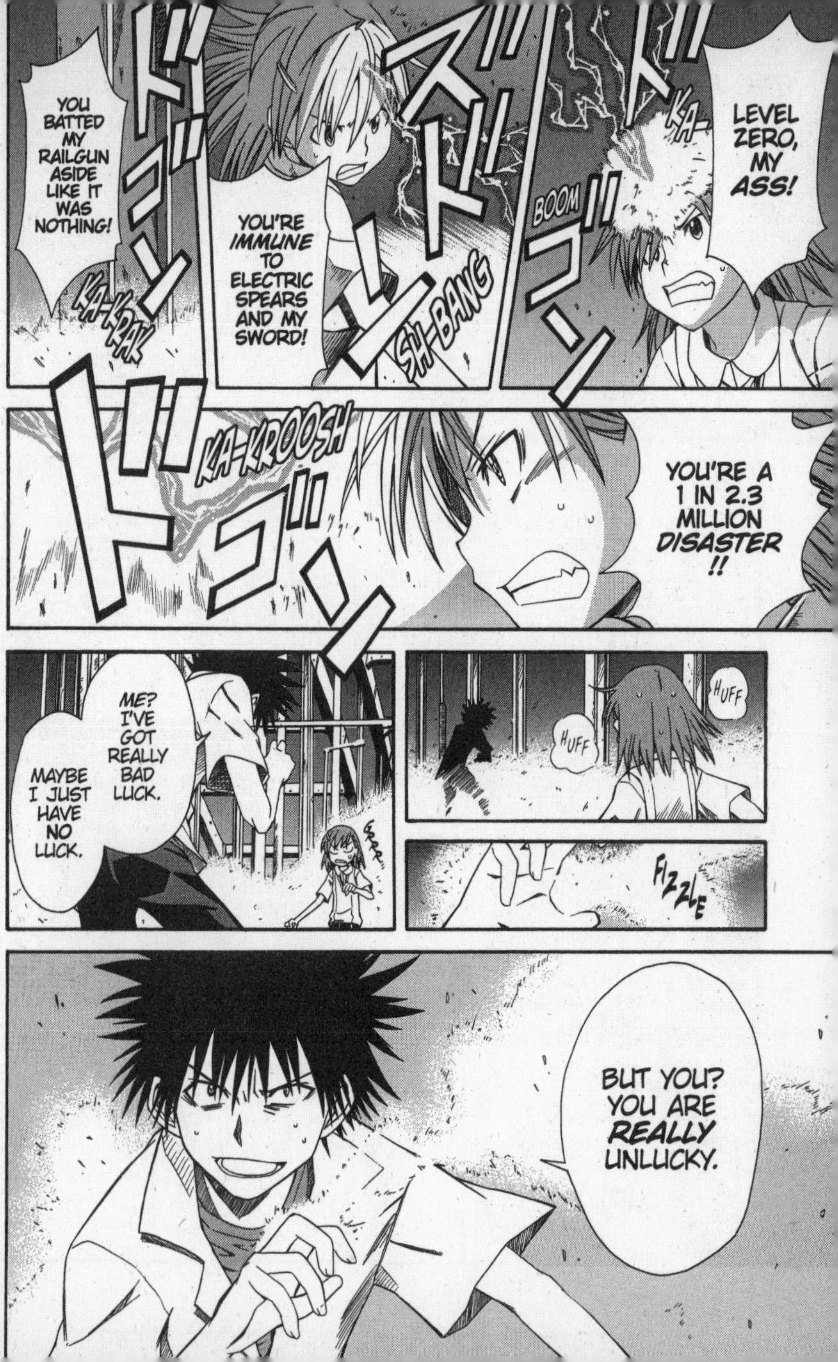
LEVEL ZERO, MY ASS!
KA-
BOOM
YOU'RE IMMUNE TO ELECTRIC SPEARS AND MY SWORD!
SH-BANG
YOU BATTED MY RAILGUN ASIDE LIKE IT WAS NOTHING!
KA-KRAK
YOU'RE A 1 IN 2.3 MILLION DISASTER!!
KA-KROOSH
HUFF
HUFF
FIZZLE
ME? I'VE GOT REALLY BAD LUCK.
MAYBE I JUST HAVE NO LUCK.
GRRR
BUT YOU? YOU ARE REALLY UNLUCKY.

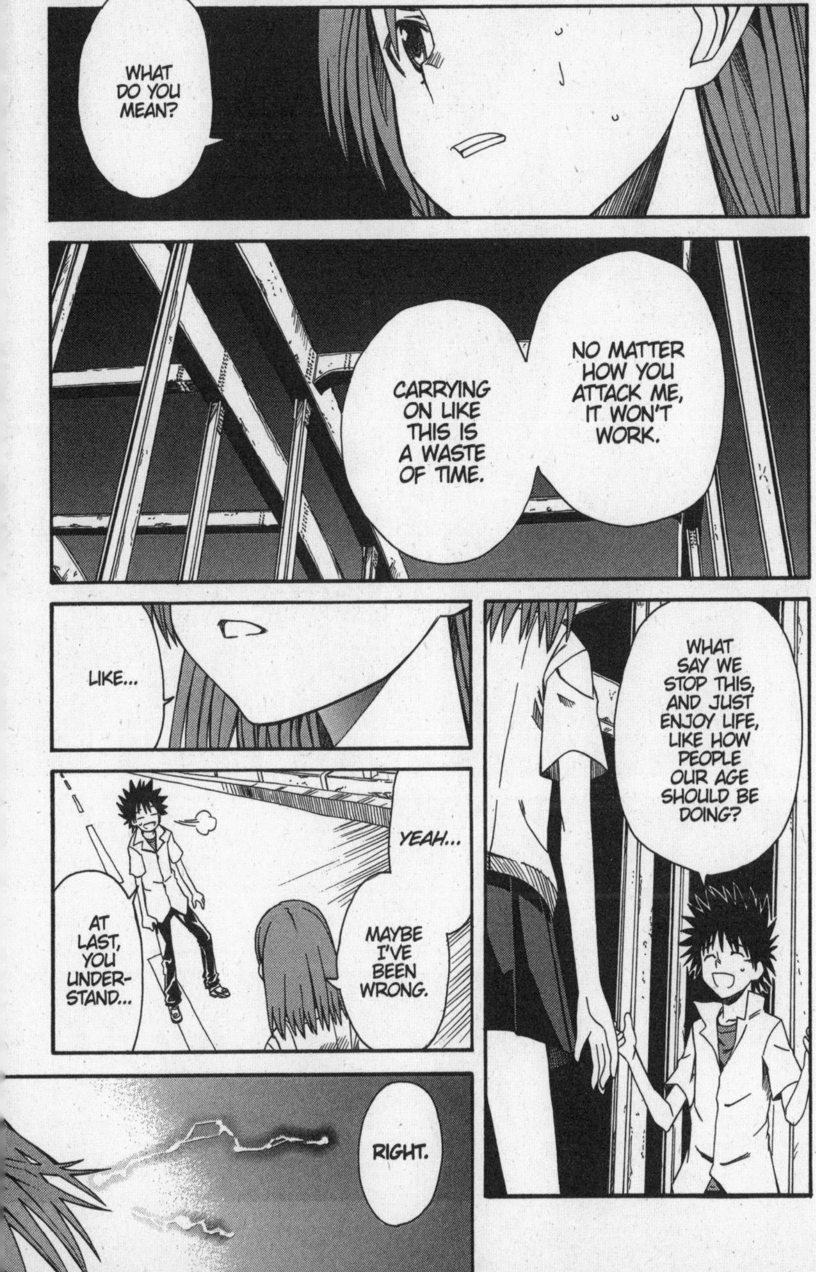
WHAT DO YOU MEAN?
NO MATTER HOW YOU ATTACK ME, IT WON'T WORK.
CARRYING ON LIKE THIS IS A WASTE OF TIME.
WHAT SAY WE STOP THIS, AND JUST ENJOY LIFE, LIKE HOW PEOPLE OUR AGE SHOULD BE DOING?
LIKE...
YEAH...
MAYBE I'VE BEEN WRONG.
AT LAST, YOU UNDER-STAND...
RIGHT.

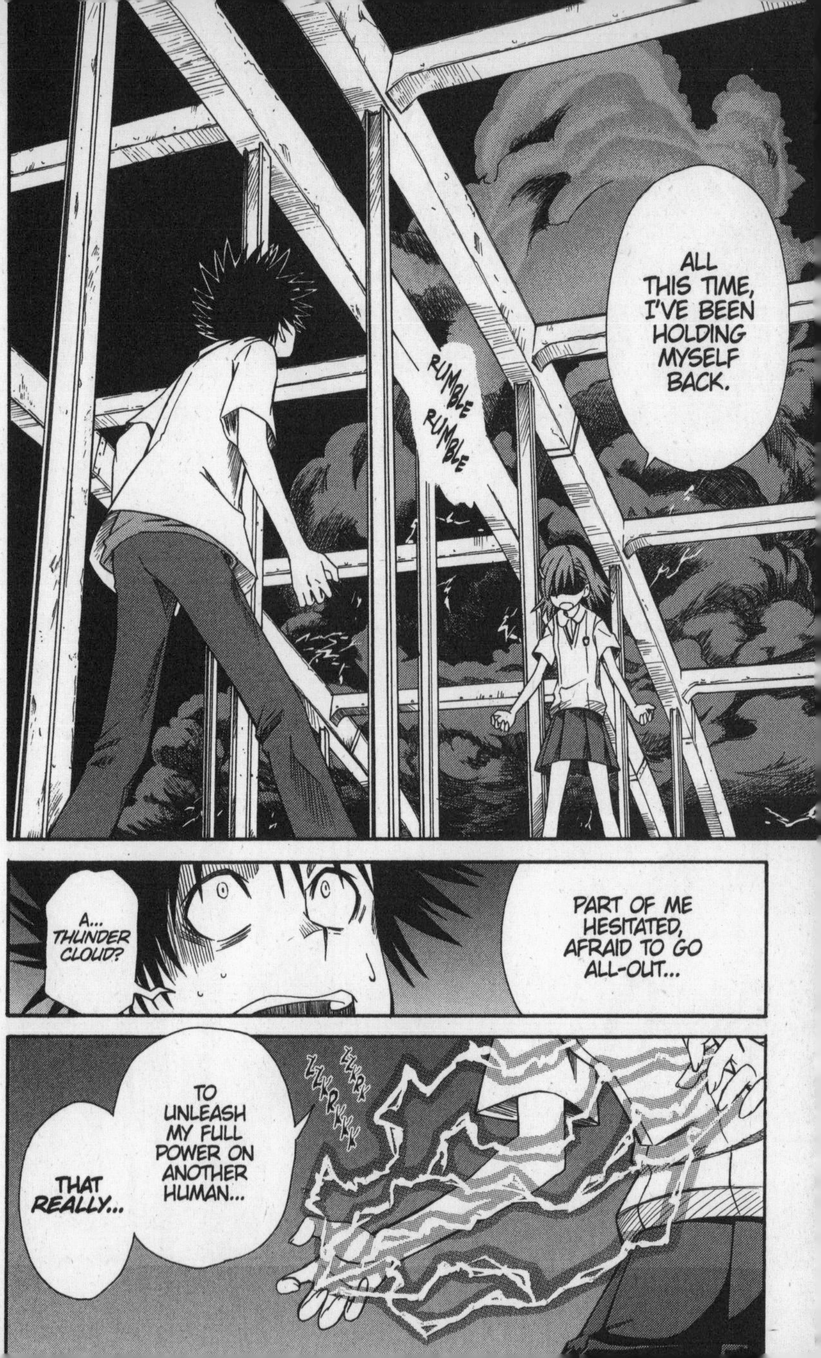
ALL THIS TIME, I'VE BEEN HOLDING MYSELF BACK.
RUMBLE RUMBLE
PART OF ME HESITATED, AFRAID TO GO ALL-OUT...
A... THUNDER CLOUD?
ZZKRK
ZZKRKKK
TO UNLEASH MY FULL POWER ON ANOTHER HUMAN...
THAT REALLY...

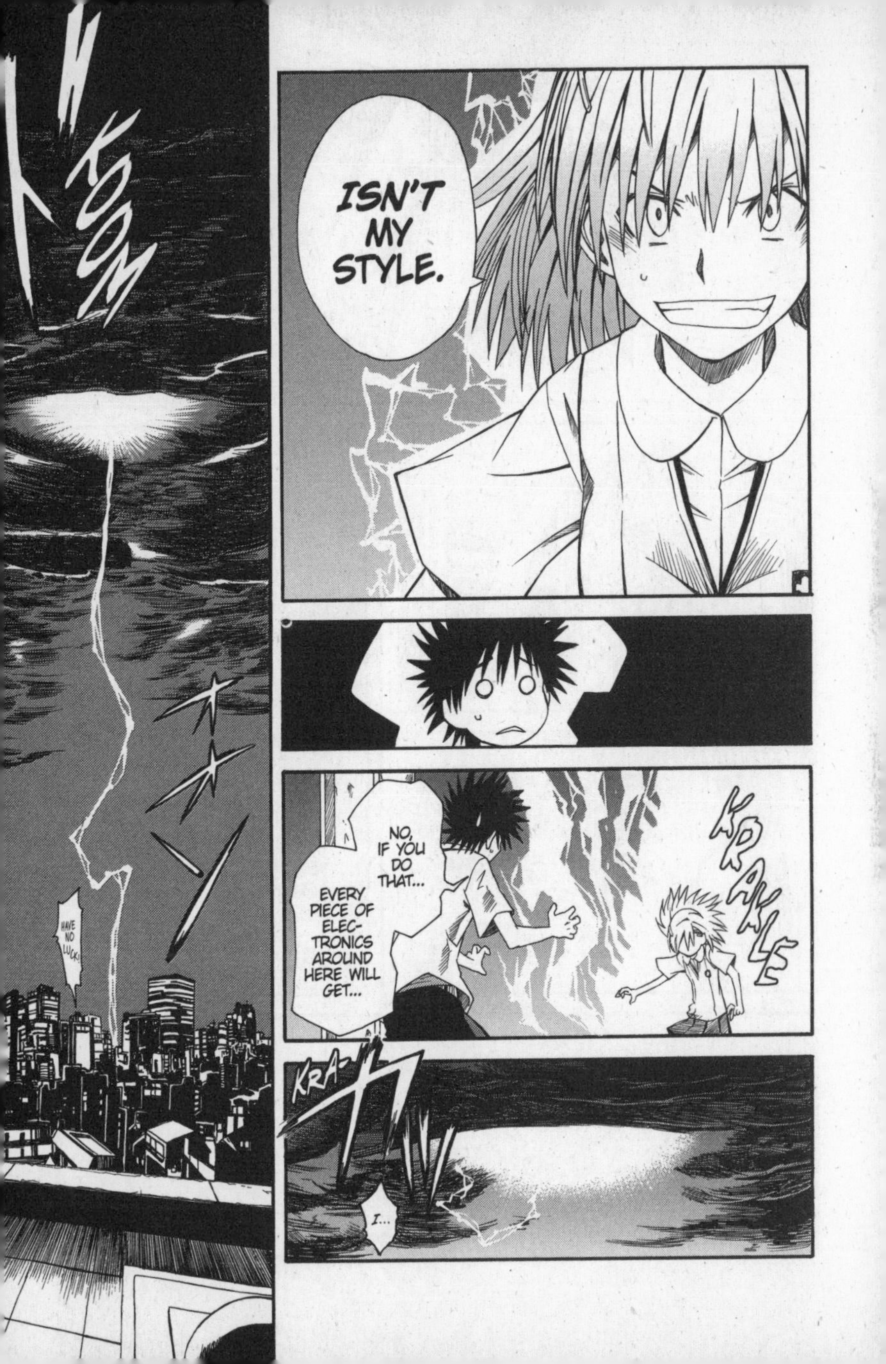
ISN'T MY STYLE.
NO, IF YOU DO THAT...
EVERY PIECE OF ELECTRONICS AROUND HERE WILL GET...
KRAKLE
KRA-
I...
KOOM
HAVE NO LUCK!

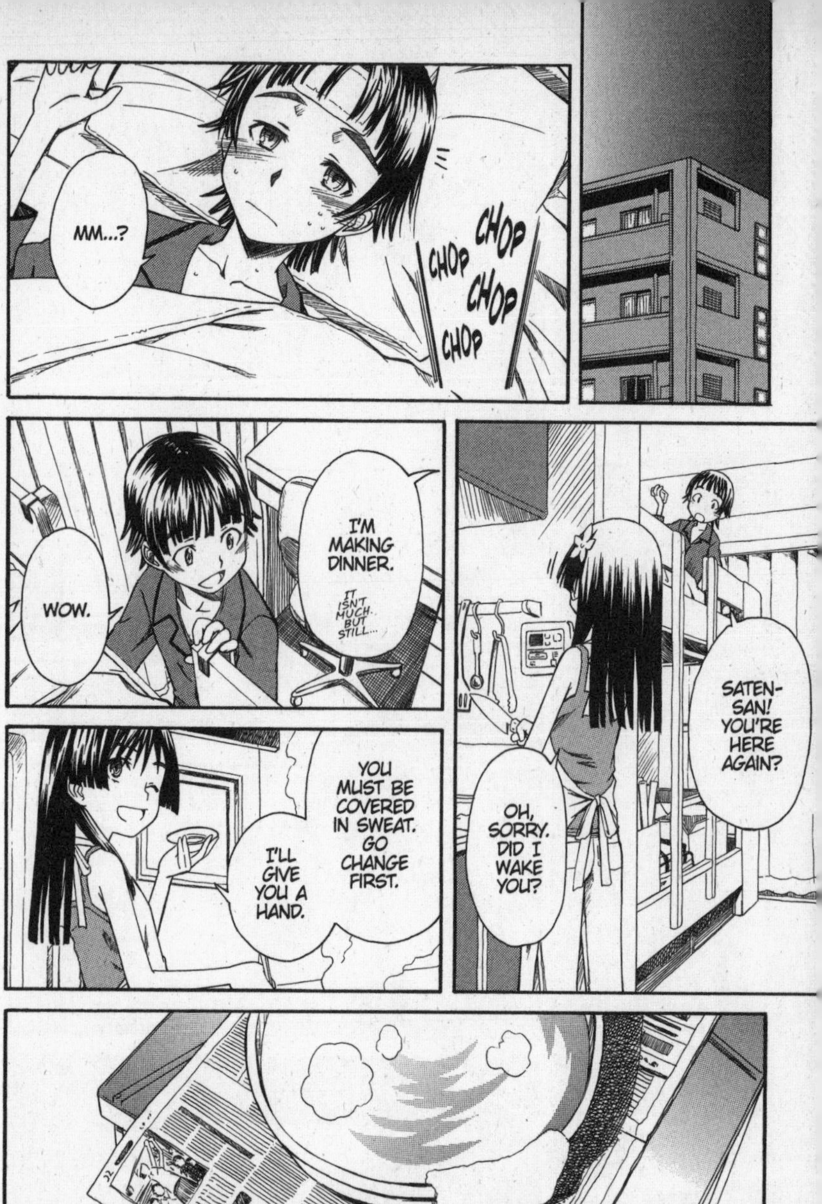
CHOP CHOP CHOP CHOP
MM...?
SATEN-SAN! YOU'RE HERE AGAIN?
OH, SORRY. DID I WAKE YOU?
I'M MAKING DINNER.
IT ISN'T MUCH. BUT STILL...
WOW.
YOU MUST BE COVERED IN SWEAT. GO CHANGE FIRST.
I'LL GIVE YOU A HAND.

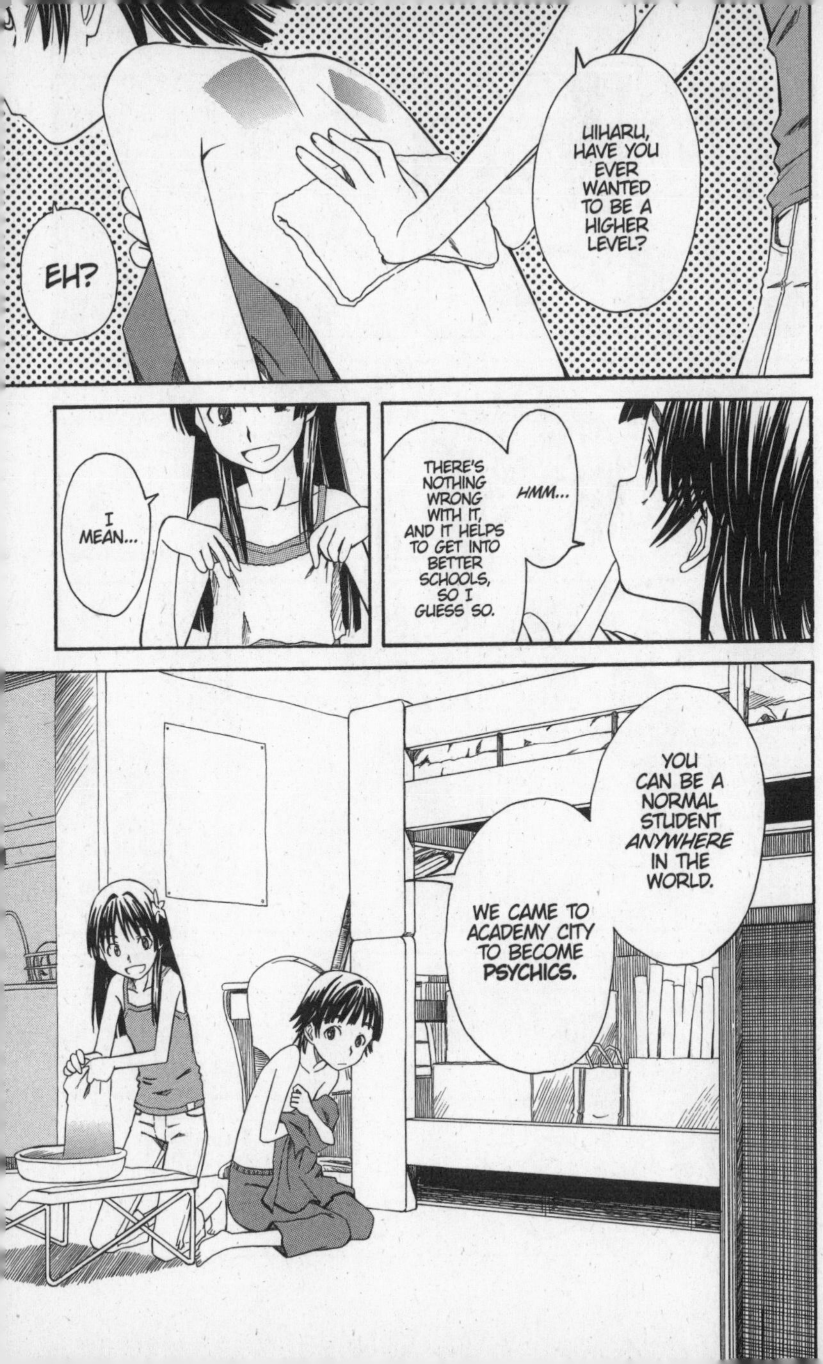
UIHARU, HAVE YOU EVER WANTED TO BE A HIGHER LEVEL?
EH?
HMM...
THERE'S NOTHING WRONG WITH IT, AND IT HELPS TO GET INTO BETTER SCHOOLS, SO I GUESS SO.
I MEAN...
YOU CAN BE A NORMAL STUDENT *ANYWHERE* IN THE WORLD.
WE CAME TO ACADEMY CITY TO BECOME **PSYCHICS.**

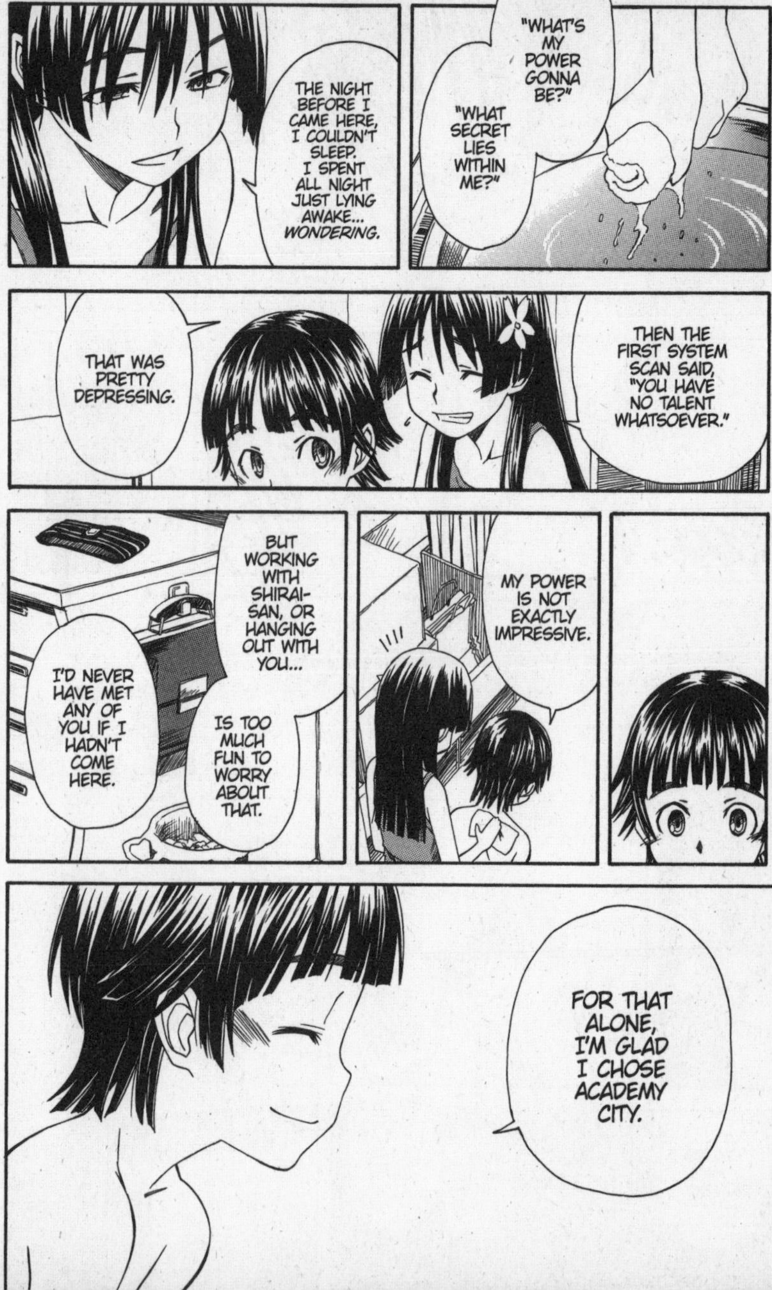
"WHAT'S MY POWER GONNA BE?"
"WHAT SECRET LIES WITHIN ME?"
THE NIGHT BEFORE I CAME HERE, I COULDN'T SLEEP. I SPENT ALL NIGHT JUST LYING AWAKE... *WONDERING.*
THEN THE FIRST SYSTEM SCAN SAID, "YOU HAVE NO TALENT WHATSOEVER."
THAT WAS PRETTY DEPRESSING.
MY POWER IS NOT EXACTLY IMPRESSIVE.
BUT WORKING WITH SHIRAI-SAN, OR HANGING OUT WITH YOU...
IS TOO MUCH FUN TO WORRY ABOUT THAT.
I'D NEVER HAVE MET ANY OF YOU IF I HADN'T COME HERE.
FOR THAT ALONE, I'M GLAD I CHOSE ACADEMY CITY.

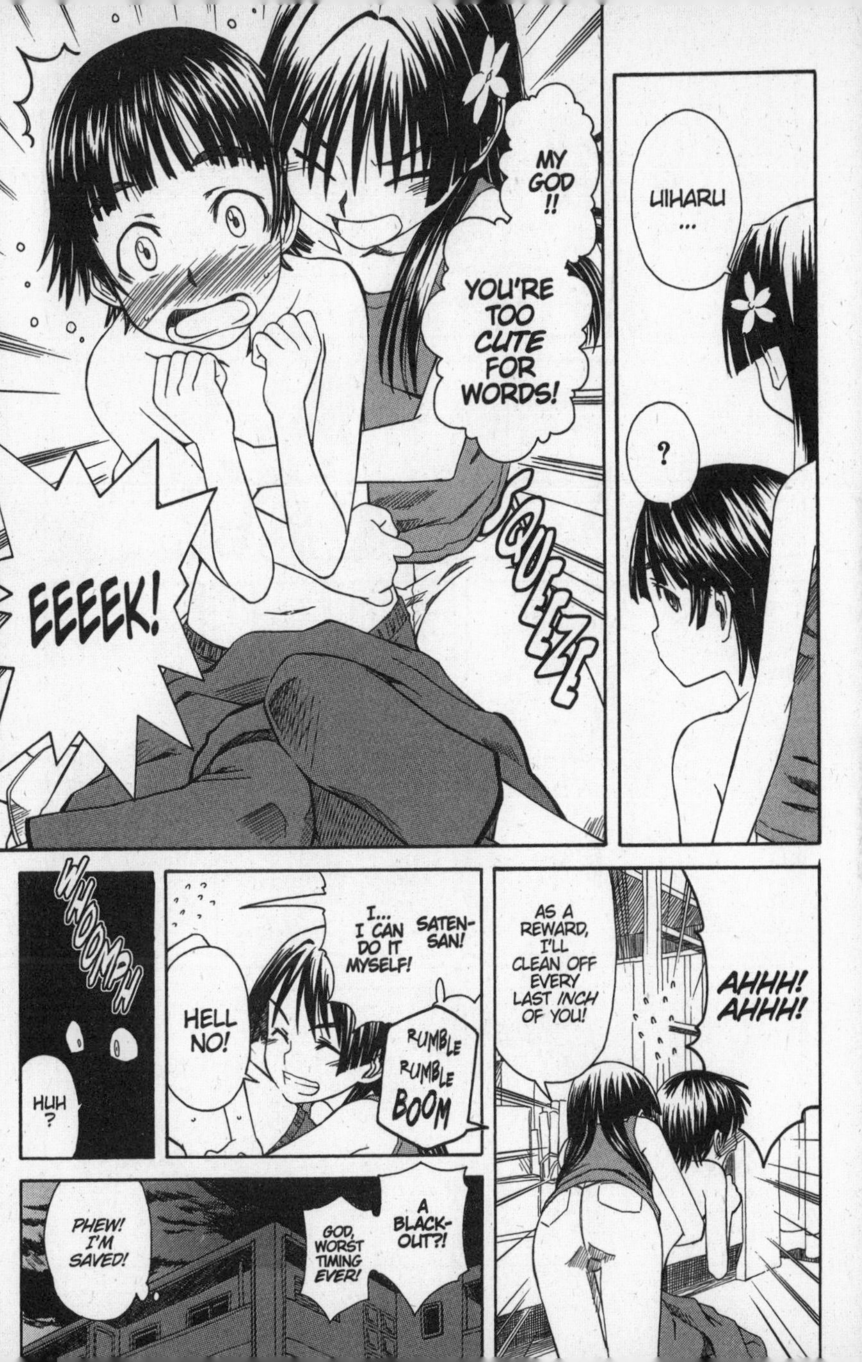
UIHARU ...
?
MY GOD !!
YOU'RE TOO CUTE FOR WORDS!
SQUEEZE
EEEEK!
AHHH! AHHH!
AS A REWARD, I'LL CLEAN OFF EVERY LAST INCH OF YOU!
SATEN-SAN!
I... I CAN DO IT MYSELF!
HELL NO!
RUMBLE RUMBLE BOOM
WHOOMPH
HUH ?
A BLACK-OUT?!
GOD, WORST TIMING EVER!
PHEW! I'M SAVED!

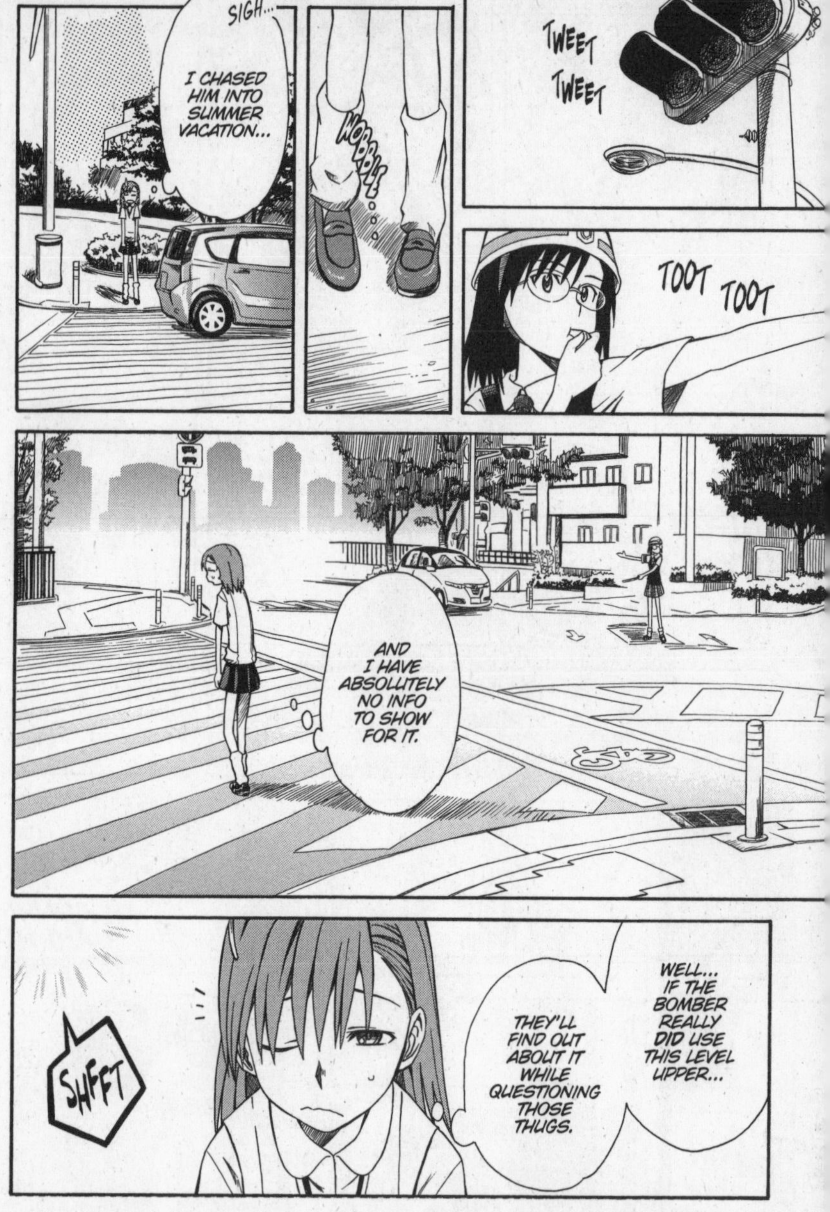
TWEET
TWEET
TOOT TOOT
WOBBLE...
SIGH...
I CHASED HIM INTO SUMMER VACATION...
AND I HAVE ABSOLUTELY NO INFO TO SHOW FOR IT.
WELL... IF THE BOMBER REALLY DID USE THIS LEVEL UPPER...
THEY'LL FIND OUT ABOUT IT WHILE QUESTIONING THOSE THUGS.
SHFFT

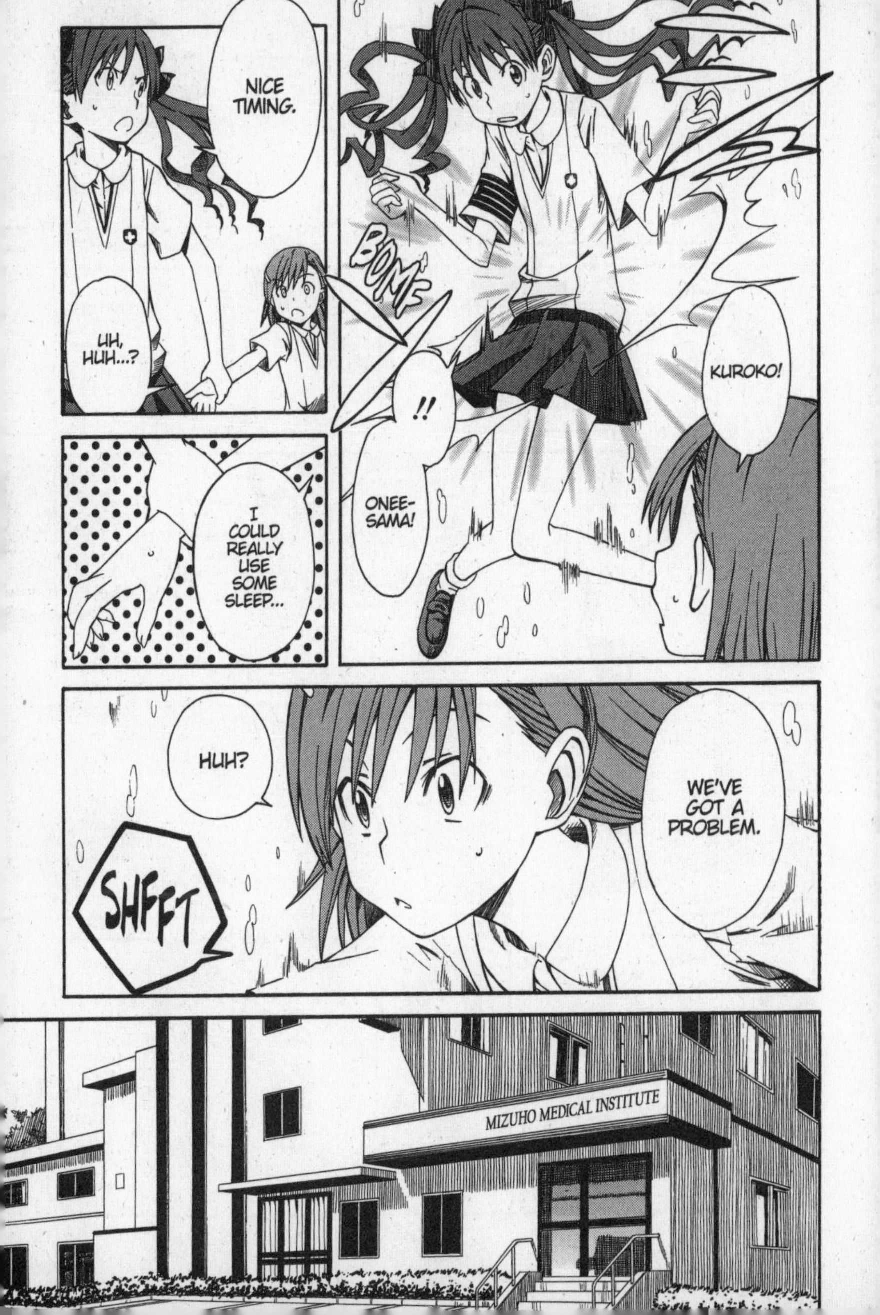
BOMF
KUROKO!
!!
ONEE-SAMA!
NICE TIMING.
UH, HUH...?
I COULD REALLY USE SOME SLEEP...
WE'VE GOT A PROBLEM.
HUH?
SHFFT
MIZUHO MEDICAL INSTITUTE

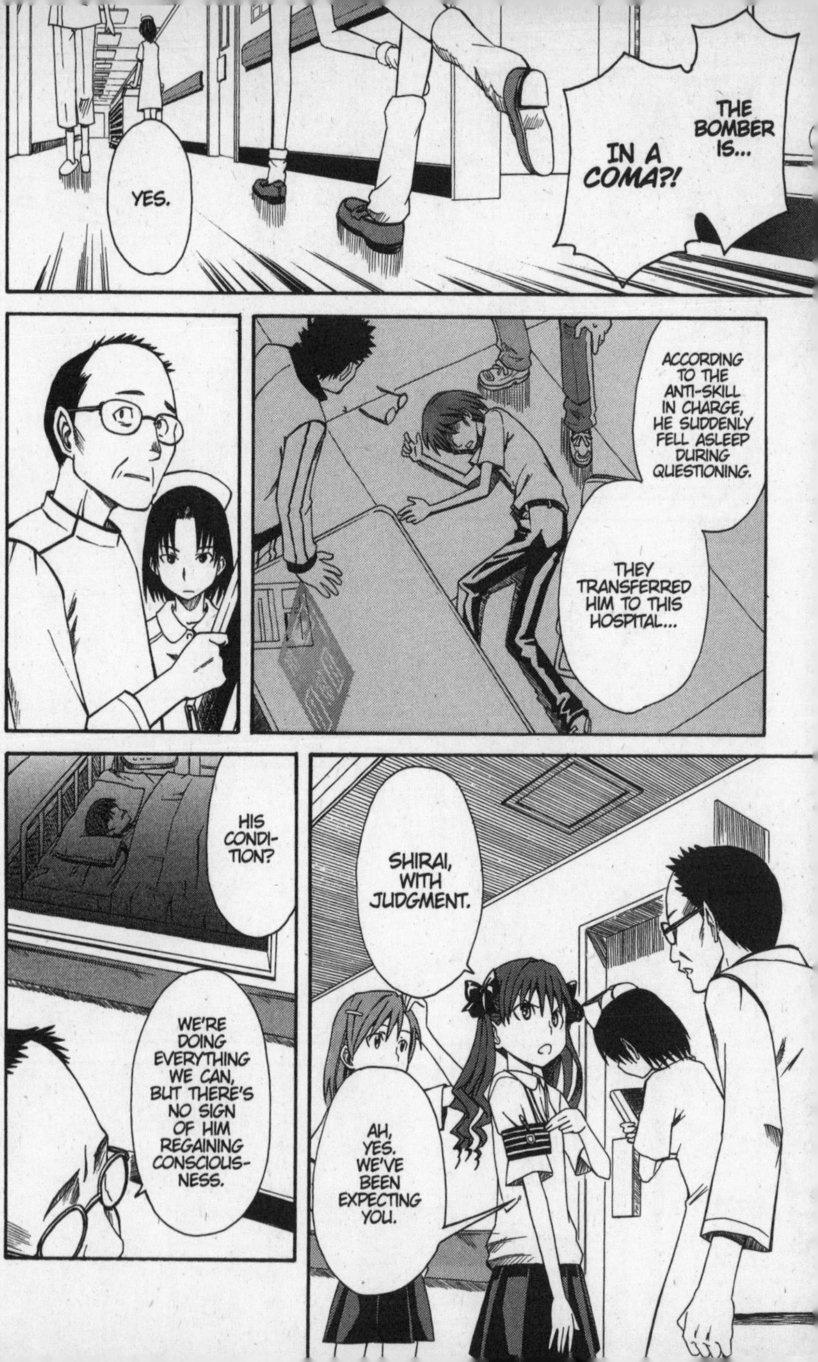
THE BOMBER IS...
IN A COMA?!
YES.
ACCORDING TO THE ANTI-SKILL IN CHARGE, HE SUDDENLY FELL ASLEEP DURING QUESTIONING.
THEY TRANSFERRED HIM TO THIS HOSPITAL...
SHIRAI, WITH JUDGMENT.
AH, YES. WE'VE BEEN EXPECTING YOU.
HIS CONDI-TION?
WE'RE DOING EVERYTHING WE CAN, BUT THERE'S NO SIGN OF HIM REGAINING CONSCIOUS-NESS.

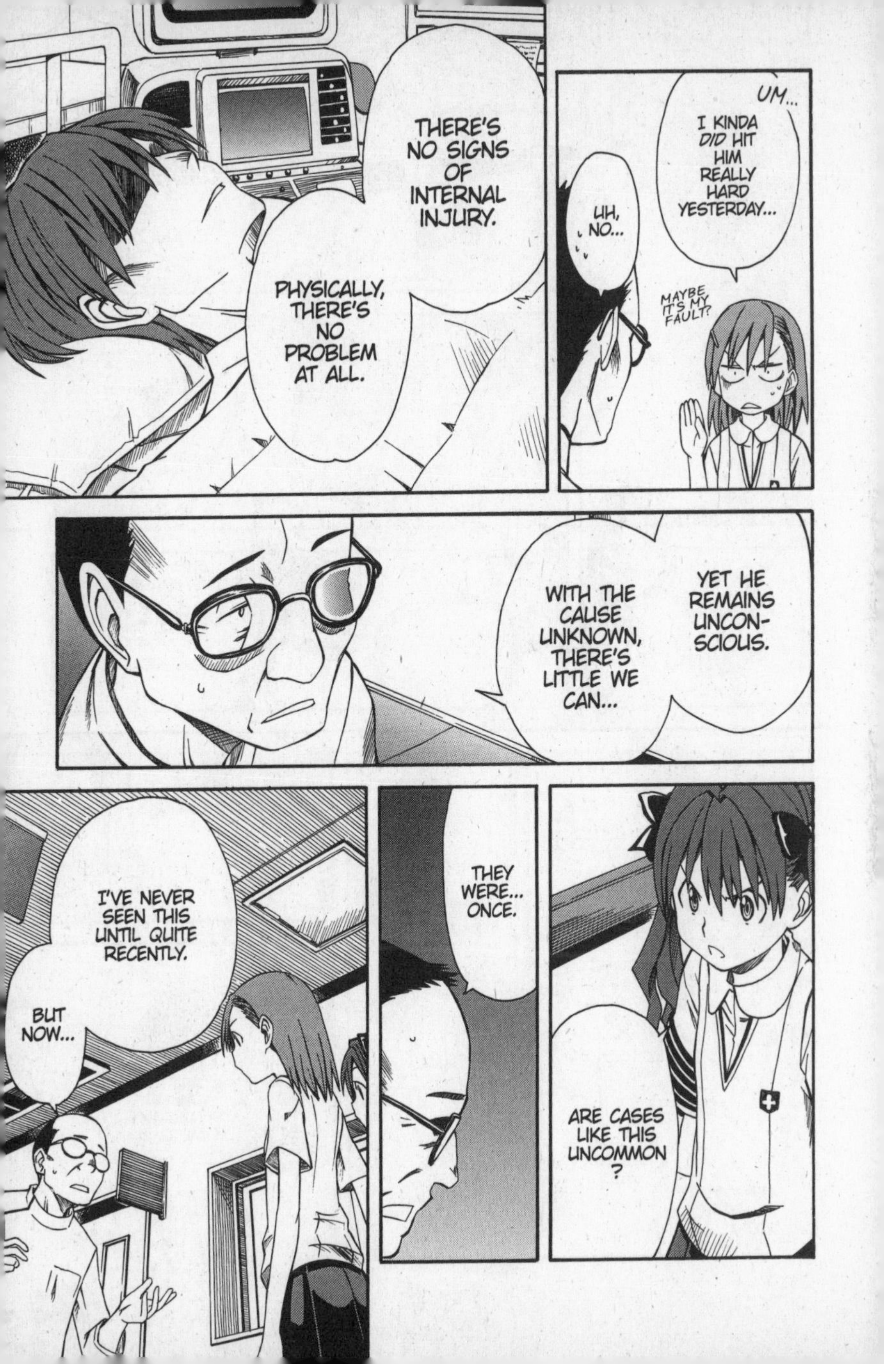
UM... I KINDA DID HIT HIM REALLY HARD YESTERDAY...
MAYBE IT'S MY FAULT?
UH, NO...
THERE'S NO SIGNS OF INTERNAL INJURY.
PHYSICALLY, THERE'S NO PROBLEM AT ALL.
YET HE REMAINS UNCONSCIOUS.
WITH THE CAUSE UNKNOWN, THERE'S LITTLE WE CAN...
ARE CASES LIKE THIS UNCOMMON?
THEY WERE... ONCE.
I'VE NEVER SEEN THIS UNTIL QUITE RECENTLY.
BUT NOW...

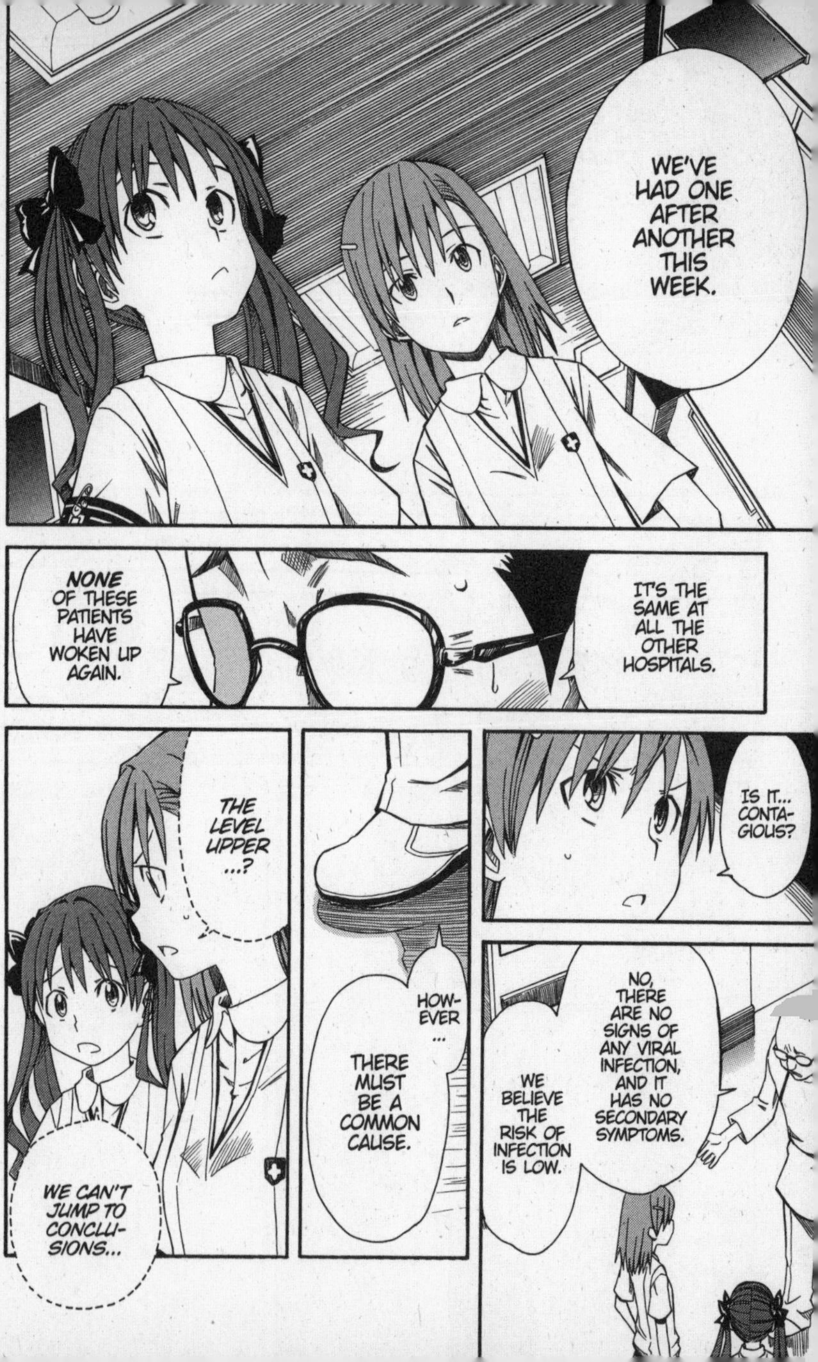
WE'VE HAD ONE AFTER ANOTHER THIS WEEK.
IT'S THE SAME AT ALL THE OTHER HOSPITALS.
NONE OF THESE PATIENTS HAVE WOKEN UP AGAIN.
IS IT... CONTAGIOUS?
NO, THERE ARE NO SIGNS OF ANY VIRAL INFECTION, AND IT HAS NO SECONDARY SYMPTOMS.
WE BELIEVE THE RISK OF INFECTION IS LOW.
HOW-EVER ...
THERE MUST BE A COMMON CAUSE.
THE LEVEL UPPER ...?
WE CAN'T JUMP TO CONCLUSIONS...

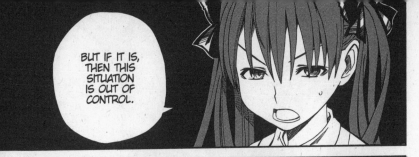

BUT IF IT IS, THEN THIS SITUATION IS OUT OF CONTROL.
I HATE TO ADMIT IT...
BUT THIS IS BEYOND OUR CAPABILITIES.
WE'VE CALLED IN A TEAM OF NEUROLOGY SPECIALISTS.
THEY SHOULD BE HERE ANY MINUTE NOW.

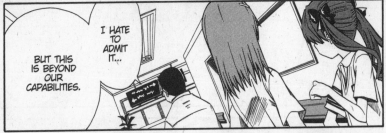

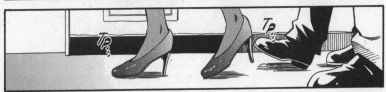

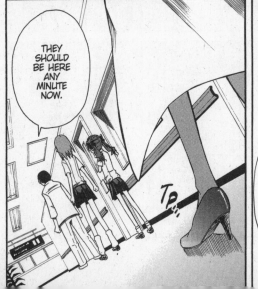

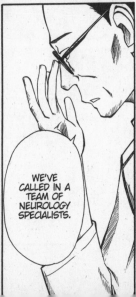

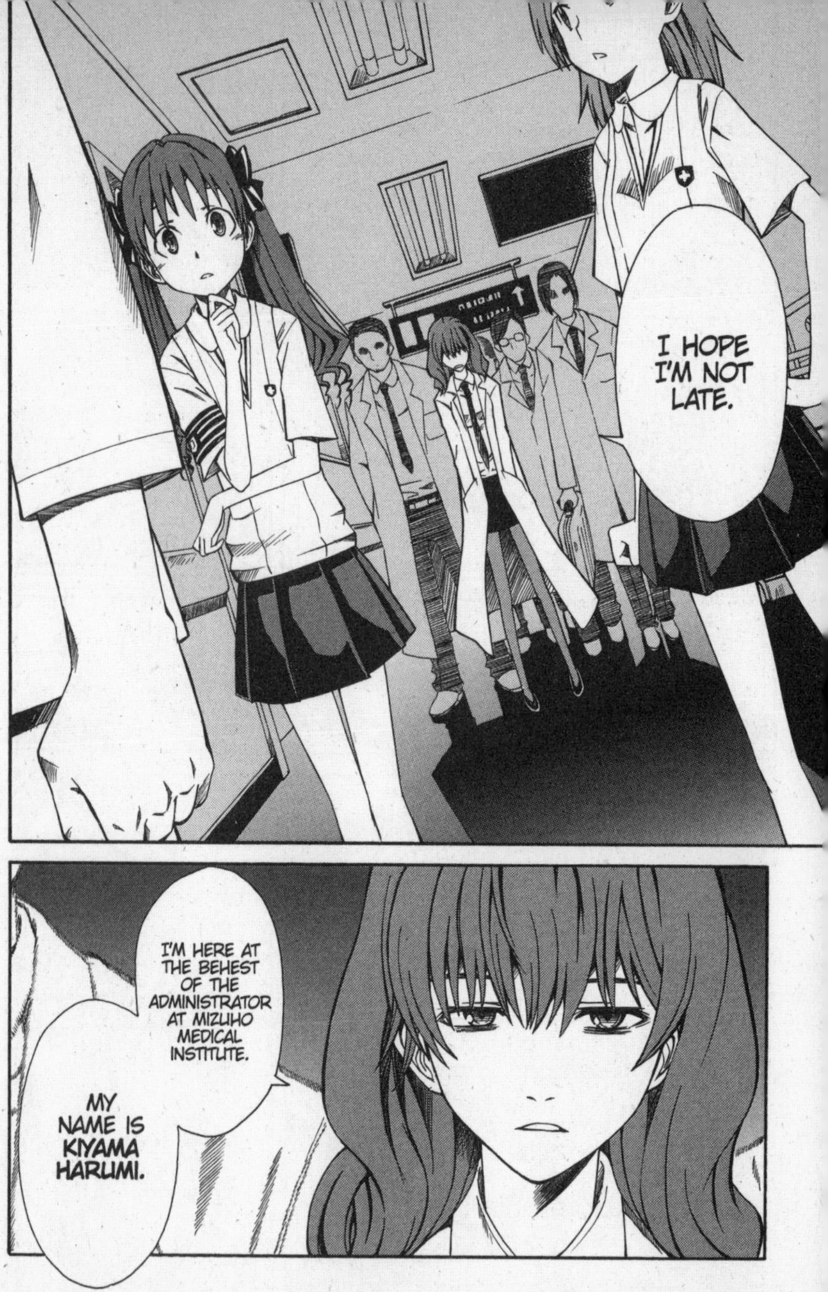
I HOPE I'M NOT LATE.
I'M HERE AT THE BEHEST OF THE ADMINISTRATOR AT MIZUHO MEDICAL INSTITUTE.
MY NAME IS KIYAMA HARUMI.

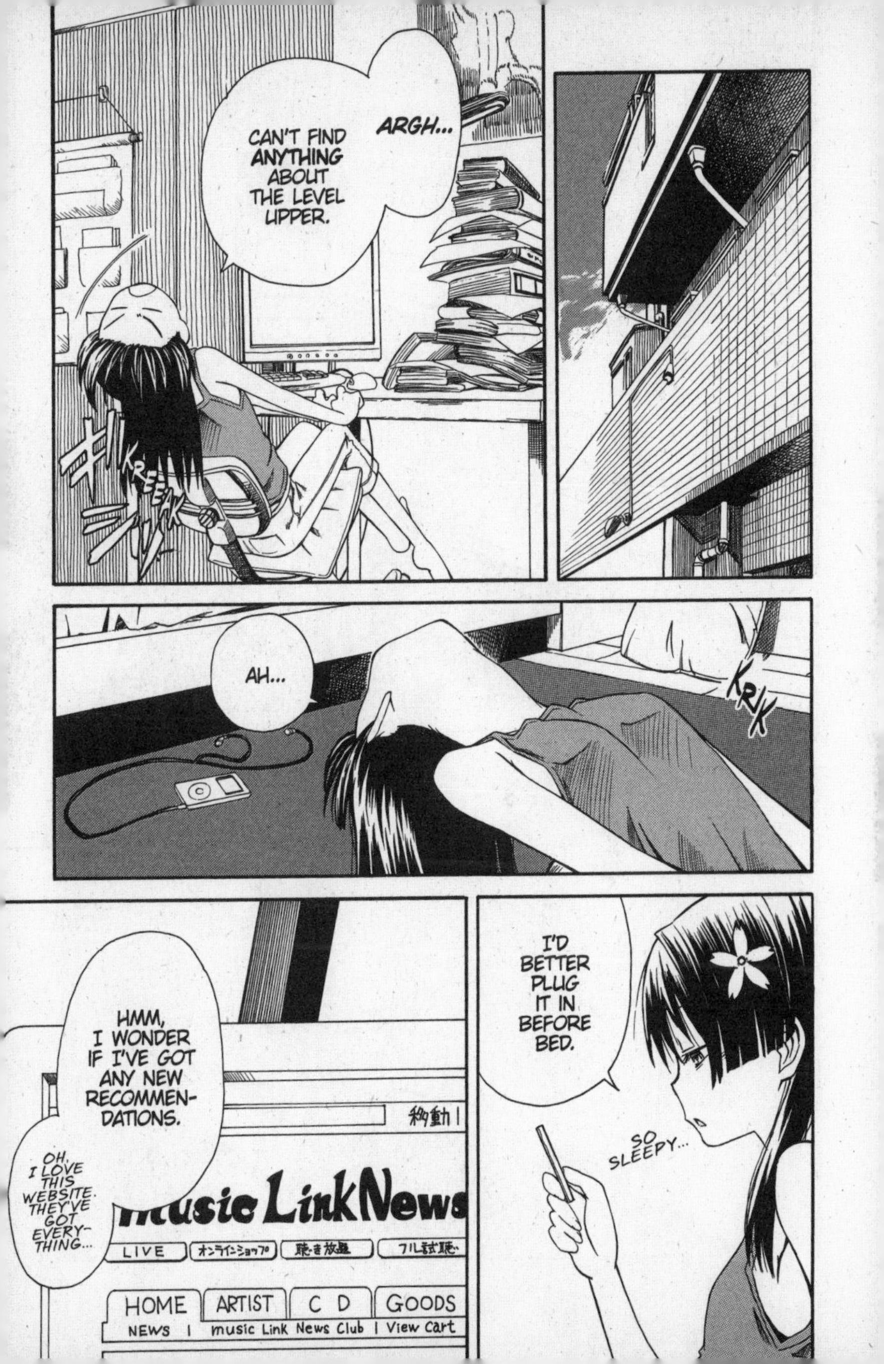

ARGH...
CAN'T FIND ANYTHING ABOUT THE LEVEL UPPER.
KREEAK
AH...
KRIK
I'D BETTER PLUG IT IN BEFORE BED.
SO SLEEPY...
HMM, I WONDER IF I'VE GOT ANY NEW RECOMMEN-DATIONS.
OH, I LOVE THIS WEBSITE. THEY'VE GOT EVERY-THING...
music Link News
LIVE
オンラインショップ
聴き放題
フル試聴
HOME
ARTIST
C D
GOODS
NEWS | music Link News Club | View Cart

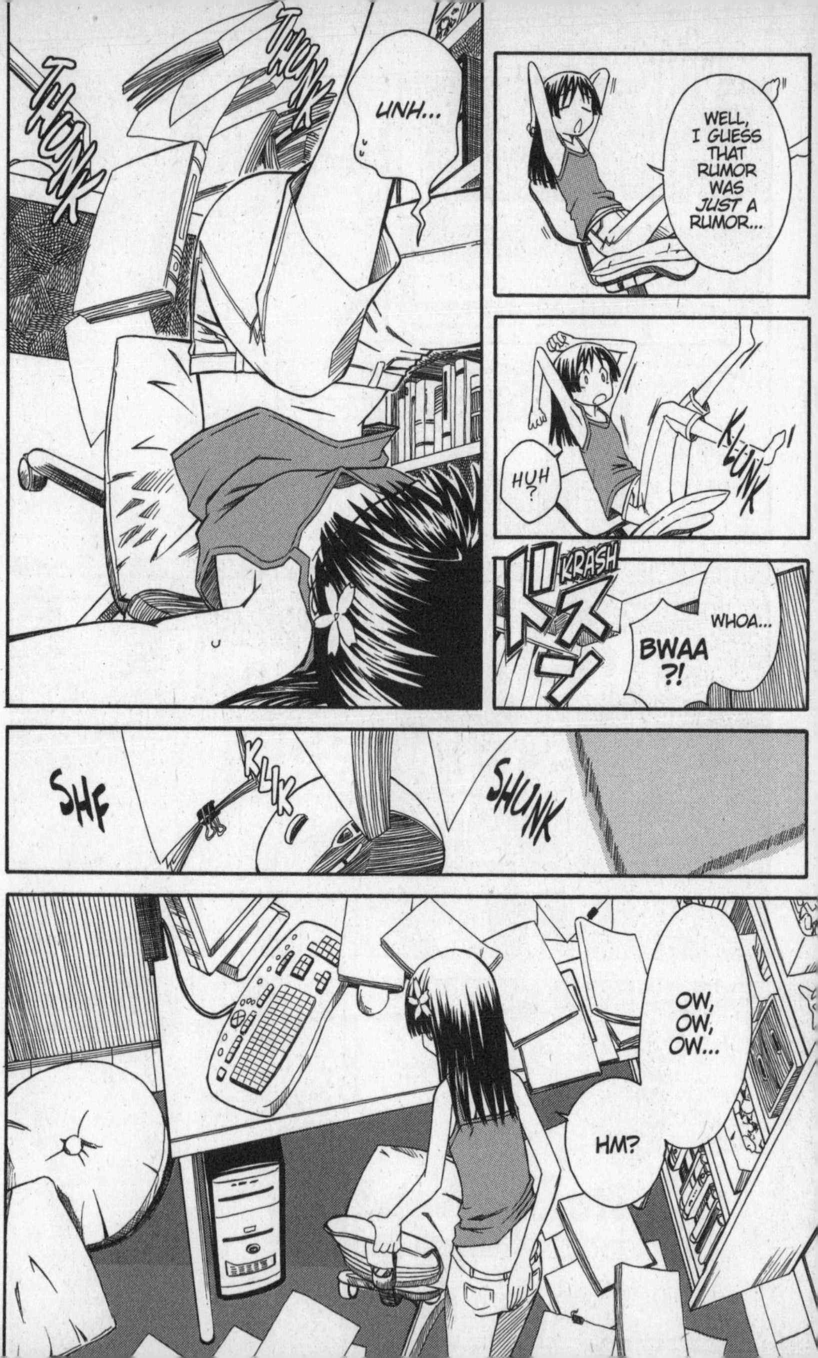
WELL, I GUESS THAT RUMOR WAS JUST A RUMOR...
KLUNK
HUH?
WHOA...
BWAA?!
KRASH
ドスーッ
THUNK
UNH...
THUNK
SHUNK
KLIK
SHF
OW, OW, OW...
HM?

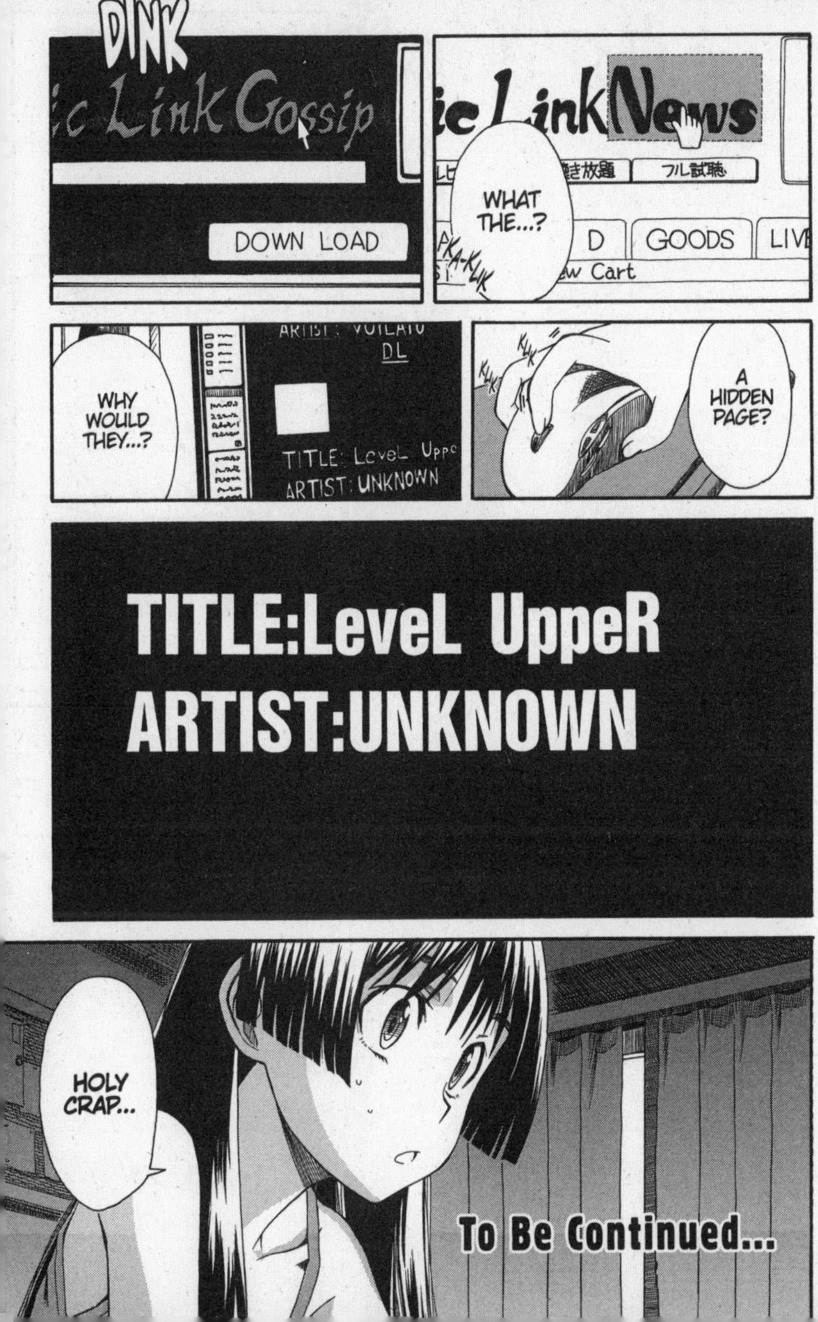
ic Link News
フル試聴
WHAT THE...?
KA-KA-KLIK
D
GOODS
ew Cart
DINK
ic Link Gossip
DOWN LOAD
KLIK KLIK
A HIDDEN PAGE?
WHY WOULD THEY...?
DL
TITLE: LeveL Uppe
ARTIST: UNKNOWN
TITLE:LeveL UppeR
ARTIST:UNKNOWN
HOLY CRAP...
To Be Continued...

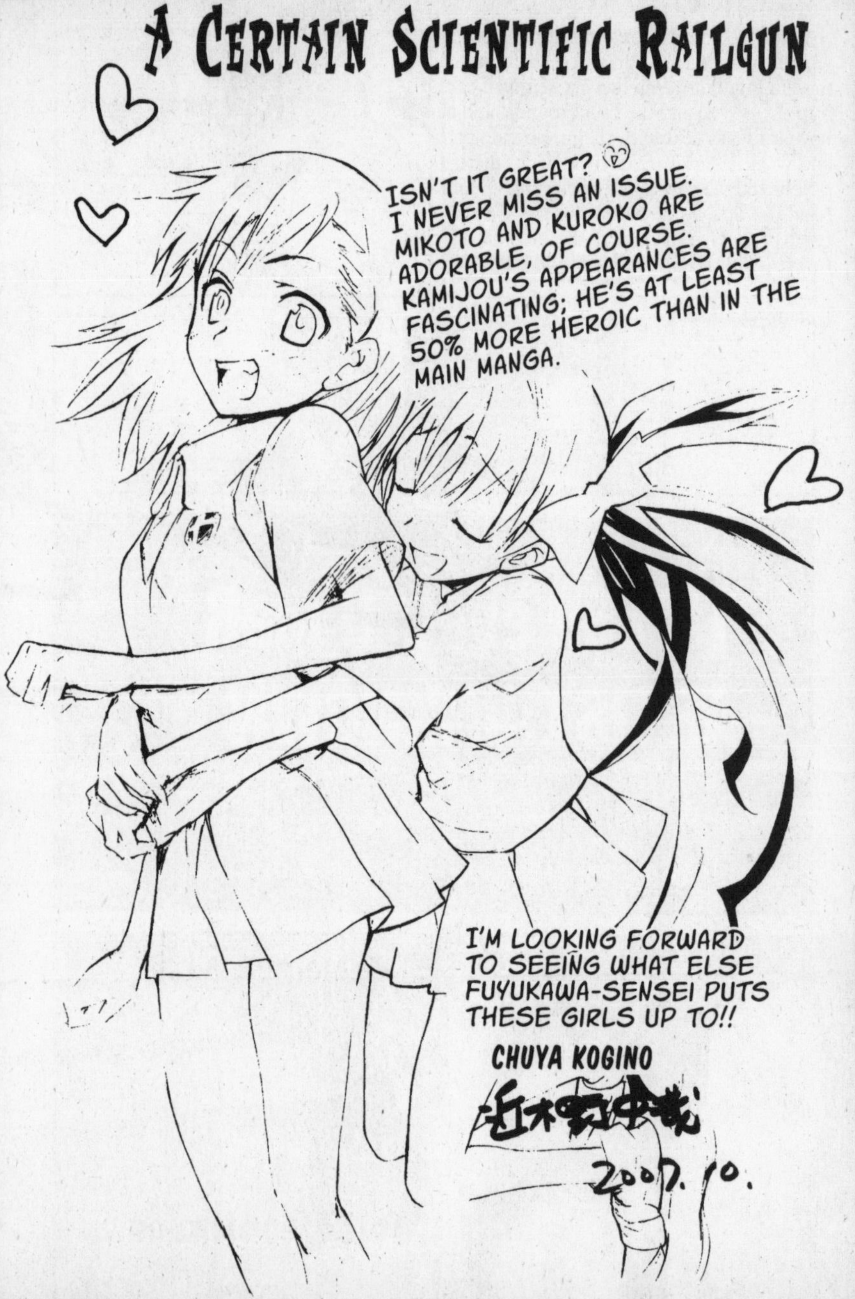
A CERTAIN SCIENTIFIC RAILGUN
ISN'T IT GREAT? I NEVER MISS AN ISSUE. MIKOTO AND KUROKO ARE ADORABLE, OF COURSE. KAMIJOU'S APPEARANCES ARE FASCINATING; HE'S AT LEAST 50% MORE HEROIC THAN IN THE MAIN MANGA.
I'M LOOKING FORWARD TO SEEING WHAT ELSE FUYUKAWA-SENSEI PUTS THESE GIRLS UP TO!!
CHUYA KOGINO
2007. 10.

A Certain Scientific Railgun is finally out. Congratulations to all involved, including myself. Fuyukawa-san has put so much care into the people and the backgrounds, and to how students deal with their own strengths and weaknesses in an environment where psychic powers are a part of the curriculum. I feel like he's really made Academy City come to life. I'm sincerely grateful for that. I can't wait to see what he does next.

Kazuma Kamachi

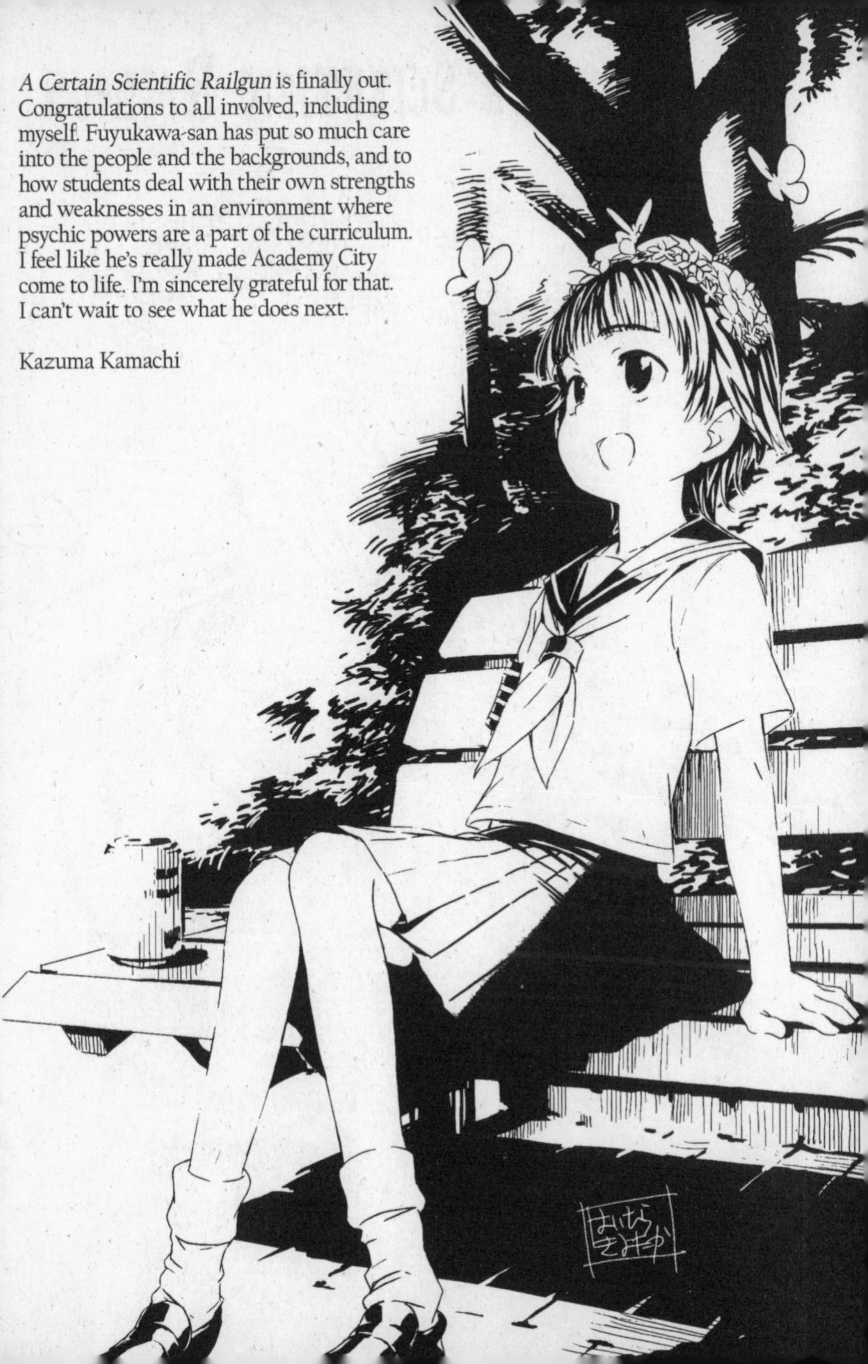

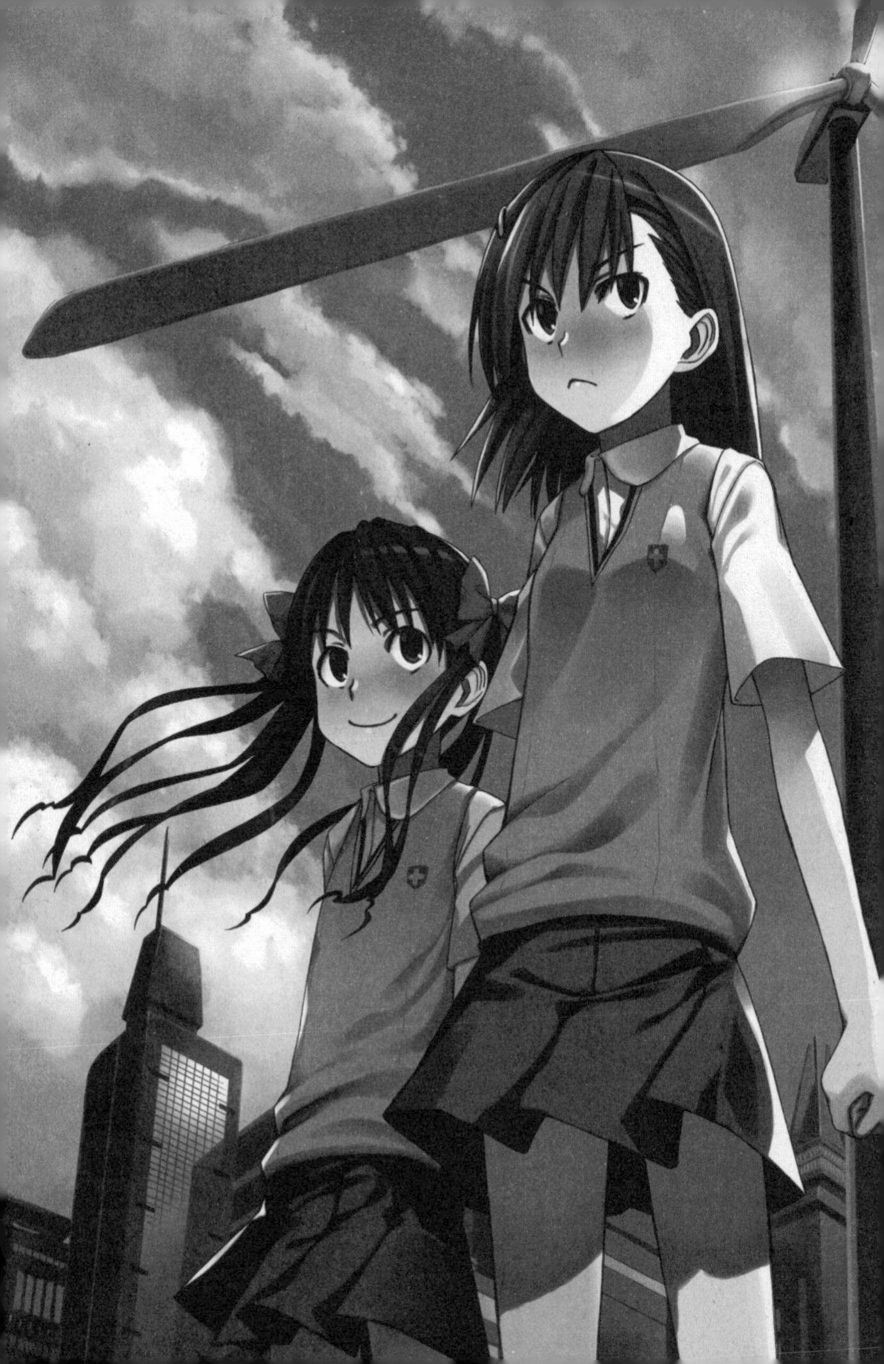

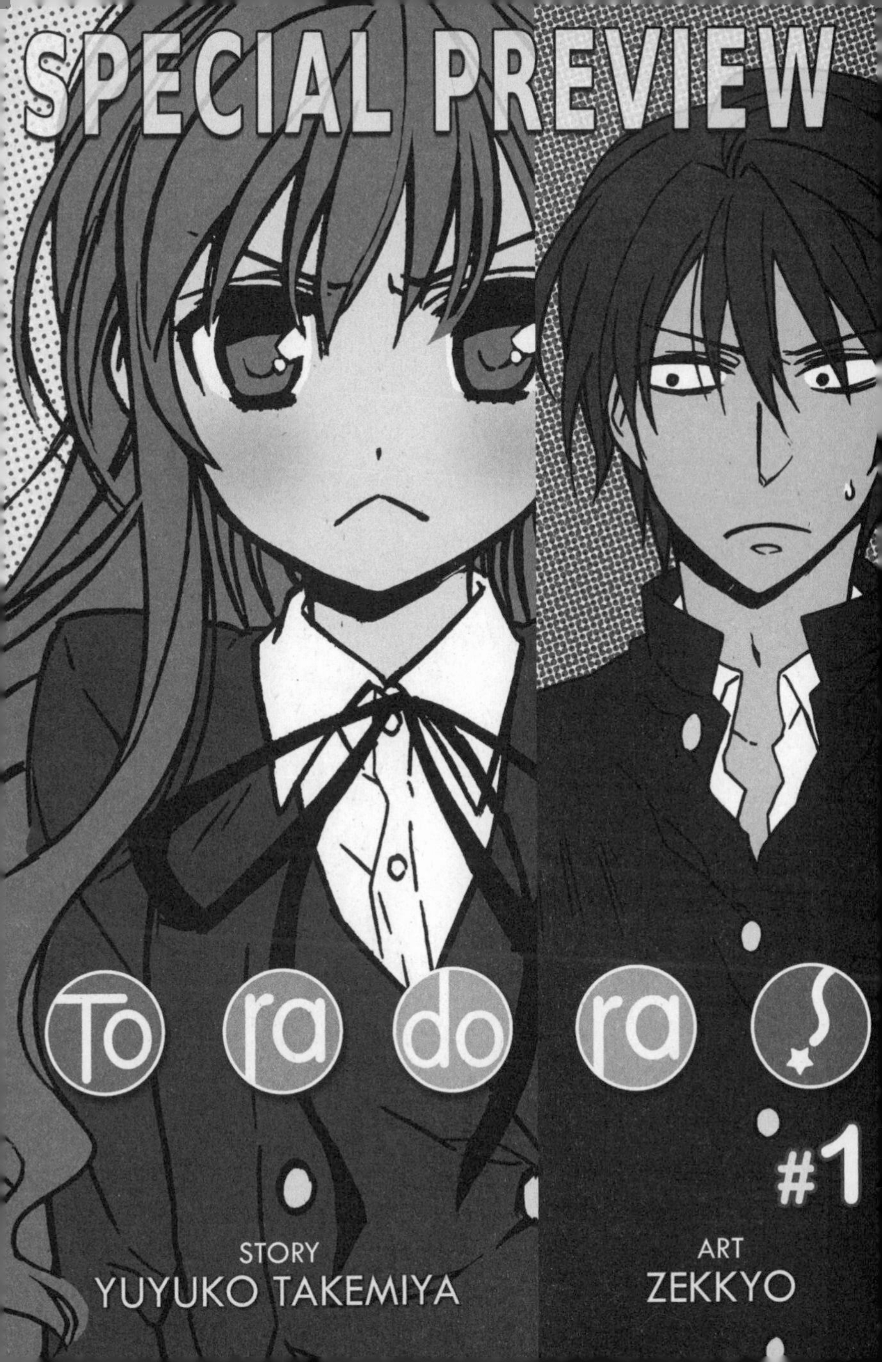
SPECIAL PREVIEW
Toradora!
#1
STORY
YUYUKO TAKEMIYA
ART
ZEKKYO

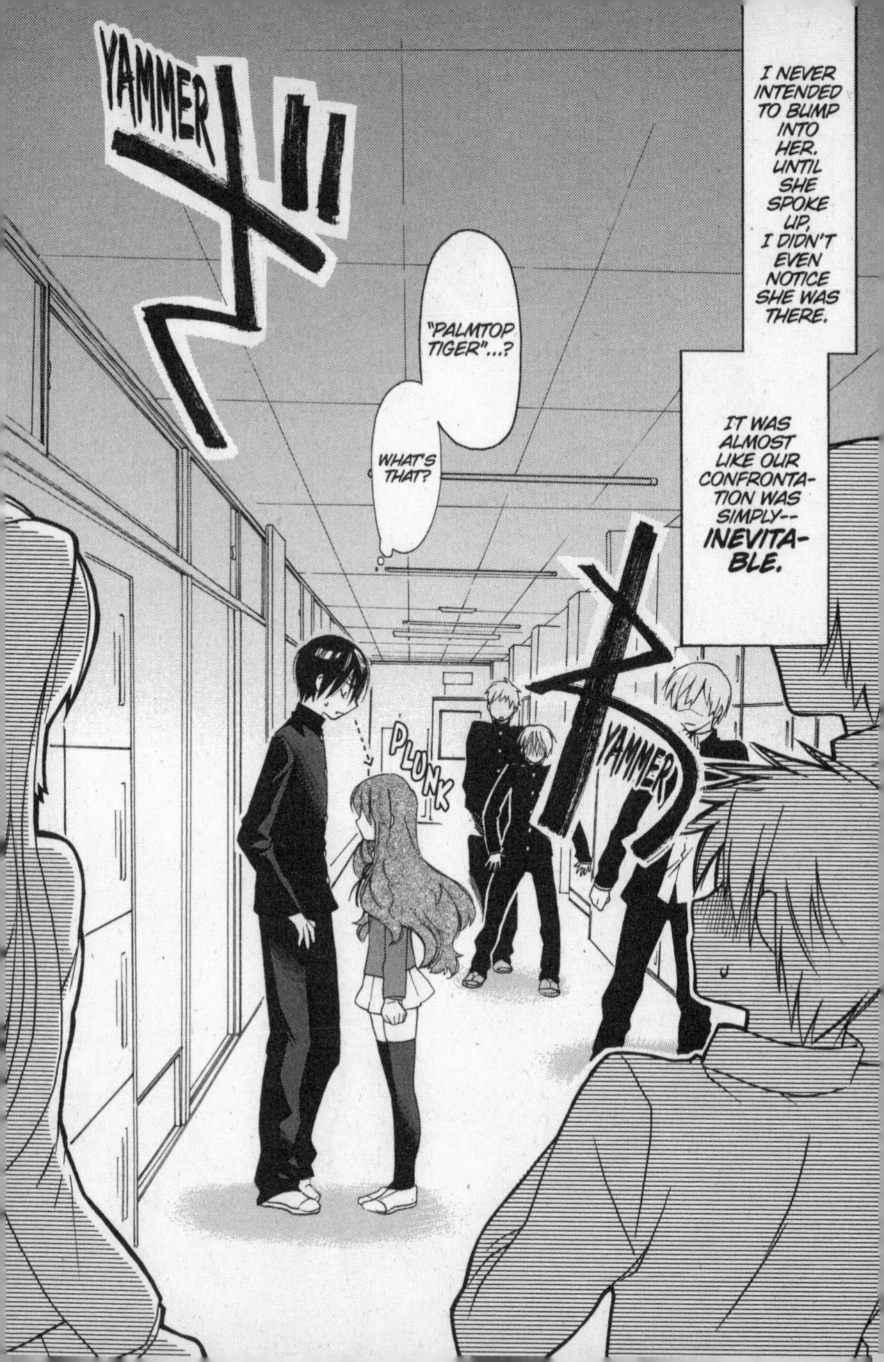
I NEVER INTENDED TO BUMP INTO HER. UNTIL SHE SPOKE UP, I DIDN'T EVEN NOTICE SHE WAS THERE.
IT WAS ALMOST LIKE OUR CONFRONTATION WAS SIMPLY-- **INEVITABLE.**
YAMMER
"PALMTOP TIGER"...?
WHAT'S THAT?
YAMMER
PLUNK

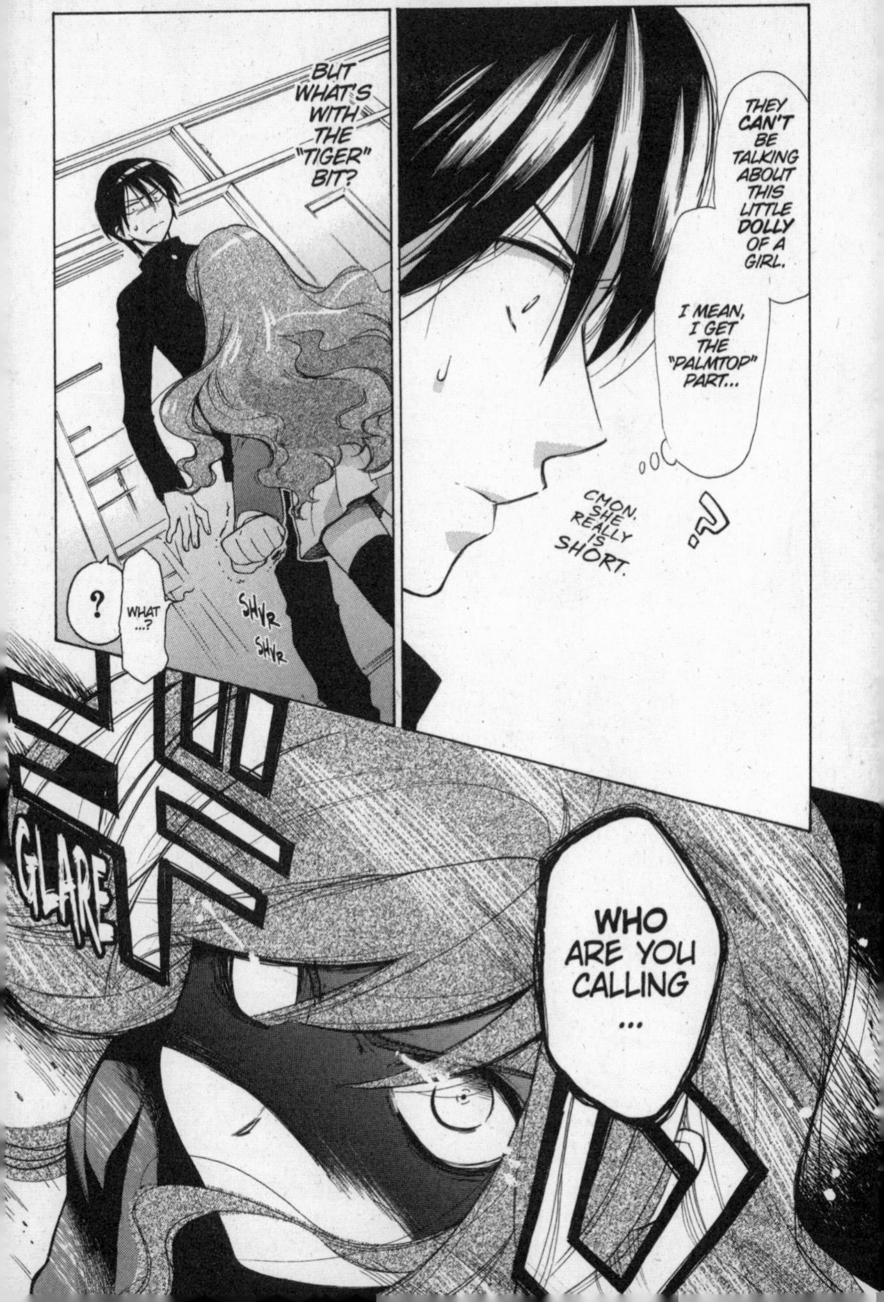
THEY CAN'T BE TALKING ABOUT THIS LITTLE DOLLY OF A GIRL.
I MEAN, I GET THE "PALMTOP" PART...
CMON, SHE REALLY IS SHORT.
BUT WHAT'S WITH THE "TIGER" BIT?
?
WHAT ...?
SHVR
SHVR
GLARE
WHO ARE YOU CALLING ...

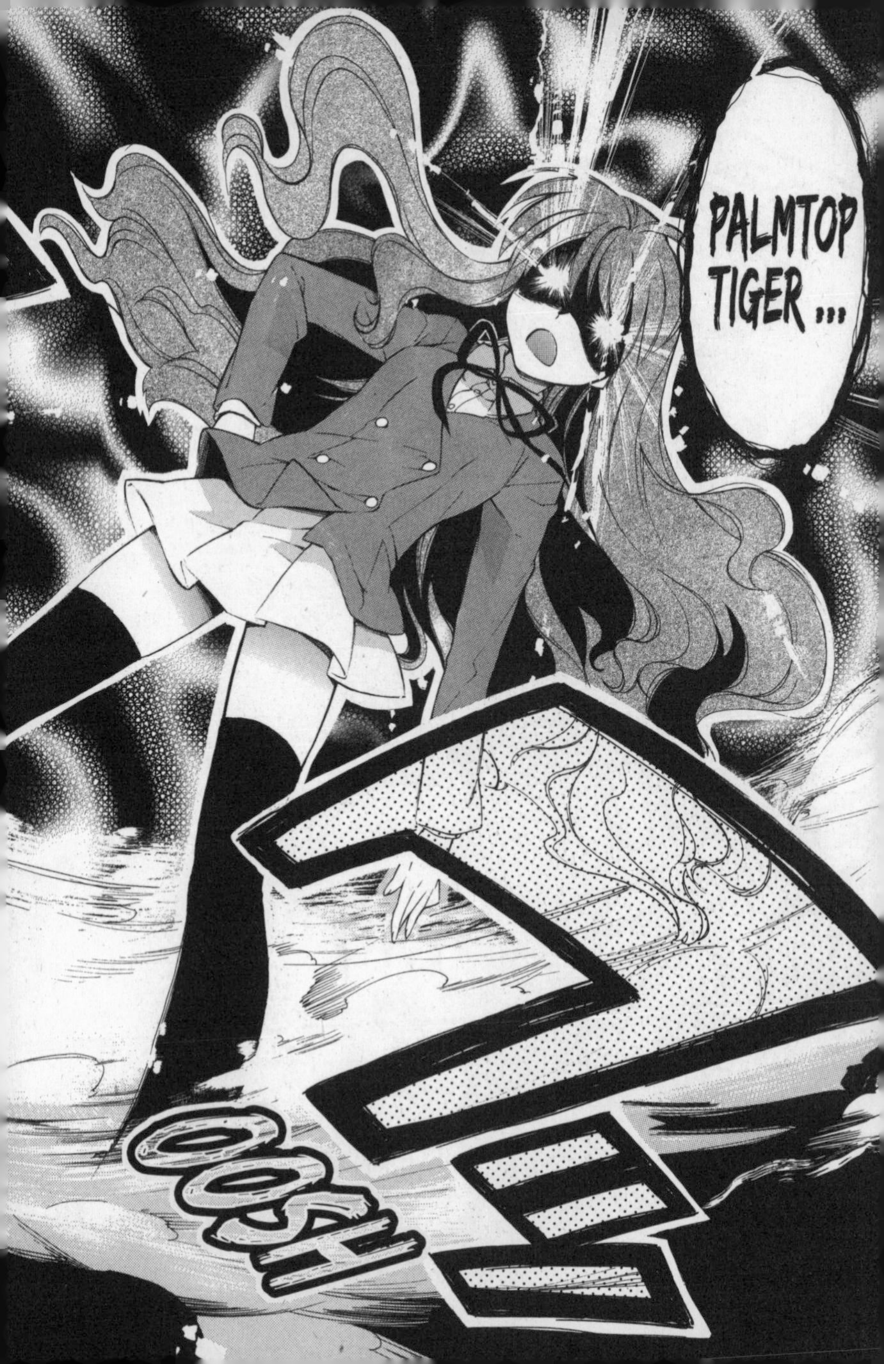
PALMTOP TIGER ...
OOSH!

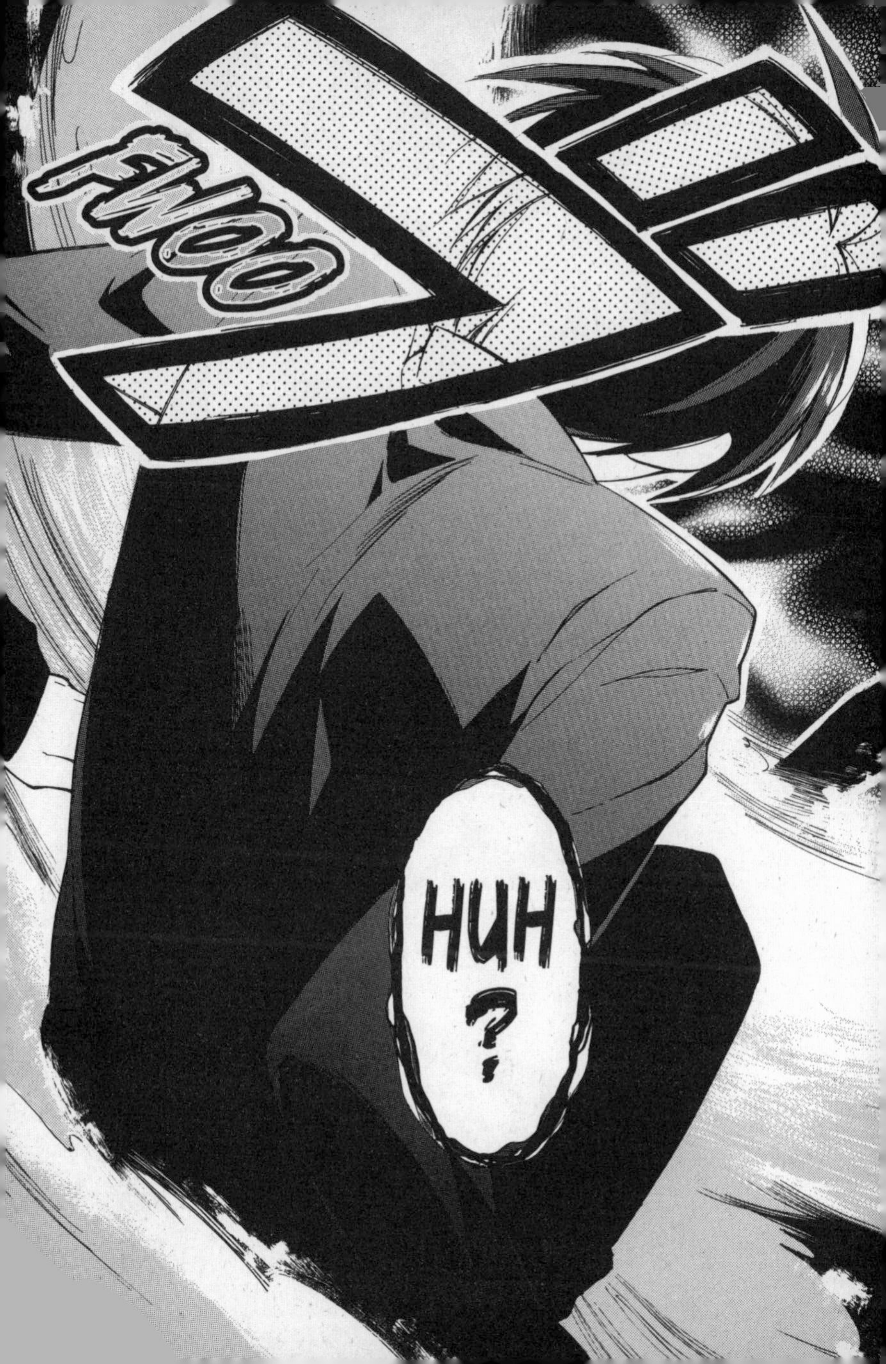
FWOO
HUH ?

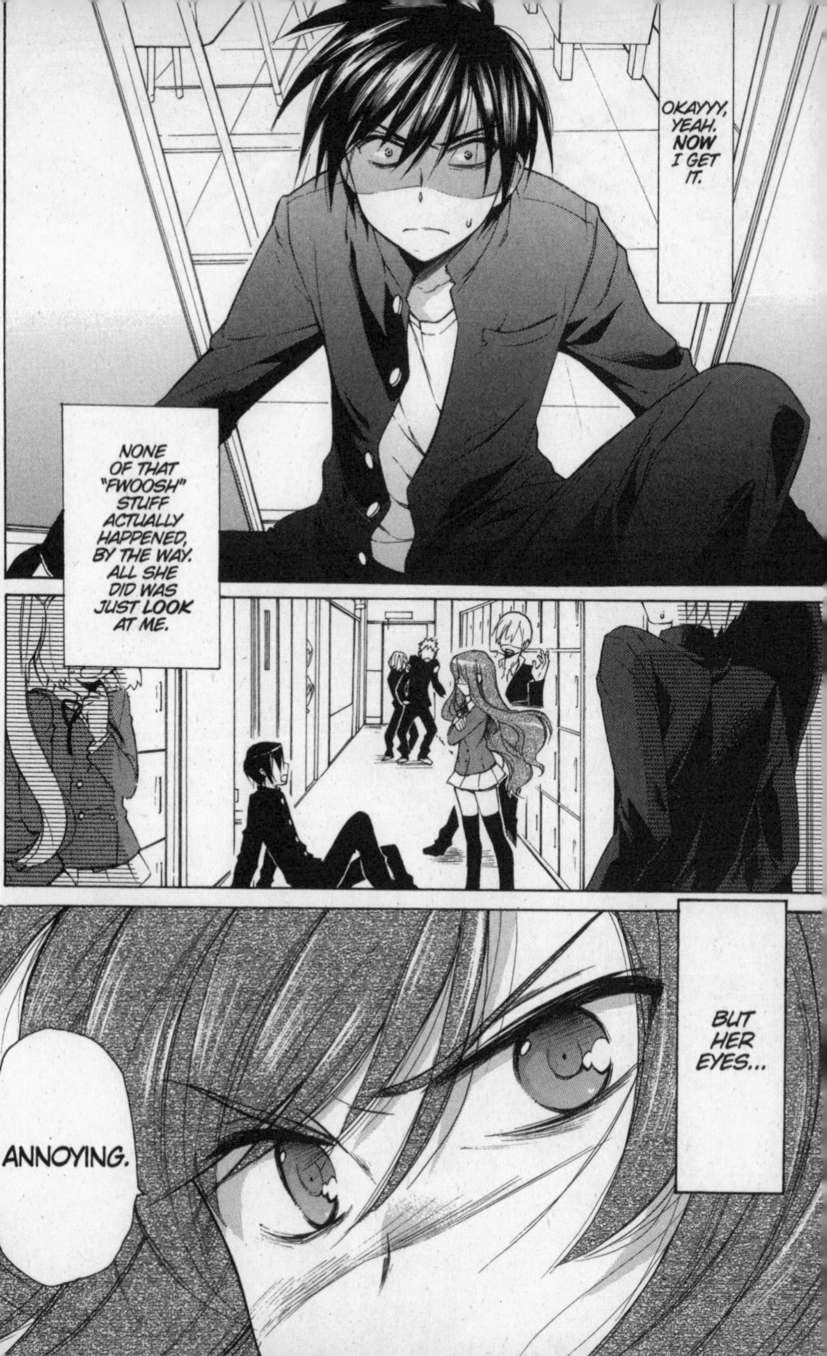
OKAYYY, YEAH. NOW I GET IT.
NONE OF THAT "FWOOSH" STUFF ACTUALLY HAPPENED, BY THE WAY. ALL SHE DID WAS JUST LOOK AT ME.
BUT HER EYES...
ANNOYING.

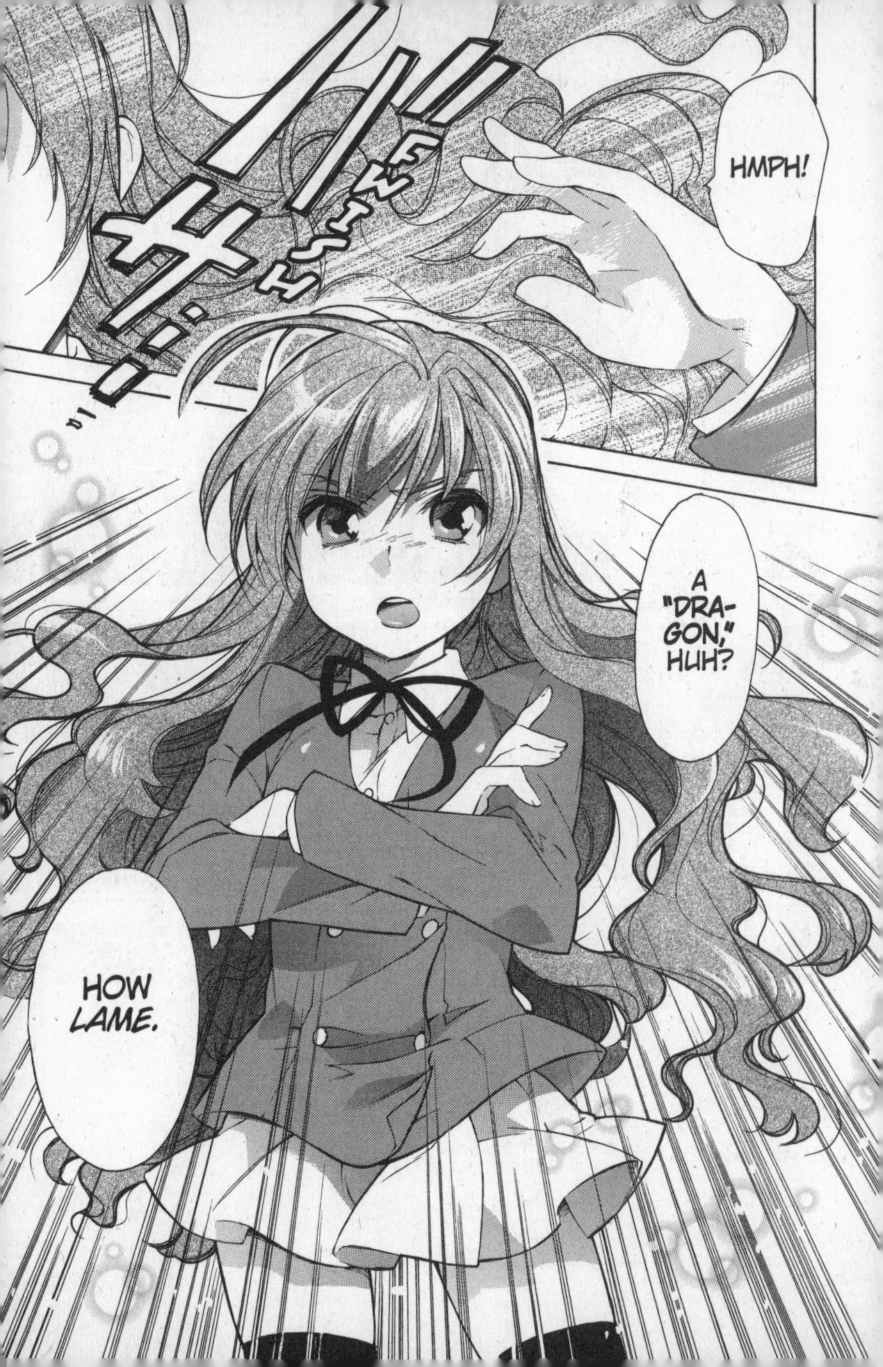
HMPH!
FWISH
A "DRA-GON," HUH?
HOW LAME.

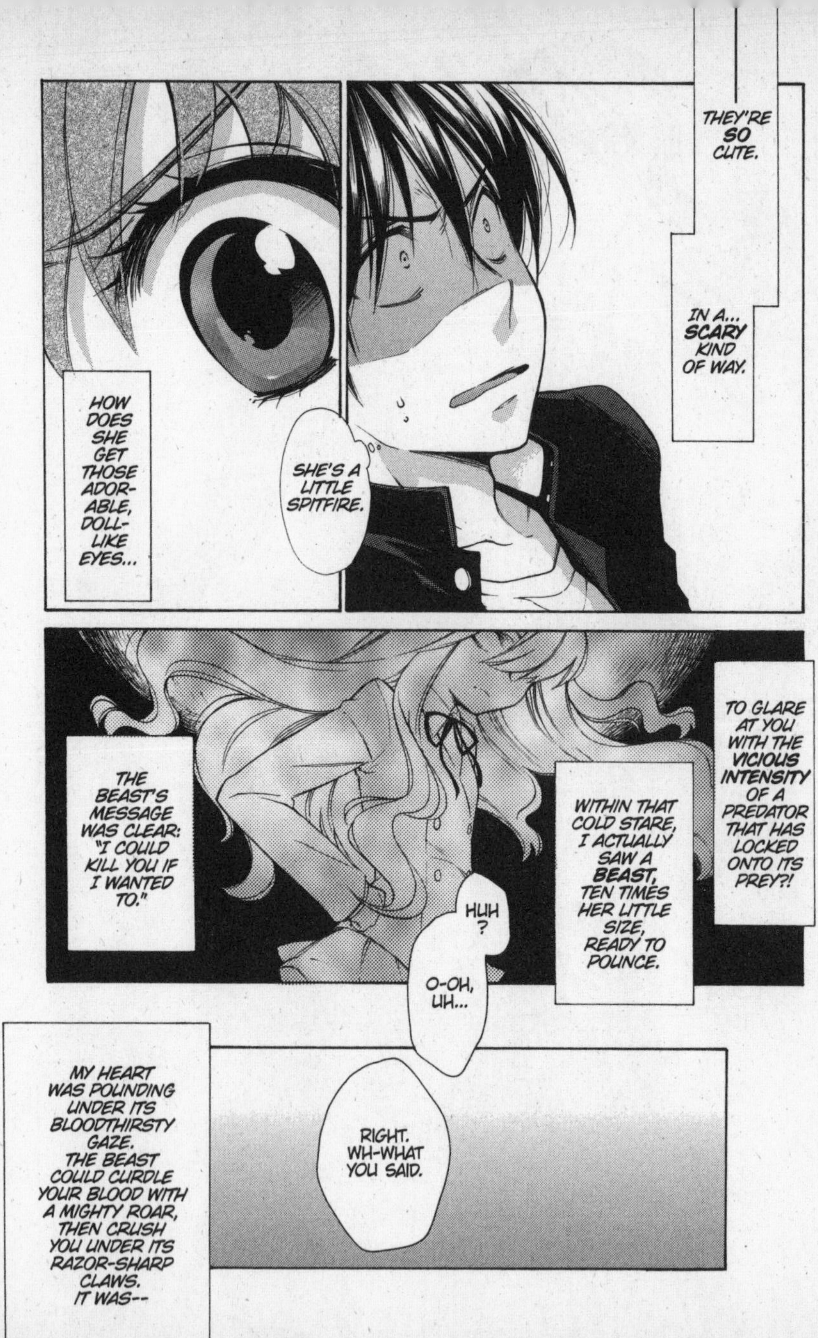
THEY'RE SO CUTE.
IN A... SCARY KIND OF WAY.
SHE'S A LITTLE SPITFIRE.
HOW DOES SHE GET THOSE ADORABLE, DOLL-LIKE EYES...
TO GLARE AT YOU WITH THE VICIOUS INTENSITY OF A PREDATOR THAT HAS LOCKED ONTO ITS PREY?!
WITHIN THAT COLD STARE, I ACTUALLY SAW A BEAST, TEN TIMES HER LITTLE SIZE, READY TO POUNCE.
HUH?
THE BEAST'S MESSAGE WAS CLEAR: "I COULD KILL YOU IF I WANTED TO."
O-OH, UH...
RIGHT. WH-WHAT YOU SAID.
MY HEART WAS POUNDING UNDER ITS BLOODTHIRSTY GAZE. THE BEAST COULD CURDLE YOUR BLOOD WITH A MIGHTY ROAR, THEN CRUSH YOU UNDER ITS RAZOR-SHARP CLAWS. IT WAS--

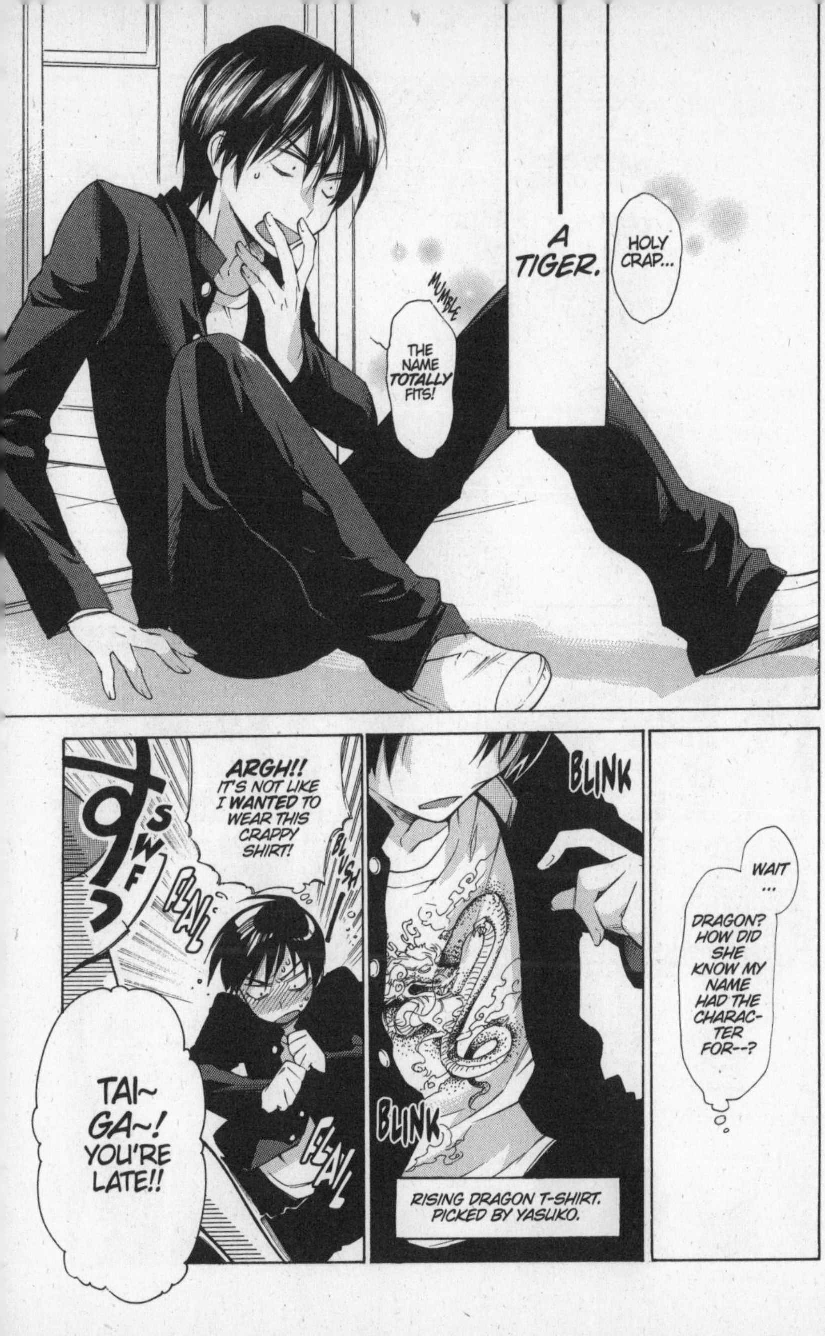
HOLY CRAP...
A TIGER.
MUMBLE
THE NAME TOTALLY FITS!
WAIT ... DRAGON? HOW DID SHE KNOW MY NAME HAD THE CHARACTER FOR--?
BLINK
BLINK
RISING DRAGON T-SHIRT. PICKED BY YASUKO.
ARGH!! IT'S NOT LIKE I WANTED TO WEAR THIS CRAPPY SHIRT!
BLUSH
SWF
FLAIL
FLAIL
TAI~ GA~! YOU'RE LATE!!

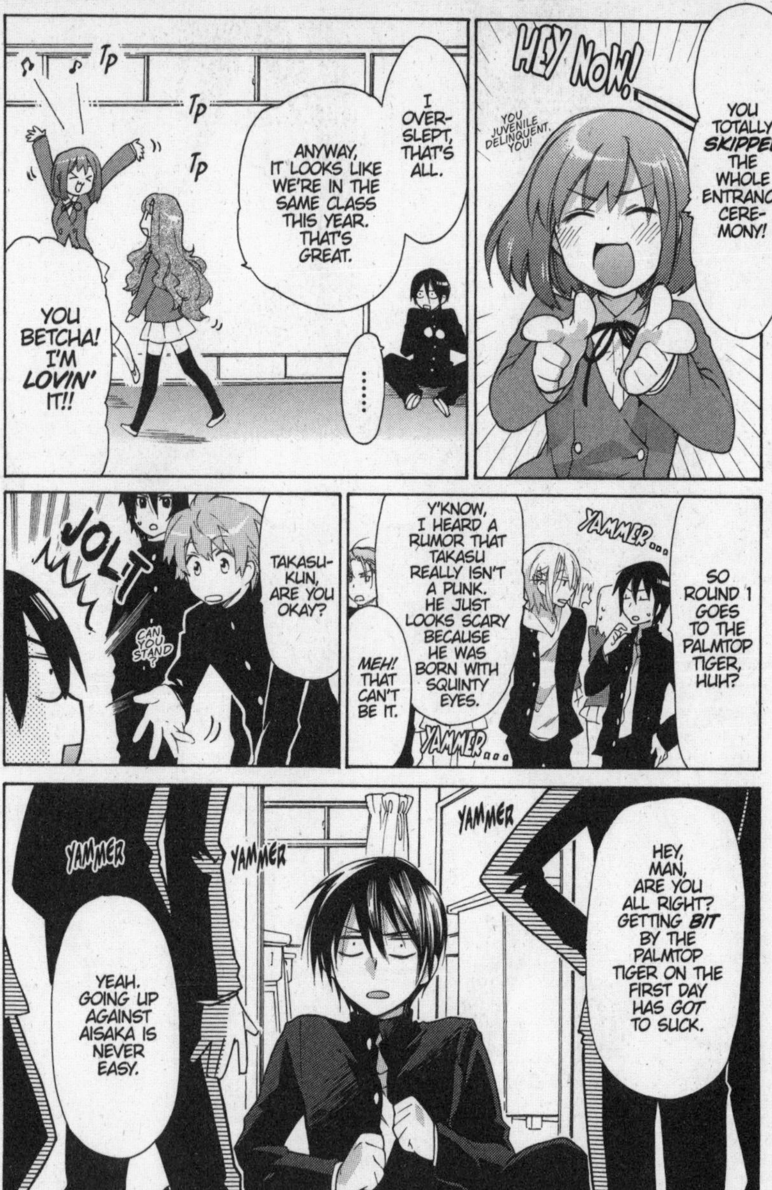
HEY NOW!
YOU TOTALLY SKIPPED THE WHOLE ENTRANCE CEREMONY!
YOU JUVENILE DELINQUENT, YOU!
I OVER-SLEPT, THAT'S ALL.
ANYWAY, IT LOOKS LIKE WE'RE IN THE SAME CLASS THIS YEAR. THAT'S GREAT.
Tp
Tp
Tp
......
YOU BETCHA! I'M LOVIN' IT!!
YAMMER...
SO ROUND 1 GOES TO THE PALMTOP TIGER, HUH?
Y'KNOW, I HEARD A RUMOR THAT TAKASU REALLY ISN'T A PUNK. HE JUST LOOKS SCARY BECAUSE HE WAS BORN WITH SQUINTY EYES.
MEH! THAT CAN'T BE IT.
YAMMER...
TAKASU-KUN, ARE YOU OKAY?
JOLT
CAN YOU STAND?
YAMMER
HEY, MAN, ARE YOU ALL RIGHT? GETTING BIT BY THE PALMTOP TIGER ON THE FIRST DAY HAS GOT TO SUCK.
YAMMER
YAMMER
YEAH. GOING UP AGAINST AISAKA IS NEVER EASY.

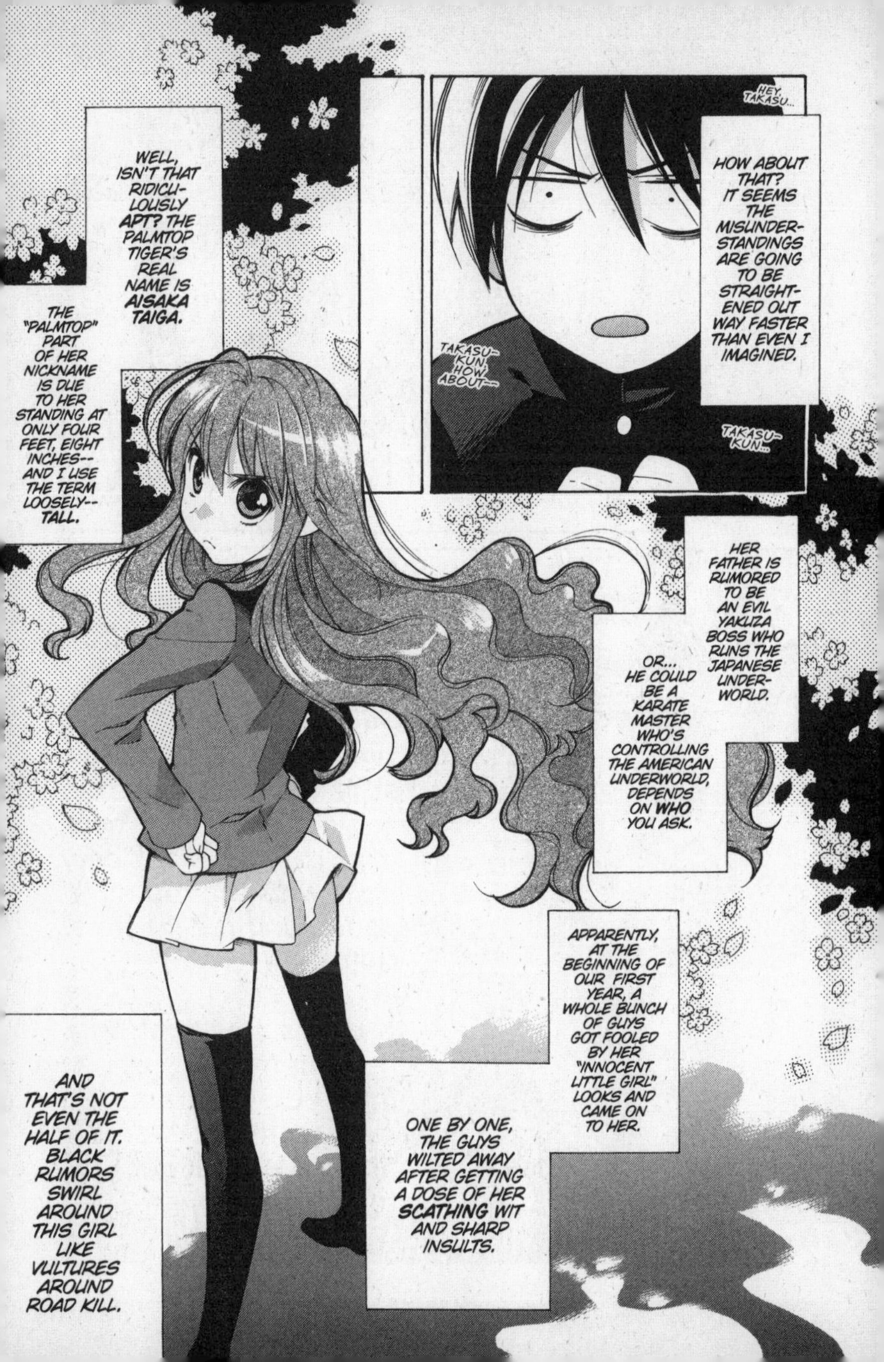
HEY, TAKASU...
HOW ABOUT THAT? IT SEEMS THE MISUNDERSTANDINGS ARE GOING TO BE STRAIGHTENED OUT WAY FASTER THAN EVEN I IMAGINED.
TAKASU-KUN, HOW ABOUT--
TAKASU-KUN...
WELL, ISN'T THAT RIDICULOUSLY APT? THE PALMTOP TIGER'S REAL NAME IS AISAKA TAIGA.
THE "PALMTOP" PART OF HER NICKNAME IS DUE TO HER STANDING AT ONLY FOUR FEET, EIGHT INCHES-- AND I USE THE TERM LOOSELY-- TALL.
HER FATHER IS RUMORED TO BE AN EVIL YAKUZA BOSS WHO RUNS THE JAPANESE UNDERWORLD.
OR... HE COULD BE A KARATE MASTER WHO'S CONTROLLING THE AMERICAN UNDERWORLD, DEPENDS ON WHO YOU ASK.
APPARENTLY, AT THE BEGINNING OF OUR FIRST YEAR, A WHOLE BUNCH OF GUYS GOT FOOLED BY HER "INNOCENT LITTLE GIRL" LOOKS AND CAME ON TO HER.
ONE BY ONE, THE GUYS WILTED AWAY AFTER GETTING A DOSE OF HER SCATHING WIT AND SHARP INSULTS.
AND THAT'S NOT EVEN THE HALF OF IT. BLACK RUMORS SWIRL AROUND THIS GIRL LIKE VULTURES AROUND ROAD KILL.

THE END

YOU'RE READING THE WRONG WAY

This is the last page of
A Certain Scientific Railgun
Volume 1

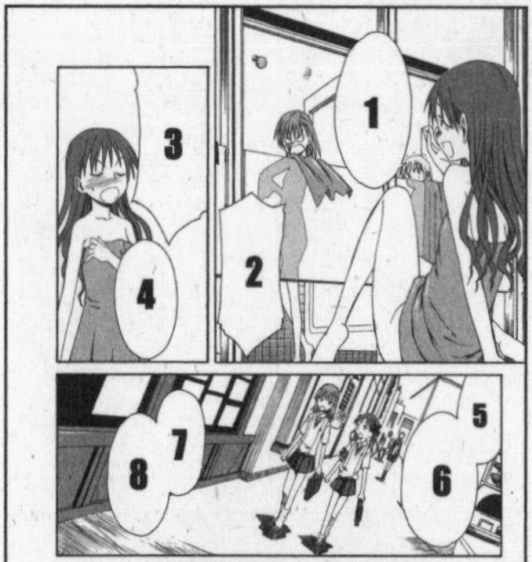
1
2
3
4
5
6
7
8
9
10
11
CREPES
12

This book reads from right to left, Japanese style. To read from the beginning, flip the book over to the other side, start with the top right panel, and take it from there.

If this is your first time reading manga, just follow the diagram. It may seem backwards at first, but you'll get used to it! Have fun!